For Granny and Auntie,
with much affection for years
of love and support.

Dan

Identifying the Image of God

Recent titles in
RELIGION IN AMERICA SERIES
Harry S. Stout, General Editor

IDENTIFYING THE IMAGE OF GOD

Radical Christians and Nonviolent Power
in the Antebellum United States

Dan McKanan

OXFORD
UNIVERSITY PRESS

2002

OXFORD
UNIVERSITY PRESS

Oxford   New York
Auckland   Bangkok   Buenos Aires   Cape Town   Chennai
Dar es Salaam   Delhi   Hong Kong   Istanbul   Karachi   Kolkata
Kuala Lumpur   Madrid   Melbourne   Mexico City   Mumbai   Nairobi
São Paulo   Shanghai   Singapore   Taipei   Tokyo   Toronto

Copyright © 2002 by Dan McKanan

Published by Oxford University Press, Inc.,
198 Madison Avenue, New York, New York 10016

www.oup.com

Oxford is a registered trademark of Oxford University Press

Library of Congress Cataloging-in-Publication Data
McKanan, Dan, 1967–
Identifying the image of God : radical Christian and nonviolent power in antebellum
United States / Dan McKanan.
p. cm. – (Religion in America series)
Includes bibliographical references and index.
ISBN 0-19-514532-1
1. Sociology, Christian–United States–History–19th century.   2. Liberalism
(Religion)–United States–History–19th century.   3. Image of God–Social
aspects–United States–History–19th century.   I. Title.   II. Religion in America series
(Oxford University Press)
BR517 .M385 2002
261.8'0973'09034–dc21   2002074933

1 3 5 7 9 8 6 4 2

Printed in the United States of America
on acid-free paper

In memory of
Nellie Yates and Nancy Jay

Acknowledgments

The completion of this book has been a long journey, and many friends have shared part or all of the walk with me. I am grateful, first of all, for the financial support of the Institute for the Advanced Study of Religion and the Pew Program in Religion and American History, which allowed me to be fairly single-minded about my research and writing between 1996 and 1998. Both the Institute and the Pew Program are communities of scholars, as well as funding institutions, and I am grateful to Frank Reynolds, Harry Stout, and Jon Butler for making them fruitful centers of dialogue. More recently, Saint John's School of Theology provided me with release time during each of the past three years.

I am grateful to the American Society of Church History, the American Academy of Religion, and the Society for the Interdisciplinary Study of Social Imagery for allowing me to present my research publicly. The advice of Tom Davis and the anonymous reviewers for *Religion and American Culture* contributed immeasurably to the first chapter. The two anonymous reviewers for Oxford University Press helped give shape and focus to the final manuscript.

I wrote the earliest precursors of this project under the supervision of Dale Johnson, Elisabeth Israels Perry, and Lewis Baldwin, all at Vanderbilt University. I am grateful to all three for stimulating my interest in nineteenth-century social reform movements, and to my coworkers at the Project to End Abuse Through Counseling and Education in Nashville, Tennessee, for shaping my early understanding of the connections between theology and violence. Still earlier, my scholarly vocation was shaped by the example and influence of three professors at Harvard. Elaine Scarry's conviction that it is possible to say something useful about violence continues to push me forward, while to Gordon Kaufman and James Engell I owe an ever-deepening appreciation of the religious importance of the human imagination.

At the University of Chicago, I benefited immeasurably from the guidance of Catherine Brekus, Clark Gilpin, Martin Marty, and Laura Rigal, each of whom attended to the unfolding of this project for nearly five years. As dissertation readers, they did not wait passively for a finished project but stimulated my thinking at every step of the way. Catherine Brekus was, and is, both adviser and friend, reading each draft with care and listening patiently to my excitements, insecurities, and ambivalences. I am also thankful for the input, direct or indirect, of Professors Kathleen Conzen, Dwight Hopkins, Mark Krupnick, Bernard McGinn, Martin Riesebrodt, David Tracy, Richard Rosengarten, David Reynolds, and Mark Noll; and of my colleagues Sarah Sadowski, Jonathan Moore, Ben Leff, Laura Ammon, Phil Harrold, Rob Wilson-Black, Robert Alvis, Jim Perkinson, and Kristin Boyce. I am also grateful to the Chicago Fifty Years Is Enough Campaign and the Chicago local support committee of the Lutheran Volunteer Corps, communities that supported me emotionally even as they stoked my radical commitments. During the Chicago years, also, I gained much from the intellectual companionship of Amy Carr, whose own scholarship is intertwined with this project in innumerable ways.

Since moving to Minnesota, I have drawn spiritual sustenance from the Community of Saint Martin and Camphill Village Minnesota, and constant hospitality from Bob Hulteen, Susan Masters, Korla Masters, Ella Masters, and Steve Heymans. My commitment to radical Christian liberalism has been sharpened by my ongoing debate with Bob Hulteen, Steve Heymans, and Ron Pagnucco. The love and support of Tammy McKenna, now McKanan, has been a joy-filled surprise of the past year and a half, and her critical reading of the manuscript has sharpened my understanding of both my message and my audience.

Finally, this book is dedicated to two of my foremothers. As a white Southern woman, my great-grandmother Nellie Yates struggled to identify with the victims of slavery and handed that ongoing struggle on to her descendents. And, as a teacher, Nancy Jay inspired me and many others to see the *imago dei* in every child born of woman.

March 2002   D. M.
Collegeville, Minnesota

Contents

Identifying the Image of God

Introduction

The Power of Identification

In a famous scene in *Uncle Tom's Cabin*, Harriet Beecher Stowe (1811–96) describes the dilemma faced by an Ohio senator when, days after voting for the Fugitive Slave Act, he encounters a fugitive mother and child at his own doorstep. Senator Bird is a warmhearted man but also a conscientious statesman who is convinced that "private feeling" must not take precedence over "great public interests." When his wife questions his vote, he tells her that the act—which required citizens of Northern states to assist in the capture of escaped slaves—was necessary to maintain harmony between North and South. But this principle dissolves as soon as the senator gets a look at Eliza and Harry, escaped slaves who have just fled across a half-frozen Ohio River to avoid being sold to a slave trader. Almost immediately he sees them as part of his own family: he suggests that his wife alter one of her gowns to fit Eliza, cries when Eliza tells of losing two of her children, and insists that Harry take a drawerful of clothing that had belonged to his own dead son. The transformation of Senator Bird, the narrator concludes, shows that "a senator is but a man." He can stand on political principle so long as "his idea of a fugitive [is] only an idea of the letters that spell the word," but "the magic of the real presence of distress,—the imploring human eye, the frail, trembling human hand, the despairing appeal of helpless agony" is enough to push his humanity to the fore.[1]

Twenty years before the publication of *Uncle Tom's Cabin*, the abolitionist newspaper the *Liberator* unveiled a new masthead intended to effect the same "magic" as Stowe's scene. The masthead illustration centers on a family of four slaves at a slave auction in Washington, D.C. Both mother and father cover their faces in grief, while the son and daughter look up to their mother in desperate expectation. They are surrounded by smiling spectators in business attire, one of whom examines another slave. Above them perches an auctioneer standing behind a sign that reads, callously, "Slaves Horses & Other Cattle to Be Sold." In the background one can glimpse a slave being whipped, the United States Capitol with a banner reading "Liberty," and a pile of Indian treaties lying in the dust. The viewer is clearly intended to identify with the grieving family, to recoil from the auctioneer's dehumanizing sign, and to feel the bitter irony of a government that announces but cannot embody "Liberty."

3

Stowe's vignette of Senator Bird and the *Liberator* masthead exemplify a central practice of early nineteenth-century social reform movements in the United States. Whether their cause was the abolition of slavery, the promotion of peace, the restraint of alcohol abuse, an end to corporal punishment, or equal rights for women, antebellum social reformers invited their neighbors to *identify* with those caught up in systems of violence and oppression. They lifted up Southern slaves, battered women, alcoholics, Native Americans, and children as representative human beings, fully entitled to the liberty and equality promised by the Declaration of Independence. To help others in the work of identification, social reform writers placed the victims of oppression in situations understood to be universally human. They depicted them as loving members of families and as sensitive individuals vulnerable to physical and emotional pain. The goal of such depictions was to get other individuals to place themselves in the victims' shoes, and then to join the victims in working for a just society.

The Cultural Roots of Identification

This "politics of identification" had deep but paradoxical roots in the culture of the early United States. Politically, its proponents were inspired by the words of the Declaration of Independence: "We hold these truths to be self-evident: that all men are created equal; that they are endowed by their creator with certain inalienable rights; that among these are life, liberty and the pursuit of happiness." To promote identifications among free and equal individuals, reformers could plausibly argue, was to fulfill the nation's central vision. Yet they also knew that the United States Constitution denied voting rights to women and many poor people and sanctioned the enslavement of blacks. The Constitution assumed, moreover, that the nation would be held together not by identification but by military force and judicial coercion. Hence Stowe assumed that Senator Bird's impulse to identification was at odds with his senatorial duty, while the *Liberator* masthead implied that the nation's promotion of "Liberty" was a sham. For the *Liberator*'s editor, William Lloyd Garrison (1805–79), the national irony could be encapsulated in the tension between what he called the "solemn and heaven-attested Declaration" and a Constitution he denounced as "a covenant with death, an agreement with hell."[2]

The politics of identification was at least as dependent on Christian theology as on Jefferson's manifesto of democratic politics. For many reformers, Jesus' nonviolent Sermon on the Mount and his insistence that his followers love their neighbors as themselves were the first and most authoritative calls for identification. Social reformers also drew on the ancient Christian doctrine of the *imago dei*—the belief that each human individual is created in the image of God. To identify with the full humanity of another person was to identity with his or her underlying divinity and to unleash powers that were divine as well as human. Yet the theological roots of identification were also paradoxical. Many social reformers had to conclude that their understanding of God's presence in humanity was at odds with traditional Protestant doctrine, which stressed God's difference from humanity and the awesomeness of divine power. They could not believe that a God who identifies with humanity would, as orthodox Protestants taught, make arbitrary distinctions among individuals, predestining some to heaven and others to hell. Nor could they accept the sacrificial theory of the atonement, according to which

God unleashed salvific power only by demanding the violent death of his sinless son. The God whose image they hoped to embody was a perfectly loving parent who identified with, cared for, and shared the sufferings of every human individual.

The theology and politics of identification were thus both grounded in and at odds with the larger culture of the antebellum United States. Reformers who promoted identification pitted the Declaration of Independence against constitutional government, and the Sermon on the Mount against the established churches. They appealed to consensual values of equality, freedom, and benevolent love but insisted that existing social institutions fell far short of embodying those values. The most consistent reformers may be characterized as "radical Christian liberals," for they took to revolutionary extremes the Christian values of the Gospels and the liberal values of the Declaration of Independence. Radical Christian liberals were a tiny minority of the United States population, and even within social reform organizations they rarely constituted a majority. Yet they played a central role in the shaping of United States culture between 1820 and 1860. In their activism and, especially, in their literature, they promoted a utopian vision of a society free of violence and coercion, organized entirely around its citizens' recognition of the divine image in one another.

The Sentimental Practice of Identification

This utopian vision appeared with special clarity in the narrative literature of social reform. During the antebellum decades, social reformers created an array of new genres: historical novels that celebrated identification between whites and Indians; "temperance tales" that traced the dynamics of addiction and recovery; fugitive slave narratives; and full-blown novels of social reform. Such texts as *Ten Nights in a Bar-Room*, *The Narrative of Frederick Douglass*, and *Uncle Tom's Cabin* were well suited to the politics of identification. They presented extended portraits of the victims of social injustice, inviting readers to sympathize and identify with them. They also offered imaginative glimpses of what society might be like if everyone rose to the challenge of identifying with victims.

Social reform authors articulated a sentimental theology that was as sophisticated and compelling as the systematic writings of professional theologians. Because the term "sentimentality" has been assigned quite divergent meanings, a careful definition is needed here. I take sentimentality to be a practice that asks one individual to acknowledge the full, equal humanity of another by appealing to common experiences of relationship, bodily pain, or both. I might ask you to recognize John's humanity because he is a father and you are a father, because he has broken his arm and you have broken your leg, or because both of you have lost a beloved child to consumption. All of these are sentimental strategies. First promoted by philosophers like Jean-Jacques Rousseau and novelists like Samuel Richardson, sentimentality presupposes the liberal faith in human equality and in the divine origin of human powers. The sentimentalist is convinced that humans have enough in common that each of us can imaginatively stand in anyone else's shoes. She is also convinced that when this happens, both individuals will gain in power because they will be able to work together for the common good. By the early nineteenth century, sentimentality had become the primary means of expanding the community of political discourse in Europe and North America. Through sentimental appeals, elites came to see first women, then children, and ultimately slaves, as fully human.[3]

Sentimental power is based in the body—indeed, in the broken, suffering body. Yet it is the antithesis of violent power. Just as violence "works" only when the perpetrator derives a sense of invulnerability (felt subjectively and acknowledged by others) from the victim's vulnerable body, so sentimentality works when the victim's bodily suffering generates a bodily response in the weeping, sympathetic observer.[4] As one critic has noted, "Reading sentimental fiction is . . . a bodily act, and the success of a story is gauged, in part, by its ability to translate words into pulse beats and sobs."[5] But why should this apparent multiplication of suffering be a source of power? The reason, I believe, is that the broken body is in most cases also a body in the process of healing. To acknowledge and share the reality of bodily pain is, paradoxically, to ensure that the power that inflicted the pain has not had the last word—that life, after all, goes on.[6]

Sentimentality combines this appeal to the body with an appeal to the relational powers inherent in family life. This may seem odd. Radical Christian liberals were deeply suspicious of institutions that relied on coercion rather than the power of identification, and historically the family has been the locus of as much coercion and injustice as any other institution. Radical Christian liberals acknowledged and repudiated many oppressive dimensions of family life, including the unilateral authority of fathers, the law of primogeniture, restrictions on married women's property rights, and the corporal punishment of children. Yet they also asserted that, in its essence, the family was not like other institutions. As the spontaneous expression of divinely implanted affections rather than a by-product of tyranny, it was capable of existing apart from coercive power.

The goal of family life, as radical Christian liberals understood it, was the full, equal selfhood of each member. "In a family of true order," wrote novelist and activist Lydia Maria Child (1802–80), "each one would think, feel, and act as an individual, with respectful regard to the freedom of the other members."[7] The parent's sentimental identification with the sufferings of the child began a long developmental process, eventuating in the child's mature selfhood and in adults' acknowledgment of that selfhood. This emphasis on the development of selfhood allowed liberals to assert the full humanity even of those vulnerable people who could not ground their claims to recognition in their moral autonomy or tangible contributions to society.[8] The family model also allowed them to downplay the challenge of ethnic differences to sentimental identification. For them, the family transcended ethnic difference, since people of all cultures form families. It also offered a concrete mechanism for uniting ethnically diverse individuals, who could always form families together.[9] At their most radical, sentimental writers celebrated the conscientious individual and the loving family as dual sources of a nonviolent power that might overthrow all other institutions and usher in an age of perfect freedom.

The embodied, familial power of sentimentality was very different from that associated with the military and judicial apparatus of the state. From the liberal perspective, the latter was a zero-sum game in which the strong took whatever power they could from the weak. Rejecting Saint Paul's claim that the ruling powers had been "established by God" (Romans 13:1), liberals held that states were the product of tyrannical usurpation. In other words, they saw coercive power as derivative, while sentimental power was grounded in the very character of Creation. As a consequence, coercive power was always weaker than what abolitionist Frederick Douglass (1817–95) called the "magic power of human sympathy." "It is beyond the power of slavery," he explained, "to annihilate affinities recognized and established by the Almighty. The slave is bound to mankind, by the powerful and inextricable net-work of human brotherhood."[10]

The Modern Critique of Identification

Ultimately, however, sentimental power was not able to bring about a nonviolent revolution or a society free of coercion. The Civil War came instead. For many, the war experience gave the lie to radical liberal faith. The liberal goal of freedom for the slaves was achieved, but through military action rather than through the mutual recognition of the *imago dei*. In the years after the Civil War, most Americans embraced the more moderate tradition of liberalism associated with Abraham Lincoln, who was willing to use coercive institutions to preserve and gradually to expand the scope of individual freedom. As a "martyr" to his cause, Lincoln gave it a prestige that has still not worn off. Ever since the Civil War, our vision of what American democracy might mean has been narrower than it was in the decades before.

The radical Christian liberal tradition faced additional challenges in the late nineteenth and early twentieth centuries. During that time, Marxism emerged as the leading revolutionary movement in the Western world. Though Marxism drew on previous revolutionary traditions, it dissented from radical liberalism in profound ways. For Marx, the notion of sentimental identification among all people was a pious mystification: true social change could occur only through a class conflict that pitted the workers against the owners of capital. Marx also assumed that violence would be an intrinsic part of the revolution. He advocated the creation of a vanguard party that would concentrate political and military power in its own hands. His ultimate goal of a decentralized society in which each person would work with both hands and mind was similar to that of utopian liberals, but he believed that the state must become more powerful first and wither away only later. Because of Marx's far-reaching influence, few people today can even imagine the possibility of a nonviolent revolution that seeks to dismantle the state rather than merely transfer state power to a new group.

In the early twentieth century, Christian liberalism was dealt a nearly fatal blow by the "neo-orthodox" movement associated with Karl Barth in Europe and the Niebuhr brothers (Reinhold and H. Richard) in the United States. Rejecting the liberal emphasis on human goodness and the kinship between God and humanity, these theologians reasserted orthodox understandings of God's mysterious sovereignty and the sinful depravity of humans. Liberalism, they charged, simply made things too easy, denying the tragedies and ironies of human existence. In H. Richard Niebuhr's famous account, it taught that "a God without wrath brought men without sin into a kingdom without judgment through the ministrations of a Christ without a cross."[11] Such a theology provided no basis for responsible action in a deeply flawed world.

Politically, the Niebuhrs remained sympathetic to the pragmatic, institutional liberalism of Abraham Lincoln, whom they also regarded as a theological precursor because of his deep sense of the difference between God's ways and human ways. But they were harshly critical of the liberal tradition of social reform. The liberal faith in the goodness of human nature was, they believed, the source of much that was wrong with the United

States because it could blind people to their own capacity for evil and violence. Liberal pacifism was particularly dangerous because it discouraged thoughtful people from using limited coercion to restrict the violence of others. By positing perfect peace as an achievable goal, liberalism actually made a limited justice more difficult to attain. This conclusion reflected Reinhold Niebuhr's personal experience as a Christian pacifist who embraced just war theory once he recognized the depth of evil posed by fascism.

Scholars in a variety of disciplines have embraced similar arguments, even if they do not share the Niebuhrs' theological commitments. Historian Stanley Elkins faulted the abolitionists—and, by extension, other radical social reformers—for their irresponsible disconnection from established social institutions. Noting the close ties between Transcendentalists and abolitionists, Elkins wrote that "by the 1830's the closest thing to an intellectual community in the United States consisted of men with no concrete commitment to the system at all. . . . They were truly men without responsibility." This was a problem, from Elkins's perspective, because only responsible men could have worked within the system to make changes without disrupting society as a whole.[12]

The literary critic Ann Douglas, in her influential 1977 study of nineteenth-century sentimental fiction, drew an extremely unfavorable contrast between the liberalism of the nineteenth century and the orthodoxy of the eighteenth. The orthodox theologians associated with Jonathan Edwards, she claimed, produced "the most persuasive example of independent yet institutionalized thought to which our society has even temporarily given credence." In the nineteenth century, though, the liberal clergy had lost much of their social standing and formed a "sentimental" alliance with equally disempowered middle-class women. By creating a literature celebrating the power of moral "influence," they obscured the fact of their real impotence and thus failed to take constructive action to overcome it. "Sentimentalism," Douglas wrote, "provides a way to protest a power to which one has already in part capitulated. . . . The fakery involved was finally crippling for all concerned." Though Douglas stressed the powerlessness rather than the excessive radicalism of the liberals, her point is similar to that of Elkins and the Niebuhrs: the real power is inside the "system," and responsible people must be willing to use it.[13]

Even the Niebuhrs' theological critics have little good to say about liberalism. In today's academy, the case for Christian pacifism has been made most eloquently by John Howard Yoder and Stanley Hauerwas. Like the radical Christian liberals described in this book, Yoder and Hauerwas regard the Sermon on the Mount as a practical blueprint for Christian life. Like them, they do not believe that Christians should restrict themselves to working within the system. But Yoder and Hauerwas see no connections between the "politics of Jesus" and the liberal values of the United States. Nonviolence is not about honoring the "inalienable rights" of other people, nor is it a way of expressing the divine power that is naturally present in every human soul. It is, rather, a supernatural grace that is possible only in the context of Christian discipleship. Christians should practice nonviolence not to identify more fully with others but to honor their particular identity as Christians. The anticipated fruit of nonviolence, moreover, is not revolutionary social change. It is a fuller participation in the mystery of the cross.[14]

The many scholars influenced by Michel Foucault have proposed a rather different critique of American liberalism. Like the Niebuhrs, Foucault viewed the attempt to purge society of all forms of coercion as essentially unrealistic. Indeed, he believed that each epoch of human history has its own distinctive form of coercion. From this perspective, the eighteenth- and nineteenth-century liberal campaign against physical coercion merely masked the transition to a new, more oppressive epoch, in which the coercive powers of the state were internalized in the pysche, making physical coercion unnecessary.[15] (This theory makes it hard to explain why twentieth-century states have committed far *more* violence than in previous epochs!) From an extreme Foucauldian perspective, the social reform campaigns against slavery, corporal punishment, and war were not really "about" these things at all. They were simply a means by which the new style of discipline was inculcated in the American middle class.[16] Foucault's skepticism about the liberal belief in a shared human nature has also led some academics to embrace an extreme "politics of identity," in which any connection between diverse cultural groups is simply impossible.[17]

The Abiding Power of Identification

Despite these criticisms, radical Christian liberalism remains the most viable revolutionary tradition in the United States. It has little stature in the academy, but it is the implicit ideology of many of the most committed political activists of our day. This was most apparent during the civil rights movement, when Martin Luther King Jr. and other leaders invited all Americans to identify with the victims of southern segregation, discrimination, and violence. Like the social reformers described in this book, King appealed to the political and religious values shared by most Americans, even as he challenged many of the United States' most powerful institutions. In the "I Have a Dream" speech, for example, he referred to "the magnificent words of the Constitution and the Declaration of Independence" as a "promissory note" on which the nation had defaulted. Mixing references to biblical prophecy and patriotic hymns, he anticipated the "day [when] this nation will rise up and live out the true meaning of its creed" by allowing "little black boys and black girls [to] join hands with little white boys and white girls as sisters and brothers."[18] At the time of his assassination, King was a true revolutionary who believed that the American creed demanded the dismantling of racism, militarism, and capitalism.

Ironically, though, few people recognize that King stood in an American tradition that was more than a century old. Most know that King drew on Mohandas Gandhi's theory of active nonviolence, but only a handful are aware of the chain of influences that connected Gandhi to Leo Tolstoy and Tolstoy to the Garrisonian nonresistants of the nineteenth century. Similarly, some people know that Gandhian nonviolence is based on the Hindu teaching that there is a piece of God in every human being, but very few realize that, for many nineteenth-century activists, this was also a fundamental Christian teaching. The tradition of radical Christian liberalism has nearly been lost to historical memory.

My hope is that the present study will help revive that tradition. As a historian, I believe that we seriously misunderstand antebellum social reform if we fail to recognize its roots in liberal Christian theology. As a theologian, I believe that the liberal theology of the *imago dei* is valuable both as a spur to radical action and as a basis for interfaith dialogue with other traditions that posit a deep connection between God and humanity. Most important, as an activist, I believe that the peace and justice movement will be enriched by a deeper awareness of how fully it is *at home*, both in America and in Christianity. Activists are rightly critical of the complacency and otherworldliness of the American churches, and of the planet-threatening hubris of the American government. Many of our social institutions deserve to be overthrown—*must* be overthrown, perhaps, if the planet and we are to survive. But the deepest values of both Christianity and the United States remain reliable guides to a transformed world.

1

Wheat and Tares

The Liberal Encounter with Puritan Violence

In *Leaves from Margaret Smith's Journal*, John Greenleaf Whittier's 1849 fictionalization of early New England history, the heroine visits Elnathan Stone, a veteran of the wars with the Indians. On his deathbed, Elnathan is a model of Christian piety who professes to have "no feeling of anger or unkindness left towards any one, for all seemed kind to him beyond his deserts, and like brothers and sisters." He loves even the Indian enemies who inflicted his mortal wounds, and chides his mother for referring to them as "bloody heathen." "I used to feel as mother does," he tells Margaret and her cousin; indeed, he had originally hoped to "spare neither young nor old of the enemy." Yet in the heat of battle God had used Elnathan's own natural affections to help him identify with the enemy: "I thank God that even in that dark season my heart relented at the sight of the poor starving women and children, chased from place to place like partridges. Even the Indian fighters, I found, had sorrows of their own, and grievous wrongs to avenge." After his capture he had been adopted by an Indian chief, Squando, whose own son had been drowned by white settlers, and their extended relationship had made him aware of the evils of white policy and the capacity of human benevolence to transcend race.[1]

A participant in the antebellum peace, antislavery, and temperance movements, as well as a popular poet and fiction writer, Whittier (1807-92) infused his writings with social purpose. Like other reformers, he called on his neighbors to identify with the victims of violence and oppression, and his depiction of Elnathan Stone exemplifies this sentimental practice. Elnathan identifies with his enemies and, by telling his story, induces Margaret to identify with him; by depicting these two identifications, Whittier invites his readers to identify successively with Margaret, with Elnathan, and with Squando and the other Indians. Like Elnathan, we are expected to regard all people as brothers and sisters. This chain of identifications is possible because Whittier depicts each link as both physically vulnerable and emotionally related. The Indians suffer from hunger and worry about their children; Elnathan is mortally wounded and close to his mother; Margaret is far from home and yet linked to her cousin Rebecca. Each character, in short, recapitulates the primordial human experience of being a vulnerable infant, utterly dependent on the nurture of others. Social reformers hoped that such appeals to early experience might make one family of the whole human race.

But why did Whittier lodge his call for identification in a work of historical fiction? Why was it important to depict the transformative potential of identification in a society—Puritan New England—that had been dead for more than a century? Whittier's turn to history was not accidental or idiosyncratic; on the contrary, he continued a tradition of liberal depictions of Puritan New England that was a generation old by 1849. Beginning in the early 1820s, such writers as Catharine Maria Sedgwick (1789–1867), Lydia Maria Child (1802–80), Lydia Sigourney (1791–1865), and Eliza Buckminster Lee (1788/94–1864)—all descendants of the Puritans with deep reservations about Puritan theology—had applied to Puritan history the very practices of identification that would be embraced by social reformers in the 1830s and 1840s. In a sense, historical fiction about the Puritans was the founding genre of antebellum social reform literature. Why was this?

The social reformers' practice of identification rested on a set of theological assumptions at odds with the orthodox Reformed doctrine that had been normative for Puritanism and remained authoritative, in theory, for the most prominent groups of antebellum Protestants.[2] In appealing to the primordial experiences of vulnerability and relation, social reformers assumed that humans are born with a capacity to identify creatively and constructively with others. Orthodox theology, by contrast, taught that infants are innately depraved and capable of no virtues until they have been infused with supernatural grace. The practice of identification aspired to forge familial connections among *all* people, while orthodox theology insisted that many or most people have been predestined to ultimate exclusion from the human family. Perhaps most important, social reformers believed that their efforts to build a better society would be guaranteed by divine power, while the orthodox held that God rules history according to purposes utterly inscrutable to the human mind. Orthodoxy, in short, offered no hope that humans might overcome the violence of history through the exercise of nonviolent power. The repudiation of orthodox theology was thus a prerequisite to radical social reform.

And yet few antebellum liberals were willing to disown the heritage of Puritanism altogether. Indeed, they saw their particular projects of social reform as extensions of the sixteenth-century Reformation, which they understood as a struggle for gospel liberty and freedom from feudal oppression. Though liberal reformers rejected Martin Luther and John Calvin's interpretation of the gospel, they shared the Reformers' conviction that the gospel—whatever it might be—was the most powerful force in human history. It was more powerful than the established church, more powerful than the Holy Roman Empire, more powerful even than the demonic forces of violence. Liberal reformers believed that this conviction had inspired the Puritans to found a new society in North America, and they could not help but see their own hopes for social transformation as a continuation of the Puritan dream.

Antebellum liberals turned to Puritan history with a twofold purpose: to dismantle the orthodox theology that inhibited hopes of social transformation, and simultaneously to enlist Puritan zeal on behalf of a radical vision. To accomplish this they used sentimental identification in diverse ways: sometimes identifying with the Puritans' enemies (Indians, Quakers, and accused witches) to expose the violence inherent in Puritan doctrine, at other times identifying with the Puritans themselves to demonstrate the underlying power of the Puritan vision. This did not involve duplicity, for the ultimate goal was to forge a chain of identifications from which no one was excluded. But it did involve ambivalence and uncertainty. Was it possible to square God's omnipotence,

God't benevolence, and the continuing existence of violence in the world? Was the liberal imagination truly broad enough to identify with all people, including all victims of oppression? These questions would haunt every phase of antebellum social reform.

In the present chapter I shall look at a series of imaginative representations of Puritan history penned by liberals between 1820 and 1860, with an emphasis on the influential early texts of the 1820s.[3] Liberals used Puritan "tares" to expose the violence inherent in orthodox theology and Puritan "wheat" to illustrate the nonviolent power inherent in all people. They did so with considerable ambivalence, struggling in particular to mold the Puritan doctrine of Providence to their own ends. And, ultimately, they failed fully to include Native Americans in their imagined community of identification.

The Liberal Renewal of *Imago Dei* Theology

Liberal theology revolved around the doctrine of the *imago dei*. This, of course, was no innovation of the nineteenth century. It placed the reformers in a long, if somewhat discontinuous, tradition. In Genesis God creates humanity "in our image, after our likeness" (1:26). In the context of the Hellenistic world, this teaching fit nicely with the Platonic doctrines that each human soul is a seed or spark of divinity, and that likeness is the basis of love. Christian Platonists taught that the essential kinship between God and the soul allowed humans to grow steadily in likeness to God, ultimately achieving full divinization. Various schools of esoteric and mystical Christianity have preserved this view through the centuries.

Among more mainstream Christians, however, it gradually lost favor. Early in the patristic period, most theologians repudiated the Platonic doctrine that human souls are naturally divine. In the fifth century, Saint Augustine articulated what would become the orthodox understanding of original sin: the Fall effaced the divine image in humanity, leaving us incapable of willing any good without the assistance of supernatural grace. Still, most medieval Catholic theologians continued to teach that redemption was a process of loving identification between God and humanity, in which nature and grace worked together to draw out the divine image in each person.

During the Protestant Reformation, theologians like Luther and Calvin radicalized Augustine's teaching. For them, the fallen human will was entirely in bondage to sin, incapable of contributing in any way to its salvation. God, for the Reformers, was less a loving father than an absolute sovereign who saved some humans and damned others for his own mysterious purposes. Redemption was based not on active love of God but on a passive faith in God's once-for-all gift of grace. Christ's dual nature as both divine and human did not open a path by which other humans could become divine, but it enabled Christ to do what others could not: pay the sacrificial price of humanity's original rebellion. This was the "orthodoxy" of nineteenth-century American Protestantism.

The notion that God can be truly known only on the basis of kinship began to be revived in eighteenth-century New England. Congregationalist ministers Charles Chauncy, Jonathan Mayhew, and Ebenezer Gay challenged the orthodox doctrines of the absolute sovereignty of God and the total depravity of humankind. Drawing on Enlightenment philosophy, these divines taught that God is a loving father whose "benevolence" is easily comprehended by the human intellect, and that humans possess an inborn "moral sense" that allows us to fulfill God's will. They were also quite critical of the revivals of the Great Awakening, although this was partly because eighteenth-century revivalists like Jonathan Edwards were such ardent defenders of Reformed orthodoxy. Gradually, party lines hardened in the Massachusetts church: while the Connecticut River valley was the heartland of revivalist orthodoxy, most Boston ministers, with the faculty of Harvard College, went over to the liberal or "Arminian" side.[4]

The underlying conflict came to the surface in 1805, when Harvard College appointed the stridently liberal Henry Ware Sr. as Hollis Professor. By this time, most liberals had accepted the "universalist" position that all humans will eventually be saved, were committed to a rationalist study of the Bible, and taught that the doctrine of the Trinity was both irrational and unbiblical. (Though the last of these positions gave a name to the new denomination, antitrinitarianism was never as important to the Unitarian movement as its emphases on divine benevolence and human moral ability.)[5] These new positions were deeply offensive even to those revivalists who had accepted the Arminian position on free will. Orthodox Congregationalists, for their part, bitterly protested Ware's appointment. A protracted rhetorical battle ensued, culminating in the founding of the American Unitarian Association in 1825.

The significance of the Unitarian controversy was that it inspired liberals to promote their cause actively. Eighteenth-century Arminians had been so committed to maintaining harmony with their orthodox brethren that they rarely spelled out their theology; many, moreover, were elitists who had no interest in persuading the masses. In the context of controversy, however, nineteenth-century liberals became indefatigable producers of tracts, journals, and educational institutions. Like their orthodox brothers and sisters, they were committed to the work of "benevolent" societies to help the poor. When permitted to do so, they cooperated with orthodox societies; when excluded, they formed their own.[6] Still, the Unitarian Church never emerged as the organizing center of Christian liberalism in the United States. Beyond the neighborhood of Boston, most liberals remained Congregationalists, joined the more doctrinally inclusive Episcopalian Church, or flocked to the more populist Universalists. In Boston itself, the most daring liberal thinkers chafed at the remaining doctrinal restrictions and "corpse-cold" style of official Unitarianism. Many turned to a noninstitutional piety or, as in Lydia Maria Child's case, to the more mystical Swedenborgian church. In 1829 the Unitarian novelist Catharine Sedgwick summed up the situation by noting "I do not know that the course of *unitarianism* as such makes very rapid progress, but liberal principles— sure pioneers—are fast gaining ground."[7]

The individual closest to the heart of the Unitarian Reformation was William Ellery Channing (1780-1842). A powerful preacher, he articulated the movement's guiding principles in an 1819 ordination sermon that rallied dozens of young people to the cause. He was also a philosophical theologian who paved the way for Transcendentalism—and was usually spared the harsh attacks that Transcendentalists directed against other Unitarian leaders. Channing placed special emphasis on the *imago dei*. Alluding pointedly to Plato, he noted that the idea "that God can be known and enjoyed only through sympathy or kindred attributes, is a doctrine which even Gentile philosophy discerned." He knocked the orthodox emphasis on faith rather than morals, suggesting that "God becomes a real being to us, in proportion as his own nature is unfolded within us. To a man who is growing in the likeness of God, faith begins even here to change into vision."[8]

Three slogans popular with liberal Christians were intimately linked to this "vision" of the *imago dei*. Against traditional images of God as a king and judge, they preached "the fatherhood of God and the brotherhood of man," thus asserting a basic kinship between the human and the divine. Against the orthodox doctrine of total depravity, they claimed that people possess a "moral sense" that inclines us to identify with others and continually grow in likeness to God. Finally, they sought to continue the work of the Reformation and the United States Revolution by rooting out all vestiges of "tyranny and priestcraft" that threatened violence against God's image in the human individual.

God's Parental Character

To contemporary ears, "the fatherhood of God and the brotherhood of man" may reek of patriarchy, but in its own context it was a ringing affirmation of the kinship between God and all humanity. Liberals saw God as a benevolent parent who seeks not to control his children but to nurture in them a mature independence, and who has created the entire universe in accordance with his nurturant intentions. "To give our views of God in one word," proclaimed Channing, "we believe in his Parental character. . . . We believe that he has a father's concern for his creatures, a father's desire for their improvement, a father's equity in proportioning his commands to their powers, a father's joy in their progress, a father's readiness to receive the penitent, and a father's justice for the incorrigible."[9] Similarly, Lydia Maria Child told the readers of a children's history that "the Almighty requires nothing from his creatures but what is calculated for their best good, both in this life and that which is to come."[10]

The common fatherhood of God, of course, made all humanity brothers and sisters, and liberals taught that God's love enables each person to form family ties with all people. "By our Love of one another the Lord will measure our Love of Himself," John Greenleaf Whittier has a liberal minister preach in *Margaret Smith's Journal*, his novel of early Quakerism. Another character tells his sister, shortly after his conversion to Quakerism, that his love for her will only "be increased by a measure of that Divine love which, so far from destroying, doth but purify and strengthen the natural affections."[11] Lydia Maria Child even went so far as to write that "the universal brotherhood of mankind may . . . be defined as the central Idea of the Christian reform."[12]

The orthodox also referred to God as father, of course, but to liberal ears talk of divine fatherhood and human brotherhood implied a sharp critique of the orthodox understanding of divine sovereignty. The orthodox taught that God was a sovereign who created the universe in order to manifest his own glory. Though he was benevolent, his benevolence was utterly beyond human comprehension: no one could expect to recognize it as such. When they counseled humans to practice "disinterested benevolence," moreover, the orthodox referred to a radically theocentric ethic that involved the sacrifice of natural affections for the sake of obedience to God.[13]

Liberals rejected orthodoxy's God as too capricious to deserve worship, and they insisted on rooting human benevolence in the everyday affections implanted by a loving God. Since human and divine benevolence were intimately linked, the mere observation of God's love, they believed, could inspire humans to act more benevolently. "By the habit of contemplating the divine display of power, wisdom, and goodness, exhibited throughout the creation," Child promised, "we shall be preserved from those corroding passions of hatred and envy, and pride and self-conceit." Conversely, even local expressions of human kindness might expand steadily until they achieved the all-embracing character of God's love. Thus, in her first novel Catharine Sedgwick compared the sexual love of a man and a woman to God's expansive love. Their love, she wrote, "constantly enlarging its circle, embraced within its compass all that could be benefited by their active efforts and heavenly example." To love one person was a first step toward loving all humanity.[14]

The liberals linked divine and human love in part because their image of God's fatherhood was shaped by a new model of human parenthood that had been developed by John Locke and the Scottish commonsense philosophers. In various ways, these thinkers promoted a pedagogy in which the proper role of a parent, teacher, or deity was to promote the good of the child by nurturing the virtuous habits that would make mature independence possible.[15] This new pedagogy presupposed that humans are born capable of growing in virtue, a position that had been denied by the orthodox doctrine of original sin.

The Moral Sense

The first major proponent of Enlightenment anthropology was John Locke. While orthodox theology held that every human being is born with a nature corrupted by original sin, Locke taught that character is not inherited at all but constructed by a lifelong series of sense impressions and experiences. The proper parental role was thus benevolent cultivation rather than sovereign restraint: the goal was to ensure the child's exposure to influences that would nurture in him or her rational faculties and moral virtues. From a Lockean point of view, parental or divine benevolence was very important indeed.[16]

The difficulty, as Locke's successors realized, was that Locke had presented the parent with an impossible task. How could a mere accumulation of sense impressions, however carefully orchestrated, add up to a mature and virtuous mind? It could not, insisted David Hume, noting that the ideas we use to make sense of experience, such as the principle of causality, cannot themselves be grounded in experience. The threat of Humean skepticism led many thinkers to step back from Locke's position, conceding that the mind was not an *entirely* blank slate. Most influentially, Francis Hutcheson proposed that experiences are filtered not only through the physical senses of taste, touch, sight, smell, and hearing but also through a "moral sense." The moral sense inspires affection between human beings and helps us respond compassionately to others in need even before we calculate the consequences of such acts. Hutcheson's moral sense was not self-sufficient but needed to be cultivated by parents and then directed by the mature reason. Thus, his theory retained the need for Lockean pedagogy but gave it a clear starting point.[17]

Hutcheson's moral sense theory became a foundational doctrine of the Scottish commonsense school, promoted by such thinkers as Thomas Reid, Dugald Stewart, and Lord Kames. It was also widely influential in North America. Already in 1759 the Arminian

Ebenezer Gay made the moral sense the keystone of his Dudleian Lecture on natural theology, pointing to the "divine Workmanship in human nature." Jefferson was a firm adherent. Channing first encountered Hutcheson as a Harvard undergraduate and was so moved that he "longed to die and felt as if heaven alone could give room for the exercise of emotion." Catharine Sedgwick found in moral sense theory the basis for an optimistic pedagogy. It was, one of her characters suggests, "far easier to persuade the infirm to virtue than to vice. There is an unbroken chord in every human heart that vibrates to the voice of truth."[18] Christian liberals also noted the analogy between the Quaker doctrine of the inner light and moral sense theory, and they used the biblical image of "divine impressions . . . written on the heart" to refer to the moral sense.[19]

The orthodox also read Hutcheson, and even Jonathan Edwards was prone to speak of human virtue as a matter of "affections."[20] Still, the liberals correctly pointed out that moral sense theory was not consistent with orthodox anthropology. Edwards could speak only of *supernatural* affections, for Reformed orthodoxy taught that the natural human affections were destroyed by the Fall. Humans had originally been created in God's image but had entirely lost the ability to do God's will: their noblest efforts only entangled them more deeply in sin. The Fall also disordered physical nature, which ceased to be a path by which humans might reach God. This doctrine of total depravity deeply troubled antebellum liberals. "We consider," Channing explained in one of his earliest statements of liberal doctrine, "the errors which relate to Christ's person as of little or no importance compared with the error of those who teach, that God brings us into life wholly depraved and wholly helpless, that he leaves multitudes without that aid which is indispensably necessary to their repentance, and then plunges them into everlasting burnings and unspeakable torture, for not repenting." Eliza Buckminster Lee found the doctrine so much at odds with common sense that she declared indignantly that "the natural feelings of man are ever at war with the Calvinistic theology."[21]

Those who rejected total depravity did not always move to the opposite extreme. Some held that infants were born not virtuous but morally neutral and capable of growing in virtue. Thus, such Founding Fathers as John Adams, Benjamin Franklin, and Thomas Jefferson, all deeply influenced by moral sense theory, assigned humanity a "mixed" nature. A human being, William Livingston commented, "may without vanity reflect on himself, as capable of a Participation in the Divinity: and without error rank himself with the meanest Reptile."[22] The postrevolutionary generation was not so cautious and sometimes blurred the distinction between an original capacity for virtue and original virtue itself. But if liberals became increasingly optimistic about the *potential* of human nature, they never doubted the *actuality* of human sinfulness. Even "reason and conscience," Henry Ware Sr. insisted, could be "neglected," "perverted," or "misguided."[23] Given this awareness, the liberals' optimism goaded them to attend more closely to concrete manifestations of human evil.

Tyranny and Priestcraft

Since liberals regarded both human individuals and family relationships as naturally good, they turned to larger social institutions to explain the origins of evil. Unlike the family, the church and the state could not be perceived as "natural" outgrowths of the moral affections. More often their role was to impose artificial restraints on human passions. As liberal anthropology made the need for such restraints less obvious, liberals began to focus on the tendency of church and state to degenerate into superstitious "priestcraft" and exploitative "tyranny." Such degeneration occurred whenever institutions sought to place limits on the individual's freedom of conscience. Indeed, liberals saw freedom of conscience as the supreme value, and any attack on it as a sacrilegious affront on God's image. "God's throne in heaven is unassailable," Channing explained. "The only war against God is against his image, against the divine principle in the soul, and this is waged by tyranny in all its forms." In her fictionalized account of the martyrdom of the Quaker Mary Dyer, Catharine Sedgwick made clear that her interest was not in Quakerism as such but in "that great cause, that has stimulated the highest minds to the sublimest actions; that calls its devotees from the gifted, its martyrs from the moral heroes of mankind; the best cause, the fountain of all liberty—*liberty of conscience!*"[24]

Interestingly, liberals expressed their distaste for tyranny and priestcraft in the terms of an orthodox Protestant theology of history. Protestant historians taught that from the rise of the papacy (under Gregory the Great in the late sixth century), Europe was engulfed in an "antichristian" darkness in which consciences and bodies were bound by papal and imperial machinations. Martin Luther's preaching of the gospel then inaugurated a new era in history. Though liberals rejected the content of Luther's theology, they celebrated his frontal attack on the empire and the papacy. By boldly nailing his theses to the church door and then standing up to both pope and emperor at Worms, he had restored human freedom. His work was continued by the English Puritans, who had defied the authority of king and bishops, and then set out to create a free, gospel-guided society in North America. Liberals assumed that this historical trajectory would culminate in the millennium of peace and justice, and they saw the religious and social ferment of their own day as essential to this process. Thus, in 1835 the Unitarian minister Henry Ware Jr. surveyed the "interesting discussions in various unconnected portions of the Christian church" and declared that they were "all of them growing out of the great action of the principles of the Reformation, all a part of the mighty struggle of the times for liberty and light, all . . . giving to the thoughtful observer auspicious pledges of the sure advent of a day of complete and established reform."[25]

The Antebellum Harvest of Christian Liberalism

Many antebellum liberals saw the movements for peace, abolition of slavery, and temperance as a harvest of the egalitarian seeds sown by both Martin Luther's gospel revolt and Thomas Jefferson's Declaration of Independence. They did not see themselves as promoting new ideas. Indeed, for them the principles of freedom and equality were rooted in human nature and had simply been recognized by such prophetic figures as Jesus, Luther, and Jefferson. Nevertheless, there were several new things about the style of Christian liberalism that emerged in the 1820s. It was, first of all, new to many of its outspoken proponents in the sense that their family roots were in orthodox and Federalist communities. (Indeed, one of the distinguishing features of Christian liberalism is that it is not so much an ongoing tradition that is handed down from generation to generation as a religious option that is rediscovered in each generation by those believers who cannot reconcile received doctrine with lived experience.) A postrevolutionary consciousness also shaped antebellum liberalism. While Revolutionary era liberals were concerned primarily with achieving democratic rights for white, middle-class men, antebellum liberals hoped to extend those rights to women, children, Native Americans, African Americans, and immigrants. They were willing to extend the liberal critique of tyranny to a variety of institutions that threatened the individual and family. Slavery, war, and even the "drinking system" were now targets of liberal ire.

Despite this broad reformist agenda, the tone of antebellum liberalism was initially irenic, even serene. The literature of the early national period had been suffused by anxiety: Charles Brockden Brown's novels, for example, espoused a radical social and familial vision but also hinted that the slightest mistake could cause both the family and the nation to explode in irrational violence. The ubiquitous pamphlets of Mason Locke Weems ostensibly promoted temperance and other reformist causes but used these as an excuse for wallowing in scenes of outrageous violence. And early seduction novels, such as *Charlotte Temple* and *The Coquette*, were implicitly orthodox in their assumption that a single breach of sexual propriety would lead inevitably to dissolution and death. In the antebellum novels of Catharine Sedgwick, Lydia Maria Child, and Eliza Buckminster Lee, by contrast, there are few irremediable mistakes, and hardly anyone falls entirely out of grace.

Antebellum irenicism owed much to the family circumstances of liberal writers. They were committed to theological and political liberalism, and they assumed its eventual triumph, but this confidence paradoxically enabled them to celebrate their ties to illiberal ancestors. Sedgwick, Child, and Lee all joined older brothers in repudiating their fathers' values without disowning the fathers themselves. Lee's father was an orthodox minister, while her brother, Joseph Buckminster, was an early Unitarian leader, and so she wrote a memoir to celebrate the ties of sentiment that had continued to hold the family together.[26] Child's brother, Convers Francis, was a Unitarian pastor and cofounder of the Transcendental Club who encouraged his sister's literary interests and heterodox theology.

Similarly, Sedgwick, whose father had been the arch-Federalist Speaker of the United States House of Representatives, followed her brothers in embracing Jeffersonianism but retained a fondness for New England's old Federalist order. Men like her father, she remembered, had abolished slavery in Massachusetts and sometimes taken bold stands on behalf of oppressed individuals. Indeed, Sedgwick's very liberalism compelled her to honor the moral virtues resident in illiberal Federalist hearts. Thus, in "A Reminiscence of Federalism," she told of an idealistic young Vermont Jeffersonian who must negotiate a precarious path between his tyrannical grandfather (a Jeffersonian) and his benevolent future father-in-law (a Federalist minister).[27] Sedgwick's approach was to expand the liberal constituency through familial affection and sentimental identification rather than to sharpen partisan lines dividing liberals from their enemies.

It was no accident that many of the writers who promoted this irenic liberalism were women; indeed, the prominence of women writers was another distinctive feature of antebellum liberalism. Inspired by new educational opportunities and by the revolutionary rhetoric of self-assertion, but frustrated by their lack of professional opportunities, middle-class women were eager to spread liberal virtues throughout the young nation. Virtue itself, as it had been defined in the late eighteenth century, now had a feminine gender. A male reaction would eventually set in, as James Fenimore Cooper and Natty Bumppo led male readers out of the home and into the wilderness, but for a decade or so, women writers promoted a liberal, familial virtue that appealed to both men and women.[28]

Antebellum women writers took for granted a model of family life that had emerged in the eighteenth century and became normative for the middle class by the 1820s. They assumed that affection, not economics, was the foundation of a successful marriage, that children are different from adults and in need of deliberate nurture, and that mothers have the right and duty to direct this process of nurture.[29] A few decades earlier, all these propositions were debatable, but by 1825 they were so taken for granted (among literate, native-born European Americans) that they could be used as a rhetorical springboard for more radical causes. The whole world, liberal women argued, needed to be run like a household; the nurturant norms of maternal love were valid in all walks of life. Indeed, maternal love was the paradigm of nonviolent power.

Antebellum women writers, many feminist critics have suggested, proposed "domestic ideology as serious public policy."[30] This domestic ideology was also a domestic theology, for antebellum women writers were often deeply committed to the cause of religious liberalism. Catharine Maria Sedgwick was a close family friend of William Ellery Channing, who had attended her father's deathbed, and her first novel was an expanded Unitarian tract. As sisters of prominent Unitarian leaders, both Lydia Maria Child and Eliza Buckminster Lee were equally familiar with theological liberalism. (In 1822 Child joined the Swedenborgian church, which blended liberal theology with a healthy dose of heterodox mysticism.) All three women, and to a lesser extent such liberal but non-Unitarian writers as Lydia Sigourney, wove theological concerns into their fiction. The rise of Unitarianism as an institutional center of religious liberalism was thus yet another factor in the antebellum harvest of Christian liberalism.

The Antebellum Boom in Fiction

To a remarkable extent, the newly assertive Unitarian liberals chose as their medium neither the sermon nor the theological treatise but rather religious fiction. The turn to fiction made sense for many reasons. It was a virtual necessity for liberal women, who even in Unitarianism were denied access to the pulpit and the university podium. But fiction was also *the* growth industry of intellectual life in the 1820s, a period that Sandra A. Zagarell has termed "the take-off decade of American literature."[31] In these years a few Americans—Washington Irving, James Fenimore Cooper, Catharine Sedgwick—became able to support themselves through writing. They were also the first U.S. novelists to attract readers in Europe: Sedgwick's second novel, *Redwood*, was translated into German, Swedish, Italian, and French. But domestic factors were decisive in generating the boom in fiction. The period of sustained economic growth that began in 1821, along with improvements in print technology, enabled publishing firms to create national networks for distribution, while the expansion of public education created a newly literate audience for popular fiction.

Short fiction appeared in ornate "gift books" designed to help middle-class families observe holidays and in such literary journals as the elite, mostly Unitarian *North American*

Review (founded in 1815), the *Saturday Evening Post* (1821), and *Godey's Lady's Book* (1830). Writers typically began with pieces suitable for such venues, then turned to the novel. The national output of fiction swelled from 5 volumes in 1820 to 26 in 1830 and 54 in 1835. (The panic of 1837 caused a brief downturn followed by an even more dramatic explosion; 158 volumes of fiction appeared in 1845.) These numbers were dwarfed both by the importation of English novels and by the massive output of American fiction in the 1850s, but the novels of the 1820s exerted special influence as the inaugural works of the American tradition. Most of the rhetorical strategies found in *Uncle Tom's Cabin*, for example, were pioneered by Sedgwick and her peers. Indeed, when Sedgwick died in 1867, *Harper's* eulogized her by noting that "her precedence was never seriously threatened until Mrs. Stowe wrote 'Uncle Tom.'"[32]

Antebellum writers of fiction triumphed over both a weak economic infrastructure and a widespread cultural antipathy to fiction. Even in the midst of the publishing boom, fiction was guilty until proven innocent: the highest praise a reviewer could offer a novel was to say that it was not like other novels. Antipathy to fiction was rooted in both orthodox theology and commonsense philosophy: the two traditions agreed that excessive reading of fiction enabled imagination to usurp reason as the guiding power of the psyche, and that the substitution of imagined for real events usurped God's authority as Creator. Both traditions, moreover, were concerned about the "immoral" influences of the novel of seduction, which orthodoxy thought would exacerbate the mind's natural corruption, and common sense thought would corrupt the mind's natural affections.[33]

Gradually, these concerns ceased to justify a wholesale condemnation of fiction and became a set of criteria for virtuous fiction. A good novel would be "founded in fact" or at least related to observable generalizations about human behavior, and it would subordinate the exercise of the imagination to the rational pursuit of virtue. After 1814, Sir Walter Scott's *Waverley* novels emerged as the leading model of moral fiction. By drawing his themes from history, Scott ensured that his writing would have a vital connection to factual reality. And by stressing the discernment processes of ordinary historical agents, Scott ensured that his novels would have more moral relevance than the increasingly dispassionate works of professional historians. Soon even as staunch a partisan of orthodoxy as Lyman Beecher was encouraging his children to spend time reading Scott.[34]

The Liberal Commitment to Fiction

Still, liberals were quicker than the orthodox to embrace fiction as an important theological genre. Indeed, the fiction of Sedgwick, Child, and Lee was as integral to the liberal theological corpus as either the biblical scholarship of Andrews Norton and Henry Ware Sr. or the sermons of William Ellery Channing and Jared Sparks. Fiction meshed well with the liberal agenda for several reasons. It attended in detail to the particulars of human experience, thus providing an excellent platform for the development of the liberal doctrine of the inherent dignity and ultimate perfectibility of human nature. Fiction was not inherently polemical and thus fit with the liberal conviction that theological minutiae were less important than ethical living—though liberal fiction always had a theological ax to grind.

Fiction could easily reach beyond institutional boundaries. While a sermon delivered from a Unitarian pulpit or a lecture presented at Harvard Divinity School was addressed almost exclusively to a liberal in-group, a popular novel might be picked up by anyone wanting a good story. Fiction might, moreover, be written by individuals, particularly women, for whom university training and ordination were not possible. Given the widespread liberal ambivalence about institution-building and the chronic weakness of liberal institutions, fiction helped make the fate of liberalism independent of the fate of the American Unitarian Association. Perhaps most important, liberal fiction of the 1820s was important as an incubator for the more radical liberal ideas that emerged in the 1830s and 1840s. Because liberal fiction placed ordinary human life, rather than the Bible or the church, at the center of religious reflection, it paved the way for frontal attacks on Bible and church by both Transcendentalists and "come-outer" political radicals who blasted the churches for their compromises with such social evils as slavery.[35]

Though most liberal fiction was written by women, two ordained Unitarian men played key roles in highlighting the theological potential of fiction. Henry Ware Jr., son of the noted biblical scholar and Harvard professor, was committed to shifting the Unitarian center of gravity from theory to practice and from the minister's study to the kitchen and parlor. As holder of a new chair in "pulpit eloquence and pastoral care" at Harvard Divinity School, he integrated practical concerns into the ministerial curriculum, and as editor of a series of novels entitled *Scenes and Characters Illustrating Christian Truth*, he provided institutional support for several writers committed to the liberal gospel. Sedgwick's most popular novel, *Home*, first appeared in this series.

Meanwhile, William Ellery Channing pleaded eloquently for the interdependence of literature and faith. The optimistic liberal faith in humanity promised to inspire literature in a way that the "technical, arbitrary dogmas" of orthodoxy never could, and fiction—especially women's fiction—could in turn communicate liberal truth more effectively than the traditional sermon. "Woman, if she may not speak in the church, may speak from the printing room," wrote Channing, "and her touching expositions of religion, not learned in theological institutions but in the schools of affection, of sorrow, of experience, of domestic charge, sometimes make their way to the heart more surely than the minister's homilies."[36] While orthodox critics worried that works of human imagination threatened the creative authority of God, Channing taught that literary creativity expressed humanity's kinship with the divine father. Channing also tied the work of fiction to the liberal promise of the United States. "The great subject of literature," he insisted, was a "consciousness of our nature" that is the germ of love for ourselves, for others, and for God. But that consciousness had been suppressed in Europe, where "establishments founded in force" had imposed "political and artificial distinctions" that "obscured our common nature." Europe had "kings, nobles, priests, peasants" and thus a "degraded" literature; America had conscious human beings and thus the potential for a "profounder" literature.[37]

Channing voiced an implicit antebellum consensus that literature was a source of power that might supplant the traditional, potentially violent forms of power rooted in established states and churches. The particular form this power took was that of *interest*: a powerful novel stimulated strong feelings of fascination or enchantment in the reader. Like economic interest, literary interest was not a zero-sum sort of power. Novels were powerful precisely because they enhanced the self and made the reader more powerful.[38] This was the repeated message of liberalism: people could assert themselves without dethroning God, and could love themselves and their neighbors simultaneously.

The liberal commitment to literature dated back at least to 1803, when Unitarian ministers William Emerson and Joseph Buckminster (father and brother, respectively, of Ralph Waldo Emerson and Eliza Buckminster Lee) founded the Anthology Club and the *Monthly Anthology*, a short-lived predecessor to the *North American Review*. The first novelist with strong liberal connections was probably Sarah Savage, who began publishing in 1814 and contributed to *Scenes and Characters* in the 1830s. But the defining text for the liberal novelistic tradition was Catharine Sedgwick's first novel, *A New-England Tale*. Sedgwick wrote this fictional attack on orthodox faith and morals as a tract celebrating her conversion to Unitarianism, then expanded and published it in 1822. It tells of the trials and triumphs of Jane Elton, a young orphan growing up in a town modeled on Sedgwick's own hometown of Stockbridge, Massachusetts. Beset by the cruelty of her orthodox relatives and neighbors, Jane finds sympathy and support from a Methodist maid and a variety of socially marginal characters. After a difficult romance with a cruel and violent infidel who is scarred by his orthodox background, Jane realizes that her truest love is for her longtime friend and benefactor, a Quaker widower. The novel closes as they begin a life of connubial bliss and wide-ranging benevolent service.[39]

The Liberal Approach to Historical Fiction

In the years following this publication, Sedgwick and her admirers produced a prodigious quantity of liberal fiction, treating both contemporary and historical themes. In their historical works, liberals grappled most directly with the connections between theology and social violence. The turn to history was logical, for in the 1820s history dominated American publishing. Eighty-five percent of best-sellers during the 1820s were histories, a pattern that reflected the expansion of public education and the proliferation of state historical societies. But liberal historical fiction must be distinguished from both history proper and the historical romance of James Fenimore Cooper.

The purpose of history, proponents agreed, was to instill virtuous and republican habits in the citizenry. This task was made more important by religious disestablishment, which meant that churches were no longer positioned to promote a common morality. The arena of history attracted both irenic individuals who sought a consensus history and religious partisans who hoped to keep their versions of events from being forgotten. The Plymouth bicentennial of 1820 thus sparked an intense debate between rival religious historians in New England. In that year Thomas Robbins, an orthodox minister who believed that Mosaic law should be strictly binding on all nations, edited an edition of Cotton Mather's *Magnalia Christi Americana* which proved wildly popular. For liberals, who saw Mather as the superstitious and power-mongering tyrant behind the Salem witch trials, this entailed a serious challenge, and most of the novels considered here can be read as sustained answers to Mather and Robbins. Since both liberals and orthodox claimed for themselves the evangelical faith of the Reformation, clarity about the essence of that faith was all-important.[40]

Historical fiction was the radical edge of antebellum historiography.[41] By focusing on the experiences of ordinary people rather than on official acts of institutions, histori-cal fiction anticipated the concerns of twentieth-century social history. Fiction writers were also more inclined to write polyphonically, placing the voices of historical losers—slaves, Native Americans, accused witches—on a par with those of the winners. The predominantly female writers of historical fiction, moreover, made sure that the choices and experiences of women were an integral part of the histories they told.

The liberal women novelists also offered a significant counterpoint to the historical tradition of James Fenimore Cooper. Cooper closely followed Sir Walter Scott, who promoted a "stadialist" view of history. Both authors believed that all societies move inexorably through stages: hunting-and-gathering "savagery," herding "barbarism," civi-lized agriculture, and commerce, each with its own set of beliefs, practices, and values. Though these differences were in no sense "racial" or biological, they could not be tran-scended by sheer individual effort. Conflict was inevitable when a society passed from one stage to the next, or when communities at different stages—such as Europeans and Native Americans—encountered one another. Stadialism allowed Scott and Cooper to write sympathetically and elegiacally about the victims of history even as they proclaimed the inevitability of the historical events that victimized them. They were not interested in promoting a future society in which such victimization might be undone.[42]

Sedgwick and her followers, by contrast, wrote historical fiction in order to create a better future.[43] For models they looked not only to Scott but also to Maria Edgeworth, whom Sedgwick characterized as "the beneficent genius who has made the actual social world better and happier." They took much of stadialist theory for granted—it was part of the cultural air they breathed—but also assumed that universal human commonali-ties, such as familial affection, were more significant than cultural differences. They sometimes called Native Americans "savages," but they insisted that savages had "hearts as bold and true" and "bosoms throbbing with as deep and fervent tenderness" as civi-lized Europeans.[44] Consequently, they treated events such as the Indian wars not as inevitable cultural clashes but as struggles *within* each community between violence and virtue. (More precisely, they inconsistently blended both accounts of the Indian wars.) Above all, the liberal novelists used historical fiction as a laboratory in which to test the universal validity of liberal ideas. They believed that the impulses toward freedom, equality, and affection which they felt in their own hearts were shared by people of every age, and they wondered why the historical record was still so full of bondage, privilege, and violence. In tracing the history of New England, one critic has perceptively suggested, liberal novelists were most concerned with a single question: "How would someone like me have fared at the hands of the Puritans?"[45]

The Liberal Account of Puritan Violence

The liberals' oft-repeated answer was twofold: a virtuous individual in Puritan New England would have faced the organized violence of orthodox and illiberal institutions but also would have connected with the affectionate impulses of most individual Puri-tans, and thus could have changed a violent society for the better. (The social reformer of the 1830s who challenged institutions of war, intemperance, or slavery was in an almost identical situation.) Because antebellum liberals believed that virtuous individuals did in fact exist among the Puritans, as among *all human communities*, their novelistic task was simultaneously to explain the violence of Puritan institutions and the nonviolent power of Puritan individuals. Though these two themes were interwoven in Puritan novels, I shall analyze them sequentially.

Why was New England history so full of violence—of the persecution of Quakers, the hanging of witches, and the slaughter of Native Americans? The orthodox could answer easily: violence, like all sin, has been an ineradicable part of human nature ever since the Fall, but it is channeled by God's inscrutable Providence to serve the ultimate end of divine glory. God used the violence of New England history, for example, to chastise members of his chosen community for their lapses and to ensure their triumph as a "city on a hill." This explanation was unacceptable to liberals, who believed that it excused Puritan oppression and made God a violent and arbitrary tyrant. But the liberals' faith in natural human virtue made it hard for them to explain human violence at all. Lydia Maria Child, for example, wrestled awkwardly with the problem in *The First Settlers of New England*, a fictional history written for children. When Child's narrator tells her daughter of all the abuses committed by the Puritans, the girl plausibly asks how people "by nature disposed to do right" could succumb to such wickedness.[46] Liberals could answer only by rehearsing the entire history of New England.

Their first move, typically, was to locate the Puritans at an early phase of the Reformation movement—a moment when the rediscovered gospel was just beginning to liberate human nature from institutional oppression. "I never view the thriving villages of New England," Child claimed at the outset of her first novel, "without feeling a glow of national pride, as I say, 'this is my own, my native land.'" Just two centuries earlier, North America had been desolate and Europe had been depraved, but the Reformation had uncovered a transformative, Christian light. "During many long, long ages of gloom and corruption, it seemed as if the pure flame of religion was every where quenched in blood;—but the watchful vestal had kept the sacred flame burning deeply and fervently."

After praising the "stern and unyielding" men who brought the gospel to America, however, Child responds to an invisible critic. "In this enlightened and liberal age," she says, many perceive the Puritans as "dark, discontented bigots." In fact, the "shadows" of their characters were mixed with "bold and powerful light." Their misdeeds could be ascribed to circumstance: to the harshness of their oppression in England, to all "the hardships of a remote and dreary province," and above all to the "absurd and trifling" elements of their theology. Such evils could not obscure the "conscientious, persevering fortitude" that the Puritans—like their Jesuit rivals!—brought to their cause. "Whatever merit may be attached to the cause of our forefathers, the mighty effort which they made for its support is truly wonderful; and whatever might have been their defects, they certainly possessed excellencies, which peculiarly fitted them for a van-guard in the proud and rapid march of freedom."[47]

This conventional account of the light and shadows of Puritanism was shared by all the liberal writers, and it is worth highlighting its main features. First, Child insists that the Puritans must be understood with reference *both* to the violence of history and to the future promise of America. They had lived in a period in which religious freedom in general, and gospel truth in particular, had been brutally suppressed, yet they helped inaugurate a new era of human history. Their actions reflected both the impress of the past and the promise of the future. Thus far, Child is simply echoing the Puritans' own understanding of their community as a city on a hill erected after long centuries of "papist" darkness.

Second, Child contends that light and shadows coexisted within the same community and even within the same individuals. The link to the Jesuits is telling: the Puritans' light was not their exclusive possession but something they shared with even their bitterest enemies. Third and finally, Child suggests that the Puritan shadows can best be understood as the consequence of contingent historical and environmental factors, including the intricacies of their own theology. It is here that she departs most radically from the Puritan version of the New England story: the Puritans often admitted their faults, but they never would have traced them to the caprice of circumstance, much less to their own theology. For them, every human failing was evidence of innate depravity and of Satan's machinations, and the explanations so ardently sought by the liberals were quite beside the point.

Despite their half-apologetic stance, liberals were unsparing in their depictions of the specific violent practices of the Puritans. The Puritans, they contended, ruthlessly persecuted dissenters, moving from "fine, imprisonment, scourging with the 'three-corded whip,' cutting off the ears, and boring the tongue with a red-hot iron" to public executions. In describing Puritan treatment of the Quakers, they repeatedly deployed the sentimental tactic of placing the victims of violence in their familial context. Thus, Whittier depicted a woman still holding her newborn as she is stripped for a lashing, and Lee described a Quaker woman being dragged through the streets as her Puritan husband follows, desperately trying to block the sheriff's whip. Liberals also linked Puritan violence to the repression of the individual's spiritual integrity: by sparing innocent women only if they confessed to witchcraft, the Puritans did violence to the conscience as well as the body.[48]

The liberal novelists expected little dissent from their readers when they condemned witch-hunts and the execution of Quakers, for such activities had long been discredited in the larger society. They trod on more controversial ground when they laid the genocide of Native Americans at the feet of the Puritans. Violent attacks on Indians had hardly ended in the 1820s: the frontier resistance of the Creeks, the Seminoles, and Tecumseh's Confederation had been crushed just a few years earlier, and by the end of the decade Andrew Jackson's administration began a series of devastating removals of those nations that had sought to coexist with whites in the Southeast. Even in New England, the popular school texts of Hannah Adams, Emma Willard, and Augusta Berard justified genocide by demonizing all Indians as a violent menace to the New England experiment.[49]

Lydia Sigourney, by contrast, wrote her epic poem, *Traits of the Native Americans*, from a pro-Indian standpoint, and in *A New-England Tale* Sedgwick had Jane Elton contrast Puritan and Quaker Indian policies: "Our fathers . . . refused to acknowledge the image of God in the poor Indian . . . while Penn, and his peaceful people, won their confidence, their devotion, by treating them with even-handed justice, with brotherly kindness." Both Sedgwick and Child quoted ironically from the spate of recently republished Puritan histories to illustrate the horrific ways in which the Puritans had interpreted even the burning of Pequod villages as a "sweet sacrifice" to God. Child summed up the liberals' most radical perspective in a later text, the "Appeal for the

Indians"; "The plain truth is, our relations with the red and black members of the human family, have been one almost unvaried history of violence and fraud. Our ancestors, whether Catholics or Puritans, were accustomed to regard heathen tribes as Philistines, whom 'the Lord's people' were commissioned to exterminate root and branch, or to hold them as bondmen and bondwomen."[50]

Liberals did not consider colonial violence to be entirely the fault of Puritanism. They believed that members of all three colonial cultures—English Puritans, French Catholics, and Native Americans—perpetrated violence because their benevolent "affections" had been suppressed and their destructive "passions" enflamed. Though affections were naturally stronger than passions, each culture had "prejudices" or "superstitions" that could, in Child's words, stifle "the voice of conscience" and paralyze "the natural emotions of compassion." In one story, for example, Child described a Jesuit whose practice of celibacy and asceticism had "turned back many a gentle current of affection, which might have soothed and refreshed his heart." Similarly, in the novel *Hope Leslie*, Sedgwick told of an Indian chief who is naturally given to the "human virtues" but succumbs to the passion of vengeance when his oldest son is killed and his other children are kidnapped by the whites. His temporary instability is reinforced and encouraged because of his community's religious belief "that an insane person is inspired."[51]

Liberals gave more detailed attention to the affection-twisting tendencies of Puritanism, and out of their theological critique they developed an interesting and systematic sociocultural theory of violence. This generally followed the "moral" argument against Calvinism that Channing had first articulated in his Baltimore Sermon of 1819. Channing argued that while the actual behavior of orthodox individuals generally reflects the positive influences of "nature, conscience, common sense" and the gospel, the doctrines of total depravity and predestination tend "to discourage the timid, to give excuses to the bad, to feed the vanity of the fanatical, and to offer shelter to the bad feelings of the malignant . . . to pervert the moral faculty, to form a gloomy, forbidding, and servile religion, and to lead men to substitute censoriousness, bitterness, and persecution, for a tender and impartial charity."[52] Orthodox theology, in other words, always threatened the moral integrity of orthodox individuals and sometimes succeeded in depraving them.

In *A New-England Tale*, Sedgwick so insistently traced human villainy to the malignant effects of Calvinist doctrine that a reader might conclude that the *doctrine* of original sin had caused all the depravity traditionally ascribed to original sin itself. The argument focuses on an orthodox woman, Mrs. Wilson, who enthusiastically espouses Samuel Hopkins's teaching that a true Christian should gladly accept God's predestination of some people to heaven and others to hell, even if this entails the damnation of beloved relatives. When Mrs. Wilson's liberal niece, Jane Elton, is orphaned, she presents the girl with an incomprehensible doctrinal test: "I put it to her conscience, whether if she was sure her mother had gone where the worm dieth not and the fire is not quenched, she should be reconciled to the character of God, and be willing herself to promote his glory, by suffering that just condemnation." Though Jane steadfastly resists her aunt's theology, Mrs. Wilson's own son is so demoralized by his mother's views on reprobation (that is, predestination to damnation) that he becomes a violent criminal. Even then, his mother does not seek to redirect him but embraces his fall as a providential affliction: "The saints of old, David, and Samuel, and Eli, were afflicted as I am, with rebellious children. I have planted and I have watered, and if it is the Lord's will to withhold the increase, I must submit."[53] Sedgwick's account inspired a whole literature of post-Calvinist hypocrites, misers, duelers, seducers, and murderers that culminated in Harriet Beecher Stowe's portrait of Aaron Burr (the wayward grandson of Jonathan Edwards) in *A Minister's Wooing*.

More historical versions of the moral argument appeared in Child's *First Settlers* and in two novels by Eliza Buckminster Lee. Child's argument turned on the orthodox doctrines of the substitutionary atonement and of election. Channing had said that the former placed a gallows at the center of the universe, and Child agreed that it represented God as a violent parent who had "formed rational creatures for the express purpose of inflicting on them torments the most excruciating and endless" and who gladly sacrificed his own sinless son. People who worshiped such a God, she suggested, could easily believe "themselves authorized to inflict all the evil in their power on wretches who are born to suffer."[54] The point was clear: people who believe in a violent God are likely to perpetrate violence themselves.

Child laid even heavier stress on the Reformed doctrine of election, which she portrayed as the logical extension of the Jewish chosen people tradition. In the introduction to *First Settlers*, she noted that while her first goal was to expose the evils of the conquest, her second was to show "that the conduct and sanguinary institutions of the Jews, from which we have derived our cruel and unworthy notions respecting the Deity, can have no connection with the pure and heavenly religion of Jesus." (Here she echoed an anti-Judaism widespread among Enlightenment thinkers.)[55]

In the body of the text, the narrator tells her daughters that the Puritans, like the Israelites, believed they had been chosen and "authorized by God to destroy or drive out the heathen, as they styled the Indians." She further explains that confidence in one's own election breeds moral irresponsibility, as illustrated by the case of a dishonest cook who defends herself from criticism by quipping that "where sin abounds, grace much more abounds." "Mary's temper was not really bad," the liberal mother elaborates, "but she had been accustomed to cherish bad passions, instead of repressing them, by the odious doctrines set forth by Calvinistic preachers, of their sect being the only favored people who cannot err."[56] This is of course a caricature of Puritan piety, but even so Child's critique is selective. It is directed not at the Puritan community as such but more narrowly at their "odious doctrines." Mary is presented not as a typical Puritan but as an unusually consistent one who is morally hypocritical precisely because of her theological consistency. Other Puritans, Child implies, were better Christians because they were sloppier theologians.

Despite its harshness, Child's theory was partly continuous with the orthodox view of sin: it linked violence to an excess of self-assertion. Other liberals placed more emphasis on the depressive side of orthodoxy—on its tendency to inhibit the cultivation of a responsible self. Eliza Buckminster Lee suggested that orthodoxy produced not just arrogant perpetrators of genocide but also passive parents, sinners too depressed to reform, and spectators of violence too timid to intervene. She focused on the doctrines of total depravity, which led people to distrust their own best affections, and reprobation, which led people to despair rather than to repentance and conversion.[57]

In *Delusion*, Lee paints a picture of Seymore, a well-meaning ministerial student who ultimately votes to condemn his own lover as a witch. He takes the doctrine of original sin so seriously that he succumbs to "a morbid sensitiveness to moral evil, an exaggerated sense of his own sins, and of the strictest requisitions of the spirit of the times." He cannot trust himself. When Edith is accused of witchcraft, consequently, Seymore interprets his love for her not as a divinely implanted natural affection but as a form of idolatry to be rooted out: "He trembled when he thought of his almost idolatrous love, and with a faith which he fancied resembled that of Abraham, he believed the time had now come when he must cut off a right hand, and pluck out a right eye, to give evidence of his submission to the will of God." This embrace of a sacrificial logic only separates him from God, however, for it was Edith who had previously helped him experience a positive sense of divine presence.[58]

Seymore illustrates Channing's comment that "the history of the church proves, that men may trust their faculties too little as well as too much." Though Channing's reference was to the intellectual timidity of those who doubt their ability to understand God, his remark suggests that liberals understood that a lack of self-assertion could be as sinful as too much self-assertion. This had profound implications for their understanding of violence. While the orthodox could plausibly assume that Providence might use violence to chasten excessively assertive selves, liberals insisted that violence was invariably destructive for all involved. The attempt to instill virtue through terror, Channing insisted, "generally injures the character, breaks men into cowards and slaves, brings the intellect to cringe before human authority, makes man abject before his Maker, and, by a natural reaction of the mind, often terminates in a presumptuous confidence."[59]

In *Florence, the Parish Orphan*, Lee traced another trajectory of violence, in which orthodoxy inspires first neglect of the self and then its tyrannical repression. Where Seymore had been weighed down with total depravity, Ralph Leonard is raised without any constraints whatsoever. His Aunt Molly believes in total depravity but is too lazy to pursue a regime of discipline: "To spare herself the trouble of inflicting punishment, she allowed him in bursts of uncontrolled passion, from the effects of which she could not always herself escape." This confirms her belief in his depravity and justifies a violent response to his misdeeds. Soon Molly and Ralph are locked in an escalating cycle of reprisals, played out on their farm animals. Ralph trains his dog to kill Molly's chickens; Molly has a hired man shoot the dog; Ralph, genuinely sorrowful but unable to channel that sorrow properly, takes the gun and shoots an innocent calf.[60]

Ralph's downward path is temporarily checked by his romance with Flory, a virtuous girl who draws out in him affections that are "gentle, humble, humane." But she cannot prevail over the "counteracting influence at home" or Ralph's jealousy of an apparent rival, George Lovell. When George gives Flory some orphaned birds, Ralph reacts violently: "With a jerk of his thumb and finger he had wrung the frail necks of two of the birds, and cast them far from him, before Florence could spring towards him and save the older bird from the same fate." At this point, fear dampens Flory's affection, but she also does not trust herself enough to recognize that theirs is "not the instinctive attachment of two young hearts, twined together, as it were, in heaven." She remains pledged to him when he goes off to sea. On his return years later, Ralph finds Flory and George together near a cliff and pushes Flory to her death "by accident or design." The precise degree of Ralph's guilt remains ambiguous, but its roots are crystal clear.[61]

Lee's point was that even batterers like Ralph were not naturally depraved but were victims of the entire system of orthodox "superstition." Similarly, Child wrote that "no superstition could be compared to Calvinism in its demoralizing, petrifying effects." This was more than a pejorative. "Superstition" suggested that both the system and its violent effects were contingent, even ephemeral. Violence was rooted not in cosmic necessity but in a particularly insidious and far-reaching error. There was no need for a cosmic struggle between good and evil *groups* of people; the real contest existed between the inner nature and superficial beliefs of people caught in the superstition. Orthodox views, Lee insisted, were often held by individuals whose souls were "daily fed with charity and prayer, and filled to overflowing with tender, human love; but their faith; their tenets, are no part of themselves." Violence became possible when these people allowed extrinsic beliefs to take priority over the affectionate powers that were truly "part of themselves."[62]

References to "superstition" also indicate an appreciation for scientific rationality. Liberals linked Puritan violence to a belief in an enchanted universe of angels and demons, in which the heavens and earth were filled with meaningful signs. Fearful of both God and the devil, the Puritans had readily interpreted unusual natural events as indications, in Lee's words, "that God demanded of them . . . the destruction of his enemies." Lee elaborated this point in her writings about witchcraft, in which she juxtaposed an enlightened liberal view of witchcraft to Puritan beliefs. The Salem witch craze, she suggested in *Delusion*, was the result of the malicious deceptions of the "afflicted" girls. By refusing to confess falsely, Lee's heroine Edith defends not only truth but also a rational theology in which "God suffers us to be tempted by our own passions and unrestrained imaginations, but not by visible or invisible evil spirits."[63]

Yet Lee suggested that the ultimate problem with Puritan superstition was not so much that it was false and irrational but that it was allowed to trump nonviolent and affectionate impulses. In an earlier story, a woman named Miriam is accused of witchcraft because she is able to calm her epileptic brother by simply gazing at him. He is brought to her trial as a test of her diabolical powers and, as expected, suffers a fit when he sees his sister's distressed appearance. Though she knows it will only seal her guilt in the judges' eyes, she cannot subdue the affectionate impulse to calm her brother. The judges' subsequent condemnation of Miriam is not merely wrong; it is dangerous because it so completely misrecognizes natural family affection.[64]

For liberals, this misrecognition was the basic orthodox error. Violence occurred when well-meaning people failed to recognize the nonviolent powers resident in every human soul. Certainly, the mistake was widespread. "I know," wrote Channing, "that the doctrine of ages has been, that terror, restraint, and bondage are the chief safeguards of human virtue and peace." Yet it could be corrected: "We have begun to learn that affection, confidence, respect, and freedom are mightier as well as nobler agents."[65] Liberals hoped that by disenchanting violence—by exposing it as no more than a mistake—they would liberate those agents to transform not just family life but society as a whole.

The Liberal Sacralization of Nonviolent Power

Even as liberals disenchanted violence, they found new religious significance in nonviolent power. Despite their occasional use of scientific-sounding arguments, the liberals were not empiricists seeking to banish God's hand from all explanations of earthly events.

Their goal was to see the divine presence in a new way. God was active in the world as a loving parent, gently prodding human beings to exercise their affections in ever wider contexts. To see this, however, one had to break down the wall separating divine from human power, and "religion" from everyday life. Thus, Channing insisted that he could best understand God by "reverencing" the "marks of a divine origin and the pledges of a celestial inheritance" in human nature. Sedgwick admonished her readers "that our religion is not like that of the ancients, something set aside from the ordinary concerns of life, . . . but is 'the leaven that leaveneth the whole lump,' a spirit to be infused into the common affairs of life."[66] This argument echoed the Puritan concern not to set certain times or places apart as especially sacred; as in so many ways, the liberals based their critique of orthodoxy on fundamental Puritan values.

Liberals could draw especially direct links between God's power and earthly existence because they denied the doctrine of original sin, which had historically marked the boundary between heaven and earth. While liberals and orthodox agreed in seeing divine Providence as the most overarching context of human existence, the orthodox held that original sin and the other consequences of the Fall provided the next most encompassing context, while the family (and other social institutions) was a local, fragile manifestation of order amid the chaos of sin. The encompassing character of original sin meant that Providence could act only paradoxically, by "overruling" sinful human actions. This made it easy for the orthodox to see God's hand in violent events and difficult for them to draw a more direct, nonparadoxical connection between Providence and human affections. Indeed, they assumed that even the most benevolent affections were corrupted by sin and thus needed to be transcended by the true Christian. Liberals, by contrast, saw the exercise of human love as an extension of divine love that provided the second most encompassing context of human life, while sin and violence were contingent and local. Human love did not therefore need to be transcended: it was a path to God.

Liberals articulated this theology by telling stories about the family. When parents recognized the divine image in their children and directed that image toward maturity, God's power was manifest on earth. Family life was the truest form of worship. "Madame de Stael," recalls the narrator of Lee's *Delusion*, "says that a mother with a sick child must have invented prayer; and she is right: a woman would first pray, not for herself, but for the object of her tenderness." Liberal novels are thus filled with examples of family worship. Children are encouraged to share their faith with adults alienated from the church; parents and children join in conducting a sabbath school for their neighbors; a son heading to war is sent off first by the minister and then by his family in "a sacred service more informal, and far more intensely felt." All of these means fulfilled Sedgwick's dictum that familial and religious affections be nurtured together: "How easy it is to interweave the religious with the domestic affections, and how sadly do those sin against the lights of nature, who neglect to form this natural union!"[67]

Since the definitive task of the liberal family was education, liberals found particular religious meaning in educational activities. Liberal novelists promoted a familial model of religious education, encouraging parents to introduce biblical themes into everyday conversations, teach concrete Bible stories before abstruse doctrines, and "improve every opportunity" to illustrate gospel truths via natural phenomena. They also urged Christian parents to model their disciplinary actions on the steady presence of Providence:

"When a young child finds its mother uniform—not one day weakly indulgent, and the next capriciously severe, but always the same mild, firm being—she is to the child like a beneficent but unchanging Providence; and he no more expects his own will to prevail, than children of an older growth expect the sun to stand still, and the seasons to change their order, for their convenience."[68] Here the doctrine of Providence functions not to distinguish divine sovereignty from human subjection but to suggest a basic continuity between divine and human activity.

The goal of such pedagogical practices, liberals affirmed, was no less than to make human children like God. "Religious instruction," Channing insisted, "should aim chiefly to turn men's aspirations and efforts to that perfection of the soul, which constitutes it a bright image of God." The narrator of one of Sedgwick's novels agreed, suggesting that "a perfectly disinterested action is a demonstration to the Spirit of its alliance and communion with the divine nature—an entrance into the joy of its Lord." Nearly all liberal novelists reinforced the point by repeatedly referring to benevolent or affectionate characters as "angels." Sedgwick's Jane Elton is identified as "an angel upon earth" by her friend Polly, who heeds Jane's advice "just as much as if it were spoken to me right out of Heaven." Eliza Lee's Naomi "has the form and expression of an angel visitant," while in the same novel John Eliot's offer to support a ministerial student is "a benevolent errand, a message of hope, that gave to his countenance an expression of angelic goodness."[69]

Liberal novels are also filled with angelic mothers whose orphaned children pray as often to them as to God. When Sedgwick's Hope Leslie is in trouble, she goes to the churchyard, looks at the moon, and exclaims, "Oh, my mother! if ever thy presence is permitted to me, be with me now!" Her lover, Everell Fletcher, likewise feels a "celestial spirit" in his soul when he is facing possible death at the hands of Pequod captors, and he reflects that "it may be . . . that my mother and sisters are permitted to minister to me." And Edith, in Lee's *Delusion*, seeks out "a particular spot in the evening sky where she fancied the spirit of her mother to dwell; and there, in all her childish griefs, she sought sympathy and turned her eyes towards it in childlike devotion."[70]

Liberals even referred to infants, who presumably had not yet matured into the full likeness of God, as angels. The significance of these child angels was twofold: their affections had not yet been distorted by violent institutions, and they could inspire in the adults around them redemptive, familial feelings. Eliza Cabot Follen's contribution to *Scenes and Characters*, for example, centers on a sickly little girl, Fanny Grey, who is to her parents "an angel from heaven." Her mother reads the Bible with Fanny in her lap because "both speak to me of the kingdom of Heaven, where there are no harsh words," and Fanny's complete faith in immortality rescues her father from skepticism and infidelity. When Fanny dies, the narrator sums up her significance: "Such beings seem to hold a more exalted place, to have a higher mission in this life, than the rest of mankind. They come as messengers from heaven to us; their angelic looks, their pure lives, are their credentials. They come to declare to us the existence of the spiritual world." Similarly, in Sedgwick's *Hope Leslie* an infant is the only member of the Fletcher family able to stop an Indian massacre—by perceiving the Pequod chief as a father rather than an enemy and directing to him "a piteous supplication that no words could have expressed."[71]

It is not clear how literally the novelists meant for readers to take their angelic references. They placed many in the mouths of naive or ill-educated characters, and occasionally a so-called angel will disavow the label. When Jane Elton's unworthy suitor, Edward Erskine, calls her a saint, for example, she demurs: "There are, and there ought to be, few believers in earth-born angels."[72] (The interchangeability of saints and angels is typical of these texts and also seems to point to a metaphorical reading.) Yet it may be significant that Edward is an infidel: perhaps Sedgwick meant to suggest that the *language* of faith is meaningless apart from the *life* of faith. Probably the liberal novelists did not want to force their readers to choose between a literal and a metaphorical reading. By leaving the question open, they destabilized the boundary between the natural and the supernatural and thus reinforced their main point, which is that God is to be found in the midst of ordinary phenomena.

The liberals' goal was not merely to exhibit the angelic virtues of benevolent individuals but also to demonstrate the effectiveness of nonviolent power in the midst of institutional and superstitious violence. By showing how angelic Puritans could overcome the violence surrounding them, they suggested that the legacy of Puritanism lay not in the errors of Puritan theology but in the affections of Puritan families. This was all the more important because liberals saw the Puritans as transmitters of the Reformation's gospel message to North America. Leaders like John Winthrop and John Eliot, Sedgwick sincerely believed, "were men selected of Heaven to achieve a great work. In the quaint language of the time, 'the Lord sifted three nations for precious seed to sow the wilderness.'"[73] Puritans had espoused, albeit in imperfect form, the liberal doctrine of religious liberty; they had staunchly opposed Stuart tyranny; they had created roughly egalitarian social institutions and promoted universal liberty; they had even instituted early restrictions on cruelty to animals. There was, in short, much wheat to be extracted from the tares of Puritan violence.

Liberal Interlopers

One way liberal novelists extracted this Puritan wheat was by filling their stories with Puritan characters who repudiate their community's violent or persecutory practices. These "liberal interlopers," as I shall call them, function as mouthpieces for the authors' perspective on Puritanism, but they also reflect an honest belief that liberalism was not a monopoly of the early nineteenth century. Thus, Catharine Sedgwick's William Fletcher, a leading character in *Hope Leslie*, chides his wife when she says that an unconverted Pequod woman had died "in her sins." "We should not suit God's mercy," he says, "to the narrow frame of our thoughts." Then, as a good Puritan, he cites a supporting scriptural text. Whittier's Margaret Smith anticipates the nineteenth-century liberal agenda even more explicitly when she scolds a Puritan deacon for holding a slave, for supplying him with liquor, and for subjecting him to physical punishment. In other texts, liberal interlopers quietly dissent from witch-hunting, adapt religious ceremonies to the needs of Catholic visitors, rescue prisoners from the Puritan authorities, question the Indian policy, and boldly assert the irrelevance of sectarian divisions.[74]

Liberal interlopers typically appear as lonely individualists or outsiders, but they are unique not so much in their possession of liberal sentiment as in their ability to articulate it. The majority of Puritans, the novelists suggested, quietly opposed persecution and violence because they felt a kinship with the victims or simply possessed a "mildness of . . . disposition." They could be expected to ransom an accused Quaker, aid a fugitive, or even support direct challenges to the Puritan authorities. Even the most persecutory Puritans had not fully stifled the "voice of nature" in their hearts, to which liberal interlopers repeatedly appealed. Lee thus describes a Puritan cleric at the execution of Mary Dyer: "The heart of the man was melting and full of love, but the soul of the Calvinist was fierce and bitter."[75]

Modern readers have a ready label for this sort of narrative strategy: anachronism. But we should not be too quick to accuse the liberal novelists of naive anachronism. They knew what anachronism was; indeed, they repeatedly warned their readers against it. Lee's *Naomi*, which contains the most fully developed picture of a liberal interloper in its title character, is peppered with reminders that the Puritans were "men of the day," that their actions were shaped by the "spirit of the times," and that all their misdeeds were palliated by the fact that they were deprived of "all these genial influences" enjoyed by later generations. Even when she describes a young woman whose "simple good-sense" allowed her to recognize Quaker virtues, Lee suggests that such context-transcending behavior was ordinarily impossible for the Puritans: "If the light of toleration had not dawned in England, how could it be expected to shine upon these western shores?"[76]

This is not as contradictory as it seems. The liberal novelists could simultaneously assert and transcend the historical distance between the Puritans and nineteenth-century readers because their very notion of historical distance was based on a particular model of historical progress. Unlike Cooper and Scott, they did not believe that the Puritans were rigidly bound by the worldview associated with a distinct cultural stage. Instead, they placed them at a particular point along a continuous pathway of reform, which was itself simply the ongoing liberation of human powers that had existed all along.[77] From this progressive point of view, it was reasonable to suppose that some individuals may have had a good sense of where the larger community was headed. Interestingly, however, the liberal novelists did not unconditionally valorize such individuals. Instead, they portrayed them as fully immersed in the ambivalence of history. Catharine Sedgwick, for example, described her interlopers as "visionaries" who were "impatient of detail," "too rapid in their anticipations," and "like children, who, setting out on a journey, are impatient after the first few paces to be at the end of it."[78]

Liberal novelists connected the progressivism of liberal interlopers to their family backgrounds. When parents were affectionate toward their children and encouraged in them habits of self-assertion, those children grew up to challenge the repressive activities of social institutions. When parents' love for one another overcame sectarian differences, their children were especially likely to become liberal interlopers. Sedgwick, for example, says of one heroine that because "those persons she most loved . . . were of variant religious sentiments," she was able to soar like a bird "beyond the contracted boundaries of sectarian faith."[79] Although liberal beliefs may have been fully articulated only in the nineteenth century, they corresponded to all people's ability to extend their moral affections to others, even others who are different.

At their most fully developed, liberal interlopers model a practice of liberal faith and devotion independent of violent social structures. The title character of Lee's novel *Naomi* is a Quaker convert from a religiously diverse family, and all her actions are dictated by a familial faithfulness that does not compromise her principles but, indeed, makes them possible. Raised in England by her father's Anglican relatives and a Quaker nurse, Naomi rers sail for America when she learns that her Puritan mother is dying. En route she is comforted by the Quaker doctrine of inner light: "She felt that the soul was alone with God; that he was near to her, and that it needed no intervention of church or priest, or even the Bible, to make her feel that he held her, and all things, in the hollow of his hand." In Massachusetts she finds her mother dead, her stepfather a self-serving hypocrite, and herself torn between the persecuting faith of the community and the "extravagances and follies" of her fellow Quakers. Though she remains devoted to the family, her very affections seem to have left her alone with God: "She had obeyed the voice of her mother and of her own heart in coming, and it was in consequence of the providence of God that she was left alone to bear the responsibilities and the trials of her new faith."[80]

In an orthodox text, this moment of aloneness would likely be the occasion for Naomi's conversion to a faith transcending all earthly affection. But for Lee, Naomi's challenge is to hold fast to her liberalism even when it isolates her, *and yet* to maintain hope that her affections will ultimately find a this-worldly outlet. This hope begins to bear fruit late in the novel, when she at last encounters Herbert, a young Harvard graduate who rejects the persecution of Quakers on the basis of an almost Transcendentalist natural religion. Naomi's sense of spiritual kinship with Herbert sustains her as she intervenes on behalf of her nurse, rescues her from jail, and ultimately proclaims her own faith before the Puritan authorities. After further trials and separations, Naomi and Herbert are at last married, beneficiaries of a friend's "silent prayer" that "drew down upon this perfect union of their young hearts the bliss of perfect faith in each other, and trust in God, that never failed through long years of absence."[81]

Ruthian Genealogy

The happy ending of Naomi's story suggests the logic of a narrative strategy which I call "Ruthian genealogy." In historical novels and more memoiristic village sketches, liberal writers forged links between contemporary readers and their Puritan ancestors by means of genealogies, or accounts of how Puritan virtues were passed from one generation to the next. Typically, these genealogies employed narrative strategies similar to those found in the biblical Book of Ruth, in which a Moabite widow follows her mother-in-law to Israel, where she actively pursues a husband, who in turn fathers a son from whom King David will eventually descend. Like Ruth, the heroines of liberal genealogies are able to pass their virtues on to new generations because they care deeply about their mothers, their sisters, their lovers, and even those who are not biologically their kin. They trust their natural affections, and it pays off in both this-worldly and otherworldly terms.[82]

Ruthian genealogy is an alternative to the "Abrahamic genealogy" found in the Book of Genesis. In that story, Abraham receives a divine promise that will descend to future generations only if he is willing to sacrifice (or almost sacrifice) his son Isaac. God's support for the family is paradoxical, dependent on the repeated *breaking* of affectionate ties. The promise descends from father to son, on a path marked by the exclusions of first Ishmael and then Esau, both of whom become fathers of rival communities.[83] The Christian liberals were utterly opposed to the basic logic of Abrahamic genealogy: they disliked the notion of an exclusive chosen people and found the idea of God demanding the sacrifice of children to be reprehensible. (Unfortunately, they identified the Jewish tradition exclusively with this sacrificial theology, failing to recognize the more inclusive counterpoint found in the Book of Ruth and other parts of the Hebrew Bible.)[84] By constructing Ruthian genealogies—by insisting on the capacity of affection to hold the generations together—liberals offered an alternative vision of how a society might be ordered and reproduced without violence.

Significantly, Ruthian genealogies do not simply invert Abrahamic genealogy. Abrahamic genealogy depends on the exclusion of women; Ruthian genealogy excludes no one on principle but postulates that all possess the natural affections on which families and societies are founded. Men may have more trouble accessing those affections, especially if they are already invested in a patriarchal system, but this simply means that others must be patient in drawing out paternal affection even as they resist patriarchal authority. This concern for the fathers, in fact, gives many Ruthian genealogies an apparently conservative cast.

Among the liberal novelists, Catharine Sedgwick was the most determined proponent of Ruthian genealogy. Her major novels are all marriage comedies in which lovers from different communities (a Southerner and a New Englander, a Puritan and a liberal Englishwoman, a New York Tory and a New England Patriot, an upper-class woman and a middle-class man) remain faithful to their affection despite patriarchal opposition, only to discover that they have fulfilled not only their own but also their fathers' deepest longings.[85] By reconciling diverse communities and repudiating patriarchal tyranny, such romances overcame the need for violence in a double sense. This plot line undoubtedly appealed to Sedgwick in part because of her own family situation: she longed to see her own Jeffersonian and Unitarian commitments as faithful to the legacy of her Federalist father and Edwardsean ancestors. But she readily connected her personal circumstances to what she perceived as the larger culture's need to appropriate Puritan virtues without being ruled by them or doomed to recapitulate Puritan violence.

Hope Leslie, Sedgwick's Puritan novel, turns on an elaborate romantic dilemma. William Fletcher, a young Englishman, is destined by a wealthy uncle to marry his cousin Alice. The uncle has a change of heart when he learns of William's Puritanism, and after a failed elopement William sails alone to New England. Separated, both he and Alice marry and have children. William's son Everell grows up in the frontier town of Springfield, where he is imbued with his father's independent spirit and deeply influenced by the kindness of a Pequod girl, Magawisca. As for Alice, she heads to New England after the death of her husband but dies en route, entrusting her two daughters to the Fletchers' care. Everell's romance with the elder daughter, Hope Leslie, is thus inevitable. It not only fulfills William Fletcher's sentimental dream but also has great reconciliatory potential: Hope's implicit religious liberalism balances Everell's Puritanism, while his strong commitment to racial justice helps her overcome the trauma of seeing her younger sister carried off by Indians.

The Puritan fathers oppose the marriage of Hope and Everell. They would rather see such independent-minded youths married to more conventional and controllable partners. Hope in particular, John Winthrop opines, needs "some one who should add to affection the modest authority of a husband."[86] It is significant that the leader of the patriarchal group in this story is John Winthrop—a man whom Sedgwick and other liberals regarded as the paragon of Puritan virtue. Patriarchal tyranny, for Sedgwick, could not be reduced to the isolated actions of individual bad men: it was an oppressive system in which even the best could be entangled.[87] But, by the same token, it was not an inevitable, inescapable system. Because the benevolent Winthrop truly desired what was best for Hope Leslie, his conflict with her was rooted not in necessity but in his own theologically confused distrust of her natural affections. He faced "superfluous trials" because of his belief that "whatever gratified the natural desires of the heart was questionable."[88]

Because Winthrop is on her side without knowing it, Hope can triumph over patriarchal tyranny through simple faithfulness to both her affections and her principles. It is not easy, to be sure, for Hope has a double genealogical task. She needs to marry Everell and also to reconnect with her sister, Faith, who is captured by the Pequods early in the story, marries her adoptive brother Oneco, and converts to missionary Catholicism. Because the Puritans are on the verge of renewed war with the Pequods, Hope must negotiate secretly with Oneco's sister Magawisca for a rendezvous with Faith. Her disappearance on a stormy night rouses the suspicions of John Winthrop, who is hardly mollified by her liberal appeals to a higher duty: "I have offended, I know; but I should commit a worse offence—an offence against my own conscience and heart—if I explained the cause of my absence." When Everell echoes Winthrop's distrust, Hope further appeals to liberal principle: "I would not be a machine, to be moved at the pleasure of anybody that happened to be a littler older than myself."[89]

Ultimately Hope's principles allow her to meet her sister, marry Everell, and make peace with Winthrop. The result is not a radical social vision: Hope triumphs by working around the fathers rather than overthrowing them, and the novel ends with them still in places of power, still forcing idealistic youth to work around them. One might imagine that real-world Hopes would have to make far more compromises to achieve harmony with real-world John Winthrops. Yet for all its easy answers, the novel challenges its readers to take seriously the social power of everyday affections—to consider that they might have more influence than armies and coercive institutions. In the 1840s, writers with far more radical commitments began to promote the same vision.

Ruthian Genealogy and Racial Reconciliation

Ruthian genealogy might have held more radical implications had it been applied more consistently to issues of race. The liberals did not really challenge their readers by suggesting new ways of understanding their relation to the Puritans (since all agreed that they were in *some* sense related to the Puritans), but to propose a model of kinship between whites and Indians was genuinely challenging. Curiously, however, the liberals had trouble fully integrating Native American characters into their genealogies. *Hope Leslie* and *Hobomok* are among the very few antebellum novels to feature interracial marriages in a positive light, but these marriages carry little genealogical significance. Sedgwick tells us little about the marriage of Faith and Oneco except that both are happy; at the end of the novel they head west with the rest of the Pequod community and are lost to history. In *Hobomok*, Mary Conant's marriage to Hobomok is motivated not by affection on her part but by her confusion when she thinks her British lover has drowned. When the lover reappears, Hobomok willingly renounces Mary and, like Faith and Oneco, heads west.[90]

Perhaps the most effective use of Ruthian genealogy to promote racial harmony is the touching story of Oriana, which appears at the end of Lydia Sigourney's *Sketch of Connecticut*. Although this village history contains several stereotypical references to the Indian proclivity for revenge and brutal violence, Oriana's tale is a poignant and daring liberal reworking of the Puritan captivity narrative. Oriana is introduced as the mysterious white woman who lives with two Indians, Zachary and Martha. When she falls sick, she summons an Anglican minister to her deathbed and entrusts to him her life story. She is, she says, the widow of a British soldier. She recalls the Revolution with unmitigated horror: the cannonballs that "rend in atoms whatever opposes them," the "severed, mangled limbs of several British soldiers thrown into the air by their explosion," the death of her husband. She then tells a seemingly Puritan tale of her capture by Indians: "Thus was I in the power of beings, whom I had ever contemplated, as the most savage of mankind. I followed them, as we rove in a terrible dream unable either to resist, or to awake. Stupefied with grief, I was for many days unequal to the sense of my misery." But her captors demonstrated their possession of an innate moral sense by supplying her with ample food and sometimes carrying her on a litter. Some contemplated sacrificing her, but when she arrived in the village, old Zachary arranged for her adoption. She was amazed: "Can it be that *an Indian* thinks of God?" She decided not to return to England, where she no longer had any relatives, but to embrace her new family.[91]

Oriana's final words to her Anglican confessor suggest that she has discovered a familial virtue that fully transcends race. "Here," she says, "I have learned to estimate a race, to which I had ever done injustice." Newly aware of the "philanthropy, intellect and devotion" of Native Americans, she is able to repudiate the Old World valorization of status and wealth. She concludes that "the Almighty has here appointed me to realize the nature of those phantoms which often held me in bondage, that renouncing all other dominion, my affections might own supreme allegiance to him. It was necessary that the pride of my heart should be subdued by affliction: and affliction having had her perfect work, has terminated in peace."[92] This invocation of the theme of providential affliction only betrays how far Sigourney has strayed from orthodox doctrine. For the Puritans, the turn to God involved the breaking of earthly ties. For Oriana it involves only the loss of "phantoms" such as racism and social hierarchy. Her affections "own supreme allegiance" to God precisely when they are turned back to their natural channels in a mutually caring, familial relationship.

Nonviolent Power and Religious Pluralism

The inclusion of Native American and Roman Catholic characters in Ruthian genealogy suggests that, for liberals, affectionate virtue was not a Puritan monopoly. They celebrated the wheat of Puritanism as just one example of the liberal virtue inherent in all faith traditions. Thus, Sedgwick and Lee also argued that the liberal belief in the *imago dei* was implicit in the Catholic doctrine of the saints. "It is not necessary to be a Catholic," wrote Lee in *Delusion*, "to believe in the intercession of saints. To a tender heart, a mother lost in infancy is the beautiful Madonna of the church; and the heart turns as instinctively to her as the devout Catholic turns to the holy mother and child."

Lee also described Naomi as a "pure poetical soul" who, like a painting of the Madonna, simply embodied divinity. Sedgwick made the same point in a scene in which a pious Italian sailor mistakes Hope Leslie for the Virgin Mary. Agitated by threats from the sailor's shipmates, Hope appears luminous when she wakes him up: "Her deep sense of the presence and favour of heaven heightened her natural beauty with a touch of religious inspiration." Reluctant to impersonate Mary, Hope persuades the sailor that she is in fact his "own peculiar saint," Petronilla, commands him to row her to safety, and bestows on him a relic in gratitude for his services. In a sense this is just a humorous and condescending scene, but Sedgwick nevertheless suggests that the Italian's pious belief expresses an inner awareness of the sanctity of simple kindness.[93]

Liberals even more frequently sought Native American sanction for their theories of nonviolent power. Indians, they claimed, taught three of the central tenets of the liberal faith: that God is revealed in the natural creation, that all faiths have access to divine truth, and that children are born possessing a spark of divinity. Thus, Sedgwick's Indian heroine Magawisca teaches that "the Great Spirit and his ministers are everywhere present and visible to the eye of the soul that loves him; nature is but his interpreter; her forms are but bodies for his spirit," and that while the Bible "contains thy rule" and may be authoritative for whites and those of mixed race, "the Great Spirit has written his laws on the hearts of his original children, and we need it not." Earlier in *Hope Leslie,* Sedgwick has an elderly woman say of a white child (the one who will stop the massacre of the Fletchers) that "the baby is like a flower just opened to the sun, with no stain upon it—that he better pass now to the Great Spirit." A few years later Child argued that interracial marriage was a good idea because Indians had always embraced the gospel principles of which Europeans needed to be reminded. Jesus, she claimed, was a teacher sent "to illustrate and confirm those divine impressions, which [God] hath graciously written on the heart"—and which the Natives had never "darkened or corrupted by superstition."[94]

Liberals admired Native American religion in part for its keen awareness of God's presence in physical nature. Anticipating the themes of Transcendentalism, liberal novelists accorded the book of nature equal authority with the scriptural text and frequently portrayed their heroes and heroines "worshiping" through communion with nature. In Sedgwick's *New-England Tale,* Jane Elton remains happy amid adversity because she practices a regular discipline of reading the Bible in the early morning: "She would steal from her bed at the dawn of day, when the songs of the birds were interpreting the stillness of nature, and beauty and fragrance breathing incense to the Maker, and join her devotions to the choral praise." In Sedgwick's *Home,* the Barclay family spends Sunday morning at church but devotes the afternoon to nature walks and such activities as the drawing of animals. And in *Naomi,* Lee archly contrasted the "mysterious psalmody" of frogs and insects on a Sabbath evening to the shuttered indoor devotions of observant Puritans.[95]

Liberals assumed that God's presence in nature was opposed to human violence, and they often prefaced accounts of violence with evocations of natural harmony. "This sabbath of our little world, this silent hymn of nature," wrote Lee before describing the execution of Mary Dyer, "was soon to be broken by rude sounds, and the lovely beauty of God's creation profaned by the bleeding offering of man's passion." In *A New-England Tale,* Sedgwick set the stage for a duel thus: "The morning of which they were going to make so unhallowed a use, was a most beautiful one. Nature was in a poetic mood; in a humour to give her votaries an opportunity to diversify her realities with the bright creations of their imaginations. . . . But this appeal of Nature was unheeded and unnoticed by these rash young men." And in *Naomi*, Lee's Harvard-educated hero can challenge the persecution of Quakers only by appealing to "that elder scripture that was all around them, in the boundless forest, and in the old, mysterious ocean."[96] Violence, however horrible, was for the liberals never more than a local blemish on the beauty of God's universe.

Liberal Ambivalence and the Limits of Providence

Liberals, in short, saw the signs of God's presence both inside and all around them—in "divine impressions" written on their hearts, in the bosom of the family, at the core of the Puritan tradition, in the best insights of other faiths, and in physical nature from the spires of the forest to the depths of the ocean. God was everywhere, prodding humans to a fuller expression of divine affections. Yet omnipresence is not omnipotence, and in some respects liberal notions of divine power were a pale shadow of the orthodox alternative. The peace of nature could not prevent duels or executions from taking place, and the moral sense was hardly a perfect vaccine against superstition and violence. By conceding that God sometimes works in a left-handed way, by overruling evil, the orthodox could assert that divine power lies behind every earthly event: their God was truly sovereign. Liberals wanted God to be a father rather than a tyrant, and they could not quite decide if such a God could be sovereign in a tyrannical world. Their ambivalence came out most clearly when they invoked the doctrine of Providence.

The liberals' fascination with Providence is evident throughout their novels. They clearly wanted their readers to know that the Puritans had believed in Providence. In *Hope Leslie*, two Puritans planning to rescue some captives pause first to share "a fervent prayer—a duty never omitted in any emergency by the Pilgrims, whose faith in the minute superintendence of Providence was practical." In *Naomi* the narrator comments that to the Puritan community "it seemed as though the Quaker iruption, as it might be called, was permitted by Providence to try their souls, to see how far prosperity had hardened their hearts." And quite frequently the authors highlight the doctrine gratuitously by attributing something first to chance and then correcting themselves: "an accident, or what we term an accident—the instrument that Providence provides to shape our destiny."[97]

While liberals were quick to embrace the familial affections of Puritans and to repudiate their violent practices, they avoided passing judgment one way or the other on Puritan providentialism. The occasional evaluations they did offer were strictly contextual and pragmatic: if providential belief inspires a character to face adversity confident of God's love, it is good; if it contributes to passivity or malevolence, it is invalid and superstitious. Thus, in Lydia Sigourney's *Sketch of Connecticut* the leading character's providential interpretation of her children's death is praised because it helps her connect with another bereaved mother and thus remain grounded in earthly existence. The two women meet frequently to share their faith in "the Hand that rules, both under the cloud, and in the sun-shine." By contrast, when a character in Sedgwick's *Clarence* uses Providence to justify passivity in the face of injustice, the heroine chides her. "Whatever is, is best," Gertrude insists, only if "we cannot by our efforts make it better."[98]

Liberals were particularly critical of anyone who used providential theology to impose his or her will on others, or to justify misdeeds. In *Hope Leslie*, when John Winthrop urges William Fletcher to emigrate without his Anglican lover, the narrator wryly comments that "with that characteristic zeal which then made all the intentions of Providence so obvious to the eye of faith, and the interpretation of all the events of life so easy, Mr. Winthrop assured his friend that the designs of Heaven in relation to him were plain." Later in the same novel the villain Philip Gardiner excuses himself by claiming that "the stars—destiny—Providence, what are they all but various terms for the same invisible, irresistible agency." Gardiner's cynicism was, to liberals, an echo of the Puritan belief that Providence had mandated the destruction of the Indians. "How very wicked and odious," Child exclaimed, "it seems to speak of God as guiding and assisting to destroy a people so worthy of respect and esteem, and to whom they were so much indebted!"[99]

Still, liberals admired individuals who integrated providential doctrine into their spiritual paths. They psychologized Providence, treating it as a useful, indeed essential, component of the Christian individual's self-understanding but not a reliable account of cosmic or historical phenomena. They were fond of quoting Milton: "The mind is its own place, and in itself, / Can make a heaven of hell, a hell of heaven." This slogan could be used to deny the reality of violence and suffering, but more often it indicated that courageous resistance to violence had eternal significance. Thus, in Sedgwick's telling of the Mary Dyer story, Dyer proclaims from the gallows that she is already in heaven, and the narrator concurs: "She spoke truly. Her mind was the paradise of God."[100]

Perhaps the most complete expression of this psychological providentialism appears in Lee's *Delusion*. The novel's preface provides a good context for understanding Lee's version of Providence. "The object of the author," she writes, "has not been to write a tale of witchcraft, but to show how circumstances may unfold the inward strength of a timid woman, so that she may at last be willing to die rather than yield to the delusion that would have preserved her life."[101] From the beginning we know that this feminist novel will not be about passively accepting the will of God but rather about a woman's gaining power through encounters with what appear to be manifestations of that will.

The heroine, Edith, strives to "solve the mysteries of Providence" even as a child. The story of Lady Ursula, who was massacred by Indians while awaiting her long-lost lover, suggests to her that Providence may sometimes break deep affections in order to purify the self for a practice of broader benevolence. But still she asks, "Why do we suffer?" Her benevolent father's happy death brings her closer to a solution. "A change had been wrought in her character by that nightly death-bed, and by four days of lonely sorrow. She felt that she must rely on herself." Like the ocean polishing a pearl, time and sorrow "reveal to one's self the inward pearl beyond all price, on which we must forever rely to guide us."[102] Here Lee is engaged in a subtle reworking of providential doctrine. As in orthodoxy, Providence breaks affections, but this culminates not in the self's subordination to the divine will but in the discovery of the *imago dei* at the heart of one's own identity.

This discovery makes the rebuilding of affective bonds possible, and soon Edith falls in love with a young ministerial student. Together they discuss their community's concern with alleged witchcraft. Edith realizes that it is one thing to make sense of her own life providentially and quite another to impose a providential reading on social conflicts. She chides her lover for his ready belief in witchcraft: "God forbid that I should limit his power! but I fear these poor children are wicked or diseased, and that Satan has nothing to do with it." Such words seem to deny God's involvement in earthly events, but really Lee is getting at something different. Edith's attack on witchcraft belief comes at the conclusion of a long letter to her lover in which she describes her faith that the divine presence pervades both their individual romance and the entire universe. Her critique of Seymore is not that he is too quick to see God's hand in earthly events, but that his view of divine agency focuses too superficially on violent and miraculous events. Religion, she tells him, "is not a distinct thing from everyday life," but "like the air we breathe." Their love for one another is inseparable from God's love and should make "every hour . . . an act of adoration and praise." Paradoxically, then, it is Edith's profound sense of God's presence that allows her to identify those situations in which God is *not* involved.[103]

Edith's "inward pearl" of self-reliance allows her to challenge her lover's narrow theology, but it suffers a more severe trial when she adopts Phoebe, the troubled granddaughter of a suspected witch. Here she succumbs to the prevailing belief in the minute superintendence of Providence, which the narrator faults for being too close to the tragic Fate of the ancients. Belief in fate, she complains, fostered fortitude in suffering but not the benevolent discipline and hope in eternity promoted by genuine Christianity. Thus, Edith cannot "free herself from a superstitious feeling that this child was to have, in some way or other, she knew not how, an unfortunate influence upon her happiness." When Phoebe accuses Edith of witchcraft, she initially succumbs to a fatalistic despair: "Of what avail has been a life of self-denial, of benevolence? . . . In one moment, by that child of my own cherishing, . . . I am suspected of a horrible, contemptible crime; humiliated to the very dust."[104]

Paradoxically, it is Seymore's betrayal—he first urges Edith to confess falsely and then joins her persecutors—that puts Edith back on the right track. Suddenly she appears stronger in the face of all her afflictions and resolves to tell the truth forthrightly, even though, as the narrator repeatedly reminds us, "it is easy for the accused to believe themselves guilty." She now has "the spirit of a martyr" and faces death confident that God will give her the requisite courage. In Lee's text, this acceptance of victimization—not as the expression of God's will but simply as a consequence of sticking to principle in a violent situation—is something that each self-reliant individual can only do for herself. Edith can affirm an abiding faith in Providence—"I see his hand even from the moment when that child was committed to my care"—just as her black friend Dinah can see God's hand in her own capture and enslavement. But Dinah *cannot* accept Edith's suffering as providential, and she must act to prevent it. The novel concludes when she concocts a successful rescue plan, and Edith begins a new life far from her persecutors.[105]

By imposing a happy ending on her tale, Lee evaded the liberals' most pressing theological dilemma: what to make of the victimization of other people. Could it be part of God's plan? If so, when and under what circumstances? If not, would God's nonviolent power ever triumph over the violent effects of tyranny and priestcraft? When would this happen? The force of these questions was blunted by the liberals' faith in the immortality of the soul. This doctrine allowed them to assert that, while God did not will the suffering and death of innocent victims, God would ensure that such victims would be compensated with eternal felicity. This argument easily shaded into the notion that the suffering of the innocent was itself a source of nonviolent power. Thus, in describing the deaths of infants, liberals often suggested that their affectionate powers became fully effective only in death: the baby who stops a massacre in *Hope Leslie* is himself killed in the process. This narrative device was consistent with the repudiated orthodox doctrine of the sacrificial atonement, and it was more common in the writings of liberals who retained some ties to orthodoxy, such as Harriet Beecher Stowe. Its presence even in Sedgwick's work reveals the ambivalence and inconsistency of even the most committed liberals.

Providential Theology and the Meaning of Genocide

Liberals were even more inconsistent when they attempted to relate God's power to the group victimization of Native American communities. None could entirely resist the appeal of the stadialist theory, which made the decline of Indian societies a regrettable but necessary consequence of historical progress. Stadialism allowed liberals to condemn genocidal violence without holding out the hope that nonviolent power could save Native culture: it was wrong to kill the Indians even if they were going to die anyway. Rather than promoting a full sentimental identification between whites and Indians, Liberals contributed to the elegiac myth of the noble yet disappearing Indian, which was of course most famously presented by James Fenimore Cooper. In *Redwood*, a novel of contemporary life written three years before *Hope Leslie*, Sedgwick referred to Indians "who like the remnants of their sacrifice rocks, remain among us monuments of past ages," and this was as close as many writers came to imagining a living Indian in the present day. Both *Hope Leslie* and *Hobomok* featured a range of Native American characters and depicted interracial marriage in a positive light, but by the end of both novels all the Indians have begun, in Sedgwick's words, "their pilgrimage to the far western forests. That which remains of their story is lost in the deep, voiceless obscurity of those unknown regions."[106]

In her *Sketch*, Lydia Sigourney offered a fairly nuanced but ultimately elegiac rendition of the voluntary removal west of Connecticut's Mohegan community. In Sigourney's telling, the Mohegans themselves openly wonder "if the sentence of extinction were indeed passing upon our race," but they resolve to trust in God. The Mohegan pastor Samson Occom seems to speak for Sigourney when he suggests that perhaps racial integration, based on conversion to Christianity, will be possible in their new home in New York. Yet Sigourney also gives voice to a more pessimistic point of view in the words of an anti-Christian chief: "Why are Christians so eager to wrest from others lands, when they profess that it is *gain* for them to leave all, and die?" Occom cannot really answer this, so he simply reasserts his claim that Christianity is a fitting religion for the Mohegans' unhappy circumstance: "To whom do the promises of the gospel address themselves with more force, than to a race like ours, homeless and despised?"[107] Sigourney clearly means to suggest that Christianity is a religion not of sacrificers but of victims, yet she offers little hope that Native American victims might become survivors.

Of the writers considered in this chapter, only Child explicitly moved from sentimental identification with historical Indians to solidarity with their nineteenth-century descendants. This occurred not in the completely elegiac *Hobomok* but in *The First Settlers of New England*, which was written at the onset of the Jacksonian Indian removals. Child persistently linked the genocides of Puritan New England to contemporary Indian policies, which she feared would undo the promise of the Revolution and trap the young republic within the violence of Old World history. "This crooked and narrowminded policy, which we have adopted in reference to the Indians," she wrote, "will assuredly subject us to the calamitous reverses which have fallen on other nations, whose path to empire has been marked by the blood and ruin of their fellow men." Child even suggested that contemporary policies were less excusable than those of the Puritans, who had after all been afflicted with "darkness and superstition."[108]

Child recognized that elegy promoted a passivity incompatible with genuine solidarity. "It is, in my opinion, decidedly wrong, to speak of the removal, or extinction of the Indians as inevitable; it surely implies that the people of these states have not sufficient virtue of magnanimity to redeem their past offences, by affording the sad remnant, which still exist, succour and protection." Though she pessimistically conceded that the Indian "will in all probability soon be blotted from the face of the earth," she insisted that that probability was no cause for inaction. After citing favorably a writer sympathetic to the Indians, she blasted him for assuming that white culture is superior and Indian culture must give way: "For what purpose does the writer of the article . . . so forcibly describe their wrongs, and in some instances, point out the mode of alleviation; when, after all, he can so coldly consign them to destruction?" The most viable solution, she contended, was intermarriage on the basis of cultural equality. In support of this position she cited both the glories of mixed-race cultures in Egypt and India and the authority of Scripture: "The English, though they laid great stress on some portions of scripture, appear to have overlooked . . . that which informs us that God hath made of one blood all the nations of the earth, that they may dwell together."[109]

There is here an eloquent opening to interracial genealogy, but it is not one that Child fleshes out. *First Settlers* is not a novel but a thinly fictionalized didactic history, and as such it offered Child little space to develop imaginatively her social aspirations or to explain whether she believed divine power would ultimately guarantee their realization. She *tells* her readers that solidarity is a moral necessity, but she does not show them what it might look like. The closest thing to an imaginative vision of solidarity in liberal literature is thus Sedgwick's portrait of her Pequod heroine, Magawisca. As a member of the tribe most hated by New Englanders, Magawisca is different from Cooper's noble Indians, all of whom come from tribes that supported the "right" side of the frontier wars. Sedgwick's point is thus not to map the cosmic struggle of good and evil onto tribal divisions but to suggest that nobility and natural affection are the common inheritance of all humanity. Magawisca occupies a curious position with respect to the genealogical plot line of *Hope Leslie*. Adopted into the Fletcher family early on (after John Winthrop intervenes to prevent her being sold into West Indian slavery), she nearly becomes a permanent member. Indeed, her precipitous departure west at the novel's close and her invocation of a classically elegiac justification—"it matters not whether we fall by the tempest that lays the forest low, or are cut down alone by the stroke of the axe"—surprise the reader almost as much as they do her friends Hope and Everell.[110] This final failure of genealogical identification, Sedgwick makes abundantly clear, resulted from the moral failure of the white community, not the cultural failures of the Indians.

Prior to this point, Sedgwick develops her picture of Magawisca's character primarily through her relationships with Everell and Hope. Magawisca and Everell spend their childhood years together, and their friendship is one of deep intimacy and mutual learning. Everell, in particular, learns much from Magawisca. She tells him the story of the genocide of her people, accenting the fact that in violent situations some victims never regain their voices: "Those fearful guns that we had never heard before—the shouts of your people—our own battle yell—the piteous cries of the little children—the groans of our mothers; and oh! worse than all, the silence of those that could not speak." He is persuaded by her argument that the Indians should not convert to the Puritans' hypocritical faith and comes to see her as bearing her own revelation: "She seemed to him to imbody nature's best gifts, and her feelings to be the inspiration of heaven."[111] When Mononotto captures Everell, Magawisca intervenes to prevent his sacrifice, losing her own arm in the process; later, both Hope and Everell help Magawisca escape from a Puritan prison.

Magawisca's relationship to Hope is more ambivalent, yet all of the ambivalence is on the side of the otherwise angelic Hope. Apparently deeply committed to maintaining an interracial sense of family, Magawisca goes out of her way to arrange a reunion between Hope and her sister, Faith, a captive who has married Magawisca's brother Oneco. Hope shows considerable fortitude in making the arrangements but stumbles when she actually encounters her sister. She cannot quite imagine that Faith can be family with both Oneco and herself, and she even tries to bribe Faith to return to the white community. Magawisca patiently translates many offensive things for Hope: "tell her," says Hope, "that our mother, now a saint in heaven, stoops from her happy place to entreat her to return to our God and our father's God." Faith, a missionized Catholic, pulls out a crucifix in response. Magawisca carefully explains to Hope that Faith and Oneco are happily married, and that Hope must respect that bond if she is to rebuild the bond of sisterhood. The difficult reunion is ended by the governor's guards, who take Magawisca as a prisoner of war and thus begin the final dissolution of the Fletchers as an interracial family.[112]

Despite her more perfect embodiment of liberal virtue, then, Magawisca ultimately must surrender both her lover and her land to Hope. In a more pessimistic novel this might be interpreted as hard-boiled realism. Perhaps Sedgwick's point was that sentimental identification, despite its basis in human nature and divine power, was less powerful—at least in this life—than the contingent structures of violence and superstition. But she did not say this, and the happy ending of Hope's story suggests that she believed natural affections were omnipotent within the white world. Apparently Sedgwick—like the other liberals—did not plumb the depths of the theodicy question her novel raised, and as a consequence she drew a color line within the divine nature. For whites, God was certainly good and perhaps great as well; for Indians, God was great but not good.

Sedgwick's problem stemmed in large part from the fact that she had few opportunities to interact with flesh-and-blood Native Americans. She had trouble imagining interracial genealogy in her fiction because she had not experienced it in her life. In the 1830s, however, the emergence of radical reform movements gave liberals the chance to build concrete relationships with fugitive slaves, battered women, and alcoholics. These transformative encounters would push sentimental theology in an increasingly radical direction.

2

From Sentimentality to Social Reform

The Emergence of Radical Christian Liberalism

The sentimental practices pioneered by Sedgwick, Child, Lee, and Sigourney were soon embraced by a range of authors involved in the great social reform movements of the antebellum period. Such movements as temperance, abolitionism, and nonresistant pacifism gave concrete expression to the liberal belief that humans have the power to transcend our sinful past and create a society in which the image of God shines brightly in each person. Many reformers, however, took liberal principles to radical extremes. For these radical Christian liberals, to unleash the power of the *imago dei* was to overthrow any and all social institutions—even constitutional government and organized churches—that stood in the way of human freedom.

A few definitions may clarify the connection between radical Christian liberalism and antebellum social reform. I suggest that key leaders of the temperance, abolitionist, and nonresistant movements were *liberal* insofar as they affirmed the inherent goodness of humanity and sought to liberate human individuals from all forms of violence and coercion. They were *Christian* insofar as they grounded their liberalism in central claims of the Christian faith, particularly the belief that humans are created in the image of God. Finally, they were *radical* insofar as they were willing to contemplate the overthrow of all social institutions, even ostensibly liberal or Christian ones, that blocked the free expression of the *imago dei*. The abolitionist leader Maria Weston Chapman summed up the logic of radical Christian liberalism by suggesting that "Christianity, in every age, has ever presented herself as the antagonist of its crying abomination." Whether the menace was "idolatry," "the unclean spirit of intemperance," or slavery, Christianity would rise to vindicate "that groundwork of the human soul,—its Freedom."[1]

I define social reform as any attempt to transform the economic, political, and cultural building blocks of society. Such attempts may be modest or extremely far-reaching. In using the term "reform," therefore, I am simply following nineteenth-century usage and do not intend to draw a sharp distinction between "reformist" and "revolutionary" approaches to social change. The major antebellum reform movements had both revolutionary and nonrevolutionary wings, and my emphasis in this study will be on "reformers" who were also "revolutionaries," either implicitly or explicitly. I will focus particularly on three movements: the temperance campaign against alcohol, the abolitionist struggle against slavery, and the nonresistant movement against war and violence.

Each of these reforms is important for a particular reason. Temperance was the most inclusive and the most outwardly successful of all antebellum reforms. People of all classes, races, and regions—including virtually all abolitionists and nonresistants—came together in a movement that more than halved per capita alcohol consumption in a single decade.[2] Arguably, the early temperance movement achieved more by noncoercive "moral suasion" than its successors did by means of legislative prohibition. Abolitionism was the most overtly revolutionary of the major reform movements. Though it did not succeed alone in abolishing slavery, it certainly helped pave the way for the most dramatic social transformation in the history of the United States. Nonresistant pacifism rejected all forms of coercion (and thus all existing governments), countenancing only "moral and spiritual resistance of evil and evildoers" through practices of active nonviolence.[3] Compared with temperance and abolition, it attracted few supporters and had little effect on national policy. But it was the reform most intimately associated with what I am calling radical Christian liberalism. While radical Christian liberals worked alongside more orthodox Christians and more moderate liberals in the temperance and abolitionist movements, they were virtually alone on the nonresistance platform.

Each of these movements relied primarily on what was then known as "moral suasion." That is, reformers sought primarily to change the hearts and minds of their neighbors, assuming that institutional changes would follow inevitably from changed persons. Lydia Maria Child, who was an early supporter of all the reforms examined here, was also one of the most articulate theorists of moral suasion. "The union of individual influence," she wrote in 1833, "produces a vast amount of moral force, which is not the less powerful because it is often unperceived." Just by avoiding the "desire of retaliation," she promised readers nine years later, they could do "much to abolish gallows, chains, and prisons, though thou hast never written or spoken a word on the criminal code."[4]

This theory was radically democratic. Only male citizens could vote; only ministers could preach; only the strong could fight—but anyone could stir up the consciences of his or her neighbors. This did not imply, however, that suasion had to work entirely apart from social structures. Rather, as Child explained, once people's consciences were aroused, they would be free to act in an infinite variety of ways. She conceded that some reformers might choose to focus more narrowly on political, ecclesial, or even military action. Personally, however, she insisted that the ultimate goal was to "purify the *fountain*, whence all these streams flow."[5]

I have excluded several other reform movements for reasons of space. The "moral purity" movement against prostitution attracted many of the same supporters as temperance and abolition. Campaigns against capital and corporal punishment gave concrete expression to the ideals of nonresistance. Many social reformers were eventually drawn to the utopian socialist communities at Northampton, Hopedale, Brook Farm, Fruitlands, and dozens of Fourierist "phalanxes." But by far the most significant omission in this study is the lack of sustained attention to the women's rights movement. This movement was as significant in its long-term consequences as abolition, though it met with few concrete successes before the end of the nineteenth century. And it was, for a time, as fully identified with radical Christian liberalism as nonresistance. Indeed, the women's rights movement was almost alone in preserving radical Christian liberal ideas in the decades after the Civil War. But, for precisely this reason, to give adequate attention to women's rights would force me to move well beyond the chronological bounds of this study. Probably the most significant text for studying the theological dimensions of the movement is the *Women's Bible*, which appeared only in 1895. I am not presently able to explain why postbellum feminists were able to preserve the radical Christian liberal tradition at a time when it was otherwise in retreat, and to do so adequately might double the length of what is already a very long book.

The Causes of Social Reform

The great social reform movements of temperance, abolitionism, and nonresistant pacifism all emerged between 1826 and 1840, though each had roots stretching much further back in history. During those fourteen years, social reform endeavors brought together both liberal and revivalist Christians, both social conservatives and radicals, both victims of oppression and those who hoped to stand in solidarity with victims. Together these diverse groups created national societies that demanded the attention of the country—and then split apart as the tensions increased between the various factions. Several of the resulting splinter groups—most notably the Washingtonian temperance movement, the American Anti-Slavery Society, and the New England Non-Resistance Society—proved to be especially congenial contexts for the articulation of radical Christian liberal ideas in literature. The 1840s and 1850s, as a result, were the golden years of social reform literature.

No single cause fully explains the emergence of social reform in the years following 1826.[6] In part, the various movements were fruits of the revolutionary tree planted fifty years earlier. Most leading social reformers were part of the first generation to grow up as United States citizens. As such they believed implicitly that "all men are created equal" and were willing to take radical action to make this truth manifest. A substantial group of reformers had also participated in the religious struggles that led to the creation of the Unitarian and Hicksite Quaker churches. For these women and men, social reform was part of a larger campaign for religious liberalism and freedom of conscience. A larger group of reformers came out of the religious revivals that swept the nation in the early decades of the nineteenth century. Though many of these individuals eventually repudiated orthodox doctrine, the revivals gave them a zeal for personal transformation and a knack for creating effective organizations. Perhaps the most important cause of social reform, however, was the simple fact of identification. When diverse people came together—sober middle-class reformers and impoverished "drunkards," industrious New England farmers and courageous fugitive slaves—the resulting identifications helped them imagine a new society.

A wide range of reformers expressed the power of identification by appealing to the doctrine of the *imago dei*. These people became involved in reform because they recognized God's image in their oppressed brothers and sisters—and because they believed they possessed the divinely implanted power to overcome oppression. Thus, the eloquent fugitive slave Frederick Douglass identified as his cause the pursuit of "that freedom which every being made after God's image instinctively feels is his birthright."

Maria W. Stewart (1803–79), another African American activist, reminded the black community that God "hath formed and fashioned you in his own glorious image." The white abolitionist Theodore Weld (1803–95) opined that "it is the *perfection* of *reason* to *be like* God." And Gerrit Smith (1797–1874) a wealthy land speculator who participated in nearly every antebellum reform, believed that "this religion, then, which recognizes man's capacity for resembling his God . . . is the only religion which can . . . shut up the dram-shop, and put an end to slavery and the other outrages upon the high nature of man."[7]

By appealing to the *imago dei*, these reformers implied that the emergence of social reform did not really need to be explained. From their perspective, it flowed naturally from the moral principles implanted in every human conscience. (Perhaps the fact that it did not appear earlier is what needed explanation!) Thus, in an address given in 1855, Frederick Douglass argued that the antislavery movement had not been born but merely "revived" in 1830. Indeed, its underlying principles, "like the great forces of the physical world, fire, steam, and lightning, have slumbered in the bosom of nature since the world began." They were created by the "Great Mind" of "nature's God" for the sake of the "moral safety" of humanity. "In the very heart of humanity," Douglass said, "are garnered up, as from everlasting to everlasting, all those elementary principles, whose vital action constitutes what we now term the Anti-Slavery movement." Despite "ages of oppression, and iron-hearted selfishness," the principles continued to be articulated anew in the "noble testimonies" of "good men." Interestingly, Douglass included even Thomas Jefferson and the other slaveholding Founding Fathers among those "good men" who witnessed to eternal truth.[8]

The Jeffersonian Heritage of Social Reform

Jefferson's unique contribution was to make a liberal understanding of the *imago dei* part of the patriotic heritage of an entire nation. While most pre-Revolutionary Americans believed that the *imago dei* had been partly or wholly alienated from humanity as the result of the Fall, Jefferson claimed that "life, liberty, and the pursuit of happiness" were the "inalienable" birthright of every individual. While Jefferson could not deny the ubiquity of violence and oppression in history, he relegated these to a secondary status. Oppression was rooted not in human nature but in the tyrannical denial of that nature, and as such it could be rooted out of human societies. The surprising success of the American Revolution gave this utopian notion an almost revelatory status.[9]

For the generation that grew up with Jefferson's words, the Declaration of Independence was the blueprint for the millennial transformation of the world. No one yet knew what shape American democracy would ultimately take; it was plausible to hope that the sordidness of party politics might soon give way to a system in which popular sentiment would translate immediately into social reality. It was equally plausible to suppose that those social practices that violated the Jeffersonian vision of equality—most notably slavery but also war and the violence apparently spawned by alcohol abuse— were rooted less in an unchanging human nature than in the aftereffects of a now deposed tyranny. (Admirers of the Declaration naturally believed Jefferson's curious claim that the British Empire had somehow foisted slavery upon a reluctant colonial community.) The antebellum period was the high point of a century of progressive hope, which Alfred North Whitehead aptly described as a time when "wise men hoped, and . . . as yet no circumstance had arisen to throw doubt upon the grounds of such hope."[10]

When reformers sought to translate their hopes into manifestos for action, they often turned to the Declaration—a text that has been called "the mainstay of American radicals."[11] Both the American Anti-Slavery Society and the New England Non-Resistance Society (like the Workingmen's party before them and the women's rights movement after) prepared "Declarations of Sentiments" outlining their grievances and the principles of their reform. Appeals to the Declaration struck a special chord in the late 1820s and early 1830s. This period was marked by the fiftieth anniversary of national independence, the simultaneous deaths of John Adams and Thomas Jefferson on that very anniversary, and the inauguration of the first president born after the Revolution, John Quincy Adams. Commemorative events such as the Plymouth Bicentennial, the erection of the Bunker Hill monument, and the national tour of Lafayette (the French hero of the American Revolution) helped United States citizens reflect on the meaning of their national identity.[12] These events reinforced liberalism's place as a shared heritage of all Americans and at the same time inspired a few Americans to launch new revolutionary campaigns against war, intemperance, and slavery.

The Revolutions of Liberal Religion

Such campaigns had special meaning for members of two small Christian denominations that had just undergone their own revolutionary struggles. In the 1820s the Unitarians and Hicksite Quakers had split, respectively, from the established Congregational Church of Massachusetts and the de facto Quaker establishment of Pennsylvania. Both groups placed more emphasis on Christian ethics than on doctrinal correctness, though both were also quite critical of traditional doctrines—particularly the doctrine of original sin—that seemed to inhibit earnest moral effort. Both groups placed enormous emphasis on the freedom of the individual conscience, which they sought to safeguard against both institutional oppression and excessive formalism in ritual. As a result, neither group put its whole heart into ecclesial institution-building, and both denominations remained small and decentralized. Individual Hicksites and Unitarians, however, did put their whole hearts into the various tasks of social reform.[13]

Unitarian social reformers often followed the lead of William Ellery Channing. Though he was no radical, Channing was a founding member of the American Peace Society, a longtime supporter of temperance, and the author of influential treatises on both war and slavery.[14] For him, the liberal doctrine of the innate virtue and inherent dignity of all individuals created in God's image was the best reason to be involved in social reform. Though he did not contemplate the overthrow of all social institutions, he believed that individual freedom was the criterion by which all institutions must be judged. Society was not the product of written constitutions or a Hobbesian social contract but rather of the "spiritual ties" of loving individuals; consequently, the needs of society or state could never come before those of individuals. "The human soul," he proclaimed, "is to outlive all earthly institutions. The distinction of nations is to pass away. . . . But the individual mind survives, and the obscurest subject, if true to God, will rise to a power never wielded by earthly potentates."[15] Channing encouraged his parishioners and admirers to follow the leadings of their individual minds beyond the limits of his own theology, and thus his congregation provided a comfortable home for many of Boston's most influential reformers.

Just as Channing inspired many of Boston's brightest reformers, so a widely scattered circle of Quaker activists took their lead from Elias Hicks (1748–1830). The so-called Hicksites were a diverse group with a range of concerns about the direction of Quaker life. Some were troubled by the increasing "worldliness" and prosperity of the Philadelphia Quaker community; some hoped to strengthen the Quaker testimony against slavery; some wanted to safeguard the Quaker tradition of silent worship. All opposed the tendency of Quaker leaders, in both Philadelphia and London, to downplay differences between Quakers and orthodox Protestants. For some, though, this opposition stemmed from a desire to preserve the community's character as a "peculiar people," set apart from the larger society, while others were eager to explore connections with the more liberal wing of Christianity.[16]

Hicks himself was a Long Island farmer, popular traveling preacher, and vitriolic controversialist. A fervent champion of his own rural lifestyle, Hicks could shake up the Philadelphia aristocracy with his denunciations of luxury, education, and the involvement of many Quaker merchants in the sale of cotton and other goods produced by slaves. Hicks was the primary initiator of the "free produce" movement, which eventually would lead many abolitionists to choose wool, beet sugar, and other products that could be produced without exploitation. Above all, Hicks insisted on the centrality of the "inward light" to Quaker life, arguing that outward forms like the Bible and worship were merely prods "to lead the minds of the children of men home to this divine inward principle manifested in their own hearts and minds."[17] This teaching led Hicks to a Christology that many found heretical: Christ, for him, was simply a human being who had absorbed himself fully in the divine light that exists to some degree in every human soul.

Hicks did not create the movement that came to bear his name. Indeed, it had multiple sources. Just after the War of 1812, the so-called New Lights of Massachusetts had promoted a more radical understanding of the "inward light," leading to the expulsion of many from their Quaker meetings. In Wilmington, Delaware, a cluster of Friends sought to integrate Quaker theology with the ideology of the French Revolution. Hicks's role was to link such radical movements to the underlying traditionalism of rural Friends, and he did so with a pungency that forced people to take sides. In 1819 he spoke before the Men's Meeting at Pine Street in Philadelphia, chastising his hearers for their compromises with slavery and urging the young men to heed their consciences rather than their elders. This led to several attempts to discipline him, and finally in 1827 his Philadelphia followers simply withdrew from their Yearly Meeting. In a statement of explanation, they appealed to "the glorious truth that God alone is the sovereign lord of conscience, and that with this unalienable right, no power, civil or ecclesiastical, should ever interfere."[18]

Both the Hicksites and their "orthodox" opponents recognized the parallels between the Unitarian and Hicksite movements. Probably the leading charge against Hicks was that he denied the divinity of Christ. His defenders could not decide whether this was true or not. Some sought to prove his essential orthodoxy, while others argued that even such a rudimentary standard of orthodoxy was an unwarranted "creed." Though Hicks's rural followers probably knew little of Channing and the Unitarians, the educated leaders who produced the movement's propaganda were quite conversant with liberal theology, often preferring the label "liberal" to that of "Hicksite." Their wing of the movement was quick to embrace the radical social reforms of the 1830s, often working side by side with non-Quakers in temperance, abolitionist, and pacifist enterprises.

For Unitarians like Samuel J. May and Hicksites like Lucretia Mott, the denominational schisms provided an important impetus to reform. In various ways, these individuals were inspired by the liberal theology of the *imago dei*, energized by the revolutionary struggles of the liberals, and dispirited by the resulting estrangement of Christian communities. By 1830 they were ready to shift their energies from the narrowly ecclesial context to the wider field of social transformation. Both the denominational struggles and their passing, in short, led these reformers to social reform.

Samuel J. May, for example, was one of the brightest young Unitarian pastors to come of age during the decades of controversy. May was descended from such leading Boston families as the Sewalls and the Quincys, and his father, Joseph May, was a co-founder of both King's Chapel (Boston's first Unitarian congregation) and the American Unitarian Association. May attended Harvard College and the newly formed Harvard Divinity School, where he studied under such Unitarian luminaries as Henry Ware and Andrews Norton. Though May was highly recommended by his friend William Ellery Channing, he chose to accept his first call at out-of-the-way Brooklyn, Connecticut, in 1825. As Connecticut's first Unitarian pastor, May made ample use of his talents for bridge-building and reconciliation—for example, he urged his parishioners not to use legal action to recover the communion vessels that had been taken by a seceding, orthodox faction.[19]

While in Brooklyn, though, May devoted his greatest energies to the various causes of social reform. He had met the Unitarian peace activist Noah Worcester while a student, and one of his first actions in Brooklyn was to found the Windham County Peace Society. He also joined the Massachusetts Society for the Suppression of Intemperance, resolving early on to forgo wine as well as hard liquors. In 1829 he organized an affiliate of the American Colonization Society, but he abandoned this cause as soon as William Lloyd Garrison introduced him to the more radical position of immediate emancipation. Within a week of meeting Garrison, May preached a guest sermon in Boston in which he warned that "if need be, the very foundations of the Republic must be broken up" to end slavery. This semitreasonous sentiment led all of Boston's Unitarian ministers except William Ellery Channing and Ralph Waldo Emerson to bar him from their pulpits.[20] Undeterred, he went on to tell Emerson's congregation that the proslavery parts of the federal Constitution could not be morally binding on the nation. For the next thirty years, May maintained a steady commitment to both universal reform and the Unitarian ministry, serving long pastorates in Scituate, Massachusetts, and Syracuse, New York.

Like May, Lucretia Mott (1793–1880) had deep roots in her faith tradition: her family was one of the original Quaker families on Nantucket Island. She attended the noted Quaker school, Nine Partners, where she met and married another birthright Quaker, James Mott. After the Motts settled in Philadelphia, Lucretia's preaching skills gained her local, and soon national, prominence as an "acknowledged minister." One of the

most important models for her ministry was Elias Hicks, whom she had first encountered while a student. In 1825 his testimony inspired her to refrain from using any
slave produce in her household; five years later her husband followed suit by switching
his commission business from cotton to wool. Mott believed that Hicks's ethical concerns were part of a Quaker tradition that stretched back at least to William Penn; she
was fond of shocking the orthodox by quoting Penn's dictum that "men are to be judged
by their likeness to Christ, rather than by their notions of Christ."[21]

Mott was also drawn to the liberal implications of Hicks's emphasis on the "inward
light." "Truth for authority, not authority for truth," was her lifelong motto, and she
found support for this position both in Hicks's preaching and in the writings of William
Ellery Channing, whom she started reading in the 1820s and eventually got to know
fairly well. In particular, she cherished Channing's emphasis on the *imago dei* in the
individual conscience. One favorite quote, for example, speaks of "the *sense* of *duty*" as
"the inward monitor which speaks in the name of God."[22]

Despite her esteem for Elias Hicks, however, Lucretia Mott did not immediately side
with the Hicksites at the time of the schism. Her husband, James, was quick to declare
himself, but Lucretia hesitated as she weighed the cost to long-standing friendships and
family ties. Even after her decision to affiliate with the Hicksites, she made a double
effort to stay connected with those who had chosen differently. Ironically, she had more
trouble staying connected with the Hicksites themselves. She was disturbed that they
continued the traditional practice of disowning young people who married outside the
church. In 1830 she spoke out against a letter that some Hicksite leaders had written to
reassure London Friends of their orthodoxy; such a letter, she argued, compromised
the fundamental principle of freedom of conscience and implicitly accepted a creedal
test for church membership.[23]

These experiences, as well as her disappointment at the rancor of the split, led Mott
to shift her energies toward such social reforms as temperance, abolition, peace, and
women's rights. Within these movements, she played a special role in linking each specific
cause to the underlying principles of liberal theology. Thus, at the American Anti-Slavery
Society's founding meeting, she befriended a Presbyterian seminarian named James Miller
McKim and introduced him to the thought of Channing, Hicks, and other liberals. At
a London convention in 1840, she met Elizabeth Cady Stanton, who was then associated with the more orthodox wing of abolitionism, and inspired her to commit her life
to women's rights. Even Garrison credited Mott with his own liberalization, writing in
1848 that "if my mind has become liberalized in any degree (and I think it has burst
every sectarian trammel) . . . I am largely indebted to James and Lucretia Mott for the
change." Mott's enthusiasm for liberal theology stemmed from her conviction that the
divinity within each person provided the only sure basis for social reform. "All the leading reforms of the age,—Anti-Slavery, Temperance, and all the benevolent and philanthropic movements of the day," she told an audience in 1855, "have sprung not by the
dogmas propounded by either the Church of Rome or England, or any other material
organization, but from the individual soul of man, from the Divinity rising within man,
from the Divinity of which Christ was the most celestial exemplar."[24]

May and Mott were far from unique. Indeed, the liberal reformations of Channing
and Hicks influenced even reformers who were quite orthodox in their theology. Lewis
Tappan, a reformer who was sharply critical of theological liberalism, got his start as a

member of Channing's congregation and the first secretary of the American Unitarian Association. Tappan's dissatisfaction with the complacency of wealthy Unitarians soon led him back to his mother's orthodox faith, but he never lost his regard for Channing as his first and most beloved spiritual mentor.[25] Another of Channing's early parishioners, George Barrell Cheever, became a popular orthodox preacher in New York City and a stalwart of the temperance and abolitionist movements. (Evidently, Tappan's and Cheever's early flirtations with Unitarianism got something out of their systems, for they were among very few leading reformers to preserve their orthodoxy unscathed.)

Revivalists and Reformers

Men like Cheever and Tappan cannot, of course, be counted as liberal reformers. They were part of the much larger group whose impulse to reform came primarily from the revivals of the Second Great Awakening.[26] In particular, both Cheever and Tappan were key players in the network of mission and reform societies often referred to as the "benevolent empire." The benevolent empire was largely the brainchild of Lyman Beecher (1775–1863), a powerful preacher who sought to link the theological heritage of the Puritans to the energy of the new revivals. Originally, he was also committed to preserving the social prestige of Congregationalism as the established church in much of New England. (The federal Bill of Rights had forbidden any *national* establishment of religion, but it left open the possibility of individual states maintaining their own religious establishments.) When the Connecticut legislature voted to dismantle the Congregationalist establishment in 1817, Beecher was deeply disappointed—but only for a time. He soon realized that the churches could do more to regulate public morality as autonomous "voluntary societies" than as departments of state. He poured his energy into the creation of "societies" to distribute Bibles and tracts, to send missionaries to the frontier and overseas, to sponsor Sunday schools, and to promote a stricter observance of the Christian Sabbath.

The societies, funded largely by New York merchants, were powerful instruments of ecumenism, drawing Presbyterians and Congregationalists—twin heirs of the Puritans—very closely together, while Methodists and Baptists were affiliated a bit more loosely. All of these churches came together in a united front determined to preserve the Christian, Protestant character of America. Though the initial goals of the societies were either socially conservative or narrowly ecclesiastical, they soon branched out into areas of social reform. In 1826 the American Temperance Society was created to promote abstinence from hard liquor, and in 1816 the American Colonization Society had begun to seek an end to slavery by means of gradual emancipation and the transporting of free blacks "back" to Africa. Each society was led by a board of directors with substantial clerical representation, and each hired "agents" who fanned out across the nation to gain supporters, village by village.

The societies were pushed in a more radical direction by the Finney revival in upstate New York. Charles Grandison Finney (1792–1875) was nominally Presbyterian, but he rejected the understanding of revivals traditionally espoused by Presbyterians, Congregationalists, and other denominations in the orthodox Reformed tradition. According to that tradition, ever since the Fall, human nature has been totally depraved, incapable of earning salvation or performing any truly good work. Christian conversion was possible only through the gift of supernatural grace, and that was extended only to a predestined few, following God's own timetable. According to Finney, by contrast, original sin was simply a voluntary selfishness that could be abandoned through sheer force of will. Conversion was thus a choice, available immediately to anyone. This "Arminian" understanding of sin had been standard Unitarian and Methodist doctrine for decades, but Finney's innovation was to connect it to the social activism of the benevolent empire.

Finney's young converts, as a consequence, threw themselves into social activism. The emotional experience of "rebirth" gave these reformers the fervor they needed to devote long hours to reform activities, sacrifice personal respectability, and even withstand the onslaughts of hostile mobs.[27] Theodore Dwight Weld, for example, destroyed his voice with nonstop campaigning for abolition and then trained seventy new "apostles" to continue the work. Reformers also pioneered new rituals that looked a lot like religious conversion. Temperance activists "took the pledge" to abstain from alcohol and gave "testimony" about how this act changed their lives. Abolitionists, similarly, "came out" from institutions that supported (or failed to condemn) slavery, particularly the "proslavery" churches. On occasion, "coming out" involved the symbolic disruption of worship services.

These conversion-style rituals did not, however, appeal only to revivalists. Many of those who placed most emphasis on the fervor of their conversion to reform actually had nonrevivalist backgrounds. Lydia Maria Child, for example, reported that when she became an abolitionist she found "the whole pattern of my life-web" transformed. And Samuel J. May recalled that when he first heard Garrison speak, "my soul was baptized in his spirit, and ever since I have been a disciple and fellow-laborer."[28] Perhaps these individuals were drawn to the emotional intensity of the revivals but could not stomach the revivalist assumption that human depravity necessitated an entirely new birth. Social reform rituals appealed because these involved the renunciation of corrupt social institutions but not of human nature itself.[29]

Most people who did experience conversion, moreover, did not take the second step of embracing social reform. Those who did were generally lifelong spiritual seekers for whom the conversion experience was simply the first of many stages. In some cases, they turned to social reform only after the fervor of the revivals had worn off.[30] Encounters with a wide range of reformers also helped them to embrace an increasingly liberal theology. The case of Theodore Dwight Weld is illustrative.

Weld was one of the first of Finney's converts to embrace immediate abolition, and his charismatic influence galvanized hundreds of other revivalists in New York and Ohio to the cause. By the time Weld married the Quaker abolitionist Angelina Grimké (1805–79) in 1838, however, they refused to have any minister participate in the ceremony. In 1843 Weld told Lewis Tappan that he believed all church structures interfered with the individual's relationship with God. Shortly thereafter, Weld founded the Eagleswood School at a Fourierist colony in New Jersey. His inclusion of prominent Transcendentalists Elizabeth Peabody and William Henry Channing on the faculty did not dissuade other ex-Finneyites like Henry B. Stanton and Gerrit Smith from enrolling their children. After the Civil War, Weld moved to Boston and was a cofounder of a Unitarian congregation that "exact[ed] no sectarian or theological test of membership, and [strove] for no dead uniformity of speculative belief, as a means of obtaining that living unity with God, which first of all we should seek."[31] Other reformers who followed a similar trajectory include Elizabeth Cady Stanton, Henry B. Stanton, James Birney, Gerrit Smith, Elizur Wright Jr., Antoinette Brown Blackwell, Joshua R. Giddings, Lucy Stone, and J. Miller McKim.[32]

Many historians credit Finneyite revivalism with a significant change in tone that occurred in most reform movements around 1830. At that time, reformers began speaking of "immediate" solutions to long-standing social evils. Antialcohol activists redefined "temperance" to mean not moderation but abstinence from both fermented and distilled beverages, and thousands rallied to take the "teetotal" pledge. Peace activists began talking about total abstinence from both defensive and offensive wars. And antislavery activists like Garrison and Weld denounced the old strategy of African colonization as a racist compromise with sin, calling instead for the "immediate emancipation" of all slaves.

The reason for these changes, these historians suggest, is that Finneyites understood social evils as sins that could be voluntarily given up.[33] This understanding of sin, however, was little different from that held by liberal Unitarians and Quakers.[34] Liberals and revivalists alike rejected the orthodox notion that sin was an inherent component of fallen human nature that could not be rooted out by a mere act of will, since the will was equally fallen. Both groups were thus attracted to a "perfectionist" ethic in which all sins were to be given up immediately.[35]

The logic of social reform also pushed many activists beyond revivalist notions of sin as something that inheres primarily in the individual. Reformers sometimes *began* with a desire to achieve personal purity through renunciation of sin, but they gradually came to understand intemperance, slavery, and war as "systems" of sin, rather than as mere accumulations of individual misdeeds. Individuals were to renounce these systems not only for the sake of their personal salvation but also for the benefit of the many victims caught up in them. Thus, temperance activists held respectable "moderate" drinkers responsible for the misdeeds of alcoholics who could not control their drinking, while abolitionists held white Northerners responsible for perpetuating a slave system that was guaranteed by the federal Constitution. After visiting a prison in 1842, Lydia Maria Child reported that "society" had made the prisoners sinful, and that she personally had participated in the process "by yielding to popular prejudices, obeying false customs, and suppressing vital truths." By arguing for "the moral renovation of SOCIETY, as well as of the *individuals* of whom society is composed," social reformers anticipated the models of structural sin espoused by twentieth-century liberation theologians.[36] But this fact is obscured by the many historians who insist that the reformers' revivalist understanding of sin blinded them to the institutional dimensions of the evils they fought.[37]

Encounters with the Oppressed

The changed understanding of sin cannot fully account for the emergence of "immediatist" styles of reform around 1830. An equally important factor was the fact that around that time reformers began to listen to the victims of social evils.[38] This occurred simultaneously in several contexts. In upstate New York, Gerrit Smith got to know the local "drunkards" who had taken the temperance pledge, even though the temperance campaign had not originally targeted them. In Baltimore, antislavery editors Benjamin Lundy and William Lloyd Garrison got to know the black activists who read their newspaper and sometimes served as its agents. In Philadelphia, Lucretia Mott was invited to preach at a black church and met James Forten, a wealthy sailmaker who had fought in the United States Revolution. And at Cincinnati's Lane Seminary, a group of students under the leadership of Theodore Dwight Weld began tutoring and befriending the large population of fugitive slaves and free blacks in the city.

All of these people had a common message for the earnest young reformers: gradual amelioration of social evil was not enough! Garrison discovered that the free blacks' "convention" movement already had a well-established critique of colonization as a racist plot to purge the United States of its black citizens. Lucretia Mott heard the same argument from James Forten, who pointed out that he had lived his whole life in the United States and was offended by suggestions that Africa was his home. And the alcoholics of Peterboro told Gerrit Smith that moderate drinking would never do for them: the only solution to their addiction was immediate abstinence, modeled by the respectable leaders of society.[39]

The combined voices of all these witnesses, as much as any new conception of sin, led the reformers of the 1830s to demand an immediate end to intemperance and slavery. But they likely would not have listened to the victims at all if Jefferson's liberal ideology had not first been widely disseminated. From the perspective of the orthodox reformers of previous decades, slaves and drunkards were totally depraved individuals who had not yet been transformed by the light of the gospel. At best, the goal was to convert them by means of effective preaching; at worst, it was to rid the nation of slavery and intemperance by shipping the slaves to Africa and letting the drunkards die. For those who took the Declaration of Independence seriously, however, slaves and drunkards were images of the invisible God whose rights could never be alienated. As such, they deserved a place in the social reform movement alongside the disciples of Beecher, Finney, Channing, and Hicks.

The Boston Ultraists

One of the most important meeting grounds for reformers of diverse backgrounds was Boston.[40] It was here that William Lloyd Garrison, himself an upstart editor with Baptist and Federalist roots, brought fugitive slaves, working-class blacks, rural Baptists and Quakers, patrician Unitarians, scholarly Transcendentalists, and angry rebels from the orthodox churches together to explore their common humanity. It was here, too, that such liberal writers as Lydia Maria Child and John Greenleaf Whittier signed on to the cause of reform, risking their reputations but ensuring that sentimental identification would have a central place among reform strategies. All these people created the first and most logically consistent strand of radical Christian liberalism, a tradition that was generally known as "ultraism." (Chapter 3 will focus particularly on the "ultraist" wing of radical Christian liberalism.)

At the heart of Boston ultraism was the idea of "universal reform." Everyone in the circle around Garrison shared his commitment to temperance, abolition, and women's rights; many also supported his nonresistant pacifism and increasingly harsh critique of orthodox theology and religious ritualism. Eventually, ultraists were also attracted to utopian socialism, spiritualism, and such "body reforms" as the Graham diet, feminist dress reform, phrenology, and manual labor.[41] They sometimes tried to keep all these causes "mechanically separate" for the sake of alliances with more moderate reformers, but they could scarcely conceal their conviction that "TRUTH is one and indivisible." Ultimately, they aspired to the liberation "of the whole earth from sin and suffering."[42]

The ultraists, above all, were "agitators." With few links to the benevolent empire, they did not build as vigorous societies as did their revivalist brothers and sisters, but they made up for it with the fervor of their publications and their theatrical activism.[43] The role of the agitator was not to transform institutions or even to persuade individuals directly. Rather, it was to get people thinking about an issue so that their divinely inspired consciences would eventually lead them to the truth. "Do all you can," Elizabeth Cady Stanton explained, "*no matter what*, to get people to think on your reform, and then, if the reform is good, it will come about in due season." In the face of self-evident evils, agitators did not hesitate to provoke offense or even hostility if these would dispel public apathy. "At a time like this," Frederick Douglass commented, "scorching irony, not convincing argument, is needed." Agitators also cared more about disseminating ideas than recruiting full-fledged members of their cause. The techniques of reformist agitation were derived from journalistic provocation rather than revivalist persuasion, and they fit nicely with the liberal principle that freedom of conscience is the starting point of genuine reform.[44]

The first and foremost venue for Boston ultraism was Garrison's newspaper, the *Liberator*, which was founded in 1831 and ran until the close of the Civil War. Unlike most other social reform papers, this was not the journal of any specific organization. Instead, it was a vehicle for free debate, guided by its editor's idiosyncratic and inclusive vision. Though Garrison never abandoned his central focus on slavery, he offended some readers with his advocacy of women's rights, others with his nonresistance, and still others with his harsh attacks on the "pro-slavery" clergy. The *Liberator*'s provocative style gave it a high profile, and soon many reformers wanted to dissociate themselves from it and its editor. This, in large part, was the source of the schisms in the abolitionist and peace movements at the end of the 1830s.

The peace movement split in 1838, when ultraists began denouncing not only defensive war but also all coercive functions of government. This led to the creation of the New England Non-Resistance Society, which was largely controlled by Garrison and his allies. Around the same time, some temperance activists began insisting that the churches stop using fermented communion wine, a demand that unsettled biblical literalists. Others shifted their energies away from moral suasion to the passage of so-called Maine Laws that legislated abstinence. Still others moved into the new "Washingtonian" movement, in which reformed drunkards rather than ministers took the leading role.

The abolitionist movement, for its part, split over a whole host of issues. The ultraists stridently attacked the established churches for their support of slavery, thus offending

New York abolitionists with closer ties to the benevolent empire. New York City leaders were also troubled by the ultraists' insistence on agitating such issues as nonresistance, women's rights, and even Transcendentalist theology. Meanwhile, many western abolitionists, equally frustrated with clerical conservatism, wanted to shift their efforts out of the churches and into partisan politics—a move that was anathema to leaders in both Boston and New York. All these issues came to a head in 1840, when the annual convention of the American Anti-Slavery Society split over whether women could vote and hold office. Ultraist supporters of women's rights won the vote, in large part because they had mobilized their delegates more effectively. Their opponents in New York City formed a rival organization, the American and Foreign Anti-Slavery Society, while the "political" abolitionists sponsored a new Liberty Party. Ultimately, no faction was able to create an effective national organization, and abolitionist initiative fell to an ideologically diverse array of local societies.

Deeply disappointed, Theodore Dwight Weld complained that the division in anti-slavery ranks "crucifies the savior afresh."[45] Similarly, some historians believe that the splintering of the movement, and particularly the harsh attacks on the churches, destroyed the great dream of a united phalanx of Christians building God's kingdom on earth.[46] Others share the view of William Goodell, a Finneyite, who reflected that "abolitionism, before the division, was a powerful elixir, in the phial of one anti-slavery organization, corked up tight, and carried about for exhibition. By the division the phial was broken and the contents spilled over the whole surface of society, where it has been working as a leaven, ever since, till the mass is beginning to upheave."[47] From this perspective, which may be extended to other social reform movements, what happened in 1840 was not disaster but devolution. The reform impulse was spread out among a diverse array of groups and individuals, who worked more effectively because they did not have to follow orders from any central authority.[48]

For the ultraists, the schisms simply opened the door to a freer exploration of universal reform. Unencumbered by their revivalist allies in reform, they took a closer look at the religious institutions of ministry, church, and Sabbath at the Chardon Street Convention on Universal Reform, in 1840. A few years later they considered the authority and inspiration of the Bible—once a shibboleth for Unitarians as well as the orthodox. In keeping with the ultraist commitment to freedom of conscience, these conventions were not designed to promote a single position but provided a forum for anyone willing to join the dialogue. The Free Convention of 1858, for example, attracted Shakers, suffragists, and spiritualists to a conversation that embraced marriage, immortality, and the Sabbath as well as women's rights and slavery.

Despite their diversity, all ultraist causes were intimately linked to the doctrine of the *imago dei*.[49] Ultraists honored the freedom of conscience because they regarded conscience as a spark of divinity at the center of each person. From this flowed their preference for agitation over systematic society-building. (In a letter sent to William Lloyd Garrison in 1845, for example, Douglass referred to the "God-like approach" of "free discussion.")[50] They were, moreover, willing to attack cherished social institutions because they placed ultimate faith in the God within the soul. And they were especially concerned with violence in all its forms because it was for them a sacrilegious assault on God's image. Their consistent adherence to such principles places them at the heart of the movement I call "radical Christian liberalism."

Sentimental Reformers

Boston ultraists were not, however, the only radical Christian liberals in the social reform movement. A much broader group of reformers, whom I shall call "sentimental reformers," translated the theology of the *imago dei* into literary form. Refusing to draw sharp lines between divine and human activity, they promoted social reform by telling stories of God's work in ordinary human lives. Often these stories emerged from transformative encounters between reformers and the victims of violence. T. S. Arthur composed "temperance tales" after hearing the testimony of reformed drunkards; Harriet Beecher Stowe based *Uncle Tom's Cabin* on her youthful encounters with former slaves in Cincinnati; fugitive slaves composed their own autobiographies after realizing how much white reformers wanted to hear from them. In the struggles and triumphs of victims, sentimental reformers glimpsed God's power to transform the world. Not all could embrace the ultraists' entire renunciation of coercion, but all did place their first hope in the nonviolent power of storytelling.

Sentimental reformers came from a variety of religious backgrounds. T. S. Arthur was a Swedenborgian, and thus a participant in a tradition that blended liberal and mystical themes. Harriet Beecher Stowe was the daughter of the most prominent orthodox preacher of the day, but she personally had not had a theologically correct conversion experience and would eventually become an Episcopalian. These writers, unlike the ultraists, were not concerned to set themselves in sharp opposition to orthodoxy. But they borrowed heavily from the literary style of Catharine Sedgwick, and the theology implicit in their writings was usually quite liberal. (All of the writers discussed in chapters 4, 5, and 6 might be classified as sentimental reformers, though some would also fit in my "ultraist" and "revolutionary" categories.)

Revolutionary Reformers

After 1840, sentimentalists and ultraists often worked alongside (or in tension with) a third circle of radical Christian liberals, led by Gerrit Smith and—after his break with Garrison around 1851—Frederick Douglass. Deeply committed to temperance, abolition, and peace, these "revolutionaries" shared the ultraists' concern for universal reform. "It matters little," said Douglass in 1855, "which path of inquiry a man may pursue, or which great moral or spiritual fact he may investigate; he has but to honestly persevere to find himself, at last, at the portals of the whole universe of truth." Revolutionaries like Douglass also agreed with the ultraists that "there is something in the world much stronger than any human organization," and that most existing institutions were fatally compromised by their association with intemperance and slavery.[51] But they were unwilling to renounce the hope that some institutions, even mildly coercive ones, might someday contribute to the struggle against oppression.

Where ultraists emphasized the Sermon on the Mount and its call for perfect nonviolence, revolutionaries appealed to the Golden Rule, a text Douglass referred to early on as "the immutable, the eternal, and all-comprehensive principle of the sacred New Testament." "Doing unto others" entailed a presumption against violence, but it also meant being willing to use any means necessary to help one's neighbor in distress.

Douglass summed up the revolutionary spirit in an 1857 speech: "The struggle may be a moral one, or it may be a physical one, but it must be a struggle. Power concedes nothing without a demand."[52]

The roots of revolutionary liberalism lie in the experiences of Finneyite reformers during the late 1830s. Like the Boston ultraists, revolutionaries were deeply disappointed at the failure of the orthodox churches to rally to the cause of social reform in general, and that of abolition in particular. As Douglass recalled, they had trouble believing that people "loved God truly, who hated the image of God so intensely."[53] But they had little exposure to the Unitarian and Hicksite traditions, which provided the framework for the ultraists' spiritual explorations. So Gerrit Smith, Elizur Wright Jr., and others simply shifted their attention from the churches to politics, creating the Liberty Party as the vehicle for their reforming vision. This was not a sign of any particular pragmatism: the Liberty Party platform was often as utopian as Garrisonian nonresistance, although the particulars differed. Where Garrison rejected the very notion of government, Smith taught that "government in its true sense is simply the collective people, charged with the duty of protecting each one of the people." He denied the validity of unjust laws by claiming that "law is for righteousness," but he insisted that activists work through political structures whenever feasible.[54]

Following his friend Alvan Stewart, Smith came to believe that the Constitution was itself antislavery, in part because of the ideals laid out in the Preamble and in part because of the Fifth Amendment's guarantee of due process. By 1851, even Garrison's most talented disciple, Frederick Douglass, endorsed this view. "We had arrived at the firm conviction," Douglass explained, "that the Constitution, construed in the light of well established rules of legal interpretation, might be made consistent in its details with the noble purposes avowed in its preamble."[55] In some ways, the Preamble played the same role for the revolutionaries that the Declaration of Independence did for the ultraists.

The revolutionaries came to theological liberalism gradually, but ultimately most embraced a brand of Christianity that was indistinguishable from Garrison's. From the pulpit of his nonsectarian Church of Peterboro, for example, Gerrit Smith taught that the true "religion of Jesus" was a "religion of reason" opposed to "creeds and churches and a clerical order of men"—determined, indeed, "to send them all down stream." Even the authority of the Bible was unnecessary, since "the whole nature of man" spoke out against such evils as slavery and alcohol. Smith repudiated the churches' "speculations and theories respecting Trinity, Atonement, Heaven, Hell, etc.," and especially their doctrine of original sin. Faith in the goodness of humanity, he argued, "would serve mightily to lift up [people's] lives to the high level of their nature." For true Christianity was nothing other than a practical embrace of gospel ethics: "Our lives and our likeness to Christ are the precise measure of our faith in Christ."[56]

Douglass, for his part, abandoned his early calling as a Methodist preacher soon after he joined the abolitionists. He gave pointed expression to his mature faith at a celebration in 1870 following the passage of the Fifteenth Amendment. Others had resolved that the participants thank God rather than human beings for the victory. But Douglass replied, "I have no sort of sympathy with that kind of religion that expresses its devotion to God by neglect of their fellows. . . . I want to express my love to God and gratitude to God, by thanking those faithful men and women, who have devoted the great energies of their souls to the welfare of mankind. It is only through such men and such women that I can get any glimpses of God anywhere."[57]

More than the ultraists or sentimentalists, the revolutionaries anticipated the future. Their willingness to cooperate with politicians led them to affiliate cautiously with both the Free Soil Party and the and Republican Party, though neither espoused radical liberal principles. Eventually, they became the vanguard of the Republican Party, prodding it to endorse such revolutionary changes as the emancipation of the slaves and the granting of suffrage to black men. In the process, though, they lost their vision of a still more radical transformation of American society. (Chapter 7 will trace this process, focusing particularly on Frederick Douglass, John Brown, and Abraham Lincoln.)

My categories of "ultra," "sentimental," and "revolutionary" reformers are ideal types, and many reformers might be placed in more than one group.[58] Lydia Maria Child was a pioneer of sentimental reform fiction, but she was also a committed ultraist. Frederick Douglass made a deliberate switch from the ultraist to the revolutionary camp. The Transcendentalist preacher Theodore Parker was an integral part of Boston's ultraist community and a good friend of Garrison's, but his views on violence were closer to those of the revolutionaries. The categories might be imagined as concentric circles, with ultraists at the center and sentimentalists encompassing both other groups. For both "ultraists" and "revolutionaries" supported revolutionary social change, while all three groups frequently made sentimental appeals. The point of the categories is simply to demonstrate that radical Christian liberalism took multiple forms and was widely diffused throughout the social reform movement. Not all reformers were radical Christian liberals, but neither was radical Christian liberalism a minor heresy held by a few eccentrics. It was, like revivalism, a foundation stone of the entire enterprise of social reform.

Radical Christian Liberalism and Social Reform: Four Key Insights

The history I have just outlined differs somewhat from many standard accounts of antebellum social reform. While other scholars have seen revivalism as the primary or even exclusive cause of social reform, I place equal emphasis on the liberal theology that was radicalized by William Lloyd Garrison, Lydia Maria Child, Gerrit Smith, Frederick Douglass, and other activists. Since this is a somewhat novel emphasis, it may be helpful to identify the key insights it makes visible. First, it highlights the abiding religious, and indeed theological, character of social reform. Second, it suggests that nonviolence is a key to reform: liberal reformers characteristically asserted a form of nonviolent, sentimental power against the violence of oppressive institutions. Third, it reveals social reform's paradoxical character as a revolutionary movement rooted in the mainstream values of American society. Finally, my emphasis on the liberal roots of social reform exposes the underlying fragility of the movement.

Antebellum social reform preserved its religious character right up until the Civil War. Though many leading reformers abandoned the doctrines of Reformed orthodoxy, they continued to identify their enterprise as fundamentally Christian. Maria Weston Chapman spoke for many when she claimed that the principles of liberty espoused by reformers were "identical with those of Christianity herself." This was more than lip service to conventional piety. From beginning to end, Chapman and other reformers were inspired by the liberal theology of the *imago dei*. Some even went so far as to suggest that other Americans had abandoned true Christianity by condoning slavery, alcohol, and war. In 1852, for example, Frederick Douglass described the Fugitive Slave Act "as a declaration of war against religious freedom." Most churches, he said, failed to see this because they regarded religion as "an empty ceremony, and *not* a vital principle, requiring active benevolence, justice, love, and good will towards man."[59]

It was no accident that leading reformers gravitated to religious liberalism, for reform was "at home" in liberalism in ways that it could never be in most revivalist churches. Reformers who began as revivalists ultimately faced a choice: Was it more important to change society or win souls to Jesus? Liberals did not have to worry about such choices because for them the ultimate religious duty was the realization of God's presence in themselves, and of the kingdom of God on earth.

Conversely, though, liberalism was never really at home in ecclesial institutions like the Unitarian Church. What was the point of serving a single denomination when one's deepest commitment was to a universal vision of human rights? This is why so few reformers, despite their liberal ideas, officially became Unitarians (or, for that matter, Hicksites). Their real "church" was the social reform movement itself, which offered them a sense of identity, ritual, and community, without distracting them from what they considered to be God's true work on earth.[60] As a result, many of the most creative Christian liberal "theologians" of the early nineteenth century stood outside the liberal churches—a fact that has not been sufficiently acknowledged in our theological histories.

At the heart of social reform theology, I have suggested, was the doctrine of the *imago dei*. As a consequence, reformers were especially troubled by violence, which they saw as an assault on the divine image in the individual. From their perspective, violence was the thread connecting all the forms of oppression. The violence of masters against slaves, soldiers against civilians, drunkards against their families, and rumsellers against drunkards, all contributed to a "system" of oppression that defied God by attacking God's image on earth. To fight this system, radical Christian liberals relied on the nonviolent power of God's image in their own souls, and the souls of the victims. They believed that this, not military or government power, was the ultimate force in the universe. In 1838 Channing had affirmed that "deep moral convictions, unfeigned reverence and fervent love for man, and living faith in Christ, are mightier than armies." Douglass echoed this sentiment in 1847, telling Americans that while they might withstand military opposition, "You cannot build your forts so strong, nor your ramparts so high, nor arm yourself so powerfully as to be able to withstand the overwhelming MORAL SENTIMENT against Slavery now flowing into this land."[61]

The contrast between state power and sentimental power helps explain the revolutionary character of social reform. Even at their most moderate, social reformers relegated the state to a secondary significance: the most important work would be accomplished through the power of sentiment. At their most radical, reformers hoped that sentimental power would supersede the state altogether. But this made them revolutionaries of a peculiar sort: their goal was not to transfer state power to a revolutionary vanguard or new regime but to shift it back to the individual level.

Both the "ultra" and the "revolutionary" wings of the social reform movement were quite clear about the revolutionary character of their vision. (The sentimentalists were sometimes implicitly revolutionary, but they rarely used revolutionary language.) Wendell Phillips spoke for many when, in 1863, he declared his allegiance to "the great fight . . . between free institutions and caste institutions, Freedom and Democracy against institutions of privilege and class."[62] The revolutionary character of temperance was less obvious, yet the movement sought to destroy the economic power of a large group of tavernkeepers and to transform the social activities of all Americans simply to enhance the freedom of a minority of alcoholics.[63] The nonresistance movement, for its part, was emphatically revolutionary, calling for the nonviolent overthrow of the federal government and all other states.

Nevertheless, many scholars—particularly in the middle of the twentieth century— have denied the revolutionary character of antebellum social reform and have suggested that American liberalism cannot, by definition, be revolutionary.[64] It is true that American liberalism was incompatible with the Marxist theory of revolution, which relied on class conflict and the concentration of power in a vanguard party. But liberalism itself could turn revolutionary when ostensibly liberal institutions were measured by liberal principles and found wanting. From the perspective of radical Christian liberals, vestiges of "tyranny and priestcraft" were present everywhere in America: in the power wielded by rumsellers, slaveholders, soldiers, and ministers, and in the very structure of the federal Constitution. And since they were not convinced that institutions as such were even necessary, they were willing to take risks to root out those vestiges.

Yet because it was based on shared principles, the radical Christian liberals' revolutionary stance did not set them apart from the larger society. They were not sectarians appealing to a countercultural revelation but prophets calling the nation back to its founding vision. They both affirmed and rejected their culture, using texts with broad resonance—the Golden Rule, the Declaration of Independence—to judge and condemn both church and state.[65] After his first trip abroad, Frederick Douglass testified with special eloquence to this paradoxical approach to America.

In a speech defending his right to criticize American institutions even when in Great Britain, Douglass insisted that blacks could not feel "patriotism" for a nation that so consistently denied them their rights. They wished to stay in North America, to be sure, but only because of their attachment to the American soil, to family members, and to their "three million" brothers and sisters in bondage. At the same time, though, Douglass denied being anti-American. His loyalties were not narrower than the nation but broader: "I love humanity all over the globe. I am anxious to see righteousness prevail in all directions." This cosmopolitan liberalism was itself rooted in American ideals, particularly the ideals laid out so powerfully in the Declaration of Independence. Thus, Douglass took special pleasure in noting that many of the harshest British critics of American slavery had the Declaration displayed prominently in their homes.[66]

The radical Christian liberals' rootedness in American ideals gave them extraordinary power, but it was also their weakness. Because they identified so fully with their own culture, radical Christian liberals could not rely on any external power to guarantee that their vision of the future would be accomplished. To be sure, they affirmed the omnipotence of God; but they believed this was expressed only through the actions of ordinary people. Radical Christian liberalism was only as strong as its faith in humanity.

As a result, radical Christian liberals were often deeply ambivalent. Ultraists wrestled with their commitment to a standard of perfect nonviolence. They struggled valiantly to convince themselves and their neighbors that humans are naturally capable of identifying with one another and that God is able to change society entirely through nonviolent human actions. Yet these beliefs remained hopes, not certainties. Some ultraists embraced nonviolence only for a brief period or only in certain circumstances. Others, including Garrison, remained personally committed to nonviolence but entertained the hope that God might also work through the actions of their violent neighbors.

Sentimentalists, similarly, were only partly committed to the tactic of "moral suasion." For those who dared believe in its power, suasion posed a dramatic challenge to the assumption that only political and military power truly count in this world. This is why Angelina Grimké sparked such controversy merely by speaking publicly on behalf of the slave: she forced the nation to confront the possibility that a verbal act, performed by a woman, might itself change the world. But sentimentalism foundered on a paradox. If, as sentimental texts often claimed, identification depended on the actual presence of a suffering, related body, how could a mere text bring about such presence?[67] Sentimental writers tried to bridge the gap between body and text with ever more extreme rhetoric, but this gave their works an aura of unreality that made identification even more difficult.

This unreality was most apparent in the Christology of the sentimentalists. Initially, liberals like William Lloyd Garrison had emphasized Jesus' life of love and service rather than his sacrificial death. They insisted that the best way to follow Christ was to imitate his life. This was a demanding Christology, in which Christ's manifest divinity challenged others to uncover their own nascent divinity. But gradually, some liberals began to assume that only certain individuals—devout slaves, for example, or innocent children—could perfectly imitate Christ. They also began to emphasize the suffering *deaths* of these individuals more than their healing *lives*. Thus, in *Uncle Tom's Cabin* both Little Eva and Uncle Tom are most powerful—indeed capable of redeeming the sinners surrounding them—at the moment of their deaths. This led to an easier Christology, in which Christ's divinity set him apart from the rest of humanity and gave him powers not vouchsafed to mere mortals, such as the ability to give life to others by dying a perfect sacrificial death. This left the rest of us off the hook, and without a task.

Of the three groups of radical Christian liberals, the revolutionaries managed best to avoid the ambivalences inherent in liberal theology. Because they were open to a broader range of revolutionary tactics, they could recognize God's presence in a wider range of people, including both violent revolutionaries like John Brown and politicians like Abraham Lincoln. Increasingly, though, they saw God's image *only* in those who used violence. By the Civil War the revolutionaries, and with them the social reform movement generally, had abandoned the theology of nonviolent power most characteristic of radical Christian liberalism. It would be nearly a century before this theology was reborn in the civil rights movement.

3

The Gospel, the Declaration, and the Divine Child

Theology and Literature of Ultra Reform

"Ultra" reform burst onto the American stage on New Year's Day 1831, when William Lloyd Garrison published the first issue of his radical antislavery newspaper, the *Liberator*. At the close of a year marked by liberal revolutions throughout Europe, Garrison promised to extend the liberal values of freedom and equality to the most downtrodden community in North America, the slaves. He would, he declared, "lift up the standard of emancipation in the eyes of the nation" and keep it flying "till every chain be broken, and every bondman set free!" Garrison's liberalism, like that of earlier Christian liberals, found its sanction equally in the democratic tradition of North America and in the Christian faith—in Jefferson's Declaration *and* Jesus' gospel. But unlike his predecessors, Garrison was unwilling to concede that the defeat of tyranny and priestcraft would be gradual. As he wrote in his opening editorial, he had once "unreflectingly assented to the popular but pernicious doctrine of *gradual* abolition" of slavery. But now he demanded an immediate end to human bondage—and, indeed, to anything that constrained or blurred the divine image in humanity.[1]

The most characteristic feature of Garrison's activism was his ability to draw radically countercultural conclusions from widely shared values. He appealed to no new revelation, claimed no special authority for himself, and did not contemplate the creation of a new church or political party. "The anti-slavery enterprise," he wrote in 1839, "found in the doctrines of every sect and party enough, if practically carried out, to ensure the overthrow of slavery."[2] He might well have said the same for his other cherished causes of temperance, peace, and women's rights, each of which simply extended the values professed by all Americans. Yet Garrison was willing to contemplate the overthrow of any institution—church, party, even government itself—that failed to live up to its professions.

More than any other individual, Garrison epitomized the theological and political movement that I have called "radical Christian liberalism." His sons perhaps went too far, in their hagiographic biography, when they wrote that "Mr. Garrison was the incarnation of the cause which he founded."[3] After all, many abolitionists and other reformers despised Garrison as an infidel, and still more felt his outrageous opinions did the cause more harm than good. Yet Garrison served as an exemplar for a small circle of

"Garrisonians" and as a trailblazer for many more reformers who repudiated him personally but eventually embraced positions that he had been first to articulate. He had a remarkable, at times infuriating, capacity to grasp the logical implications of ideas, and he was courageous enough to embrace these implications at great personal cost.[4] In this sense, he *did* incarnate what was generally known as the "ultra" wing of the reform community—that group of reformers who did not fear to carry their principles to their logical, if revolutionary, conclusions.[5]

Ultraist tendencies were found in every major reform movement, but they found no more congenial home than in the New England Non-Resistance Society, which Garrison helped found in 1838. Nonresistance took traditional pacifism a step further, disavowing both coercion of all sorts and participation in any government willing to use coercion. The Non-Resistance Society articulated clearly the core liberal notion that unfettered individuals, with love as their only weapon, could utterly transform society. In many ways, it was the most theological of the nineteenth-century reforms, in part because nonresistants could appeal so directly to the Sermon on the Mount, and in part because they had to work so hard to refute the "war spirit" found in much of the rest of the Bible and theological tradition. In opposition to most traditional theology, the nonresistant movement relied almost exclusively on the liberal tactic of identification—both between God and the individual and among human individuals. The Non-Resistance Society, with Garrison as its guiding spirit, thus belongs at the heart of any study of radical Christian liberalism.

The liberal theology of ultra reform appears clearly in Garrison's religious and political views, and in the work of the New England Non-Resistance Society. It is also evident in two literary expressions of nonresistance: *Human Life*, the autobiography of Garrison's close ally Henry Clarke Wright (1797-1870); and *Margaret*, a Transcendentalist novel by the Unitarian peace activist Sylvester Judd (1813-53). Both of these texts gave fervent expression to the radical Christian liberal conviction that individuals and families possessed the naturally divine power to usher in a nonviolent millennium.

Though the nonresistant movement came closer than other antebellum reforms to articulating a theology of nonviolent power, it had two key shortcomings. First, most nonresistants (though not Garrison himself) downplayed the dilemmas faced by the victims of systemic violence. It was one thing to recommend "turning the other cheek" to activists seeking to end injustice, and quite another to impose it on slaves, battered women, and others who faced violence on a daily basis. Writers like Wright and Judd generally sidestepped this distinction, leaving it to temperance and abolitionist writers to explore fully the *imago dei* in the lives of victims.

Second, nonresistants had difficulty translating their *ethic* of nonviolence into an absolutely consistent *theology* of nonviolence. They had no trouble insisting on nonviolence as a binding rule of human conduct, and they had no trouble rooting this in the theological principle of the *imago dei*. God's image in the oppressor made it necessary to treat the oppressor with love, not violence, and God's image in the activist gave that person the divine power needed to overcome oppression. But nonresistants were rarely willing to claim that this was the *only* form God's power could take. Some—notably Garrison—continued to cling to the notion that God might ultimately use apocalyptic violence to overthrow oppression. Others—notably Wright and Judd—placed more and more of their faith in messianic children whose nonviolent power was supernatural and thus not available to the ordinary run of activists. By the Civil War, these two alternative theologies would help displace the vision of radical Christian liberalism.

The Religious Pilgrimage of William Lloyd Garrison

William Lloyd Garrison's religious identity has always posed a special challenge for scholars. Some, pointing to his Baptist roots and fondness for biblical quotation, label him as an "evangelical reformer"—failing to acknowledge that he never had a conversion experience, never was baptized or joined a church, and consistently infuriated his revivalist contemporaries with his heterodox views.[6] Others see him as the leader of a small heterodox faction that exercised little influence on the much larger community of revivalist reformers.[7] Though this view correctly notes the wide gulf between Garrison's views and traditional Protestant theology, it fails to see the parallels between Garrison's religious pilgrimage and that of reformers who came to similar conclusions more gradually.

Valarie Ziegler comes closer but still misconstrues Garrison when she calls him a "sectarian radical" who believed "that institutions were corrupt and that reform occurred only when righteous individuals separated themselves from the fallen world."[8] Ziegler captures well the flavor of Garrison's radicalism but misses some key distinctions between Garrison's views and those commonly labeled "sectarian." Garrison—at least by the late 1840s—did not accept the traditional doctrine of the Fall and so did not see the world as "fallen."[9] He regarded most social institutions as corrupt but hoped to transform them precisely because he did *not* believe that the corruption extended to the root of human nature. His approach to the world was thus one not of sectarian withdrawal but of active countercultural engagement.

Throughout his editorial career, Garrison sought to maintain an open dialogue with people of all faiths and convictions, and he regarded "sectarianism" as his bitterest enemy. At the end of 1837, a time of growing division in the reform community, Garrison could still remind his readers that "we care not who is found upon this broad platform of our common nature: if he will join hands with us, in good faith, to undo the heavy burdens and break the yokes of our enslaved countrymen, we shall not stop to enquire whether he is a Trinitarian or Unitarian, Baptist or Methodist, Catholic or Covenanter, Presbyterian or Quaker, Swedenborgian or Perfectionist."[10]

Garrison's most recent biographer, Henry Mayer, strikes a fine balance when he suggests that Garrison "drew upon . . . rural Protestant revivalism," with its "language of repentance and conversion," but also had "secular roots" in the "natural rights tradition" and in "romantic idealism." It is true that Garrison drew on all these traditions, though it is a bit misleading to call the latter traditions "secular." These were, at least as Garrison absorbed them, traditions of Christian liberalism with deep gospel roots. Garrison would have had trouble comprehending Mayer's claim that he "turned religious energy toward secular ends."[11] What he did, rather, was to turn his religious energy from strictly *ecclesial* ends to the Christianization of the entire social order. In this regard, he stood squarely in the broad tradition of Christian liberalism.

Garrison's distinctive brand of Christian liberalism was shaped by a variety of traditions: the Baptist piety of his mother; the competing orthodox and Unitarian traditions of

Boston, where he lived most of his adulthood; the liberal Quakerism that predominated in the early abolitionist movement; and, perhaps most significantly, the reform-minded liberalism of his in-laws, the Bensons. It is necessary, therefore, to begin an account of Garrison's religious pilgrimage with a few words about each of these traditions.

Garrison's family roots were in northern New England and Nova Scotia, where both his mother and his paternal grandmother had experienced conversion in response to the "New Light" preaching of Henry Alline and other Baptists. Alline's tradition placed enormous emphasis on an emotional "new birth," but it also had significant common-alities with liberal theology. Maritime Baptists were wary of a professionalized clergy and of formal creeds, and—significantly for Garrison's later feminist commitments—they allowed considerable scope for women's leadership. Indeed, Garrison's mother played an important role in transplanting the Nova Scotian tradition of women's prayer meet-ings to new communities whenever her family relocated.[12]

Garrison himself was an obedient child who absorbed his mother's piety, even as his older brother inherited their father's alcoholism. As a young printer's apprentice, Garrison was "a complete Baptist according to the tenets" who attended church regu-larly and observed the Sabbath scrupulously, even though he had not experienced con-version or been baptized himself.[13] Throughout his apprenticeship, Garrison contin-ued to attend his mother's Baptist church in Newburyport, Massachusetts, and for several years thereafter his writing was peppered with blasts against Sunday mail delivery and the "infidelity" of Thomas Jefferson.[14] Even after he had renounced these views, he retained much of the flavor of revivalism. When he spoke, he called upon his hearers to renounce the sin of slavery and experience a conversion to abolitionism. Indeed, part of Garrison's appeal for Unitarian liberals was the fact that he allowed them a vicarious experience of revivalism. Lydia Maria Child, for example, recalled the early days of abolition as a "missionary" time when "the Holy Spirit did actually descend upon men and women in tongues of flame."[15] She also recalled, in an obituary of Garrison, that "his character, had . . . a strong stamp of Puritanism."[16]

Despite this persistent revivalist style, the *content* of Garrison's faith began to broaden in 1826, when he moved to Boston. (He would live in Boston on and off for the next five years, then settle there permanently after founding the *Liberator* in 1831.) A bud-ding interest in social reform led him to attend the sermons of both William Ellery Channing and his evangelical archrival, Lyman Beecher. Despite their theological dif-ferences, both Channing and Beecher stressed "disinterested benevolence" as a cardi-nal rule for all Christians, and it was this that Garrison absorbed most eagerly at their feet.[17] Soon he signed on as editor of a temperance newspaper, the *National Philanthro-pist*. From this editorial perch, he began to articulate a broad-based vision of reform, which was proudly American and focused on the causes of peace, antislavery, and tem-perance. "The brightest traits in the American character," he wrote in 1828, "will de-rive their lustre, not from the laurels picked from the field of blood . . . but from our exertions to banish war from the earth, to stay the ravages of intemperance among all that is beautiful and fair, to unfetter those who have been enthralled by chains which we have forged, and to spread the light of knowledge and religious liberty wherever darkness and superstition reign."[18]

Garrison's reform commitments quickly led him to forge strong ties to the Hicksite Quaker community. He had actually known Quakers from very early in his life; one of his first apprenticeships was with a Quaker cordwainer named Gamaliel Oliver, and in 1826 editor Garrison had discovered the shy Quaker poet John Greenleaf Whittier. He embraced immediate abolition while working for another Quaker, Benjamin Lundy, at the *Genius of Universal Emancipation.* Lucretia Mott, as noted earlier, was a key theological influence, and a more personal influence came from the philanthropic Benson family of Brooklyn, Connecticut. The Bensons shared Garrison's Baptist background but had fallen out with their minister and gravitated toward the more reform-minded Quakers. Two of their daughters actually became Quakers, but the rest of the family found a congenial home in the local Unitarian congregation pastored by Samuel J. May.[19] Garrison married Helen Eliza Benson in 1834 and soon thereafter wrote to his new brother-in-law, "I am growing more and more hostile to outward forms and ceremonies and observances, as a religious duty, and trust I am more and more appreciating the nature and enjoying the privileges of that liberty wherewith the obedient soul is made free." A year later, the British traveler Harriet Martineau met Garrison and reported that he had "a good deal of a Quaker air."[20]

If reform commitments drew Garrison closer to the Quakers, they also pushed him away from both of the rival religious establishments of Boston. At the beginning of his career, Garrison firmly believed that the churches held the key to a national regeneration of morals, but he was repeatedly disappointed in his hope that they would rise to that challenge. Even as editor of the *Philanthropist,* he complained of the lack of "*reasoning* Christians" with a "definite perception of what constitutes duty," and in the *Genius* he bemoaned "a religion which is graduated by the corrupt, defective laws of the State, and not by the pure, perfect laws of God."[21] A more telling disappointment came when he could not find a single Boston church willing to host his first immediatist lecture and thus had to settle for Abner Kneeland's "infidel" Society of Free Enquirers. Though such luminaries as Beecher and Channing showed up for the lecture, they rebuffed Garrison's subsequent requests for support.[22]

Garrison understood radical agitation well enough that he was probably not surprised by his failure to attract the support of established religious leaders, and this alone would probably not have alienated him from the churches. A more crushing blow came when ministers who *were* committed to abolition began criticizing Garrison for his "unchristian" language and support for Quaker positions on peace, the Sabbath, and women's rights. Interestingly, the earliest of these "clerical" attacks came from the Unitarians: in 1834 Henry Ware Jr. and other members of the Cambridge Anti-Slavery Society sought to impose a censorship committee on the *Liberator.*[23] A year later, Ware helped create a rival organization as an antidote to Garrisonianism. Soon, however, this group fell under the control of the orthodox party, which from then on took the lead in the anti-Garrisonian campaign.

Garrison provoked the orthodox by criticizing Lyman Beecher for caring more about the Sabbath than the slave. Though his intent (at that time!) was not to undermine Sabbath observance but simply to highlight Beecher's hypocrisy, the comments unleashed a flood of criticisms, some of which pointed out Garrison's unbaptized status. Garrison explained that "religious scruples" did not allow him to "become the partisan of a religious sect, nor to bind ourselves to a human creed, nor to unite in the observance of certain forms and ceremonies," but this probably sounded too Quaker to calm his critics. By September 1836 Garrison confided to Samuel J. May that "a mighty sectarian conspiracy is forming to crush me," and within a few years the abolitionist community had split into Garrisonian and "clerical" wings.[24]

By this time the "clerical" opposition was almost entirely orthodox. Garrison's relationship with Unitarianism evolved in a considerably more complex manner. His contacts with the leadership remained chilly. Even when Channing himself published an antislavery book that some Garrisonians admired, Garrison privately branded it as "an inflated, inconsistent, and slanderous production."[25] Channing himself avoided making Garrison's acquaintance, though he once unwittingly shook his hand at a legislative hearing. But many of Garrison's earliest allies were Unitarians, including some members of Channing's elite congregation. People like Samuel Sewall, Francis Jackson, and especially Maria Weston Chapman kept open indirect lines of communication. In 1836, for example, Garrison twice joined friends to hear Channing preach and found the sermons "full of beauty and power, worthy to be written in starry letters upon the sky"— and certainly superior to Beecher's. Channing, for his part, was a longtime subscriber to the *Liberator* and the Unitarian establishment's staunchest supporter of Garrisonian pastors like Samuel J. May and Charles Follen. After Channing's death, Garrison eulogized him generously, noting that "he believed in eternal progress, and therefore never stood still, but went onward—if not rapidly, without faltering."[26]

The Unitarian movement itself did not stand still but evolved in a manner that allowed Garrison to build ever stronger connections with its radical wing. In 1841 the popular preacher Theodore Parker broke with the leadership over his reform commitments and Transcendentalist theology, and Parker's congregation provided a sort of church home for the Garrison family. The children attended Sunday school there, and Garrison occasionally filled in for Parker in the pulpit.[27] Garrison also made many friends, notably Henry Clarke Wright, who had experienced traumatic breaks with orthodox theology. Though these friends were not all Unitarians, they embraced the classic Unitarian critique of orthodoxy and imparted it to Garrison. This critique appears, for example, in an 1855 letter in which Garrison praised Francis Jackson for throwing off "the fetters of that terrible theology which has so long held mastery over the New England mind, making one universal blight of human existence here below, and filling a future state of existence with inconceivable dangers and unutterable horrors." The alternative, Garrison went on, was simply to believe that "God shall be all, and in all; which is saying, in other words, that nothing but goodness is immutable, all-conquering, everlasting."[28]

By 1840 the break in the antislavery movement gave Garrison a freer hand to participate in the liberal religious ferment of Boston. He joined in the Chardon Street Convention, which met three times in 1840 and 1841 to debate Sabbath observance, the authority of the ministry, and the nature of the church. This was understood as a free-speech convention, open to people of all points of view. Emerson's famous account captures the scene, albeit with a pinch of exaggeration: "Dunkers, Muggletonians, Come-outers, Groaners, Agrarians, Seventh-day Baptists, Quakers, Abolitionists, Calvinists, Unitarians, and Philosophers—all came successively to the top, and seized their moment, if not their *hour*, wherein to chide, or pray, or preach, or protest."[29] Though Garrison did not participate in the initial call for the convention, he argued vigorously against a mandatory Sabbath at its first meeting. At the final gathering, in October 1841, he proposed three resolutions on the church. The first held "that the true church is independent of all human organizations, creeds, or compacts"; the second that no "one who is created in the divine image" may be excluded from the church by other humans; the third that religious associations should be strictly voluntary: "all are left free to act singly, or in conjunction with others, according to their own free choice." In the pages of the *Liberator* he followed up on the convention with a series of poems celebrating the Bible's "sacred origin" and the value of free worship: "The freeman of the Lord no chain can bear— / His soul is free to worship everywhere."[30] Clearly, Garrison's antislavery commitments continued to inform his thinking even when he appeared to be far afield.

Despite the essentially Quaker cast of Garrison's resolutions, he was branded in the press as having led an "infidel convention." A Quaker friend in England questioned him about this, which gave him occasion to issue one of his most comprehensive statements of faith:

> I am an "infidel," forsooth, because I do *not* believe in the inherent holiness of the first day of the week; in a regular priesthood; in a mere flesh-and-blood corporation as constituting the true church of Christ; in temple worship as a part of the new dispensation; in being baptized with holy water, and observing the "ordinance" of the supper &c &c &c. I am an "infidel" because I *do* believe in "a royal priesthood, a chosen generation": in a spiritual church, built up of lively stones, the head of which is Christ; in worshipping God in spirit and in truth, without regard to time or place; in being baptized with the Holy Spirit, and enjoying spiritual communion with the Father &c &c. If this be infidelity, then is Quakerism infidelity.[31]

Garrison was reluctant, however, to give a comprehensive public statement of his faith— in part because of his antipathy to "sectarianism," in part because his views on many issues were still in flux. "Much as it might gratify" his critics, he wrote in 1841, "to have us publish the articles of our religious creed in the Liberator, we shall select our own time, and consult our own leisure, on this subject. . . . They must take what we choose to give them."[32]

Over the next several years, Garrison experienced a final momentous shift in his religious views: he began to doubt the divine authority of the Bible.[33] In part, this stemmed from his friendship with Theodore Parker, who was busily importing the latest German biblical scholarship. More fundamentally, though, it reflected a dilemma for the antislavery and other reform movements: Could these movements stand without the sanction of the Bible? Though reformers had appealed to the Bible from the beginning, they knew very well that their opponents could easily make counterappeals. The Old Testament presupposed the existence of slavery and actively celebrated war, while a case for women's rights could scarcely be found in Scripture. The dilemma was apparent even at the founding of the Anti-Slavery Society, when Garrison's Declaration was amended to make explicit the scriptural basis for calling slaveholders "man-stealers." Recalling this in 1863, Garrison said that at the time he felt this weakened the Declaration: "It makes the rights of man depend upon a text. . . . They never originated in any parchment . . . but are in the nature of man himself, written upon the human faculties and powers by the finger of God."[34]

Most likely, this reflects faulty memory, for at the time of Chardon Street he "expressly declared that I stood upon the Bible and the Bible alone . . . and that I felt if I could not stand triumphantly on that foundation, I could stand nowhere in the universe." He also refused to support a proposal for a convention on "the authority of the Scriptures" put forth by Ralph Waldo Emerson, A. Bronson Alcott, Edmund Quincy, and Maria Weston Chapman. Still, his mind was in motion. In 1845 a new edition of Thomas Paine's works gave him occasion to read for himself the attacks on the Bible of a man he had once regarded as "a master of iniquity." To his surprise, Garrison realized that biblical authority rested on the same coercive foundation as slavery and war. People generally believed in it out of fear, having been told that they will be "cast into the lake of fire and brimstone" if they do not believe. But "imposture may always be suspected when reason is commanded to abdicate the throne . . . when the bodies or spirits of men are threatened with pains and penalties if they do not subscribe to the popular belief."[35]

Garrison expressed this insight by giving a new twist to his long-standing conviction that slavery is sin. When told that there was no scriptural injunction against slavery, he simply placed his hand on his heart and said that "the injunction is here—inside of every human being." In 1852 the *Liberator* published an article attacking the Bible as proslavery, and a year later it ran an advertisement (soon signed by Garrison) for a convention "for the purpose of freely and fully canvassing the origin, authority, and influence of the Jewish and Christian Scriptures." At the convention itself, Garrison proposed a series of resolutions, including one that offered a startling new definition of the "Word of God": "Like its Divine Author, [it] was before all books, and is everywhere present, and from everlasting to everlasting—ever enunciating the same law, and requiring the same obedience . . . the Bible itself being witness."[36]

Even some who shared this theology were a bit disconcerted by Garrison's transformation. "It was so convenient," complained Edmund Quincy in 1843, "to be able to reply to those who were calling him infidel, that he believed as much as anybody, and swallowed the whole Bible in a lump, from Genesis to Revelation, both included." The effect was more powerful on those who had lagged somewhat behind Garrison in their own religious pilgrimages. Elizabeth Cady Stanton, who came out of the more evangelical wing of abolitionism, credited Garrison with her own religious transformation and that of "many others": "In the darkness and gloom of a false theology, I was slowly sawing off the chains of my spiritual bondage when, for the first time, I met Garrison in London. A few bold strokes from the hammer of his truth, I was free! . . . To Garrison we owe, more than to any other one man of our day, all that we have of religious freedom."[37]

Still, at the practical level not everything had changed. Garrison's new view of scriptural authority did not, according to his sons, alter "his regard for the scriptures, or . . . his use of them as a moral engine."[38] Indeed, it was the moral engine of the Scriptures—particularly the Sermon on the Mount and the doctrine of the *imago dei*—that compelled him, finally and reluctantly, to renounce the authority of any theology not rooted in the individual conscience.

Garrisonian Politics: Radical Liberal Agitation

A similar transformation occurred, somewhat more rapidly, in Garrison's political views. Here it was the "moral engine" of the Declaration of Independence, with its ringing endorsement of human equality, that led Garrison finally to repudiate the government the

Declaration had brought into being. Garrison's political formation began in his home-town of Newburyport, Massachusetts, one of the most significant bastions of New England Federalism. As a young apprentice, Garrison worked for a Federalist newspaper and participated actively in the young men's debating societies of the day. This experience made him a popular Independence Day speaker, and throughout his career Garrison continued to use the Fourth of July as an occasion for his most significant speeches.

From the beginning, Garrison refused simply to celebrate America but rather set American ideals in sharp juxtaposition to American realities. In an 1826 editorial in the *Newburyport Free Press* (the first paper Garrison edited), he argued that the Fourth of July was a time not only for "rhapsodies upon the deeds of our fathers" but also that "our follies and virtues should be dwelt upon till our whole country is free from the curse—it is SLAVERY." A few years later, in his first major antislavery speech, Garrison sharpened the contrast between the ideals of human rights found in the Declaration of Independence and the reality of official support for slavery. The original Fourth of July, he said, was "a proud day for our country," which "clearly and accurately defined the rights of man" and "presented a revelation adapted to the common sense of mankind." But he then contrasted the Founding Fathers' "pitiful detail of grievances" with "the wrongs our slaves endure!" It was like "the stings of the wasp compared with the tortures of the Inquisition." Similarly, in the "Letter to the Public" that introduced the *Liberator*, Garrison cited "the self-evident truth maintained in the American Declaration of Independence" as the basis for immediate emancipation. But he also quoted the Irish patriot O'Connell's sharp critique of the American citizen: "I run from the Declaration of Independence, and I tell him that he has declared to God and man a lie, and before God and man I arraign him as a hypocrite."[39]

In 1833 Garrison wrote the "Declaration of Sentiments," which introduced the new American Anti-Slavery Society to the world. The title is quite significant: Garrison clearly intended to echo Jefferson's Declaration, but he also signalled that the new society would operate through the power of "sentiments" rather than the coercive measures of government. Since the new society was meeting in Philadelphia, Garrison began by recalling the original meeting of the Founding Fathers:

> More than fifty-seven years have elapsed since a band of patriots convened in this place to devise measures for the deliverance of this country from a foreign yoke. The corner-stone upon which they founded the Temple of Freedom was broadly this—"that all men are created equal; that they are endowed by their Creator with certain inalienable rights; that among these are life, LIBERTY, and the pursuit of happiness."

Garrison went on to draw a double contrast between the Founding Fathers and the Anti-Slavery Society: the latter challenged a far more serious injustice, and did so without the immoral means of violence. "We have met together," he wrote, "for the achievement of an enterprise without which that of our fathers is incomplete; and which, for its magnitude, solemnity, and probable results upon the destiny of the world, as far transcends theirs as moral truth does physical force."[40]

Garrison also drew a contrast that proved more offensive to his compatriots: he set the Declaration, with its vision of human rights, over against the Constitution, with its "three-fifths" clause sanctioning slavery. The Constitution, he said in a speech in 1832, was an "infamous bargain" by which the Fathers "virtually dethroned the Most High

God, and trampled beneath their feet their own solemn and heaven-attested Declaration." Within a few years his critique of the Constitution had expanded into a thoroughgoing rejection of coercive government: even without the slavery clauses, the Constitution would have undermined the Declaration's principle that the sanctity of each person could not be violated. This anarchist sensibility made it easier for Garrison to mount, in the 1850s, a "disunion" campaign aimed at separating the free North from the slaveholding South. That campaign climaxed with an 1854 rally in Framingham, Massachusetts, where Garrison burned the Constitution before a crowd of thousands, calling it "a covenant with death, an agreement with hell."[41]

Such actions were clearly not designed to make Garrison widely popular. But neither did they reflect any desire to withdraw from the larger society. Garrison's vision was one not of sectarian purity but of cosmopolitan liberalism; that is why the *Liberator*'s masthead always bore the motto "Our Country Is the World—Our Countrymen Are Mankind." Again and again, Garrison used the rhetoric of American patriotism to invite others to embrace this broader vision. And if he used harsh and provocative language, it was in part because he was not willing to use any means *but* language to transform society. Above all, Garrison was an "agitator." Because he placed a radical faith in the individual conscience, he believed that anything that gets people thinking and talking about an injustice would eventually contribute to its overthrow. "There is nothing," he wrote in 1838, "like agitation. Free discussion will finally break all fetters and put down all usurpation." Agitation was the ultimate political tool of the radical liberal, for it sought revolutionary change without coercion.[42]

Garrison's liberal faith in agitation allowed him to maintain an open, ongoing dialogue with many people who had not yet embraced his most radical positions. (He was, unfortunately, far less charitable to those who had once held his own views but then abandoned them.) The *Liberator*'s "Refuge of Oppression" section always gave ample space to proslavery (or anti-Garrisonian) perspectives—partly to denounce them, of course, but partly to underscore the liberal value of free speech. Though Garrison personally renounced all violence and participation in government, he acknowledged that more moderate activists could do much good. "Thousands who are not prepared to come into the fulness of our principles," he wrote in 1839, "have been aroused by the light they cast upon the corruption of governments to labor to purify them."[43]

Garrison even offered measured praise to those—from Nat Turner to John Brown to Abraham Lincoln—who would use violence on behalf of the slaves. When Theodore Parker invited Garrison to speak at his church in 1858, Garrison chose "peace" as his theme, even though he knew that Parker did not share his nonresistant views. "Be true to your own convictions," Garrison wrote Parker afterward, "and I will be true to mine— holding the mind open to receive any new light that may be shed in any direction."[44] And at the height of the disunion campaign, Garrison reminded an audience of his own youthful patriotism and acknowledged that it was not reasonable to expect others to come quickly to the "high position" of disunionism. Indeed, had others done so, he would have dismissed it as "the mere impulse of the moment." He took greater comfort when people "hesitate, and hold back, and forbear to the last . . . for when such men move, it is with the force of the thunderbolt; they are as reliable as the everlasting hills."[45]

It is no accident that Garrison applied to his antislavery comrades metaphors more commonly associated with God. For the beginning and end of his political creed was the doctrine of the *imago dei*. He believed that all people deserved the same respect as God, and that all people possessed the divine power to create a society in which such respect was universal. This doctrine was most apparent in Garrison's advocacy of "nonresistant" pacifism. It is now time to consider this movement in more depth.

The Roots of Nonresistance

Garrisonian nonresistance was the consummate expression of "ultra" reform. For the handful of people who espoused it, it was, with its doctrine of sacred respect for every person, the key to all other reform commitments. "I could never separate N.R. from my idea of reform generally," commented Maria Weston Chapman in 1843. "It is the temper of mind in which all enterprises for humanity should be undertaken, rather than a distinct enterprise of itself." Similarly, in their biography of their father, Garrison's sons commented that the reforms of the age "were all summed up in the doctrine of Peace arrived at, enunciated, and exemplified by the subject of this biography."[46] The movement briefly took on institutional form in the New England Non-Resistance Society, founded in Boston on 18 September 1838. But it had roots both in abolitionism and in the earlier, more moderate peace movement.

If antebellum social reform was a poor relation of the larger benevolent and missionary movement, peace activism was the poor relation of social reform. Dwarfed in numbers by participants in the temperance and abolitionist movements, peace activists could only dream of tasting the successes enjoyed by other reformers (more precisely, successes they themselves had enjoyed in other capacities, for nearly all antebellum pacifists also supported temperance and abolition). As drinking declined precipitously and Northern attitudes about slavery began to shift, pacifists helplessly watched the federal government commit itself to one military adventure after another: the War of 1812, the Creek War and the war against Tecumseh's Confederation, the two Seminole Wars and the Black Hawk War, and, most disappointing, the Mexican War, a cynical ploy to gain new lands for slaveholders.

The marginality of the peace movement gave it a distinctive flavor. Unlike temperance and abolition (though like the later women's rights movement), it was not numerically dominated by orthodox revivalists. Indeed, in some communities orthodox pacifists hesitated to join peace societies because they were perceived as Unitarian front groups. (Mennonites and orthodox Quakers also hesitated, both for this reason and because the societies rarely espoused absolute pacifism.) It is not hard to see why peace sentiment correlated more closely with theological liberalism than did other social reforms. The liberal "faith in the indestructible principles of human virtue," as Sylvester Judd pointed out, made it easy for liberals to renounce coercive governmental measures, while belief in total depravity led most of the orthodox to conclude that some coercion would always be needed to prevent anarchy.[47] By contrast, slavery and intemperance might be opposed *either* as affronts to human dignity *or* as examples of depravity.

The antebellum peace movement got its start, appropriately, during the War of 1812. By 1812 concern about the devastating effects of the Napoleonic Wars was widespread on both sides of the Atlantic, and in the northeastern United States this concern was heightened by the economic dislocations of "Mr. Madison's War." (In mercantile towns like Newburyport, pacifist sentiment flowed easily from Federalist loyalties, and this in part explains Garrison's early attraction to pacifism.) In this context it was easy to be persuaded, as one activist recalled, of both "the unchristian character, and ruinous policy of war."[48] Though most New Englanders did not embrace pacifism, those who did found the region to be a congenial place to express their sentiments. Thus, during the war years two influential peace manuals appeared: David Low Dodge's *War Inconsistent with the Religion of Jesus Christ* (1812) and Noah Worcester's *Solemn Review of the Custom of War* (1814). At the close of the war, Dodge and Worcester each created a peace society, the New York Peace Society (NYPS) and the Massachusetts Peace Society (MPS). A third society was created in Ohio at virtually the same time.[49]

Dodge was a surprising and quite idiosyncratic peace activist. As an orthodox Presbyterian, he regarded God as an absolute sovereign who controlled the actions of violent, reprobate individuals as well as pacific Christians. But he was also a pacifist hardliner who repudiated all wars, both offensive and defensive, as well as personal self-defense and participation in government. Jesus' teaching about not resisting evil in the Sermon on the Mount was, for Dodge, an absolute rule binding on all Christians. This combination of beliefs was not illogical, but it was as unusual as it was uncompromising. Like Christian sectarians of all ages, Dodge drew a sharp line between the Christian and the depraved "world," and he refused to cooperate with either moderate pacifists or Quakers. As a consequence, his peace society quickly faded into obscurity.[50]

Noah Worcester, by contrast, represented the mainstream of antebellum pacifism and was long recognized as the movement's founding spirit. A Unitarian minister, he found his denomination supportive of his efforts. William Ellery Channing hosted the society's founding meeting, and both Henry Ware Sr. and James Freeman served as officers. (Channing also published an influential discourse titled "War" in 1816, and another in 1835.) As the first editor of the *Christian Disciple*, Worcester was free to give peace concerns a prominent place in that Unitarian journal. He soon found the resources to edit another journal devoted solely to peace, and his *Friend of Peace* was widely distributed by other peace societies. Worcester's style of activism fit well with the moderate liberalism of official Unitarianism. He was, in one scholar's apt phrase, a "cultural Christian": confident about the human capacity for self-improvement and willing to countenance the continued existence of most social institutions so long as they generally supported liberal principles.[51]

Worcester personally sympathized with Dodge's critique of defensive war, but he tried to make the Massachusetts Peace Society a big tent open to both pacifists and just war advocates. Channing, for example, believed that "national subjugation is a greater evil than a war of defence," and he warned that the "cause of peace" not "be injured by the assertion of extreme and indefensible principles." Worcester also believed that Paul had endorsed human governments in Romans 13, and he actively recruited political and educational leaders for his society. In 1819 the MPS membership included two former governors and the sitting lieutenant governor of Massachusetts, the state's chief justice, and the president of Harvard. Worcester even persuaded Thomas Jefferson to enroll as an honorary member, though John Adams declined on the ground that the application of peace principles would leave the people with no defense against tyranny.[52]

In the late 1820s Worcester's mantle passed to William Ladd, a retired Maine sea captain, a Unitarian, and—like Worcester and Dodge—author of an influential manual of pacifism. As the founder of the American Peace Society (APS) in 1828, Ladd helped spread the MPS's irenic, big-tent style of activism around the nation. His society was open even to individuals like Henry Clarke Wright's former classmate George Beckwith, an orthodox minister who was sure that some government coercion would always be needed to rein in the excesses of a reprobate world. But Ladd's personal views were both more liberal and more radical. He had little taste for just war theory or orthodox notions of human nature. Under his leadership, the APS became a somewhat congenial home for Hicksites and Garrisonians, including the Grimkés, the Motts, Samuel J. May, and Henry Clarke Wright.

Maria Weston Chapman would later recall that most Garrisonians came to pacifism "*through* their abolition principles, as the eye fastens upon the farthest surface of a diamond through the transparent medium of the nearest."[53] In fact, the progression was not always so linear. Garrison may well have been a pacifist before he was an abolitionist; certainly, he had been committed to peace as one of his three cardinal reforms since his days at the *Philanthropist*. Garrison espoused a consistent pacifism in the original prospectus for the *Liberator*, arguing "that war is fruitful in crime, misery, revenge, murder, and everything abominable and bloody—and, whether offensive or defensive, contrary to the precepts and example of Jesus Christ, and to the heavenly spirit of the gospel." He also incorporated peace principles into the Anti-Slavery Society's Declaration by noting that the Founding Fathers' "principles led them to wage war against their oppressors, and to spill human blood like water, in order to be free. Ours forbid the doing of evil that good might come, and lead us to reject, and to entreat the oppressed to reject, the use of all carnal weapons for deliverance from bondage."[54]

For Garrison's friend Henry Clarke Wright, a pacifist commitment grew more out of his rebellion against orthodoxy than out of his abolitionism. Wright had once been an orthodox seminarian who was so disciplined that he translated half of the Old Testament during his first year of studies. But as he grew disappointed at the orthodox clergy's lack of interest in social reform, he became increasingly disgusted with the violence of the Old Testament God. In 1835 he began a series of earnest dialogues with Garrison, whose understanding of nonviolence was deepening as the result of his encounters with mob violence. Garrison's views were "not yet clear and enlarged," Wright reported at the time, "though he has got hold of the right principle." Garrison, meanwhile, was confiding to his sister-in-law, "I am more and more convinced that it is the duty of the followers of Christ to suffer themselves to be defrauded, calumniated, and barbarously treated, without resorting either to their own physical energies, or to the force of human law, for restitution or punishment. It is a difficult lesson to learn."[55]

Within a few years both Garrison and Wright were prepared to mount a direct challenge to the existing peace movement. In 1836 they succeeded in introducing a condemnation of defensive war into the society's constitution. But a year later George Beckwith succeeded Ladd as APS secretary and began pushing for repeal of the new clause. Also in that year, a series of Boston lectures on peace (by such prominent Unitarians as Channing and Henry Ware Jr.) provoked Garrison to condemn the APS's inclusion of military men among its members and to threaten that "unless they alter their present course, the first thing I shall do will be to serve our Peace Societies as I have done the Colonization Societies."[56]

A few months later Garrison clarified his opposition to both offensive and defensive wars and to all coercive functions of government, noting that such opposition was only consistent with the widespread antipathy to slave rebellions: "If the slaves of the South have not an undoubted right to resist their masters in the last resort, then no man, or body of men, may appeal to the law of violence in self-defence—for none have ever suffered, or can suffer, more than they." Wright, for his part, had expounded similarly extreme views during his brief tenure as an APS agent, and he wrote *Liberator* articles that described schools, governments, churches, and even most families as "engine[s] to crush the soul."[57] Though William Ladd tried to ease the tension, neither the conservatives nor the radicals were inclined to cooperate.

In September 1838 a meeting held (nominally) under APS auspices evolved into the founding convention of the New England Non-Resistance Society. With the notable exception of Adin Ballou (a Universalist pastor turned "Practical Christian" whose theology lay midway between Dodge's sectarianism and Garrison's liberalism), most members of the new society—Henry Clarke Wright, Abby Kelly, Maria Weston Chapman, the Southwick sisters, Edmund Quincy—belonged to the Garrisonian inner circle and shared their leader's distaste for orthodox theology. Wanting to oppose both war and interpersonal violence, they struggled to find a name for what Quincy called "the anti-man-killing principle," until Garrison suggested "non-resistance." Garrisonian nonresistants embraced an ethic of absolute nonviolence, repudiating offensive and defensive wars, capital punishment, the physical discipline of children, and even police forces. But their most distinctive position was their denial of the authority of all existing governments.

Garrison himself wrote the Society's "Declaration of Sentiments," which he described proudly as the most "'fanatical' [and] 'disorganizing' instrument penned by man. It swept the whole surface of society, and upturned almost every existing institution on earth." "We cannot acknowledge allegiance to any human government," the document announced, "neither can we oppose any such government by a resort to physical force." Fidelity to God compelled the nonresistants to "come out" of earthly governments and profess allegiance to "a kingdom which is not of this world, . . . which has no state lines, no national partitions, no geographical boundaries; in which there is no distinction of rank, or division of caste, or inequality of sex."[58]

As these quotations suggest, nonresistant rhetoric blended gospel and Jeffersonian elements. Adin Ballou, who was most insistent about the *Christian* character of nonresistance, defined it as "simply non-resistance of injury with injury—evil with evil," noting that this definition derives from Jesus' teaching in Matthew 5:39.[59] But Matthew 5:39 says nothing about rank, caste, or sex—references that owe more to the egalitarianism of Jefferson's Declaration. Of course, from the nonresistant perspective, the gospel and the Declaration implied one another: to refrain from injury was to recognize the full equality of the neighbor, and to recognize equality was to renounce all coercion between individuals.

Given their fidelity to the gospel and the Declaration, the nonresistants did not deserve Lyman Beecher's accusation that they had withdrawn from both the American experiment and Christianity itself. But they were willing to pit the core values of the larger society against its institutional forms. They did so most characteristically in their efforts to repudiate the violent legacy of the American Revolution without renouncing its liberal principles. Thomas Grimké set the tone for nonresistants in 1832 when he attacked the Revolution in a speech before the Connecticut state legislature. "*I shrink not*," he said, "*from the accountability of condemning universally, unconditionally, the* MEANS *employed to accomplish the revolution.*" Its ends, Grimké conceded, were wholly meritorious, but they could have been achieved through a humble and long-suffering appeal to the "feeling, sentiment and principle" of the British people, who "had too generous and manly a spirit" to tolerate the tyranny of their leaders. (Clearly, an optimistic liberal anthropology undergirded Grimké's argument.) By fighting a war for liberty, the Americans had missed a chance to offer an authentic Christian witness to the world. But all was not lost: the United States' possession of a democratic tradition, an active press, and a wide array of reform societies proved that it was providentially "destined to be the noblest monument of the principles of peace."[60]

A year earlier, Garrison had made a similar argument in a manner that reflected his passionate commitment to abolitionism and his keen awareness of the dilemmas faced by the victims of violence. Like Grimké, he believed that revolutionary resistance to tyranny and the defense of human rights were the noblest of causes, though they did not merit doing evil that good might come. But, Garrison added significantly, anyone who believed that the revolutionary cause had merited the use of violence should be consistent. If it was right for Washington to resist taxation without representation violently, it was more right to resist the worse tyranny of slavery with violence. Yet most white Americans clung to a double standard: "A white man, who kills a tyrant, is a hero, and deserves a monument. If a slave kills his master, he is a murderer, and deserves to be burnt." Garrison came within inches of endorsing slave rebellion, but his real point was to distinguish between his own authentic pacifism and the cynical promotion of nonviolence as a virtue only for the oppressed. Garrison made this clear in his response to the famous "Appeal" of David Walker, a free black who had called upon his enslaved brothers and sisters to revolt. As a strict pacifist *he* repudiated Walker, but he refused to acknowledge the legitimacy of any nonpacifist critique: "It is not for the American people, as a nation, to denounce [the Appeal] as bloody or monstrous." Indeed, every patriotic celebration of the Revolution was an incitement to slave revolt: "Every Fourth of July celebration must embitter and inflame the minds of the slaves."[61]

Both of the passages just cited appear in the second issue of the *Liberator*. Throughout his career, Garrison consistently maintained that while violent rebellion is never justified, slave rebellion would come closer to justice than the Revolution. Lydia Maria Child reiterated this point in an early issue of the *Liberator*, in which she chided Channing for endorsing the Revolution but not slave revolt: "It has long appeared to me that bloodshed and violence in *any* cause are in direct opposition to the spirit of the Gospel; but if resistance were *ever* justifiable, it would be so in the bereaved and persecuted *slave*."[62] I underscore this consistency because some scholars have interpreted similar arguments made late in Garrison's career as evidence that he had backtracked from his early commitment to nonviolence. Garrison's real point was that it is possible and necessary for pacifists to make ethical distinctions among forms of violence. It is possible to sympathize with victims who resist oppression violently, even to hope for their success, while still believing that they might have chosen a better form of resistance. Indeed, Garrison implied, those who did not feel this sympathy—who could not admire the *spirit* of the Revolution or of slave revolt—were perhaps not truly committed to ending tyranny.

Over the course of time, nonresistants became less and less willing to concede even the nobility of the Revolution's goals. Though they never ceased to admire the sentiments found in the Declaration of Independence, they doubted that these sentiments had in fact guided the Revolutionary struggle. Thus, when in 1836 Lyman Beecher warned that if the "experiment of human liberty" failed in the United States "no nation will try it again," Garrison responded vehemently that no such experiment had been attempted: "The wonderful 'experiment' that we are making is precisely this—to see how long we can plunder, with impunity, two millions and a half of our population; how much labor we can extort with the cart-whip, . . . how tyrannical we may be without endangering our safety!" A few years later Henry Clarke Wright denounced the Revolution without even mentioning slavery. In an account written for children and entitled "Two Hundred Thousand Men for Three Pence," he wrote that "besides actually slaying more than two hundred thousand, they mutilated the bodies of twice as many more. After they had gone on tearing each other's bodies to pieces for seven years, both sides got tired out, and agreed to stop and rest awhile. All these human beings murdered, merely because the colonies refused to pay a tax that was imposed without their consent!"[63]

Such rhetoric should not be taken as evidence that Garrison and Wright were alienated from the broadly liberal tradition of American politics. They were, rather, disgusted with the timidity of other liberals who did not dare to follow their principles to their logical conclusions. The Non-Resistance Society was committed to a progressive, expansive liberalism, in which a free agitation of the most radical ideas would gradually lead everyone closer to the truth. This vision was apparent in the Society's instruction to Wright, who served as its sole agent. He had "no obligations to silence" on any of his other reform causes, because the Society had "learned that every truth strengthens and forms a part of every other truth."[64] A similar liberal spirit infused the theology of nonresistance, which can best be understood as a radicalization of the liberal theology espoused by Channing, Worcester, and Ladd.

Nonresistance as a Liberal Theology

All nonresistants could affirm at least three things: first, that the gospel of Jesus Christ demands a practice of nonviolent love for enemies and neighbors (what I shall call the "gospel principle"); second, that human beings naturally possess sufficient virtue to fulfill the gospel mandate (the "anthropological principle"); and third, that no human being should be subordinated to any other (the "governmental principle"). Together these three principles allowed a normative agreement about the human duty of nonresistance, but they did not generate a particularly clear *descriptive* account of how the God who demands nonviolence acts in the world or why violence has been so pervasive a part of human experience for so long. Individual nonresistants often gave contradictory answers to these questions. Both in their normative agreement and in their descriptive confusion, the nonresistants extended and altered the arguments of their pacifist predecessors.

In their *gospel principle*, the nonresistants followed both Dodge and Worcester by affirming that war was forbidden by divine mandate. "The principles of war and the principles of the gospel are as unlike as heaven and hell," wrote Dodge. Worcester agreed that "war is in its nature opposed to the principles and spirit of our religion." Similarly, the Non-Resistance Society's Declaration of Sentiments held that "the penal code of the old covenant, an eye for an eye, and a tooth for a tooth, has been abrogated by JESUS CHRIST; and that, under the new covenant, the forgiveness instead of the punishment of enemies has been enjoined upon all his disciples, in all cases whatsoever." Even Henry Clarke Wright, who conceded the intrinsic authority of no text or institution, accepted that Jesus' teaching of "love to man" was authoritative because it was also "inscribed on the souls of men before they were recorded in any book."[65]

This invocation of gospel principle conflicted with orthodox theology in two ways. First, it seemed to (but did not necessarily) make Christianity into an ethical system rather than a descriptive account of God's activity in the world. For Reformers such as Luther and Calvin, the heart of the gospel was not what humans should do but what God had done—specifically, that God had become incarnate in Jesus Christ in order to redeem humanity from its fallen state. Did nonresistants mean to deny this dimension of the gospel? Dodge certainly did not, although one has to read more than halfway through his book to realize that his gospel has a descriptive as well as a normative component. Worcester, on the other hand, affirmed explicitly that Christianity "is only a system of divine instructions, relating to *duty* and *happiness*; to be used by men for their own happiness, the benefit of each other, and the honor of its Author."[66] Garrison, likewise, repeatedly privileged practical holiness over credal belief, and most nonresistants echoed this theme.

Second, while Reformed theology had balanced the authority of Old and New Testaments through a nuanced system of "typology," Christian nonresistance clearly subordinated the "penal code of the old covenant" to the "new covenant" of Jesus. Dodge, Worcester, and Ladd all anticipated this subordination by making strong use of a "dispensational" theory to deny contemporary appeals to Old Testament stories about God authorizing war, physical punishments, or slavery. According to this theory, world history was divided into distinct periods, or "dispensations," each with its own set of divinely ordained laws. The "Christian dispensation," Dodge affirmed, was distinct from the "Old Testament economy." In pre-Christian times, both war and slavery had been permitted "for reasons and on principles peculiar to the ancient economy," but it was illegitimate to use such stories as the Hebrew conquest of Canaan to justify more recent events like the Puritan conquest of New England. Grimké believed that "*the law of violence*" had once had a place in "the mysterious providence of God," but that at Christ's birth "THE LAW OF INDIVIDUAL AND SOCIAL MORALS, WAS ABSOLUTELY AND FOREVER CHANGED."[67]

Worcester and Ladd agreed that the wars of the Old Testament were exceptional because they had been directly commanded by God, who alone "had a right if he pleased, to make use of the savage customs of the age, for punishing guilty nations." In his *Brief Illustration*, Ladd recapped much of Old Testament history, arguing that the Jews were victorious whenever they relied on God's power in war but quickly defeated when they depended on "the arms of war" or violated divine commands. Adin Ballou took dispensationalism a step further, arguing that the Old Testament was not "as clearly, fully and perfectly the word of God" as the New Testament. Indeed, Ballou argued, the Old Testament itself taught that it would be superseded, and in this sense it actually confirmed the nonresistant teaching of the New Testament.[68]

Even this moderate version of dispensationalism did not sit well with other nonresistants. Because they believed that the law of nonviolence was inscribed in the human heart as well as in the text of the New Testament, they had trouble imagining that it was not binding in all eras of history.[69] To distinguish historical eras, they recognized, was to leave open the possibility that the gospel mandate did not need to be fulfilled until some point in the future. Thus, Garrison included in the "Declaration" a clear statement of immediatist principle: "It appears to us a self-evident truth, that whatever the gospel is designed to destroy at any period of the world, being contrary to it, ought NOW to be abandoned."[70] Extended backward rather than forward in time, this principle implied that the Old Testament passages permitting war were simply not divinely inspired.

In 1845 Charles Stearns published an article in the *Liberator* in which he argued that even the God of the Old Testament had no right to kill. A year later, Wright wrote that "ON NO QUESTION ON WHICH THE OLD TESTAMENT DIFFERS FROM THE NEW TESTAMENT, IS IT TO BE REGARDED AS OF THE LEAST AUTHORITY." In 1849 Garrison reported that he could no longer accept the dispensationalist notion that "Christ has superseded Moses." Instead, he wrote that "whoever or whatever asserts that the Creator has required, and may still require, one portion of his children to butcher another portion, for any purpose whatever, is libelling his goodness, and asserting what every thing in nature contradicts." And, in his autobiography, Wright asked rhetorically, "Did God move Samson to kill himself and the Philistines?" Just as much, he answered, as God had "moved the Psalmist to pray that some one might dash out the brains of the children of Babylon; just as he moved Nero to slaughter the Christians, the Catholics to burn heretics, the Puritans to hang the Quakers and witches, to hunt and shoot the Indians, and the Indians to tomahawk and scalp the Puritans." In other words, not at all.[71]

Just as nonresistants could not believe that God would command violence, they could not believe that God would make humans incapable of perfect nonviolence. Their *anthropological principle* thus set them apart from orthodox theologians, who believed that fallen humans can never measure up to the strict ethic of the gospel. Nonresistants taught that humans are inherently virtuous and capable, if their natural feelings have not been twisted by war and other corrupt institutions, of complying with the gospel decree. Noah Worcester, who as a Unitarian explicitly denied the doctrine of original sin, clearly anticipated this point. "There is nothing in the nature of mankind, which renders war necessary and unavoidable," he insisted, pointing to the practices of the Shakers and Quakers as evidence. Indeed, he claimed, "a vast majority of every civilized nation have an aversion to war." Unscrupulous but powerful minorities must use all their ingenuity to "work up" the people's passions and get them to fight. Channing, similarly, taught that war results from "excesses of passions and desires which, by right direction, would promote the best interests of humanity." William Ladd agreed that "the principles of war are not inherent in the constitution of man," citing as an example the peaceful practices of the pagan Loo-Choo islanders. These people did not need to be taught Christianity in order to embody its ethic; they did so simply because they had not been corrupted by the war spirit.[72]

The "Declaration of Sentiments" was not quite so clear in its anthropology, but it did make a link between nonviolent principles and human nature. Indeed, Garrison claimed that violence was doomed to failure because it was opposed to nature: "The history of mankind is crowded with evidences proving that physical coercion is not adapted to moral regeneration; that the sinful dispositions of men can be subdued only by love;

that evil can be exterminated from the earth only by goodness." Hence, "sound policy," as well as obedience to God, required nonviolence.[73]

This is not to suggest that nonresistants denied the presence of evil in the world. On the contrary, they followed earlier pacifists in insisting that the "war spirit" can easily twist people's natural feelings into violent passions. Worcester called the *"war spirit"* a "deleterious compound of enthusiastic ardor, ambition, malignity and revenge," but his point was that such evil passions could be traced *only* to the war spirit and *not* to any universal human condition. The war spirit was widespread, but belief in its universality was one of "the grossest delusions that ever afflicted a guilty world." To accept this "popular delusion," Ladd added, was to believe that God had deliberately created human passions in order to fill the world with evil and then destroy it—but "such injustice never came from Heaven." Adin Ballou reinforced the argument by appealing to the consensual belief in historical progress, noting that the belief in the universality of violence "derives all its plausibility from the exhibition of past and remaining barbarism" and denies the possibility of change.[74]

Liberal pacifists, in other words, replaced the concept of original sin with that of the "war system," suggesting that its effects touched almost all people. Thomas Grimké was sure that peace was "the natural state of man," but he also believed that "the law of violence" had "prevailed without mitigation from the murder of Abel to the advent of the Prince of Peace." Ladd likewise began his history of war with Cain and Abel and allowed that "scarcely a country can be found which has not been more or less infected with the war *mania*, and whose inhabitants have not, at some period or other, experienced its destructive and horrid effects." This theory allowed them to suggest that redemption from the war system would not need to overcome human nature but could instead work through it. As a good liberal, Thomas Grimké believed that ordinary people, "however ignorant and uneducated," had never truly supported war. The task of peace was to get rulers to serve the people rather than "the law of violence." Adin Ballou argued that violence could be unlearned "without annihilating or perverting any essential constituent, element, property, quality or capability of human beings." In nonresistant theology, the savior's role was simply to point people to their true selves.[75]

The most extreme exponent of this humanist soteriology was Henry Clarke Wright, who declared in his *Anthropology* (1850) that "henceforth, anthropology shall be my theology. The science of man is the science of God." The cardinal principle of Wright's anthropology was his repudiation of original sin. He took great delight in noting that despite orthodox doctrine humans persist in caring for one another in countless mundane ways. "Human nature," he reflected during a trip through Europe, "is still most beautiful and lovely, fallen though it be. They say it is *totally* depraved. If it is, it is still full of overflowing affection and sympathy. Under all conditions in which I have ever seen it, it is essentially the same—a kind and loving nature; and I can say, for myself, that I have received a thousand tokens of love from my fellow beings to one of hatred. There is no human being but has a heart to love and be loved."[76]

Once again, Wright's position was not one of complacent denial of worldly evil. To affirm "the sacredness of man" was, for Wright, to repudiate all institutions that deny the person's "absolute inviolability." It was also to repudiate all notions of God that are entangled in such institutions and even—here Wright steps beyond Ballou—the notion that one must look beyond humanity in order to encounter God. Wright felt that superhuman notions of God were abstract and dangerous, insofar as they could be used to justify the neglect of human beings. He was horrified at the popular notion that God sometimes allows people to die in order to purge their friends of excessive, "idolatrous" love. "Millions die because they are loved too little," he insisted sadly; "not one because they are loved too much." Only in the fullest expression of our natural love and devotion for others can we achieve genuine love for God.[77]

If the nonresistants' sense of nonviolent duty derived from Jesus' teachings and their optimistic anthropology from the Jeffersonian Enlightenment, they saw their *governmental principle*—that no human being should be subordinated to another—as implicit in both the gospel and the Declaration. The Christian norm of love and the liberal norm of justice converged in forbidding coercion of all sorts, even if exercised by putatively republican institutions. True government, nonresistants declared, belonged only to God. Thus, Garrison's "Declaration" explained that "every human government is upheld by physical strength, and its laws are enforced virtually at the point of the bayonet. . . . We therefore voluntarily exclude ourselves from every legislative and judicial body, and repudiate all human politics, worldly honors, and stations of authority."[78]

In some ways, this simply extended a principle that Garrison had articulated in his antislavery "Declaration"—that "all those laws . . . admitting the right of slavery, are . . . before God, utterly null and void; being an audacious usurpation of the Divine prerogative, a daring infringement on the law of nature." From the very beginning Garrison and his followers had acknowledged the existence of a higher law that superseded the unjust legislation of humans. Early in his career, Garrison assumed that the source of this higher law was the Bible, which he claimed as his "statute-book" in 1835. His emphasis gradually shifted to moral sense theory, as he made clear when he wrote that the law "above all enactments of human codes" was the "law written by the finger of God upon the heart of man."[79]

Few biblical literalists or moral sense theorists would have accepted the notion that *all* human governments are at odds with that of God. Garrison might have borrowed that notion from David Low Dodge, who wrote that "God reserved to himself the government of man, whom he created in his own image." More likely he was influenced by John Humphrey Noyes, a "perfectionist" with whom he carried on a public dialogue in 1837. Noyes wrote to Garrison, "I have subscribed my name to an instrument similar to the Declaration of '76, renouncing all allegiance to the government of the United States, and asserting the title of Jesus Christ to the throne of the world."[80]

Noyes's description of his "instrument" might lead us to suspect that Garrison's "Declaration" was plagiarized, but in fact there was a significant difference between the two men's antigovernmental visions. For Noyes, as for Dodge and perhaps even for Ballou, to proclaim divine government was to express a complete indifference to the various forms of human government. He felt no allegiance to the liberal ideals of the American or French Revolutions; indeed, he anticipated a coming "convulsion" that would be "the French Revolution reversed."[81]

Garrison, on the other hand, saw divine government as the omega point of the progressive liberalization of human governments. Nonresistance carried forward the revolutionary tradition of 1776, 1789, and 1830, simply adding a refusal to "do evil that good may come." Garrison had lauded the European revolutions of 1830 in the *Liberator*'s first issue, and he sounded the same theme in an article written well after his embrace of nonresistance. Addressing the "tyrants of the old world," Garrison argued that the imminent demise of the United States would not harm true republicanism. The "rights of man," he insisted, were guaranteed not by human governments but by God, and God would ensure that "your thrones must crumble to dust; your sceptre of dominion drop from your powerless hands; your rod of oppression be broken." And for precisely the same reasons God would destroy the United States: "its subversion is essential to the triumph of justice," for "it was conceived in sin, and brought forth in iniquity, and its career has been marked by unparalled hypocrisy, by high-handed tyranny, by a bold defiance of the omniscience and omnipotence of God."[82]

The Ambivalence of Nonresistant Theology

In hinting that God would destroy both European tyrannies and the United States for their sins of violence, Garrison exposed the ambivalent underside of nonresistant theology. What exactly did it mean to say that God exercises all true government in this violent world? What sort of government was this? Was it a "moral government" that established ethical norms but did not ensure their fulfillment? Garrison's claim that the divine law was inscribed in human hearts seemed to suggest this, insofar as humans were clearly capable of ignoring the moral sense. Or was divine government a "providential government" that determined the course of human events? This was the position of orthodox theologians like Dodge, who conceded that human governments served God's mysterious purposes, even though God forbade Christians to participate in them.[83] Garrison tipped his hat to orthodoxy by invoking the traditional attributes of "omniscience and omnipotence" but then suggested that human governments could defy or even usurp divine government. He seems to have been more interested in exploiting the diverse senses of divine government for rhetorical effect than in committing to a clear position on this issue.[84]

A similar ambiguity appears in the Non-Resistance Society's "Declaration," in which Garrison wrote that "the dogma that all the governments of the world are approvingly ordained of God . . . is not less absurd than impious. It makes the impartial Author of human freedom and equality, unequal and tyrannical." This sentence seems to refute Paul's teaching in Romans, but the nontechnical language used here leaves a loophole: "approvingly ordained" could be read as "ordained by God's moral as well as providential government," allowing for the inference that Paul referred only to providential government. (This is a recurring rhetorical strategy in radical liberal writings: to warn against the "impious" implications of an orthodox "dogma" without quite asserting the converse.) But Garrison went on to assert more vehemently that "THE POWERS THAT BE . . . cannot be agreeable to the will of God; and therefore, their overthrow, by a spiritual regeneration of their subjects, is inevitable."[85]

This phrase aptly expresses the radical Christian liberal faith that God would guarantee the nonviolent overthrow of all violent institutions, through the "spiritual regeneration" of individuals rather than by means of some apocalyptic intervention. A similar hope was expressed by a letter writer in the first issue of the *Liberator*. This might well have been William Ladd, for Garrison described him as a peace activist and "one of the most distinguished reformers of the age." The correspondent began by expressing his faith in Providence: "The cause in which you are engaged, will certainly prevail, and so will mine; but when? It is not for us to ask. God will accomplish it in his own time; and *perhaps* by our means." Even in this sentence, there is a significant departure from the traditional understanding of Providence, for the writer assumes that he already knows God's plan for history and must wait only for the revelation of God's timetable.

In the succeeding sentences, he undermines the tentativeness of his "perhaps," claiming that "slavery and war will be abolished throughout all of Christendom, and the abolition of them depends on public opinion; and public opinion is directed by the pulpit and the press—by speaking and writing; and there is no other way." Here the letter writer manages to have it both ways: he gives his cause moral legitimacy by portraying it as part of God's providential plan, but he also gives it urgency by suggesting that it depends on courageous human initiative. In so doing, he virtually identifies God's power with human "speaking and writing."[86]

For nonresistants, to link God's Providence to individual nonviolence was often to deny God's violent agency in the larger world. In a speech, given in 1839, for example, Garrison insisted that the "hellish artifices" of war were not among the "sufferings and calamities which naturally occur in the providence of God"—earthquakes, fires, storms.[87] Other writers labeled all pro-violence theological claims as idolatrous rather than Christian. To suggest that God could ever approve of war, Worcester insisted, was to reduce God to an idol demanding sacrifice: "To sacrifice human beings to false notions of national honor, or to the ambition or avarice of rulers, is no better than to offer them to Moloch, or any other heathen deity."[88]

Henry Clarke Wright took particular delight in this iconoclastic theology, proclaiming that he was glad to be an atheist if that meant "a denial of the popular notions of God." After all, in that sense Jesus had also been an atheist! The problem with the "popular notions," Wright explained, was that they associated God more intimately with religious and governmental institutions than with flesh-and-blood human beings. That was the root cause of violence: "What they call God, says man, is an appendage to wealth, to a Sabbath, a meeting-house, an office, a title, a bible, a constitution, a church and governmental organization. He throws his sanction around these, and stones, crucifies, hangs, shoots and stabs, men, women and children, to death, and blows their bodies to atoms." To reject such practices, for Wright, was also to reject all notions of God as external or otherworldly. He had once, he recalled, practiced a conventional spirituality by shutting his eyes in hopes of finding God, but the God he found thereby was "a phantom—a mere abstraction." In developing a mature liberal theology he resolved instead that "I shall no more go out of this world, after him, while I live in it—but shall commune with him by communing with what I find here."[89]

Wright did not mean that he was willing to "commune" with *everything* he found in this world—he referred only to human individuals apart from their participation in violent institutions. The constant liberal dilemma was to account for how those institutions came to exist at all, given that they could not be traced to the workings of providential power. One strategy was to assert optimistically that they barely existed at all, and that they would soon crumble in the face of concerted nonviolent activity. Nearly every peace manual of the day was filled with historical and anthropological anecdotes showing, in Ladd's words, that "the principles of peace have always been productive of the best good to man." In *A Kiss for a Blow*, Wright claimed again and again that quarrels could be avoided if only the aggrieved parties would respond with love: "It is impossible to continue angry with those who will not be angry with us, or to curse those who will not curse us, or to beat those who will not beat us. It is impossible to fight no-fight."[90]

This is more an evasion than an explanation of violent institutions. But it did not necessarily imply that violence was not a serious problem in the here and now. Nonresistants taught that apart from active nonviolent intervention, violence has a tendency to feed on itself, and thus to increase its destructive power. Its roots may be small, but its effects are omnipresent. "Like begets like," Ballou suggested, is a universal law that is equally applicable to violence or nonviolence. Ladd traced both the great Flood and the falls of all the great empires of history to the spiraling effects of "corruption and violence," which "increased in acts of violence" until they culminated in destruction. Ladd often attributed this destruction to Providence or "Divine Justice," but by this he meant not a mysterious external power but the immanent logic of violence itself. "Those who do not consider the fatal tendency of war principles, often adduce the destruction of those ancient nations and cities . . . as certain proofs of the supposed inevitable decree which the Almighty has imposed on states and nations." In fact, though, such "visitations of Divine Justice" are no other than the "just and natural consequences of their own works."[91]

Here Providence is assimilated not to moral government but to a vague notion of natural law. Henry Clarke Wright also tended toward this position. In *Anthropology* and later works he contended that God is not responsible for human violence or even death, and that a happy death in old age is not truly death at all. Saying otherwise provided a theological cover for violence: "The advocates of war and death-penalty say, God kills men—therefore, men may kill one another." Instead, Wright asserted, God works through immutable laws designed for the best good of all. Neither death nor violence was inevitable for those who obeyed the laws "engraven on their bodies and souls."[92]

Nonresistants were not always so confident. In their more sober moments, they conceded that the Christian duty of nonviolence might not carry a providential guarantee of earthly success. At times, they valorized "self-sacrifice" as the true core of the gospel. Garrison sounded this theme in the first issue of the *Liberator*, in which he described his own imprisonment for libel against a New England shipowner who had transported slaves. "Opposition, and abuse, and slander, and prejudice, and judicial tyranny," he proudly declared, "are like oil to the flame of my zeal. . . . If need be, who would not die a martyr to such a cause?" The same theme appears in the Non-Resistance Society's "Declaration," where Garrison draws an extended analogy between Christ's passion and the "tumults" likely to be experienced by nonviolent activists: "We shall not think it strange concerning the fiery trial which is to try us, as though some strange thing had happened unto us; but rejoice, inasmuch as we are partakers of CHRIST's sufferings." Henry Clarke Wright similarly maintained that in this world the nonviolent person must be willing to embrace suffering. He opened his children's book, *A Kiss for a Blow*, with a paean to "the spirit of self-sacrifice": "In all cases where we must suffer and die, or inflict suffering and death on our enemies, the Peace Spirit says, Suffer and die. . . . The Peace man . . . smiles at death, when he is himself the victim."[93]

On this point nonresistants agreed with Dodge, who also affirmed that "the spirit of martyrdom is the true spirit of Christianity." But their position was much more ambivalent than Dodge's, for they had to square the apparent implication that the world was hostile to Christianity with the liberal belief that humans are naturally predisposed to Christian virtue. Again and again, liberals conflated the spirit of self-sacrifice with the spirit of love, the negative willingness to suffer with the positive desire to practice kindness. This is especially apparent in the stories found in A *Kiss for a Blow*, which often feature a loving sibling who gives up the larger apple or the better toy in order to forestall a quarrel. Though Wright sometimes labels this act as a self-sacrifice, he does not imply that it is unpleasant or morally required apart from its consequence. On the contrary, he suggests that his young protagonists deeply desire to share their possessions and are rewarded with restored affection.

In addition to being almost comically optimistic, Wright's anecdotes bore a more serious and subtle flaw. Like those of his predecessors, they consistently ignored forms of violence in which there is a systemic imbalance of power between perpetrator and victim. They described quarrels between siblings and military attacks between villages or nations but never wife battering or the violence of slavery. (This is curious, given Wright's deep opposition to slavery and to wife abuse.) By restricting themselves to violent incidents in which there is a rough parity of power, they were able to suggest that the typical perpetrator wants and expects his victim to fight back. Thus, Wright told of a little boy who liked to kill woodchucks, because they fought back, but not rabbits, which always looked pitiful and forgiving.[94] He argued that victims could always interrupt the psychology of violence by refusing to fight. But systemic violence feeds on a different psychology, in which the victim's helplessness inspires not mercy but a disregard for his or her personhood. Surely Wright did not imagine that either being female or being forgiving would spare the typical slave woman any whippings, but he did not attend to this reality when he wrote about the worldly power of nonviolence.

The one nonresistant who never averted his gaze from the structural injustices underlying violence was William Lloyd Garrison. Slavery was always his paradigm of violence, and as a consequence he was less sanguine about the efficacy of individual nonviolence to overcome violent systems. To be sure, he insisted that it was an ethical duty, but as I have noted earlier, he laid a particularly heavy emphasis on the likelihood that this duty would eventuate in martyrdom. He also repeatedly hinted that God might soon restore justice by means of apocalyptic violence. In 1829 he warned that a "mighty earthquake" was coming if the United States did not take "perhaps the last opportunity that will be granted us by a long-suffering God" to abolish slavery. In an early issue of the *Liberator*, he reprinted an article from the *National Observer* which asserted that because of the sins of slavery and Indian removal, "ALMIGHTY WISDOM AND JUSTICE, will shortly scourge this country by sword, pestilence, or famine." And in the very first issue Garrison himself fantasized that both the tyrannies of Europe and the American slavocracy might soon "feel the upheavings of the earthquake which is to overthrow its strong towers, and the heat of a fire which is to melt every chain." "Have we no reason," he concluded, "to fear the judgments of Heaven upon our guilty land?"[95]

It was typical of Garrison that he framed this as a question rather than a statement of dogma. His consistent strategy was to hint at apocalypse, to pose it as a possibility that might yet be averted, and to leave ambiguous the question of whether it would be a divine intervention or simply the consequence of natural laws. This open-endedness appears clearly in a poem entitled "Universal Emancipation," which also appeared in the inaugural *Liberator*. The first stanza gives an apocalyptic vision of slavery's end: "Wo if it come with storm, and blood, and fire, / When midnight darkness veils the earth and sky! / Wo to the innocent babe—the guilty sire— / Mother and daughter—friends of kindred tie!" The final stanza, however, retracts this vision in favor of a gradual millennialism that might readily have been affirmed by Ladd or Ballou: "Not by the sword shall your deliverance be; / Not by the shedding of your masters' blood. . . . / GOD's *time is best!*—nor will it long delay: / Even now your barren cause begins to bud, / And glorious shall the fruit be!— Watch and pray, / For, lo! the kindling dawn, that ushers in the day!"[96]

In juxtaposing alternative visions of God's millennial agency, Garrison appealed to two factions within his readership: to Northern white liberals who optimistically assumed that they could change the world through sheer moral effort, and to free blacks and fugitive slaves who knew too well that pious nonresistance alone was not likely to change many slave owners. Though Garrison personally disavowed the one-sided apocalypticism of such black leaders as David Walker and Nat Turner, he insisted on including their voices in his journal as a necessary witness to the depths of slavery's evil. Thus, in the wake of Turner's Rebellion his first response was not to criticize but to suggest that his earlier apocalyptic hints might be coming true: "The first step of the earthquake, which is ultimately to shake down the fabric of oppression, leaving not one stone upon another, has been made." Only then did he step back and offer a countervailing hope that the apocalypse might still be averted: "Wo to this guilty land, unless she speedily repent of her evil doings! . . . IMMEDIATE EMANCIPATION can alone save her from the vengeance of heaven, and cancel the debt of ages!"[97]

It seems likely that Garrison personally wavered between the alternative visions of slavery's end found in these passages. In an 1837 letter to Elizabeth Pease, for example, he expressed extreme doubts about the ultimate success of his own efforts: "I have relinquished the expectation that [the slaveholding states] will ever, by mere moral suasion, consent to emancipate their victims. I believe that nothing but the exterminating judgments of heaven can shatter the chain of the slave and destroy the power of his oppressor."[98] In a public speech a few years later, though, Garrison promised his hearers that the timing of the world's regeneration "will depend, perhaps, upon ourselves, in some measure. It is an exalted privilege to be coworkers with God." Still later, a public letter to Harriet Beecher Stowe perfectly captured the old ambiguity: "My reliance for the deliverance of the oppressed universally is upon the nature of man, the inherent wrongfulness of oppression, the power of truth, and the omnipotence of God—using every rightful instrumentality to hasten the jubilee."[99]

By refusing to explain what he meant by God's omnipotence, Garrison left the very character of God's activity in the world indeterminate. If the United States immediately freed the slaves, Garrison implied, then God would act in the manner predicted by the optimistic liberals: in and through human moral activities. But if the United States did not, he warned, God might act in a manner more in keeping with Dodge's orthodoxy: violently and cataclysmically. In a sense, the project of radical liberal Christianity could only end in theological indeterminacy, for radical liberals made this-worldly experience a criterion for judgments about God, and this world is itself incomplete and indeterminate.

The Literary Nonresistance of Henry Clarke Wright and Sylvester Judd

This indeterminacy did not prevent some nonresistants from translating theological possibilities into narrative form. Lydia Maria Child, for example, continued to produce creative fiction after her conversion from moderate liberalism to Garrisonian radicalism. Two other literary exponents of radical Christian liberalism brought the fervor of orthodox upbringings into their advocacy of left-wing liberalism. Henry Clarke Wright, born in upstate New York and educated at orthodox Andover Seminary, was one of Garrison's most intimate associates and for several years served as the traveling agent of the New England Non-Resistance Society. To promote the peace cause, he wrote several tracts, a book of children's peace stories, and an autobiography entitled simply *Human Life*. Sylvester Judd, a Unitarian minister who in 1842 shocked the citizens of Maine by attacking the United States Revolution in a sermon, told his life story in *A Young Man's Account of His Conversion from Calvinism* and gave even more fervent expression to liberal ideals in his novel, *Margaret: A Tale of the Real and the Ideal*.[100] Here I shall focus on *Human Life* and *Margaret*, two works that incorporated Garrison's radical ethics into Catharine Sedgwick's liberal plot line of natural family affection bursting the dogmatic constraints of orthodox theology. Both Wright and Judd were sure that a single individual or a loving family possessed the natural power to usher in the nonviolent, millennial transformation of society.

If Wright and Judd echoed Sedgwick's theology, however, they did so with a new tone and to different effect. Sedgwick was complacent about the progress of liberal ideals within existing social institutions, and in her novels liberal heroes and heroines typically end as stable, happily married pillars of the community. In contrast, Wright and Judd believed that all social institutions except the family were inimical to affectionate power. Wright's autobiography ends with his adult career as an itinerant radical who dreams of uniting the world through a grand reform convention on a Scottish mountain, while Judd's novel culminates in a total millennial transformation of a New England village.

The difference owes something to the wave of cultural paranoia that swept the United States during the panic of 1837: Judd and Wright wrote at a time when liberal ideals seemed both more fragile and more urgently needed than they had in the 1820s. But the difference of gender may have been even more significant. Sedgwick, Wright, and Judd all promoted a model of affectionate, familial power as normative for both men and women. But their less consistently liberal contemporaries regarded this as a specifically feminine sort of virtue and were more inclined to endorse it when it came from the pen of a woman. This partly explains Sedgwick's popular success, which may in turn have made her less inclined to trace her liberal ideas to radical conclusions. Judd, and especially Wright, by contrast, experienced social dissonance because their attachment to the domestic sphere was not often validated. They were correspondingly more inclined to embrace a radical critique of all social institutions.

Despite their radicalism, Wright and Judd were not themselves immune to the popular tendency to see nonviolence as feminine. Neither could quite imagine that an adult, white male like himself could exemplify the power of familial affection. As a consequence, both *Human Life* and *Margaret* center, in a peculiarly obsessive way, on the affectionate power of a single female child. In Judd's novel this is the title character, Margaret, who is explicitly and repeatedly identified with Christ; in Wright's autobiography it is six-year-old Catharine Anderson, the daughter of a Scottish family that hosts him during the early stages of his writing. Both girls epitomize the liberal faith in the innate goodness of humanity apart from corrupt social institutions, but they also allow the authors to sidestep the characteristic liberal ambivalence about the precise mode of God's activity in a violent world. Rhapsodies about messianic children may be appealing, but they provide little guidance to those who must live to adulthood while still awaiting the millennial age.

Wright's autobiography begins, however, on a less troubling note. At first we are confronted not with the messianic Catharine but with Wright himself. He offers his story as a response to his own call for a concrete "anthropology" that would replace the abstractions of theology. Like Emerson and others in the romantic wing of New England liberalism, Wright believed that truth could only be gained through a turn away from books and to nature and individual experience: "To learn what man is, we must go to man. . . . All books must be brought to the test of nature—nature must never be tested by a book." He further believed that a single autobiography could suffice to illuminate the universal human experience, "for in the essentials of human nature, all are alike." *Human Life* thus had "two objects," a positive anthropological task and a negative theological task: "One is, to present human life as it is illustrated in the thoughts, feelings, actions, and revolutions of an individual human being; the other is, to show the absurdity of that religion which sends us away from the earth, and all human relations and obligations, into unknown regions of space to find something to love and worship as God."[101]

This defense of earthly life against its orthodox detractors might give the impression that Wright looked on the world with rose-colored glasses, denying the intractability of human evil. Wright shatters this impression in the next paragraph, when he launches into a typically radical attack on human institutions: "The history of a government is but the history of the fagot, the gallows, the sword, the bayonet and bombshell; of fraud, superstition, hypocrisy, wrath and revenge." Wright's strategy is not so much to dissolve the problematic orthodox dichotomy of heaven and earth as to transpose it into an equally rigid dichotomy of "man, as a human being," versus man "as a church or state." Significantly, Wright placed family structures (which he took to be "natural") on the first, positive side of the dichotomy: "Human life is beautiful and lovely, as it is manifested in the domestic and social relations, affections and sympathies; but as it appears in the councils and doings of religious and civil organizations, it is like a demon of superstition, wrath and revenge, whose progress is marked by tears and blood."[102]

Wright's autobiographical task was to tell of his individuality and his familial relatedness, rather than of his participation in church and state institutions. He took this to be a truly innovative project, asserting in a letter to Garrison (included in *Human Life*) that "the history of man has never been written; only that of church and governmental organizations. The history of these is written in blood." Fiction, he acknowledged, came closer to revealing "the feelings, plans, sympathies, joys and trials of human beings," but fiction paled by comparison to concrete interactions with other people. Echoing a commonsense argument, Wright alleged that novel reading had diverted his youthful sympathies away from real people, producing "in me a kind of sickly, morbid sensibility, that unfits me to feel a deep interest in human suffering."[103] Deυpite this reservation, Wright's account of his own struggles to remain affectionately connected to an orthodox community while repudiating its belief system ran parallel to the fictional histories of Jane Elton, Hope Leslie, and Naomi Worthington, as given by Sedgwick and Lee. In chapters entitled "The Child," "The Youth," and "The Man," he described the affections and relationships that shaped his childhood in upstate New York, his apprenticeship as a hatter, his conversion in a revival, his studies at the newly founded Andover Seminary, his repudiation of orthodoxy, and his career as a radical reformer.

Like Sedgwick, Child, and Lee, Wright believed that "a human heart is necessarily at war with a Calvinistic head," and he used this dichotomy to organize his early experiences. "As a child," he wrote, "the joyous, irrepressible and innocent promptings of my spirit, and the solemn rebukes and threats of religion, were ever at war within me." His account of the religious practices of his family and community is a litany of complaints. His father had diligently led the family in a Bible reading each morning, but he read the chapter straight through without comment, even if it contained "nothing but the names of persons and places totally unmeaning and unpronounceable to the children." Thus Wright "venerated the BOOK, not its contents." Sabbath observance meant the suppression of playfulness and good spirits, and "I could not understand how an act that did not injure me, nor my fellow men, could insult or injure the Deity on that day." Church attendance was a duty performed for its own sake, unconnected to his daily duty to treat his "parents, brothers and sister and playmates, more kindly." Learning the catechism by rote affected nothing but his memory: "My heart, my affections, were untouched by the process." The Bible was presented as "the only rule of faith and practice," even though young Henry "was conscious that I believed thousands of things to be right or wrong, independent of that, or any book." He was taught to regard prayer as "an *outward* observance . . . an offering unto God" rather than as a means to personal moral improvement. He believed that conversion was an instantaneous change performed by an unseen external agent and that heaven and hell were real places to be experienced only after death.[104]

After each account of an orthodox belief or practice, Wright juxtaposes the "natural" liberal alternative, using such a phrase as "I had no idea" or "I never supposed" to suggest how deeply his inherent faith was suppressed: "I had no idea conversion meant a practical change from hate to love"; "I never supposed that heaven could be enjoyed, or hell suffered, in this life." Wright proposes a few explanations of how this suppression of humanity succeeded for so long. First, the doctrine of original sin allowed the orthodox to explain away the tensions between their teaching and lived human experiences: if human nature was inherently depraved, it could not be expected to resonate with Christian truth. Thus young Henry always *knew* that saying the catechism was "a wearisome business," but for years he believed that "the only reason why it was so irksome to me was . . . my own wickedness." He believed that as soon as he could "get a new heart," he would cease to be troubled by the biblical stories in which God took "pleasure in seeing the little children and *infants* of Jericho, and the other cities of Canaan, slaughtered, because of the wickedness of their parents." Second, the orthodox assumption that religion was a matter of external performances *on* the individual rather than the cultivation of feelings and affections *within* the individual was conducive to a neglectful style of parenting and education. His teachers called on his memory but not on his reasoning or imaginative powers, and even when his mother died, most adults did not think to "call out and soothe the lacerated feelings" of him and the other children.

Third and finally, Wright's natural religious feelings were sometimes suppressed by active, violent terror. Early in his text, Wright describes an orthodox and intemperate schoolteacher whose pedagogical method was one of "prayers for the soul, and whips for the body." Each day the teacher stood in the middle of the schoolroom with whip in hand, shouted for attention, and began a prayer about "what depraved little creatures we were; how we were more inclined to be unkind than kind, to be cruel than gentle, to hate than to love, and to injure than to do good to one another"—all the while whipping any child who moved or even smiled. The prayers of this drunken elder, Wright concludes, were as loathsome as those "of spirit-dealers, of slaveholders, and of warriors, and of all who apologize for slavery or war," for it is impossible to ask God to pity the soul without oneself showing pity for the body.[105]

The passages cited here might suggest that Wright's childhood memories were bitter, but in fact the opposite was the case. Orthodox theology did not succeed in suppressing his natural affections; it only prevented him from connecting those affections to such religious categories as "God" or "conversion." The real story of his childhood and youth, as he presents it, is one of affectionate power overcoming the trauma of his mother's death, the errors of his father's theology, and the loneliness of his first separation from the family as a teenage apprentice. Indeed, even the "Sabbath observances, meeting-going, catechisings, Bible-readings and prayers of my father . . . endear his memory to my heart" because "he had the best interests of his children at heart, and only wished to influence them to love their God and to keep his commandments."[106]

Wright's account of the powers of affection is perhaps most vivid when he describes the enjoyment he took, as a young boy, in performing tasks conventionally understood as women's work. "Many an Indian meal pudding and Johnnycake have I made," he reports proudly, "and many a dish of fried ham and eggs have I prepared." He took even more pleasure in babysitting his young half sisters: "Their laughter and their tears were mine. To wander about the fields with them; to pick berries and weave nosegays for them, and make them happy, was my delight. They seemed soft and gentle to me, and this part of my nature was filled in their company." It did not occur to him that such activities might take him "out of my sphere," but if it had, he would have rejected the notion out of an "innate sense" of the real contribution he was making to family life.[107]

For Wright the free expression of natural affections was intimately linked to the practice of nonviolence. Yet he did not pretend to have been born a nonresistant. Instead, he openly wrestled with the tension between the liberal doctrine of human nature and his own less than angelic past actions. "I had not naturally a cruel disposition," he insists in good liberal fashion, "for I never could endure to see even animals in pain, much less my fellow creatures." "Yet," he admits, "I have been cruel to animals and to human beings." He was "trained" to use violence against animals "as the only mode of subjecting them to my will." As a young boy he was in the habit of whipping his cow Nimbleshanks until she learned to drop on her knees and look at him with mournful eyes whenever he reached for the whip. On another occasion, he threw a rock at a large, greedy pig that "showed a savage temper toward his fellow pigs." The rock knocked the pig's eye out of its socket, and Wright had to watch in horror for half an hour as the animal rolled about in agony. Later he adopted a sparrow's nest, then killed the mother for too jealously guarding her babies. Despite his fervent regrets, all the young birds died by the next day.[108]

Wright was not the first liberal to tell such stories or to wrestle with the implications of children's cruelty for liberal anthropology. In his memoir Channing told a similar story of caring for a nest of birds, then feeling blamed by the parent birds after another child, apparently, killed the babies. And Henry Ware Sr. acknowledged that small children seem to take pleasure "in torturing insects and small animals."[109] Consciously or unconsciously, all three authors probably realized that such stories seemed to confirm Saint Augustine's case for the purposeless depravity of youth, so famously encapsulated in the pear-stealing episode of the Confessions.

Wright managed to draw a different moral from these episodes by placing as much emphasis on his feelings as on his violent actions. Augustine claimed that in stealing the pears he "became evil for no reason" and "had no motive for my wickedness itself," while Wright surrounded his childhood violence with a thicket of benevolent feelings and intentions: his righteous indignation against the greedy pig, his earlier care for the bird's nest, his bitter remorse at the consequences of his actions. His violent actions thus reveal not his absolute depravity but the incongruity between his deepest feelings and his behavior. This incongruity is a spur to future nonviolence: "This little incident [of the birds] has held back my hand from many strong temptations to throw stones at birds. This, and the incident of the pig, gave a powerful check to my habit of cruelty to animals and birds; and sure I am, my reflections on them have greatly tended to foster in me a spirit of gentleness toward human beings." Thus, the very experience of regret makes even the perpetrator of violence bear witness against the doctrine of total depravity.[110]

The liberal anthropology that emerges from these passages is as follows: humans are naturally sensitive to violence and filled with benevolent affections toward other creatures, but they do not always know how to translate those feelings into action. If they are not taught to repress or mistrust their feelings, they will gradually learn through trial and error, and by attending to the consequences of their actions, to avoid violence. But if they are taught to look outside themselves for moral guidance, they will lose touch with their natural feelings and become capable of tremendous violence. Yet another childhood experience, of his reaction to two classmates who fought constantly, reveals how for Wright unrepressed feelings lead inevitably though not immediately to nonviolence. At first his "feelings were greatly shocked" by their violence, and he intervened to stop their fight. When they hit him, he hit back—but that demonstrated the uselessness of a violent response. Wright never tried to stop them again but continued to be affected by their violence: "It was long, however, before I could see them fight without a feeling of shuddering lest they should put out each other's eyes or kill each other."[111]

When Wright goes away to become a hatter's apprentice, his sense of "local attachments and home affections" proves so strong that for three months he suffers a "moral crucifixion" of homesickness. Gradually, however, he discovers his ability to form new connections and affections. Though he is shocked by the rough manners of the journeymen, he and his fellow apprentices coalesce into "a kind, generous, and happy company." The lessons in nonviolence learned at home serve him well in this group: he resolves never to tease his fellows, remembering how badly he felt about having done this to his younger brother. Once again, it is his sensitivity, his regret for past mistakes, and his ability to learn and to direct his behavior accordingly—and not any instantaneous ability to meet a perfect moral standard—that prove the natural goodness of humanity.[112]

Wright goes on to describe his conversion under the influence of his master's wife, who "directed me in fact to religion, as a living principle in the soul," his studies at Andover, and finally the "radical revolution" that brought the religion of his head into accordance with the feelings of his heart.[113] Yet at this point his text begins to lose its narrative center. Rather than a connected story, Wright offers the reader a confusing mix of journal entries from his early adulthood, journal entries from the present, and "anthropological" exposition. It is almost as though, now that his head is no longer at war with his heart and experience, he can simply dispense with his heart and experience! Most surprisingly, given his previous stress on family, he has virtually nothing to say about his own marriage or the family he creates as an adult.[114]

Clearly, Wright struggled to translate the conventions of the liberal marriage comedy into autobiographical form. Sedgwick's and Lee's novels typically end when the heroine achieves a stable and useful place in society through a happy marriage. But Wright's own marriage was *not* happy—at least, he chose to spend much of it living apart from his wife—and he never attained a fully stable place in society. He could thus not bring the pedagogical process begun in his accounts of his childhood violence to a fully satisfying conclusion, and for whatever reason he did not choose to give narrative expression to his continuing longing for full expression of his natural affections. Instead, his narrative turns back on itself: when he should be telling of his adulthood, he becomes increasingly obsessed with the salvific powers of children. To be sure, much of Wright's adult career was in fact focused on children. Believing "that children constitute the most influential portion of the community," he worked for a long time as a special children's minister for several Congregational parishes in Boston and also served as a visiting school inspector. As his doubts about his ministerial vocation increased, his sense of identity with children became a focus of his reflections. "Two characters seem natural to me," he wrote in his journal in 1828, "i.e., that of a daring, joyous, romping child of nature, and that of a staid, sober, severe priest."[115]

Increasingly, Wright figured his renunciation of orthodoxy in favor of nonresistant activism as a renunciation of manhood in favor of childhood. "It is sweet," he wrote in *Anthropology*, "to live in the heart of childhood. Why need we become old in spirit? We need not: we should not, if we lived less in the future and more in the present—less in an abstract Divinity and more in an ever-present humanity." "Why should not the world see me as I am," he asked in *Human Life*, "a MAN-CHILD, or CHILD-MAN, put it as you please?" During his travels as an itinerant reformer, he lodged with many families and always made a point of befriending the children, even joining as a full participant in their games and activities. He wrote *Human Life* while staying with a Scottish family near Glasgow, and consequently his autobiographical narrative is interspersed with contemporary accounts of his adventures with little Catharine Anderson, whom he called his "Wee Darling." Together they toured Glasgow, playing hide-and-seek in the middle of a busy public square; later they climbed Glen Fruen Mountain and fantasized together about hosting a convention on "human brotherhood" atop that "true temple of God."[116]

The frontispiece of *Human Life* is an engraving of Wright sitting with his arm around Catharine Anderson, clasping both her hands; it is inscribed, "My Wee Darling." The picture fittingly expresses her centrality to the book, for Wright's thesis is that one can encounter God only by attending to the human individual, and increasingly it is Catharine, not Henry, to whom we are invited to attend. In describing their visit to Glasgow Cathedral, he writes, "I saw and felt more of God in her than in all the cathedrals, churches, observances, prayers, and sermons, I ever saw or heard." "There was more of goodness, of love, of purity, of heaven, of God, in the merry laugh of this child," he writes again, "than in all the prayers, sermons and religious exercises, that were ever performed by a sectarian, war-making, ambitious clergy."[117] And he expanded the point in a long letter to Garrison, dwelling on the heavenly power of her sheer physical presence:

> Dear friend, I am glad no mortal eyes are upon me, as I thus yield my whole heart up to glee with that child, with her bright blue eyes, her rosy cheeks, her flowing hair, curling down her shoulders, her clear, merry voice, her joyous laugh, and her firm, elastic step and graceful movements. What is the kingdom of heaven but this perfect mingling of human hearts; this joyous, confiding, divine interchange of human affection and sympathy? . . . Is not this to dwell in God?[118]

Though I cannot help but wonder, reading this passage, if Wright's relationship with Catharine Anderson was sexually abusive, my suspicion is that it was not. He seems to have been more interested in infantilizing himself than in sexualizing her, and he certainly displayed little of the impulse to secrecy that is common in cases of sexual abuse. But even on this charitable assumption, the relationship is troubling on two levels. In itself, it is troubling because Catharine was surely incapable of reciprocating, or even comprehending, the intensity of Henry's emotional investment in her. His desire to be a child was so great that he seems to have forgotten that there remained some important differences between them.[119]

As a contribution to nonviolent theology, the relationship is troubling because it allows Wright to sidestep the question of how to locate God's presence in the midst of a violent and ambivalent world. At the outset of his autobiography, he promises to show the reader that God can be seen only in the midst of concrete human experience, and his nuanced account of his own encounters with violence goes partway to fulfilling this promise. But by the end he has lodged the divine vision not in his own actual experience as a child and a man but rather in a romanticized and divinized image of Catharine— an image at least as abstract and unconvincing as the Calvinists' sovereign God.

Sylvester Judd's novel *Margaret* falls into much the same trap, and indeed Judd's theological agenda mirrored Wright's. Judd was as committed as Wright to a child-centered theology. His first publication, *A Young Man's Account of His Conversion from Calvinism*, centers its attack on the doctrine of original sin, which "teaches that there is every thing in Christianity to repel the human heart." On the contrary, Judd argues, Christianity is perfectly adapted to human nature, and he cites as proof an unconverted little girl who immediately recognizes the beauty and truth of the Sermon on the Mount. Though Judd's alternative to orthodoxy is not "anthropology" but what he calls "Evangelical Unitarianism," his account of its virtues runs closely parallel to Wright's position. Only Evangelical Unitarianism, Judd contends, "does justice to human nature" and teaches "the great doctrines of humanity, which shall subvert and utterly demolish, throughout the world, every system of oppression and degradation, religious, moral, and political."[120]

Like *Human Life*, *Margaret* contends that untrammeled natural affections will lead not to a comfortable progressivism à la Sedgwick but to a radical repudiation of all violence and of existing social institutions. And like *Human Life*, *Margaret* claims that such radical affections are the common inheritance of all humanity, but ultimately it rests its case on the idealized image of a single female child. Unlike *Human Nature*, however, *Margaret* confronts the reader with the divine child from the very beginning. In the "Phantasmagorical—Introductory" first chapter, Margaret is introduced as at once a typical girl of rural New England and a panracial Everychild:

> We behold a child of eight or ten months: it has brown curly hair, dark eyes, fair-conditioned features, a healthy-glowing cheek, and well-shaped limbs. Who is it? whose is it? what is it? where is it? It is in the centre of fantastic light, and only a dimly revealed form appears. It may be Queen Victoria's or Sally Twig's. It is God's own child, as all children are. The blood of Adam and Eve, through how many soever channels diverging, runs in its veins, and the Spirit of the Eternal, that blows everywhere, has animated its soul. . . . It is God's child still, and its mother's. It is curiously and wonderfully made; the inspiration of the Almighty hath given it understanding. It will look after God, its Maker, by how many soever names he may be called; it will aspire to the Infinite, whether that Infinite be expressed in Bengalee or Arabic, English or Chinese; it will seek to know truth; it will long to be loved; it will sin and be miserable, if it has none to care for it; it will die.[121]

After quite a bit more of this, the child is identified as Margaret, a girl growing up in a drunkard's family in the New England village of Livingston. Several chapters later, we learn that she has a more romantic origin: she is the child of a clandestine romance between an impoverished German musician and his creditor's daughter. The two lovers saw God in one another, but their earthly romance was short-lived: the father died, like "a convalescing angel," just before Margaret's birth, while the mother "lingered on a few days [after], without much apparent suffering or anxiety, blessed her child, and melted away at last in the clouds of mortal vision." Thereafter Margaret was adopted by the Hart family at the behest of their eldest son, Nimrod.[122]

Margaret is a child of nature as well as of love. Mr. Hart, nursing a long-standing quarrel with the town authorities, keeps her away from the church and school. She is educated instead by an eccentric (and alcoholic) "Master," who teaches her to see herself naturalistically. "The Master says I am of the order Bipeds, and species Simulacrens," she rambles on at one point; "distinguished by thirty-two teeth. . . . For my own part I incline to the Sylvan analogy, only my clothes are not half so durable as this bark, nor my hair so becoming as the leaves, and I must undress myself at night and take to my bed, while the trees sleep standing and unhooded." With this sort of upbringing, Margaret is spared Henry Clark Wright's (and Sylvester Judd's) childhood struggle to reconcile an orthodox head with a natural heart. Her very first encounter with orthodox religion reveals her messianic status.[123]

In the middle of Margaret's childhood, her brothers convince Mr. Hart that she should experience a church at least once in her life. She heads out on the appointed day, already worshiping as she walks: "The intangible presence of God was in her soul, the universal voice of Jesus called her forward." En route, she picks a bouquet of flowers for a murderer in the jail, who tells her he once had a daughter like her. In church she sits in the section reserved for blacks but is unimpressed by the service; when an earnest churchgoer tries to explain the doctrine of universal depravity, Margaret concludes that she should avoid such an admittedly "wicked" group of people. But that night she has a dream in which Jesus Christ accepts her gift of flowers, explains that humanity is saved not by an atoning sacrifice but by "a divine union with God and Christ," and then promises her a special messianic role: "The Church has fallen. The Eve of Religion has again eaten the forbidden fruit. You shall be a co-worker with me in its second redemption. . . . I, too, was a child like you, and it is that you must be a child like me."[124]

Like Jesus, Margaret must grow in wisdom in order to fulfill her messianic role, and this occurs in part through an extended dialogue with her suitor, Mr. Evelyn, who instructs her in the doctrines of Evangelical Unitarianism and introduces her to the Gospel story. Her sympathetic reaction to Jesus' sufferings reveals that, like him, she is capable of becoming "perfect through suffering." Evelyn identifies sin with "war, intemperance, slavery and unkindness" and tells Margaret that the Fall was simply a lapse from the natural human tendency to love: "It is ever Nature *versus* the Unnatural. The institutions and organizations of men, founded upon the new basis, partake of the general corruption, and only foster evils it is their design to prevent." Sin feeds on itself, Evelyn explains, because the doctrine of total depravity leads people to regard one another with "suspicion and enmity" rather than trust and love. And so the orthodox teaching of that doctrine "consummates the Fall!"[125]

Judd makes explicit the paradoxical heart of the radical liberals' position: as liberals, they deny human depravity, but as radicals they acknowledge that all human institutions have been utterly corrupted by that doctrine, and thus they both affirm and repudiate the world. Salvation consists in the reactivation of the latent human sympathies that have been repressed, but not destroyed, by corrupt human institutions. Jesus became a savior, Evelyn tells Margaret, by giving full vent to his natural sympathies and retaining the feelings of childhood into adult life: "He wept like a child in pure sympathy with the distresses of his friends. . . . he was sparing of those feelings which are deep because they belong to our childhood. . . . God he called his Heavenly Father, and sought to create a near and filial relation with the Divinity." Just as Jesus made family connections with all humanity, Evelyn explains later, so in the coming "Kingdom of Heaven" would all become one family by means of sympathetic identification. "Faith . . . is taking Christ to yourself in this living and warm way, receiving his spirit into your spirit, imbosoming his feelings in your feelings, impressing his character on your character, whereby his whole self becomes grafted upon and fused into yourself. . . . Adoption is becoming a member of the great Divine family. THIS IS CHRISTIANITY!"[126]

Even as Margaret grows in knowledge through her conversations with Evelyn, she also deepens her sympathy through a dogged campaign against the violent practices of the community. Her sensitivity to violence begins much as Henry Clarke Wright's did, after she perpetrates violence herself. She helps her brothers burn out a beehive to get the honey within, and then realizes that they have killed the bees. But her remorse simply makes her feel more sympathy with the life of nature around her, and she does not lapse into despair: "With all that was new about her, and fitted to engross her vision, and supplant her recent sorrowful impressions, there seemed a new sense aroused, or active within her, an unconscious instinct, a hidden prompting of duty; she trod with more care than usual; a fly, beetle, or snail, she turned aside for, or stepped protectingly over; she would not jostle a spider's web."[127]

Margaret's sympathy for the human victims of violence is aroused on a militia muster day when she notices the many veterans with missing limbs or other disabilities who have to subsist on town charity. Later she learns more about war from her friend Deacon Ramsdill, who tells her of his service in the British campaign against the French Acadians: "We dragged them out of their houses, tore children from their mothers, wives from their husbands, piled them helter-skelter in their boats. Then we set fire to every thing that would kindle; burnt up houses, barns, crops, meetinghouses." His life-long struggle, Ramsdill explains, was to learn not to resist the "nature" that led him to shrink from such violence. "I had this nater," he recalled, "when I was arter the Hurons under General Webb, and it shook my firelock so when I was pulling the trigger upon a sleeping redskin, I let him go." This nonviolent nature recurred in other situations, but yet "I fought agin nater, I tell you, and a tough spell I had of it." When he looked at his infant daughter, he realized that she was part of Christ's kingdom, while he "had slided off from what I was when I was a boy, and that I had been abusing nater all my life," but still his adherence to conventional "notions and politicals" led him to resist his better impulses. Finally he took in a colt that had been abused, and as he tamed it, nature at last triumphed:

> Then the colt came, then I saw it in old brindle, our cow, and then I saw it in the sheep, then I remembered the French gal and the Indian; and at last we gave in, and it was all as plain as a pipe-stem. When I went out in the morning, I saw it in the hens and chickens, the calves, the bees, in the rocks, and in all Creation. There is nater in everybody, only if it was not for their notions and politicals. The Papists, the Negroes, and the Indians have it. Like father, like child. I believe we all have the same nater.[128]

Margaret's own campaign against violence focuses not on war but on the town's practice of corporal and capital punishment. Because her family is none too respectable, her brothers and male friends are frequently the victims of such practices. First her friend Obed is sentenced to a public whipping for his role in a brawl. "Not comprehending precisely the nature of events," Margaret rushes up and embraces Obed in the middle of the whipping, setting off a public outcry that forces the authorities to remit the punishment. Later the same day, she visits her brother Hash in jail and there befriends a condemned murderer.[129]

The novel reaches its crisis when Margaret's brother accidentally kills the local rumseller, who had tried too aggressively to steal a kiss from Margaret. Margaret loses her position as a governess, the family loses its home, and Chilion stands trial for murder. Margaret disrupts the trial, calling the community's attention to the fact that despite his error Chilion is still essentially good, but her words have no effect, and he is sentenced to death. This is the point at which affectionate human nature most directly confronts the violence of human institutions, and it is here that we might expect Judd to offer some account of how God's power continues to be manifest in the normal expressions of affection. Instead, the novel takes an apocalyptic turn. Margaret heads out to the woods, where she encounters a mysterious Indian, "Pakanawket, grandson of Pometacom, great-grandson of Massasoit, the last of the Wampanoags." He rehearses the history of white violence against his people, then calls Margaret's attention to the fact that her village is burning down in retribution for the genocide. As she watches the church spire collapse in flames, Pakanawket, holding his infant granddaughter in his arms, leaps from a cliff to his death.[130]

It is not clear what Judd intends for us to make of this curious apocalypse. The notion that it is a just punishment for genocide is undermined by the fact that, apparently, no one actually dies in the fire. Like Catharine Sedgwick, Judd was eager to celebrate Indian virtues but nevertheless found it easier to imagine Indian deaths than white deaths. Thus, the effect of Pakanawket's suicide is to exclude his people—alone of all nations—from the millennium that Margaret brings about after the fire.

After a respite in Boston, she and Mr. Evelyn resurrect Livingston as a model village. Christ Church becomes the center of a "new society" characterized by temperance, educational and building projects, and a comfortable and commodious jail. Militia days are abolished, and when a general from outside the village comes to recruit, he is dusted with flour and sent away. The villagers develop a system of monthly festivals, including Independence Day and Thanksgiving but also three new ones modeled on the beatitudes. Visitors include "Congregationalists, Presbyterians, Episcopalians, Catholics, Armenians, Russians, Greeks, Jews, Mohammedans, Hindoos." When the state sends investigators to determine why the town no longer has a militia and is sending far fewer prisoners to the state prison, they must report on the remarkable improvement of community life. Ultimately, both John Adams and Thomas Jefferson stop by to congratulate the villagers on their achievement.[131]

Margaret, of course, is at the center of all the changes. "I never could have imagined so perfect an incarnation of Christ as she is," Evelyn comments, explaining that it was her early preservation in a state of nature that allowed her "like a new-born babe, to breathe the atmosphere of Christ the moment she came in contact with it, and to drink the sincere milk of the word. I once wholly despaired of seeing a Christian; she is one! I might say, I more than despaired of fulfilling my ideal in myself; she has aided me to do it! Christ pervades every corner and cranny of her being; she is filled with the fulness of God."[132]

If one has been persuaded of the innate goodness of humanity, this is rather charming in all its exaggeration. But what Judd does not offer, even to the convinced liberal, is a concrete model of how those who have not been preserved in a state of nature can actualize natural goodness amid institutional violence. Margaret's millennium is separated from mundane reality by both the apocalyptic fire and her own idealization. Like Garrison and Wright, and like Harriet Beecher Stowe a few years later, Judd must finally concede that the truest expression of God's power on behalf of nonviolence will appear only in an unknown future. He implicitly advises us not so much to act as to await either a messianic child or the fires of Armageddon. The tragedy for radical Christian liberalism, in the 1850s and 1860s, was that the latter arrived without the former.

4

Looking for Victims

Violence and Theology in Temperance Narratives

Despite its radicalism, the antebellum nonresistance movement had trouble hearing the voices of victims. Nonresistants like Sylvester Judd and Henry Clarke Wright were eager to discern the *imago dei* in children uncorrupted by worldly violence, but what of the many children and adults who faced tyrannical violence every day? What of slaves who were whipped by their masters, wives who were tortured by their husbands, and alcoholics subject to the tyranny of addiction? Did they also possess the image of God? With the notable exception of William Lloyd Garrison, antebellum peace activists avoided this question by focusing on the ethical debate over whether the perpetration of violence could ever be justified. Presupposing autonomous, unvictimized moral agents, they argued that such agents had the God-given capacity to repudiate violence. But for the victims of violence, the first challenge was simply to survive in the face of it. Questions of whether violence could ever be justified came later.[1] Though peace activists could avoid matters of survival and self-assertion, they were inescapable for activists committed to temperance and the abolition of slavery. As a consequence, these more broad-based reforms were generally not characterized by the ethical absolutism of nonresistance. Instead, they were shaped by a series of transformative encounters between reformers and the victims of violence. These encounters gave rise to a distinctive form of radical Christian liberalism.

The parallel between temperance and abolitionism may seem surprising. Concern for the victims of slavery might appear to be the central motive for abolition, while the temperance movement has often been portrayed as the heartless attempt of a capitalist elite to impose a more disciplined lifestyle on workers. In fact, both movements were driven by a blend of economic self-interest and sentimental identification. Many opponents of slavery in the antebellum United States were indifferent to the suffering humanity of the slaves; they rejected slavery only because it was an economic rival to the emerging system of industrial capitalism and a competitor for the fertile western lands desired by free white homesteaders. Only a relative handful of "immediatists" demanded abolition and full civil rights for blacks.

Similarly, the temperance campaign against alcohol drew considerable support from traditional elites and rising capitalists who desired a sober, disciplined, and docile workforce. Yet a central core of activists, analogous to the immediatists, were motivated by concern for wives and children who were abused by intemperate husbands—and, indeed, for the "drunkards" whom they perceived as victims of a heartless and profit-seeking "alcohol system." Unlike the immediatists, temperance radicals did not separate themselves sharply from those factions of the movement that did not share their victim-centered concerns, although they did tend to find a more congenial home in the "Washingtonian" temperance societies of the 1840s than in earlier organizations such as the American Temperance Society.

The encounter between reformers and victims was demanded by the liberal faith in the *imago dei*, but it also presented that theology with grave challenges. Victims' experiences could unsettle any sanguine confidence in human nature. Liberals believed that each individual had, from birth, enough nonviolent power to transform the world, but victims could not close their eyes to their own powerlessness. The liberal faith may have resonated with victims' sense that they were not *merely* victims but possessed their own God-given powers of survival, but victims also knew that their access to those powers depended on personal transformation. If that transformation was not an orthodox conversion or rebirth, it at least involved a liberation from the demonic powers that had robbed victims of their liberal birthright. From the victims' perspective, such demons possessed far more extensive earthly powers than many liberals were comfortable conceding. Would a benevolent God really have given the demons such broad sway? Victims thus called liberals to a deeper wrestling with the ancient tension between God's goodness and God's greatness.

The encounter between reformers and victims occurred primarily in the most radical wing of the social reform movement, but it achieved broad social influence through its reproduction in reformist literature. Among abolitionists, a concern for victims led to the proliferation of fugitive slave narratives. Among temperance activists, similarly, it inspired the production of fictional vignettes, known as "temperance tales," and of autobiographical narratives. The purpose of these genres was to present the perspective of victims, whether of women and children victimized by alcoholic husbands or of drunkards themselves, victimized by heartless rumsellers and an unforgiving society.[2]

These texts found a wide audience. The inventor of the temperance tale, Lucius M. Sargent (1786-1867), was the most popular reformist author of the 1830s, and his collected tales ultimately went through 130 editions in English and several translations. In the early 1840s, Washingtonian leaders like John H. W. Hawkins (1797?-1858) and John Bartholomew Gough (1817-86) began translating their stump speeches into autobiographical narratives, and a few of these were big sellers. Gough's appeared in 1845, almost simultaneously with Frederick Douglass's first narrative, and sold thirty-two thousand copies by 1853. By far the most successful temperance writer, though, was T. S. Arthur (1809-85), who reputedly produced 5 percent of all fiction published in the United States in the 1840s and sold more than a million books by 1860.[3] Arthur's best-selling *Ten Nights in a Bar-Room* is rivaled only by Harriet Beecher Stowe's *Uncle Tom's Cabin* as *the* manifesto of antebellum social reform.

Temperance writers drew on a variety of traditions—newspaper sensationalism, the liberal family novel, and the testimonials offered by reformed drunkards at Washingtonian meetings—to give voice to their conviction that the sheer power of words might overcome the scourge of alcohol. In so doing, they developed a distinctive theology.

Like earlier liberals, they embraced a model of divine power centered on the internal workings of the *imago dei* rather than the external works of a coercive Providence. But they refused to abandon orthodoxy's emphasis on the demonic powers of this world. By stressing both the nonviolence of divine power and the earthly power of evil, they sometimes drew a Manichean dividing line between earth and heaven. They also suggested that human powers alone might be inadequate to overcome some forms of violence. In so doing they helped initiate a transition from liberal humanism to a supernatural Christology.

Temperance and the Search for Victims

Antebellum Americans had good reason to be concerned with the evils of drink. Between 1790 and 1830, annual per capita consumption of pure alcohol swelled from three to four gallons, an increase that was driven both by farmers' need to convert grain and apples into salable commodities and by the psychological pressures generated by the new market economy.[4] More and more young men, in particular, resorted to highly destructive habits of binge drinking. Antebellum economic changes also made traditional patterns of drinking less and less viable. Colonial Americans believed that moderate consumption of alcohol helped laborers work more productively, and in fact alcohol rarely interfered with the relaxed rhythms of agrarian employment. But alcohol was inimical to the discipline required by industrial production, and what Charles Sellers has called "the great American whiskey binge" threatened to nip the Industrial Revolution in the bud.[5] At the same time, antebellum Americans perceived an intimate connection between alcohol and domestic violence. Men deprived of their customary role as agrarian patriarchs sought solace in the bottle and then took out their frustrations on the bodies of their wives and children.[6]

Given all these circumstances, it is not surprising that many individuals began to question the long-standing perception of alcohol as a "good creature" and divine gift. Already in the late eighteenth century, the revolutionary partisan and influential physician Benjamin Rush embarked on an ambitious campaign against the use of hard liquor. Rush's cause was embraced by the Federalist elite of New England—both orthodox and liberal—which saw the whiskey-drinking masses as a grave threat to the old system of deference and social order. At a time when politically ascendant Jeffersonians were dismantling both church establishments and such national institutions as Hamilton's central bank, Federalists turned to voluntary societies to fill the gap and maintain order. In 1813 they founded the Massachusetts Society for the Suppression of Intemperance (MSSI). During the same decade, local Protestant churches throughout the country passed resolutions advocating abstinence from "ardent spirits"; these groups were usually motivated more by a desire to safeguard their own families than by a wish to control working-class drinking.[7]

In 1826 the many local efforts coalesced in the American Temperance Society (ATS). Inspired by Lyman Beecher's sermons against intemperance, it was an integral part of the "benevolent empire" of missionary and reform societies founded under Congregational and Presbyterian auspices. Its leaders were generally ministers, manufacturing capitalists, and prosperous farmers who had little interest, initially, in the well-being of drunkards and their families. Indeed, ATS leaders like Rev. Justin Edwards anticipated that the quick deaths of confirmed drunkards would usher in the millennium of sobriety. The ATS's primary strategy was not to "suppress" the intemperance of the whiskey-drinking classes but to encourage the wine-drinking "respectability" to set a more inspiring example. They called upon moderate drinkers with positions of social prestige, especially politicians, to pledge publicly to abstain from alcohol.[8]

The temperance "pledge" soon took on a life of its own, drawing into the movement individuals with little taste for the ATS's orthodoxy, Federalism, or elitism. By 1833 a million members, organized in six thousand local societies, had taken the pledge. Unitarians and Universalists, despite their exclusion from the national leadership, played key roles in many local chapters. More important, countless alcoholics discovered that the pledge—especially in the strict, or "teetotal," form, which proscribed fermented drinks (beer, wine, and cider) as well as distilled spirits—was a vital tool for their own recovery. As these "reformed drunkards" joined temperance societies, those who had eyes to see realized that the example of the "reformed" could be as inspiring as that of the elite.[9]

Among the most perceptive was Gerrit Smith, the wealthy Finneyite reformer who was beginning his trek to radical liberalism. In an 1833 letter to Edward C. Delavan, secretary of the New York State Temperance Society, Smith reported on changes in his village of Peterboro, New York. Fourteen years earlier, "more than every other man in [Peterboro] was a drunkard," and drunkenness was the source of all the town's miseries. Yet even temperance activists, assuming "that the drunkard is beyond cure," did not reach out. It was "almost no crime not to feel for him." Given this background, Smith could only interpret the spontaneous reformation of drunkards as divine intervention—proof that temperance "has come down to us from heaven" and that *"the Temperance Reformation is itself the work of the Holy Spirit."* Smith filled his letter with the recovery stories of all of Peterboro's drunkards, finding in these stories the evidence of God's millennial presence.[10]

Smith was ahead of the crowd. It was another seven years before the temperance movement as a whole acknowledged the revelatory authority of reformed drunkards. In the wake of the 1837 panic, the Washingtonian movement was born. On 2 April 1840 a group of working-class alcoholics in Baltimore resolved to take the pledge together and then formed a mutual aid society to help themselves keep it. Soon drinkers in dozens of other cities gathered to take the pledge, share personal testimony, sing temperance songs, offer economic assistance to brothers in need, and finally go out in search of their communities' most desperate and destitute drinkers. Above all, the Washingtonians identified with one another. "The reformed man," explained one activist, "lifts the veil from his own heart and his suffering brother sees reflected every prism of his most ardent desire. Finally, he gains his confidence by kindness, and stirs within him an emulous spirit to rise from his degraded state and become a man among men."[11] Soon leaders took to the road, bringing sensational accounts of their reformation to packed urban audiences sprinkled with members of the older temperance constituency.

The genius of Washingtonianism was the way it tapped the sociability of working-class tavern culture for the temperance cause. With their fondness for coarse humor and boisterous singing and their antipathy to traditional reform societies, Washingtonians distressed many older activists. But the Washingtonian movement was far from exclusively working-class or alcoholic. It can, in fact, be better described as a creative meeting ground for reformed drunkards and more conventional reformers. For every reformer who took offense, there was another who was attracted and fascinated by the experience of the reformed. Washingtonianism also provided a refuge for activists who dissented from the orthodox theology and Whig politics of the ATS. Liberal and unorthodox denominations from both ends of the class spectrum were well represented among the Washingtonians.[12]

Washingtonian liberalism was more than a matter of denominational affiliation. To affirm that all alcoholics are capable of reforming was implicitly to deny the orthodox doctrines of total depravity and double predestination, while to assign leadership roles to reformed drunkards was an affront to orthodox clergymen who felt they should direct movements for social betterment. It is thus no surprise that Washingtonian speakers often resorted to anticlerical rhetoric, or that one Washingtonian convention formally disavowed the doctrine of total depravity. A few Washingtonians even recognized the affinity between their emphasis on moral suasion (at least initially, Washingtonians did not support legislative prohibition) and nonresistance by founding a Peace Washingtonian Society in Maine. Orthodox temperance groups, in response to such outbreaks of liberalism, suppressed the proceedings of Washingtonian conventions and bowdlerized seemingly innocuous Washingtonian songs. When the Washingtonians prayed that "God speed and prosper every plan / Whose basis is the good of man," the orthodox substituted "God speed and prosper every plan / That strives to bless poor sinful man."[13]

Most Washingtonians, however, were not interested in developing a comprehensive ideology of ultra liberalism. In terms of my typology, they were sentimental reformers: deeply committed to the practice of identification with victims but not preoccupied with the underlying theory. As such, they accepted the sentimental belief in the family as a source of sympathetic power beset by the tyrannical violence of larger institutions. By portraying drunkards as victims of the alcohol system, they suggested that the real violence was perpetrated by merchants who sold liquor, clergymen who discouraged their parishioners from taking the pledge, and bankers who exploited the intemperate. Families were victimized both by the alcohol itself and by the social system that promoted its use, while individual drunkards figured only as intermediary perpetrators of violence—in a sense both victims *and* perpetrators. This model of alcohol's violent effects was systemic and sociological rather than individualistic.

Twentieth-century historians have generally failed to recognize the systemic character of Washingtonian analysis because it used the political categories of liberal theory rather than the economic categories of Marxism. Both Marxists and Washingtonians looked behind the individual phenomenon of drunkenness to a larger pattern of social change, but they described the pattern in quite different terms. What was really happening in the antebellum period, from a Marxist perspective, was a shift from agrarian, family-centered production to an industrial capitalism that extorted enormous amounts of labor from workers (three thousand hours per year, compared with two thousand for a United States worker today and even less for a preindustrial farmer) and exacerbated class inequality.[14] From the perspective of the Washingtonians, who had to make do without statistics on wages and working hours, what was happening was that bankers and rumsellers were grabbing the violent authority once wielded by tyrants and priests. Unlike Marxism, this theory appealed to individuals of all classes, for it called upon them simply to sympathize with the ordinary people who were the tyrants' victims.

The heyday of Washingtonianism, and of temperance liberalism, was the early 1840s. By middecade the more respectable Washingtonians had been funneled into middle-class organizations such as the Sons of Temperance. The mutual aid and outreach efforts characteristic of Washingtonianism were downplayed in favor of prohibitionary legislation like the Maine Law. Yet the Washingtonian spirit lived on in temperance narratives. Abstinent members of the middle class, who may have felt they had expelled the demon of intemperance from their homes and communities, were brought face-to-face with alcohol's victims, of all classes, in the pages of these books. Moreover, temperance literature survived as a reminder of the centrality of moral suasion to any successful reform endeavor. Though temperance writers were as enthusiastic as anyone about the Maine Law (I have not seen a temperance tale that openly criticizes legislative prohibition), it remains the case that writing is, in itself, an act of moral suasion. It is an act of word power rather than state power.[15] And temperance writers always hoped that their words would redeem the victims of intemperance even without state support. "I draw aside the veil but for a moment," Arthur wrote in an 1843 tale, "would that some one might gaze with trembling on the picture, and be saved!"[16] To read a temperance tale was to be reminded that words might yet have a role to play in the struggle to free society—or oneself—from violence.

What literary models did writers like Arthur use to present victims' experiences? In some respects, the liberal family novel pioneered by Catharine Sedgwick and her peers was an important exemplar. Liberals challenged the power of tyrannical violence by placing the experiences—and powers—of its everyday victims at the center of their stories. But early liberals assumed that tyrannical violence was on the wane, virtually an anachronism in the egalitarian nineteenth century. They described ordinary people who had to struggle against violent authorities but whose lives were not defined by their victimization. Temperance activists, on the other hand, were convinced that tyranny, in its new guise as Demon Rum, was as potent as ever. They thus blended their family liberalism with the rhetorical practices of newspaper sensationalism, a genre whose reason for being was the depiction of extreme forms of violence. Ultimately, neither genre did much to connect readers with victims' experience: family liberalism downplayed the horrors of violence too much, while sensationalism stressed the violence itself at the expense of the people involved in it. The quest for the victim reached a new level when writers, particularly T. S. Arthur, began to draw on the testimonials of Washingtonian meetings as a new source of inspiration.

The Sensational Roots of Temperance Narrative

The first temperance writer to achieve wide recognition was in some ways the most sensational. Mason Locke Weems (1759–1825), popularly known as "Parson Weems," was an Episcopal minister who made his living as an itinerant book peddler in the employ of Philadelphia publisher Matthew Carey. Through his travels in the middle and southern states, Weems helped knit together a national reading public. He was also a prolific author who self-consciously sought to cater to the tastes of that public. His biography of George Washington (the source of the cherry tree legend) was one of the most popular books of the day, and he also wrote a series of scandalous reform pamphlets against such vices as adultery, murder, and drunkenness. As Weems freely admitted in his correspondence with Carey, his goal was not to advance any particular social agenda but simply to give the people what they wanted. That, apparently, was an ambivalent mix of graphic violence and vaguely liberal moralizing. Weems's *God's Revenge Against Drunkenness*, first published in 1812, can be seen as the founding text of temperance narrative.[17]

The thesis of *God's Revenge* is that alcohol is a demon with the power to overthrow the rational and virtuous *imago dei* within the human soul. "Drunkenness is a FLOOD that drowns the whole moral birth of the soul," wrote Weems; hence the drunkard is not merely "brutalized, but *devilized* by whiskey." Weems illustrates this thesis with dozens of examples of how the demons Moloch, Belial, and Satan lead drunkards into horrifying or ludicrous acts of hate, lust, and deceit. In one representative passage, he tells of how a single drink of rum inspires a workingman to murder his closest friend. As they sit together at lunch, "Harveson" impulsively picks up a sledgehammer and gives his friend "a blow direct on his forehead." Though the "little taylor" pleads pathetically for his life, his words cannot move Harveson: "Being drunk, and brutish as the swine that devours its own young, he regarded not the cries of the poor fallen supplicant, but lifting his blood-stained hammer, he dashed out his brains." Weems declines to narrate the prehistory or the aftermath of this murder: the physical event is all in all.[18]

On the face of it, the spontaneous murder of a friend defies explanation, especially in terms of liberal anthropology. Yet Weems's reform tracts were clearly influenced by such liberal theorists as Locke and Hutcheson. Weems's approach, somewhat typical of the ideologically contentious and frequently paranoid early national period, was to begin with liberal premises and take them to starkly illiberal conclusions. Thus in an earlier text, *God's Revenge Against Murder*, Weems articulated a threefold anthropology with clear Enlightenment antecedents. Humans possess an "animal nature," a "rational nature," and a "divine nature, which *loves!*" But this Hutchesonian understanding of the *imago dei* does not lead Weems to conclude that violence is unnecessary and easily avoided. Rather, he suggests that the divine image is easily destroyed by parents who nurture only the lower natures of their children. This is what happens to the heroine of *God's Revenge Against Murder*, Polly Middleton. Because her father does not educate her "to be the companion of a gentleman and Christian," she runs off with the "blackguard" Ned Findley. Ned is a "demon incarnate" who has managed to "stifle every sentiment of humanity." To get Polly's fortune, he takes her out in a boat, knocks her overboard with the oar, and beats her until she drowns.[19]

Weems, writing before the advent of most social reform societies, does not call on his readers to vindicate human nature by putting an end to such outrages. Instead, he complacently describes Polly Middleton's death as a fitting, divinely ordained judgment against her negligent father. Similarly, in *God's Revenge Against Drunkenness*, he uses Benjamin Rush's image of alcohol as a "moral thermometer" to suggest that God created alcohol to help separate the sheep from the goats. Alcohol has no effect, Weems asserts, on virtuous persons who have had their triune nature nurtured by good parents, but it brutalizes and demonizes those who have already succumbed to unhappiness as a result of bad upbringing.[20] It does not seem to have occurred to Weems that a truly benevolent God might hesitate to visit the sins of the fathers on their children. His repeated title suggests the center of his theology: Weems's deity is preeminently a God of "Revenge."

Imitating his vengeful God, Weems indulged in little benevolent sympathy for the human victims of neglect, violence, and intemperance. Many of Weems's stories revel in mockery of the drunkard, while others involve violence perpetrated by one drunkard against another. A drunkard roused to violence kills a peddler who is sleepily intoxicated; a drunken colonel tries to rape the wife of one of his soldiers and is murdered by the soldier, himself returning from a drunken frolic.[21] For readers who did not consider themselves to be drunkards, such stories may have inspired a revulsion against alcohol, but they also encouraged a complacent sense that sin is its own punishment, and that the virtuous need simply insulate themselves from sinners.

By blending the liberal faith in natural human affections with an orthodox view of God as a vindictive sovereign, Weems offered his readers the worst of both worlds. The orthodox believed that they were innately depraved and incapable of virtue, but they could nevertheless trust that their misdeeds had a secure place in God's plan and that divine grace would ultimately liberate them from sin. True liberals could believe that violence had no necessary place in a world that was fundamentally ordered by love. In a Weemsian world, by contrast, individuals must rely on their natural affections rather than on grace, but they cannot trust those affections to protect them from violence. The slightest lapse—of oneself or one's parents—is enough to cast the anxious individual into a hell of violence.

If Weems's is the worst of both worlds, why did so many readers enjoy his tracts? Though he denied his readers both the Reformed consolation of relying entirely on a sovereign God and the reformist consolation of joining others in building a better world, he did offer an easier consolation: that of simply being spectators of the violence. Many theorists have tried to explain why violent spectatorship is pleasurable, but it seems to me that a compelling explanation must begin with the repulsiveness of violence. To witness violence is, first of all, to imagine that one might also become a victim or perpetrator, and that is terrifying. But if the violence is narrated in such a manner as to make identification impossible (that is, if it is made ridiculous, or implausible, or restricted to a particular class of people such as drunkards), the initial terror gives way to a deeply pleasurable relief. Sensationalist texts posit that the world is pervasively violent, but they do so in such an extreme manner that most readers cannot help but think, well, the violence hasn't gotten to me yet. That pleasure is further enhanced by the sense that one is absolved of the duty of understanding the violence and the people involved in it more deeply, or of working toward healing. The basic strategy of sensationalism thus militates against the sympathetic identification that is at the heart of liberalism.

The Metaphysics of Demon Rum

Given his sensational aversion to identification and his lack of connection to organized social reform, Weems cannot be regarded as a representative temperance writer. But his texts cast a long shadow over subsequent temperance writings. Later writers were more sympathetic to individuals and optimistic about society than Weems, but they were not allergic to gore. They cataloged incidents of violence with little regard for subjective experience or narrative plausibility. "Midnight broils, broken heads, and bloody noses," Lucius M. Sargent wrote in an 1835 tale, "were as common in Still-Valley, as in any other village, possessing equal facilities for intoxication." Thurlow Brown, whose novel *Minnie Hermon* (1854) was a fictional history of the temperance movement with a strong reformist appeal to the reader, could describe domestic violence with a casual offhandedness akin to that of Weems. He tells, for instance, of "an old and respectable citizen" who sends his wife and baby out into a winter storm where they freeze to death, while he buries an ax in the head of his sleeping son.[22]

Like Weems, these writers assumed a causal connection between alcohol and violence. But they did not reduce individual drunkards to embodiments of violence. By placing their countless incidents of wife beating, child abuse, barroom brawling, dueling, and cold-blooded murder alongside still more countless incidents of parental neglect, unemployment, debt, and disease, they sought to demonstrate that alcohol—not alcoholics per se or men per se or physical violence per se—was the source of most of the destruction and misery in their society. General references to alcohol as a form of violence and murder were intended to suggest the whole range of intemperate evils. Thus, in her temperance collection, *Water-Drops*, Lydia Sigourney referred to intemperance as "that lunacy, which may transform protectors into murderers," but she did not imply that all drunkards murder their wives and children. Rather, the families of drunkards were dying of poverty, neglect, emotional abuse, *and* physical violence. "We read, too, of the murderers of fathers and the murderers of mothers," proclaims a temperance lecturer in *Nora Wilmot*; "the rumseller is the murderer of fathers, and the murderer of mothers, and of innocent children."[23]

For temperance writers, in short, alcohol rather than the alcoholic was the archmurderer. The imagery with which they made this point stood in a long tradition, evoking both liberal attacks on tyranny and priestcraft and the earlier Protestant assault on the papal Antichrist. "This hydra-headed monster," declared a character in an 1858 novel, "is the sum of all iniquities." A generation earlier, ATS leader John Marsh had announced that "it needed not a fable to award the prize of greatest ingenuity in malice and murder to the demon who invented brandy, over the demon who invented war." And Thurlow Brown resorted to the most potent image in the liberal and Protestant repertoire by describing Demon Rum as presiding over a series of unholy sacrifices: "The blood-offering of one murder ceases not to smoke upon the glutted shrine, before another victim is prepared from the bar-room. . . . The great fountain-head of crime sweeps on with increasing volume, and red-handed murder stalks forth even at noonday, with the axe and the knife hot with gore."[24] Alcohol was the ultimate idol.

Sentimental Practices in Temperance Narrative

Temperance writers were not, however, wholly preoccupied with the metaphysics of Demon Rum. Even as they demonized the alcohol system, they humanized the individuals entangled in it, calling upon their readers to identify sympathetically with the wives and children of drunkards, and ultimately with the drunkards themselves. Beginning around 1834, a new generation of temperance writers departed sharply from Weems by emphasizing the psychology of violence as much as its physicality. Lucius M. Sargent, for example, suggested that a father's violence could live on in a son long after the father's physical death. In "Kitty Grafton," the drunkard's son frequently dreams that his father is chasing him; and even during the day "he found himself occasionally afflicted with violent agitation; and that, at such times, he was apt to start and look around him, in terror."[25] This account, evocative of twentieth-century descriptions of posttraumatic stress, conveys a vivid sense of the depths of victimization. But temperance writers did not mean to convey a depressing sense of the hopeless plight of victims. On the contrary, they suggested that victims and survivors of intemperate violence can be potent mediators of divine love. Sargent's young hero, for example, grows up to be a faithful provider and role model for his younger siblings. This point is also illustrated in the two tales that made the drunkard's wife a staple character in temperance literature, Lydia Sigourney's "The Intemperate" and Sargent's "My Mother's Gold Ring."

"The Intemperate," which I will discuss in detail later, was published together with Gerrit Smith's letter to Edward Delavan in 1833, appeared in the *Religious Souvenir* in 1834, and was finally anthologized with Sigourney's other temperance fiction in *Water-Drops*. Though Sigourney's heroine can neither redeem her husband nor save the life of their son, she models the liberal pedagogy promoted by such Unitarian writers as Henry Ware Jr. and Catharine Sedgwick. (Sigourney herself was a Connecticut Congregationalist who, like most Connecticut liberals, converted to Episcopalianism.) She tells her son about God's fatherly care and Jesus' love for children, and helps him recognize the divine presence both in the Bible and in nature. By so doing, she mitigates the horror of his death and ensures his safe passage to heaven.

In "My Mother's Gold Ring," a tract that claimed at least 114 editions by 1848, Sargent's heroine has more this-worldly success because she gets an earlier start. On the very first day her husband drinks alcohol, their young son says that he smells like Isaac, the village's drunken fiddler—and receives a bloody nose for his innocent honesty. Suddenly awakened to her plight as a drunkard's wife, the heroine receives little support from the rumselling deacon or from their minister, who actively opposes the temperance pledge. But when her husband is imprisoned for debt, she discovers an effective strategy. She gives him her mother's gold ring as a reminder that he has promised not to drink. After a year passes, he feels confident enough to sign a pledge, and the happiness of their marriage is restored.[26]

Sargent was a Unitarian, and this tale illustrates his wariness of ministerial authority and his faith in familial love. Another liberal, Mary Anna Fox, expressed a similar faith in the family in her subtle reworking of Weems's thesis about familial neglect as the source of intemperance. Fox's novel *George Allen, the Only Son* (1835) introduces a stock character who was almost as prominent in temperance fiction as the drunkard's wife: the "only son" who becomes a drunkard as the result of lax parental discipline. George, son of a New England farmer, has "an ardent temperament, an eager thirst for enjoyment, and . . . no strength to resist temptation."[27] Despite the warnings of a benevolent Quaker who rescues George from drowning, his parents idolize George for his ardent nature and even allow him to share their toddy. This prepares him to be further corrupted at college, where he falls under the influence of an atheist named Theodore Wilson, who leads him to drink, gaming, and atheism.[28] Wilson's doctrine is "that man was formed for pleasure" and that all biblical teachings about the restraint of desire "were invented by a sect of stern misanthropes." When these doctrines fail to bring peace of mind, George realizes that he has been ruined by his parents and would have been better off if they had built on the strong evidence of divine Providence he received when rescued from drowning.[29]

Thus far, Fox's text conforms to the Weemsian model of a child ruined by parental neglect. But Fox's point is that George is doomed not by his parents but by his own mistaken belief—fueled by the orthodox doctrine of reprobation—that he is already ruined. Possessed by despair, George resolves to live in such a way as to punish his parents for their neglect. He moves to New Orleans, where he commits in rapid succession forgery, fraud, bank robbery, and murder, then flees to South America. On his twenty-second birthday, he returns home, dying of consumption. On his deathbed George is easily persuaded of the reality of God's justice, but he refuses to accept God's mercy: "Mercy and pardon, he would not think of. His whole soul was occupied with the fearful certainty, which he could not escape, of a judgment day, and the doom which awaited him; but even now, his emotions toward God, partook more of hatred, and sullen resistance, than of repentance or fear." Interestingly, this death is mirrored by George's father. Blaming himself for the murder of George's soul, he also refuses to accept divine mercy and lingers on, "a *lonely* and *heart-broken* man."[30]

It is significant that despair, not violence or even intemperance, is the final enemy in this story. In classic Protestant demonology, despair is the devil's most potent weapon, which he directs at the penitent sinner who is on the verge of acknowledging God's unconditional mercy. In the liberal critique, this theme is turned against orthodox theology, which is accused of actually promoting despair by teaching that God's mercy is extended only to the elect.

A variant on this theme appears in the autobiography of a Washingtonian named Charles T. Woodman. Woodman lays much of the blame for his alcoholism on his early encounters with the "tyranny" of church and school. His minister, who expected the traditional deference of colonial days, terrified him: "Whenever he visited my mother, I was afraid he came to bring the news of some calamity or to thunder forth reproof." The schoolmaster, for his part, relied heavily on a "large mahogany rule which the delinquent felt for hours after it had been frequently applied to his hand." Such "coercive" practices, Woodman explains, constrained "the expanding mind of the natural genius" and repressed the natural sentiments of "reverence" that would otherwise "spring spontaneously" from "the genial influence of love." Woodman implied that most drunkards had similarly had their natural impulses to goodness thwarted by "the frown of tyranny." "How many wrecks of men are there now in our midst," he wondered, "who have fallen victim to cold calculating men, who seek to enforce truth with a scourge."[31]

Not all Washingtonians shared Woodman's negative view of the church, but most agreed with him that alcoholism was not an expression of inborn depravity. It was, rather, the consequence of external forces that thwarted the individual's natural impulses toward goodness. John Bartholomew Gough, for example, devoted the first several pages of his autobiography to describing the happiness of his childhood and his close relationship with his mother, whose "heart was a fountain, whence the pure waters of affection never ceased to flow. Her very being seemed twined with mine." This allowed him to blame his alcoholism on his subsequent mistreatment by the cruel (but *not* alcoholic) family to whom he was indentured, and on his mother's early death.[32] Similarly, the pseudonymous author of *Autobiography of a Reformed Drunkard* claimed that any drunkard, no matter how dissolute, could be redeemed "PROVIDED THAT WHEN HE IS SOBER, THERE ARE ANY GENEROUS FEELINGS IN HIS BOSOM, ANY GOOD MOTIVES, TO WHICH YOU CAN APPEAL WITH ANY SORT OF EFFECT." The only irredeemable drunkard was one for whom drinking was "merely a consequence of his badness of heart"—and often that one was not even an especially heavy drinker.[33]

Since Washingtonians believed that most drunkards were inherently good, they assumed that the simple friendship of other drunkards had the power to save them. Thus, the turning point of Gough's autobiography comes when a stranger taps him on the shoulder, despite his disheveled appearance, and invites him to sign the pledge. This simple act is enough to reawaken his dormant goodness: "It went right to my heart, and like the wing of an angel troubled the waters in that stagnant pool of affection, and made them once more reflect a little of the light of human love." Once Gough takes the pledge, another stranger approaches him and promises to assist him whenever it is necessary. These entirely human experiences play the same role that a supernatural gift of grace would play in a traditional Protestant conversion narrative. Gough feels "rescued from the slough of despond" and, indeed, resurrected. "A new desire for life seemed suddenly to spring up; the universal boundary of human sympathy included even my wretched self in its cheering circle. And all these sensations were generated by a few kind words."[34]

Gough's reference to "kind words" is telling, for the Washingtonians consistently stressed the power of words to bring about social transformation. In particular, they relied on the temperance pledge, by which the drunkard publicly expressed his commitment to renounce the evils of drink, and the experience speech, in which he shared the details of his past violence with sympathetic peers. The experience speech echoed the conversion narrative required for membership in orthodox churches, though Washingtonians stressed the fact that it did not need to conform to a set pattern. Charles T. Woodman, for example, denounced "such reformers who believed that no man could be reformed from intemperance, but who conformed to the rules which their own narrow, prejudiced mind conceived to be the only ones right."[35]

The pledge and the experience speech were believed to have instantaneous power, and the central task of Washingtonian outreach was to persuade those who had despaired of themselves ("No one ever heard of men like me reforming") that the pledge would enable even them to reform. Once a man took the pledge, his Washingtonian friends worked assiduously to maximize his exposure to additional Washingtonian language by taking him to meetings, reading aloud temperance newspapers or stories, and establishing temperance libraries. Such activities created a ready market for temperance narratives, and they also inspired individual authors to produce them. The wild excitement of Washingtonianism in Baltimore also led T. S. Arthur, a financially strapped journeyman with no direct connection to "the evils of intemperance," to devote his life to temperance writing. Arthur's *Six Nights with the Washingtonians* (1842) borrowed its structure directly from the experience speech and set the agenda for all subsequent temperance writing.[36]

Why did Arthur see language as the one source of power able to surmount that of intemperate violence? Elaine Scarry's analysis of the dynamics of torture suggests part of the answer. Scarry suggests that bodily experiences in general, and experiences of pain in particular, are extremely difficult to communicate. Pain is an intensely private experience that at its peak cuts the sufferer off from all possibility of social connection, while language is intrinsically interpersonal. The effect of violence is to exacerbate the tension between body and voice: the perpetrator monopolizes linguistic power by reducing his or her victim to a silent body. But this is a betrayal of the true purpose of language, which is to connect embodied selves at the deepest possible level. By telling the stories of victims, temperance writers sought to regain the power of the embodied voice.

This project was driven by desire and fraught with paradox. Writers like Arthur yearned to tap the fervor of the Washingtonian meeting; they may have yearned likewise for the lost sociability of the barroom or the preindustrial family workshop; they may have even yearned in a sexual sense for the open and vulnerable body of the victim. "There is no sympathy so pure and tender," comments one temperance character, "as the genuine sympathy which flows from a heart that has itself known sorrow," and temperance writers imagined that sympathy as both useful and deeply pleasurable.[37] And yet, if they had not themselves known sorrow—and no one can truly know another's sorrow—might not their representations of victimization covertly identify with the perpetrator?

Temperance writers grappled with this paradox in several ways. Some juxtaposed claims for the authenticity of their narratives and acknowledgments of the inexpressibility of violent experience. Writing for an audience that had not fully overcome the orthodox antipathy to fiction, temperance writers assumed that their texts' power depended on their truthfulness. Lucius Sargent subtitled all his tales with the words "Founded on Fact," while Mary L. Fox claimed that *The Ruined Deacon* was not "'a *story* founded on fact;' but a relation of *facts themselves*, literally and substantially *true* in all its details." The potency of the Washingtonian experience speech inspired Arthur to claim that "in every one of the stories presented, there has been, as its groundwork, a basis of real incidents; and these have been detailed without any aim at artificial effect, but simply with a view to let truth and nature speak forth in their legitimate power and pathos."[38]

Yet one of Arthur's Washingtonians can describe his wife's "sufferings" only by claiming that they were in fact "beyond the power of human language to describe" and could only be "inferred from the fact, that in one year she sank into her grave." Maria Lamas likewise claimed that *The Glass* was a true story in which only the names were changed but then added that "pen cannot tell the mental and physical sufferings of the wife, the daughter, and the mother." And the editor of Sigourney's tale "The Intemperate" practically tripped over himself praising Sigourney for her impossible achievement. The emotions of a drunkard's wife, he asserts, are "too big for utterance" and yet "vividly presented to us"; the "woes" described by Sigourney are somehow also "indescribable and untold."[39]

The practice of these writers might be compared to that of mystics who oscillate between "cataphatic" (affirmative) and "apophatic" (negative) language for God, first piling up images of the divine and then rejecting all possible images. The mystics' point is that neither words nor silence is adequate to convey the awesome immediacy of the divine presence, which must be experienced anew by each believer.[40] Likewise, by failing to represent victimization exhaustively, temperance writers passed their own yearning for the victim on to their readers, underscoring the fact that sentimental identification is an unending task. Thus, Charles T. Woodman reminded his readers that no reformed drunkard could be "so lost to modesty as to tell *all* the disgusting reality."[41]

For his part, John Bartholomew Gough used the depiction of improbable scenes of intemperate violence to spur readers to deeper identification. Against critics who contended that Washingtonians deflected sympathy by narrating "such deeds, and . . . such scenes, as had never been witnessed," Gough held that the real problem was the critics' unwillingness to seek out drunkards and their families. "Perhaps they had not been witnessed by these skeptics and cavillers. Why? because they do not go where they were to be witnessed." Using an analogy anticipating Scarry's argument, Gough compared the critics to a person merely observing another's amputation: "The one had felt the excruciating agony of the operation, while the other could but indifferently conceive what it was."[42]

Gough clearly believed that it was difficult but not impossible to achieve sympathetic identification without cutting off one's own limb, or oneself becoming a drunkard or drunkard's wife. Temperance writers who—unlike Gough—were not themselves victims of intemperance expressed this belief by incorporating their own process of sentimental identification into their texts. Sargent, for example, introduced "My Mother's Gold Ring" by explaining that the drunkard's wife had confided her story in a "valued friend" who in turn enlisted Sargent's interest and sympathy.[43]

Thurlow Brown expanded this device in his temperance novel, *Minnie Hermon*. The narrator, a traveling temperance lecturer, first makes an impression on Mr. Fenton, a wealthy rumseller. Fenton tells how his father and his sons all died of drunkenness, and his mother of a broken heart. He then gives the narrator a manuscript written by an imprisoned friend. The manuscript tells how the friend discovered his father's cruelty to his mother when he found some letters his mother had written to her sister. Finally, we are presented with the letters themselves and encounter the mother's intense response to her victimization: "He mocks me. Great God! Martha, he mocks me in his drunken madness! He wildly laughs as I weep. To-day, I held our babe to him for a caress; he cruelly struck the innocent sleeper with his hand!"[44] These chains of sympathy reassure the reader that she does not need to leap alone over the chasm separating victims and witnesses of violence. A community of sympathetic hearts is already there to guide her.

Both Arthur and Sargent varied this strategy by representing themselves as sympathetic yet detached observers of the effects of intemperance.[45] In Arthur's *Ten Nights in a Bar-Room*, the narrator is a business traveler who visits Cedarville and its tavern; in *Six Nights with the Washingtonians*, he is a citizen of Baltimore who observes the rise of Washingtonianism and affirms that "at every step of his progress in these tales, the writer has felt with the actors—sympathizing with them in their heart-aching sorrows, and rejoicing with them when the morning has broken after a long night of affliction."[46] Like the liberal interlopers of historical fiction, these narrators show readers how to immerse themselves in the experience of suffering while retaining enough independence to keep observing and, perhaps, to save the day.

All these strategies reflect the liberal conviction that violence splits people apart, while language draws them back together. By writing temperance tales, Arthur and his peers expressed their faith in the superiority of linguistic power. They also followed the example of Washingtonian lecturers, who testified that language, particularly the experience speech, was an alternative to the violence they had once perpetrated against their families. In *Six Nights*, Arthur included a sketch of one such Washingtonian, a mechanic who traces his fall from speech to silence to violence, and his redemption through a renewal of speech. The mechanic's first harsh words to his wife, he tells his fellow Washingtonians, occurred when she chastised him for not accompanying her to church, just weeks after the birth of their first child. This incident generated a mix of guilt and resentment that led him to drink more and more, until he became "insane" and "saw all things through a false and perverted medium." Yet this insanity led first not to violence but to silence: "That moody silence, the silence as of the grave to Mary's gentlest affection, continued even while we sat at the tea-table. Once or twice she made a remark, but I did not reply." Though he was conscious "of the wrong I had done," the "evil spirit" of silence conspired with his own pride to prevent him from acting on his impulse to seek Mary's love and forgiveness.[47]

The speaker explains that his habits of silence persisted for several years before he resorted to violence to quiet a crying child. When his daughter failed to "hush," he began "beating her with all my strength"; when his wife intervened, he knocked her unconscious and kicked the child across the room. But the real damage caused by this climactic event was the deepening of his silent despair. "For about a week after I had struck that blow, I was a sober man; but my reflections, while sober, were too terrible, and at last, to drown these, I drank to intoxication." Only after his wife's death—caused more by persistent sadness than by direct abuse—did he discover the Washingtonians and regain hope in himself.[48]

Like Mary Anna Fox's "only son," this Washingtonian must struggle not merely against intemperance but ultimately against his own despair. This despair is of course analogous to orthodox reprobation, a doctrine that Arthur—a Swedenborgian—saw as a powerful impediment to both social reform and the acceptance of divine forgiveness. When people became convinced of their reprobation (or their status as drunkards), they lost all hope of transformation, but if they could be persuaded to see that hopelessness as itself the key to the problem, their hope of salvation would be restored. Arthur's contribution to the liberal critique was his stress on language—telling one's story—as the means by which one might gain sufficient distance from violence to let go of its despairing implications. Yet this was at best a fragile hope. Given the extent and persistence of intemperate violence, could temperance writers really identify divine omnipotence with the speaking voices of the reformed drunkard and his victim?

Demons, Providence, and Temperance Theology

Earlier, I suggested that liberal and nonresistant writers identified divine power with the affectionate sympathies of family members, though they sometimes betrayed doubts about the capacity of those sympathies to overcome all forms of earthly violence. Temperance writers magnified those doubts tenfold. They faced an evil that was contemporary and ongoing, unlike the tyrannies, priestcrafts, and wars of the past. For those directly touched by it, intemperance seemed an all-encompassing evil that left no facet of life untouched. "The modifications of drunkenness are infinite," wrote Sargent, "and the effects of drunkenness are infinite."[49] If temperance writers after Weems refused to see that evil as a manifestation of divine sovereignty, they could not dismiss it as ephemeral. Instead, they often treated it as a metaphysical principle at war with God for earthly dominion. They often succumbed, in short, to the old heresy of Manicheism, dividing all reality between angels and devils, God and Demon Rum.

From the beginning, temperance rhetoric relied on images of the demonic. In an 1829 address, ATS leader John Marsh compared intemperance to a "demon," a "worm eating at the vitals of the nation," and a "Juggernaut" crushing innocent children beneath its wheels. Others blasted "the Demon of Drink," "the demon of intemperance," "the Angel of the Plague," and "the Devil's viceregent upon earth." They compared alcohol to the serpent in Eden or noted that it opened a pathway to hell: "Liquor-selling is the way to ruin, and they who open the gates, as well as those who enter the downward path, alike go to destruction." Still others compared the drunkard's violence to demonic possession. "Wine made me a demon," says a drunkard in *Nora Wilmot*, after murdering a friend. "Why," asks a character in *Minnie Hermon*, "should our homes be transformed into hells, and the husband and father into a demon, to torture and kill?" In addition to underscoring the presence of satanic powers in the world, such imagery helped temperance writers make the drunkard a victim of his own violence, for the man who is violent only when possessed may in truth be a perfectly gentle husband. Thus, Thurlow Brown alleged that the rumseller "deliberately manufactures a kind husband and father into a devil, and a happy home into a hell, where the victim can torment his own wife and children!"[50]

Demonic imagery also figured prominently in the many Washingtonian accounts of the delirium tremens. Evidently, the hallucinations experienced by nineteenth-century alcoholics often drew on the contemporary iconography of hell. John Bartholomew Gough, sometimes known as the "poet of the d.t.s," gave several typical accounts in his autobiography:

> The next day those devils were after me; some of them were black and some white—of all colors, and in all shapes. This appears to me like a dream, but they were all around me with pitch forks and fire-brands and gaveling irons and pincers. . . . Then I wanted they should kill me right out; but this blue-bottle, fiery-eyed devil said they were not going to kill me in that way, but with the pincers he would pull off my finger nails; then my toe nails; then a finger; then a toe; then pull off one of my arms; then the other; then pull off my legs, and with that brand of fire they should burn up my body.[51]

Images of this sort allowed Washingtonian writers to draw a sharp line between their own created goodness and the diabolical powers that beset them.

The mere invocation of demonic imagery was not inherently Manichean. In orthodox theology, demons served as the left hand of divine sovereignty, imposing chastisements that ultimately fulfilled providential purposes. And by the antebellum period, belief in demons had become something of a shibboleth for the orthodox. The orthodox minister George Barrell Cheever, who would later clash with Gerrit Smith over the centrality of the Bible to the antislavery cause, faulted liberals for teaching "that God could pardon sin without an atonement, that the words *hell* and *devil* were mere figures of speech, and that all men would certainly be saved."[52]

It was perhaps no accident, then, that Cheever was the writer who guaranteed demonology a permanent place in the temperance literary tradition. His *The Dream: or The True History of Deacon Giles's Distillery* first appeared in a local paper in Salem, Massachusetts, and it achieved notoriety when a Salem distiller with a strong resemblance to Deacon Giles successfully sued Cheever for libel. It is a simple fable. Giles is an avaricious but outwardly pious distiller. His ancient distillery looks "like one of Vulcan's Stithies, translated from the infernal regions into this world." Yet Giles callously regards it as a suitable storage place for Bibles belonging to the local Bible Society. One Sabbath, Giles's workers quarrel and quit. He replaces them with a troop of slightly disguised demons, who work productively but magically inscribe all the barrels with such messages as "Insanity and Murder. Inquire at Deacon Giles's Distillery." The true nature of his business is thus exposed.[53]

Despite Cheever's claim to believe that "devil" and "hell" were more than figures of speech, one would not know it from his story. Like many temperance writers, he used demonology in a manner that would have been possible for the most agnostic of writers: as a rhetorical device underscoring the existence of things that are very, very bad. Unlike earlier orthodox writers, he did not suggest that Christians should interpret their demonic afflictions as revelations of God's will. On the contrary, he suggested that they fight vigorously against the demons. By suggesting that humans must defeat Satan's legions, he unwittingly undercut the orthodox confidence in God's providential government.

Less orthodox temperance writers strayed even further from traditional views of Providence, yet few were willing to repudiate it outright. Arthur, for example, was willing to concede that intemperance might have had a providential purpose in the past but not the present: "Whatever of evil uses in society it has had to perform, we are bold to believe are accomplished." Thurlow Brown came a little closer to abandoning the doctrine. In *Minnie Hermon*, an antitemperance minister describes a drunkard's murder of his family as an "*afflicting dispensation of Providence,*" only to be rebuked by a reformed drunkard who counters that it is "*a providence of RUM, inflicted by human devils!*"[54] Yet Brown seems to have been concerned more with the misuse of providential doctrine than with the doctrine itself, for elsewhere he attributed the temperance movement itself to providential intervention. Still, there is an important distinction, only implicit in temperance literature, between divine *intervention* and divine *government*. Most temperance writers could affirm only the former. They believed that the heavenly realm impinged on earthly existence in countless ways, but they did not see God's hand behind all earthly events, both good and evil.

The temperance stress on divine intervention rather than divine government appears clearly in the influential early portrait of the drunkard's wife, Lydia Sigourney's "The Intemperate." Steeped in the New England tradition, Sigourney borrowed and twisted the orthodox conventions of the Indian captivity narrative, as pioneered by such seventeenth-century writers as Mary Rowlandson. Sigourney's heroine, Jane Harwood, is a devout New Englander who follows her cruel husband to an Ohio homestead, hoping that removal from his intemperate companions will allow him to resume the industrious habits of his earlier life. As James leads his family through "by-paths of underwood and tangled weeds," Jane wonders if he would destroy the children if given a chance—a fear that echoes Mary Rowlandson's concerns about her Indian captors. Jane turns to God for sustenance and is "enabled to go on: for the strength that nerves a mother's frame, toiling for her sick child, is from God. She even endeavored to press on more rapidly than usual, fearing that if she fell behind, her husband would tear the sufferer from her arms, in some paroxysm of his savage intemperance." She interprets her situation typologically, identifying with Hagar: "Feelingly might she sympathize in the distress of the poor outcast from the tent of Abraham, who laid her famishing son among the shrubs, and sat down a good way off, saying, 'Let me not see the death of the child.' But this Christian mother was not in the desert, nor in despair. She looked upward to Him who is the refuge of the forsaken, and the comforter of those whose spirits are cast down."[55]

Like Rowlandson and other Puritan narrators, Jane sees God's hand sustaining her amid her trials, but unlike them, she does not see God's hand in the trials themselves. She does not interpret her experience as a divine judgment or as any part of the divine plan, nor does she suppose that she is being weaned from her past complacency or excessive dependence on other people. Sigourney does suggest that her heroine, like Rowlandson, is developing a more theocentric piety: "She found the necessity of deriving consolation, and the power of endurance, wholly from above." But it is not clear what Sigourney means by this. She certainly does not mean that it is bad to rely on a human network for support, for as soon as Jane arrives in Ohio, she finds her life transformed by the solicitude of her new neighbors: "As if by magic, what had seemed almost a prison, assumed a different aspect, under the ministry of active benevolence." Further, Sigourney does not seem to mean that divine love can be all-sufficient. She insists that the happiness of a wife or mother, unlike that of a philosopher, is bound up in her relations with other people: "She has woven the tendrils of her soul around many props. Each revolving year renders their support more necessary. They cannot waver, or warp, or break, but she must tremble and bleed." One can only conclude that the God to whom Jane so piously turns operates through earthly mediators who are themselves far from omnipotent.[56]

Ultimately, neither Jane Harwood nor her God can restore the earthly fortunes of her family. Her husband, despite some good resolutions, proceeds from bad to worse because he never seeks out "the strength of Omnipotence." (It is a curious Omnipotence that is omnipotent only when sought out!) Her beloved son steadily succumbs to ill health, aggravated by his father's cruelty: "The timid boy, in terror of his natural protector, withered away like a blighted flower." What Jane can accomplish, with divine aid, is the facilitation of her son's passage to angelhood. His very frailty is like "a voice from heaven" that urges her to cherish him "because, like the flower of grass, he must soon fade away." Following the stock prescriptions of liberal pedagogy, she portrays God as a loving father, emphasizes the gifts of nature, calls her son's attention to the manifestation of divine power in a storm, teaches him to cherish scriptural stories, and tells him often of Jesus' love for children. Above all, "She supplicated that the pencil which was to write upon his soul, might be guided from above." She is rewarded when her son dies peacefully while his father is away. Her initial "wail of piercing sorrow" transmutes itself into "a prayer of thanksgiving to Him who had released the dove-like spirit from the prison-house of pain, that it might taste the peace and mingle in the melody of heaven." She has given, the narrator concludes, "an angel back to heaven."[57]

In this death scene Sigourney effects an all-too-neat split between the demonic (and earthly!) realm of the violent father and the heavenly realm of the suffering son, with God's power effective only in the latter. This version of divine power is not trivial: it succeeds, for example, in forging a link between the body of the son and the voice of the mother, as well as a further link to the textual word and thus the reader. But it is not at all the sort of power presupposed by the Reformed doctrine of Providence. Where the Reformed tradition had built a doctrine of Providence in large part upon its demonology, Sigourney (and most temperance writers) divorced demonology and theology and built her doctrine of heaven exclusively upon a liberal angelology. To understand this new model of divine power, it is necessary to examine temperance angelology more closely.

Temperance Angels

Any angelology is by definition an account of the mediation of divine power—as is any non-Manichean demonology. If temperance writers emphasized the demonic far more than their liberal predecessors, they placed equal emphasis on the role of angels. The result was an ambivalent theology. Their sense of the pervasiveness of present violence made them unable to share the liberal affirmation of continuity between heaven and earth, but they took that violence too seriously to view it, with the orthodox, as a manifestation of divine power. All they had to fall back on was an angelology that, however vigorously asserted, was never completely effective in the earthly realm.[58]

Temperance writers described many sorts of angels. Some spoke of an "angel—temperance" in counterpoint to the demon of drink. Others suggested that "the angels were stirring deep down" in the souls of those who joined the movement.[59] Quite a few described the temperance pledge as a talisman, that is, an object with angelic powers.[60] But, in keeping with their emphasis on the mediation of divine power, most ascribed angelic qualities to ordinary mortals—above all to the very mothers, wives, and children who were the victims of intemperate violence. Saintly mothers, dead or alive, thus figure in countless tales. The heroine of *Nora Wilmot* devotes her life to temperance because her dying mother, herself a drunkard's wife, had urged her to "use all the influence God may ever give you against the vice of intemperance."[61]

In Sigourney's tale "The Widow and Her Son," a wayward young son, who "had been heard to express contempt for the authority of women," heads out to sea to avoid his reform-minded mother and sisters. His fall into dissipation is interrupted by visions of his mother's tears in the rain and his sister's dying face in a moonbeam. When he finally reforms and returns home, he realizes that his mother's constant prayers have saved him. And in *Minnie Hermon*, a reformer appeals to a drunkard on behalf of his wife, mother, and daughter: "Your sainted mother and wife are looking down from Heaven. Angels are weeping, Henry, and at home, . . . the only being who loves you on earth, weeps and prays for her father." Clearly, these writers assumed a special connection between angelic power and femininity. But this was tempered by a conviction that the capacity for angelhood was grounded in the Hutchesonian moral sense and thus shared by all people. "The principle of the moral constitution," proclaims a temperance lecturer in *Nora Wilmot*, "which exists in some degree in us all, leading us to experience a sensation of pain at the sight of wrong or cruelty, should become an absorbing element of every nature."[62]

Angelic status was a curious compound of power and pain. In some temperance texts, simply being a victim is enough to make one an angel. Infants achieve angelic status by dying peacefully after being brutalized by their fathers. In other cases, the experience of suffering invests the earthly angel with moral authority and sympathetic power.

In Brown's *Minnie Hermon*, the title character is a rumseller's daughter who has been victimized by her father but is nevertheless able to solace his other victims. Her angelic character is somehow enhanced both by her *success* in comforting others and in her *failure* to redeem her father. When she clings to her father despite his "coarse abuse and—*blows!*" the narrator compares her "pure spirit" to "an angel in unbroken darkness." Similarly, novelist Henrietta Rose suggested that the angels in heaven could not stomach, much less prevent, earthly violence. After describing a murder that occurs "with a demon-like fury," she adds that "the angels turned away from that sickening sight, and vailed [sic] their faces, lest their gushing sympathies should be too strongly excited."[63]

The Millennium of Temperance

Yet temperance writers could also envision an angelic power that was more than pie in the sky. Temperance angelology often merged with national millennialism to generate an extravagant vision of social transformation. Temperance writers linked their cause to republican rhetoric by referring to the pledge as "this document of freedom—this charter of liberty"; by having drunkards shout "Free again!" as they sign, and by capitalizing "Temperance Reformation" to place it on a par with the Protestant Reformation and the American Revolution. The editor who published Smith's letter together with Sigourney's story promised that by "redeeming the world from a more galling than Egyptian bondage," temperance "would soon reclaim this land of the Pilgrims from the curse of intemperance, and make it the fairest of all lands." And Henrietta Rose echoed liberal paeans to the Pilgrims by having a lecturer proclaim, "A new, a glorious light has arisen, a light that I would might shine over all the broad expanse of the whole habitable globe, and be written, as with the finger of God, in glaring capitals of light, in characters of unutterable brightness, upon the margins of the heavens, that all men might read the joyful tidings."[64]

Many temperance tales, moreover, concluded with millennial fantasies about the complete transformation of a village. These follow a distinctive pattern. The village is described as an agrarian community threatened by the larger market economy in the form of a new tavern or a distillery in the place of a grain mill; often it has an allegorical name like "Groggy Harbor" or "Still-Valley." The agents of millennial transformation are generally drunkards and their children. If the drunkard's wife plays a role, it is usually as an inspiring angel in heaven, not a still-living mortal. The son of the drunkard typically contributes by courageously naming his father's vice—as the little boys do in both "My Mother's God Ring" and Sargent's "A Word in Season"—or by successfully venturing out into the wider world. In Sargent's "Fritz Hazell," for example, the hero is adopted by a temperate farmer after his intemperate father kills his mother. As a young adult, Fritz chooses the career of a sailor, converts his shipmates to temperance, and then returns home to pursue a ministerial education. The heroes of "Seed Time and Harvest" and "Kitty Grafton" both flee their fathers' violence, only to return with enough wealth to finance temperance activism. The role of the drunkard's daughter, by contrast, is to stay close to home and persistently hold out the possibility of redemption to her father. In Arthur's "The Touching Reproof," for example, little June cries frequently over her father's drunkenness, participates eagerly in the temperance projects of her

Sabbath school, and collects scrap iron and rags to buy oranges for her sick mother. This pricks her father's conscience, and he signs the pledge.[65]

Temperance writers assumed that communal responses to this millennial vanguard of drunkards and their children would break down along class lines. In most tales, the cause is supported by other drunkards, individuals who have not prospered in a changing economy, yeoman farmers, and sailors. Its opponents are respectable church and community leaders—the very individuals who formed the core constituency of the American Temperance Society. Doctors resist the millennium by prescribing alcoholic medicines, ministers by preaching against binding pledges, bankers by defaulting on drunkards' farms, politicians by putting party before principle, and the wealthy by dismissing temperance societies as "well enough for the vulgar." But perhaps the most significant millennial enemy is the rumselling deacon who is too spiritually empty "to perceive the slightest incongruity between his office of deacon, and his calling, as rum-seller to the parish." By the tale's end, such characters lose their social standing to the temperance insurgency.[66]

The particular shape of the temperance millennium exposes the ambivalences underlying the temperance writers' model of angelic power. They appealed confidently to divine power, and yet they could not discern God's hand very clearly in the present shape of social arrangements. So they displaced God's power to heaven in the person of the dead mother and to the future in the person of the drunkard's child. By having the drunkard's son succeed in the larger world and then return to the agrarian village, they expressed their repugnance for the market economy and their awareness that market powers could not simply be repudiated. By making children the agents of a millennial overthrow of traditional elites, they both promoted radical social change and undercut hope for its realization. Could a God who refused to work through doctors, lawyers, bankers, or ministers really change society?

Fathers and Daughters

A little more should be said about one aspect of the temperance millennium. At its center, often, is a particularly intense emotional bond between the drunkard and his daughter. Though the drunkard's son may play a more significant instrumental role, it is the daughter's abiding devotion that provides the theological key. Her faith in her father's potential for reformation refutes the orthodox doctrine of reprobation, and her success in reforming him proves that the greatest power may coexist with the greatest vulnerability. Yet temperance scenes of daughterly devotion can be extremely disturbing to twentieth-century readers. Repeatedly, preadolescent girls who kiss, caress, and sleep in the same bed with their fathers are described as angels who will save their fathers from sin. Literary critic Karen Sánchez-Eppler has suggested that such scenes of "temperance in the bed of a child" derive their potency from incestuous sexuality and thus reconstitute the patterns of familial abuse they claim to overcome. Since "we cannot help but recognize [them] as scenes of pederasty and incest," it is shocking that the temperance writers "define this hardly veiled erotic contact not as abuse but as the surest and best antidote to abuse."[67]

Sánchez-Eppler's argument might be dismissed as anachronistic. Conventions about physical intimacy between parents and children have shifted in the past century and a half, and even today, many people would not interpret father-daughter kisses as evidence of incest. But the crux of the matter lies deeper. Sánchez-Eppler's critique of temperance narrative ultimately depends on her repudiation of liberal anthropology. She assumes, as temperance writers did not, that all alcoholic fathers abuse their children. (Even John Bartholomew Gough, who blamed his wife and child's deaths on his neglect, stressed his nonviolence: "I was naturally of a kind and humane disposition, and would turn aside from an unwillingness to hurt a worm.")[68] And she does not believe that these fathers can reform but assumes that any intimate act performed by a once-abusive father must be a new form of abuse. Ultimately, Sánchez-Eppler follows Foucault in regarding the family as such—not merely the alcoholic or violent family—as founded on abusive, incestuous sexuality. As a consequence, she offers no picture of what healthy intimacy between fathers and daughters might be like. And she simply dismisses the possibility that young girls—or stories about young girls—might possess genuine social power. If these premises are accepted, temperance angelology appears as a cruel form of false consciousness, which "discursively endow[s] both abused child and temperance tale with a power they too often and too painfully lacked."[69]

If Sánchez-Eppler's illiberal premises are forthrightly rejected, her argument falls. Yet temperance narrative rarely contains a forthright defense of liberal anthropology. Had temperance writers truly believed that family affection was powerful enough to redeem drunkards and reconcile relationships broken by abuse, they would have depicted more reconciliations between drunkards and their wives and sons. Instead, they suggested that the wife's salvation lay in heaven and the son's in the urban market. By leaving the daughter alone with dad, they mystified the function of angelic power, vesting it not in the daughter's humanness but in her vulnerability. The temperance quest for the victim thus ended not in the discovery of her essential humanity but in the mystification of her victimization.

Temperance Christology

The temperance approach to victimization was a step back from liberal Christology, as well as from liberal anthropology. Liberals did not fault the orthodox for emphasizing the salvific role of Jesus of Nazareth; on the contrary, they tried to make Jesus' gospel message the central authority in all aspects of human existence. What they objected to was the orthodox tendency to draw a sharp line between Jesus and the rest of humanity and to vest his salvific power in his status as victim of a divinely ordained sacrifice. For liberals, Jesus was the perfect embodiment of salvific powers inherent in all humanity rather than a supernatural savior. By ascribing salvific power to the young victims of violence, temperance writers followed liberalism in not treating Jesus as the *only* savior, but they tilted toward orthodoxy insofar as they presented their angels as saving exceptions—in their purity and vulnerability—to the ordinary rules of human existence.

Temperance writers invoked Christological imagery fairly often. Thurlow Brown referred to the temperance movement as "manger born" because it was not supported by social elites. Henrietta Rose compared female temperance activists to "that element in the Divine mind, which the scriptures represent by the sublime image of an eternally interceding high priest, who, having experienced every temptation of humanity, constantly urges all that can be thought in mitigation of justice."[70] And the single most influential temperance tale, T. S. Arthur's *Ten Nights in a Bar-Room*, recapitulates the entire passion of Christ in its story of drunkard Joe Morgan and his daughter Mary.

Ten Nights is a mythic account of the battle of heaven and hell that centers on several scenes of violence. These play a dual role. They expose the demonic possession of the present world, revealing it as a hell in which the violent spiral of revenge can play itself out to exhaustion. But they also create victims who in their victimization gain special access to the powers of heaven. The first violent scene occurs on the night of the narrator's second visit to Cedarville. Late in the evening, Simon Slade, the proprietor of the "Sickle and Sheaf," throws a bottle at the local drunkard, Joe Morgan, and accidentally strikes Morgan's daughter Mary, who has come to fetch him. It is fitting that Slade perpetrates violence against Mary, for he is a false father to her—the man who has craftily orchestrated her true father's downfall. Once, the reader gradually learns, Slade had been merely a hired hand at the mill owned by Morgan and his father. But where Morgan was easygoing and intemperate, Slade was industrious and grasping—and soon gained possession of the mill. A few years later, Slade sold the mill to open a first-rate tavern. While most of the townspeople praised Slade for putting Cedarville on the map, Morgan suddenly found himself both out of work and subject to the constant temptations of the tavern.

Even before Slade's attack on her, Mary has been introduced to the reader as a typical child angel whose "little pale face" and "soft blue eyes" have the power to silence a vulgar barroom crowd. Absolutely solicitous for her father's well-being, she repeatedly refuses to sleep until he is safe at home and "if he stayed out beyond a certain hour, would go for him, and lead him back, a very angel of love and patience." As she lies dying from her injuries, her angelic nature becomes ever more manifest, and her mother comments that "she is better fitted for heaven than for earth; and it may be that God is about to take her to himself. She's been a great comfort to me—and to you, Joe, more like a guardian angel than a child."[71]

The comment is telling, for the full measure of Mary's angelic power is directed at the redemption of her father. Sick in bed, she implores him never to visit the "Sickle and Sheaf" again. He promises only to wait until she is well, but she knows she will never recover. As she joyously anticipates her coming death and ascent to heaven, he succumbs to the delirium tremens. "You're my angel—my good angel, Mary," he tells her as he begs for aid, and she performs a sort of exorcism. She drives away his demons with her "angel-look," bestows upon him a "pure and fervent kiss," and at last watches over his sleep in the safety of her own bed: "The sphere of his loving, innocent child seemed to have overcome, at least for the time, the evil influences that were getting possession even of his external senses."[72]

Once Joe is well on his way to recovery, Mary tells him that God has called her home. He wants to go to heaven with her, but she says that he is not ready. She promises that she will return to be his guardian angel, and before she dies, she has a significant dream. As so often before, she finds herself heading to the tavern to retrieve her father. Twice she is stopped by Slade's bulldog, Nero, but when she sees Slade, she gets up her courage, walks by the dog, and enters the tavern. Once inside, she discovers that the tavern has become a store, with her own father's name on the door. Joe, neatly drugged, greets her and tells her that he is her new father. When she wakes and tells this dream to her father, he promises never to drink again. She dies joyously in his arms, and her spirit ascends to "the angels of the resurrection!"[73]

Through these events, Mary recapitulates the life, death, and resurrection of Jesus Christ. She casts out demons, performs a healing, descends into hell to defeat the devil (as well as the hound of hell) and liberate Adam, rises, promises her spirit, and ascends to heaven. Significantly, though, the theory of atonement implicit in Arthur's text is not the substitutionary atonement taught by Saint Anselm and Reformed orthodoxy but the ransom theory articulated by Tertullian and other early church fathers. According to this theory, Christ's sacrificial death is demanded not by God but by Satan. By accepting a victim untainted by sin, Satan oversteps the terms of his agreement with God, and Jesus is able to use his sojourn in hell to liberate its other inhabitants. Because it dissociated God from the institutions of worldly violence, the ransom theory was most plausible in the pre-Constantinian period of church history, when Christianity was still at odds with the Roman Empire. Similarly, it appealed to Arthur because it did not interfere with his liberal disavowal of the connection between God and violence. (I have not, however, found any evidence that he was directly familiar with patristic writings.)

Mary's redemptive journey paves the way for a millennial regeneration of Cedarville, with Joe Morgan, restored to his Adamic fatherhood, at its center. But this is not instantaneous. Just as Jesus' disciples waited years in anxious anticipation of his return, so must Joe Morgan wait as things elsewhere in Cedarville go from bad to worse. First Willy Hammond, the wayward "only son" of Cedarville's leading citizen, falls deep in debt to a crafty gambler. When they quarrel, the gambler stabs Willy and is himself killed by a lynch mob. When another gambler, Judge Lyman, jokes about the murder, the crowd tramples him to death, and all hell breaks loose. Unwilling "to witness the fiend-like conduct of men, all whose worst passions were stimulated by drink into the wildest fervour," the narrator retreats to the house of a friend. He compares the move to "a passage from Pandemonium to a heavenly region." The next day he returns to count the damage: furniture is broken; a door has been destroyed; "stains of blood, in drops, marks, and even dried-up pools," are everywhere; and the landlord Slade has lost an eye. It was all done, a genial hostler comments, by "a pack of blood thirsty devils"—and yet also by "as harmless persons as you will find in Cedarville when sober."[74]

Arthur's novel concludes with a final incident of violence: young Frank Slade's murder of his father. Frank appears early on as the endangered only son of parents "a little partial and over fond." The narrator frets constantly about Frank's increasing taste for the liquor he must dispense at the bar. By novel's end, Frank's relationship with Simon Slade has deteriorated to the point that, in an argument, he kills him with a bottle. Though Frank is in no way portrayed as a savior figure, this death of the false father (and the ruin of most of Cedarville's leading citizens) opens the way for Joe Morgan to resume his proper place and for the village's regeneration to commence. Together with another bereaved and virtuous father, Joe procures the "Sickle and Sheaf" as the site of a temperance meeting, at which the villagers resolve to destroy their stock of liquor and end the liquor trade in Cedarville. The novel thus ends at the eve of the millennium.[75]

Yet I wonder if Arthur's readers felt that they personally were at heaven's gate when they finished his novel. For individuals directly affected by intemperance or domestic violence, Arthur's account of Cedarville's hellish collapse may have rung truer than his vision of its heavenly rebirth. More important, the only path to the millennium Arthur offered his readers was the death of an impossibly innocent victim. If Mary Morgan was an appealing savior figure, she was not a model for emulation. By making his victim into a supernatural Christ, Arthur denied a human example to the victims among his readers.

5

Through the Blood-Stained Gate

Violence, Birth, and the *Imago Dei* in Fugitive Slave Narratives

All liberal reformers, I have suggested, struggled to resolve the tension between their liberal faith in the intrinsic goodness of human nature and their reformist sense of the actual depravity of human institutions. They were poised, in a sense, between birth and rebirth: between a conviction that the birth of each human being constitutes that person in God's image and an awareness that often a dramatic conversion is needed before that image becomes fully manifest. Unitarian pastors confronted this dilemma when they found themselves preaching rhapsodies about likeness to God to lukewarm congregations of smug merchants who were glad to have escaped the horrors of orthodoxy but indifferent to the higher demands of liberal Christianity. But the dilemma was hardly unique to official liberalism. During the early 1820s, as William Ellery Channing was organizing the American Unitarian Association and Catharine Sedgwick was translating the liberal gospel into novelistic form, the young Maryland slave Frederick Douglass wrestled with the same problem in a vastly different context.

Separated from his mother in infancy, Douglass spent the first few, happy years of his life at the remote cabin of his grandparents, Betsey and Isaac Bailey. Betsey Bailey provided the young boy with a comfortable and nurturing home, but she lacked the power to keep him there. When he was perhaps seven years old, still too young to walk the whole distance, she brought him twelve miles to the massive plantation of Maryland politician Edward Lloyd, where he was to begin a life of coerced labor. Here young Frederick met both his mother's sister, Esther, and his master, Captain Aaron Anthony. He had a vague sense—never confirmed—that Captain Anthony was his own father. Soon his observation of Anthony and Esther's interactions gave him a vivid idea of the likely circumstances of his own conception.

Esther was "a woman of noble form, and of graceful proportions," and Anthony obviously regarded her as his sexual property. When he found her in the company of another slave, Ned Roberts, Anthony was enraged. He stripped her to the waist, cursed her, and suspended her from a hook in the ceiling of the kitchen. Then, "after rolling up his sleeves, he commenced to lay on the heavy cowskin, and soon the warm, red blood (amid heart-rending shrieks from her, and horrid oaths from him) came dripping to the floor." Watching in terror from a closet, young Frederick identified with his aunt,

wondering if he would be the next victim of his master's violence. Recalling the incident two decades later, he described it as "the blood-stained gate, the entrance to the
hell of slavery, through which I was about to pass. It was a most terrible spectacle. I
wish I could commit to paper the feelings with which I beheld it."[1]

By placing himself at "the blood-stained gate," neither fully inside nor fully outside
"the hell of slavery," Douglass encapsulated the challenge faced by fugitive slaves who
sought to share their experiences with white abolitionists. They needed to present themselves both as slaves and as free human beings—both as victims who had been alienated
from God and consigned to "hell" by the dehumanizing violence of slavery *and* as survivors whose godlike nature could never be effaced by violent men. But which identity
came first? Had Douglass been conceived in the violence of his mother's rape and thus
condemned to the original sin of enslavement until, through the "conversion" of escape, he reconstituted himself as a free human being? Or had the image of God been
instilled at his birth and cultivated by his grandmother's nurture, only to be sacrificed
at the idolatrous altar of his violent master? Was he born a slave and then reborn as a
child of God, or vice versa? Again, how did Douglass's impulse to identify with Aunt
Esther correlate with his twofold identity as slave and human being? Did he wonder if
he would be next because he realized that he and Esther shared the universal human
capacity to suffer and survive pain, or because he dreaded that he, too, would soon be
rendered a helpless victim? If the latter, was his only alternative to identify with his
master and father, making Esther's victimization a ritual of his own freedom? Could a
victimized slave truly be a human being?[2]

Douglass's explicit answer echoed the strident liberalism of the Declaration of Independence. Full humanity was conferred at birth by God and nature; only subsequently
were some humans enslaved by tyrannical violence. The historical fact that Europeans
had kidnapped and enslaved Douglass's African ancestors dissolved the mystery of
slavery: "It was not *color*, but *crime*, not God, but *man*, that afforded the true explanation of the existence of slavery."[3] By divesting his enslavement of religious meaning and
claiming freedom as his birthright, Douglass asserted that loyalty to God and identification with his mother were one and the same. The self who had been enslaved and the
self who wrote the *Narrative* were likewise one and the same, both possessing the image
of God. But Douglass could make this claim only in the face of thousands of years of
theological tradition that had associated divine power with human violence and made
rituals of sacrificial violence the precursors to religious rebirth. Christians had always
been reluctant to regard natural birth and maternal nurture as sufficient warrants of
divine kinship. Had not the near sacrifice of Isaac been required before the Abrahamic
covenant could pass to his descendants as numberless as the stars? Had not Jesus' crucifixion been the price demanded by an angry God for the restoration of the *imago dei*?
And had not other slaves, most notoriously Phillis Wheatley, accepted their enslavement as God's strategy for Christianizing them? Who was Douglass to write slavery out
of God's providential plan?

Douglass's effort to demystify violence flew in the face not only of orthodox theology
but also of a profound narrative dilemma. As someone relatively free from physical danger,
could he presume to speak for those slaves who were silenced or even killed by their
masters' whips? And as someone capable of putting his words into writing, could he

fairly represent the experience of slaves who were trapped by enforced illiteracy? Simply to claim a voice in the face of slavery might seem to have placed him on the side of the masters rather than the slaves.[4]

It is no wonder, then, that Douglass disavowed his linguistic capacity to express fully the violence of slavery: "I wish I could commit to paper the feelings with which I beheld it." To have claimed otherwise would have been to betray his more utterly silenced aunt. Yet to have remained silent would also have been a betrayal. Douglass's task was not merely to assert his own voice but to find words for the voiceless experience of suffering. This act of giving voice to the victims can have such revolutionary power that Elaine Scarry has aptly compared it to "the birth of language itself."[5] Yet it is dangerous work. To give voice to the victims is to tread perilously close to the fascinating power of violence, to risk becoming the sacrificial priest one dreads so much.[6]

Douglass was not alone in his effort to reclaim his original humanity and divinity by giving voice to the victims. By the time of his escape, there existed a substantial community of abolitionists who, like post-Holocaust theologians of the twentieth century, recognized that no theological claim was adequate unless it could be made in the face of the whipping, rape, torture, and murder of millions of African American slaves.[7] When Douglass first told his story to an audience of abolitionists gathered at Nantucket in 1841, he encountered a community well prepared to see both his sufferings and his survival as evidence of the *imago dei*. "I think I never hated slavery so intensely as at that moment," recalled William Lloyd Garrison, "certainly, my perception of the enormous outrage which is inflicted by it, on the godlike nature of its victims, was rendered far more clear than ever."[8] By joining the abolitionist movement, Douglass became part of a vast collaborative effort of liberal whites and fugitive slaves, together seeking to acknowledge the full humanity of those who had been dehumanized by slavery's violence. The literary legacy of this collaboration was the fugitive slave narrative—a new genre that told the story of a courageous individual who passes through the blood-stained gate of enslavement but then passes back out, revealing the power of God's image in the act of escape.

The fugitive slave narrative became the antebellum period's most profound testimony to the liberal theology of the *imago dei*. Fugitive slave narrators testified that all people, even the most victimized, are able to grow in likeness to God, and that in turn God's love and power are most clearly manifest in the acts of these godlike humans. They denied that a violent rebirth is a necessary precondition to divinization, treating the *imago dei* instead as a universal birthright. They reconstructed the traditional theology of Providence, seeing God's hand clearly in their own quest for freedom but not at all in the institutions of slavery. Such institutions, for fugitive slave narrators, could be explained only in terms of the contingent, God-defying, and even demonic actions of human beings. For all its power, the theology of the fugitive slave narratives was marked by deep ambivalences. Was a God whose providential rule embraced the quest for freedom but not the institutions of enslavement truly omnipotent? Could identification with such a God provide the basis for life-giving identifications among human beings—particularly between white abolitionists and fugitive slaves, and between fugitive slaves and the mothers, fathers, sisters, and brothers they left behind? Fugitive slave narrators could invite their readers to look through the blood-stained gate, but they could not tear down all the walls of separation erected by slavery's violence.

What Is a Fugitive Slave Narrative?

My claim that the fugitive slave narrative expressed a liberal theology of the *imago dei* demands a careful definition of terms. I do not mean for this claim to apply to African American slave autobiography generally. Such noted autobiographers as Olaudah Equiano and Booker T. Washington were indeed African slaves in the Americas, but they did not write fugitive slave narratives in my sense—nor did they espouse a liberal theology of the *imago dei*. I define the fugitive slave narrative as an autobiographical, biographical, or fictional narrative that traces a slave's assertion of his or her full humanity through the repudiation of, and escape from, slavery. The struggle between slavery and freedom is thus by definition the organizing center of the fugitive slave narrative. I know of no exslave autobiographer who did not offer a negative view of slavery, but a great many declined to organize their life stories around the process of freedom. Even Equiano, who clearly had antislavery motives for writing his autobiography, made his conversion to Christianity, well after his manumission, the climax of his life story.[9] In a genuine fugitive slave narrative, the act of escape usurps the narrative function of conversion and becomes a source of ultimate religious meaning. And the religious meaning that fugitive slaves found in their escapes was consistently a *liberal* meaning.

While slave autobiographies appeared sporadically from the early days of the Atlantic slave trade until the deaths of the last former slaves in the early twentieth century, the fugitive slave narrative flowered during the heyday of the abolitionist movement, from 1836 to 1860. It was a uniquely collaborative genre, inspired by white abolitionists' desire to identify with the *imago dei* in the slave, as well as by fugitive slaves' desire to tell their stories. The abolitionist desire for the slave, perhaps fueled by the same economic anxieties that led temperance activists to focus on victim stories after the panic of 1837, was so intense that the fugitive slave narrative emerged as a genre even before many former slaves had been integrated into the abolitionist community. Abolitionists, it seems, had to imagine fugitive slaves in literature before they could find them in the flesh! Thus, of the four texts that established the genre in 1836 and 1837, one was an outright fiction written by a white abolitionist who had resided briefly in Georgia, one was written by a fugitive living in England, and two were produced under mysterious circumstances by white editors. Five years later, when Frederick Douglass began his career as a fugitive slave lecturer, fugitives still seemed so hard to find that he was greeted as a "'brand new fact'—the first one out."[10]

Soon enough, the fugitive slave became a fixture of the Northern lecture circuit, and such articulate ex-slaves as Douglass, William Wells Brown (c. 1816-84), Sojourner Truth (c. 1797-1883), James W. C. Pennington (1809-70), Josiah Henson (1789-1883), Jermain Loguen (1814-72), and Henry Bibb (b. 1815) became respected leaders of an abolitionist community that struggled to bridge the gaps between white and black, slave and free.[11] Douglass's *Narrative of Frederick Douglass* (1845), which William Andrews has called "the great enabling text of the first century of Afro-American autobiography," inspired a wave of narratives, some written by highly literate ex-slaves, others transcribed and freely edited by white abolitionists. These texts quickly found their market niche. The *Narrative* sold out its first edition of 5,000 in four months and sold 30,000 copies by 1850; William Wells Brown's narrative sold 11,000 in England alone by 1849; Josiah Henson's narrative sold 6,000 in three years, then 100,000 more after he gained notoriety as the alleged prototype of Uncle Tom.[12] The fugitive slave narrative obliterated the abolitionists' memory of earlier African American literary achievements. Phillis Wheatley, once heralded as proof of the genius of the slaves, was instantly eclipsed by Douglass's rising star.[13] Reflecting on a decade of literary triumphs, Douglass concluded that "the present will be looked to by after coming generations, as the age of anti-slavery literature—when supply on the gallop could not keep pace with the ever-growing demand—when a picture of a negro on the cover was a help to the sale of a book."[14]

Douglass's keen awareness of the "ever-growing demand" highlights the collaborative character of the fugitive slave narrative: it did not burst spontaneously from the experience of fugitive slaves. By stressing the role of abolitionist collaboration in the shaping of the genre, I am offering a perspective that complements the approaches of most previous studies of slave narratives. These fall into two general categories: historical studies that use the testimony of ex-slaves as a foundation for a more comprehensive history of slavery, and literary studies that treat slave narratives as the founding genre of the African American literary tradition.[15] Both sorts of study appropriately look to the narratives as a record of the slave's *own* voice; they consequently privilege those narratives written by ex-slaves without significant editorial intervention and tend to filter out the "values of the age," that is, the sentimental conventions and standard plot devices that shaped the narratives of even (or especially!) the most literate ex-slaves.[16] My study, by contrast, will focus on the white abolitionist *desire* to hear the voice of the slave, as well as the ex-slaves' response to that desire. I shall consider fictional, heavily edited, and genuinely autobiographical texts as each in its own way a product of the contested and cooperative encounter between ex-slaves and their Northern allies.

My approach complements the other two in several ways. First, it allows me to consider on their own terms three influential but highly fictionalized texts that have been neglected by scholars concerned to recover the authentic voice of the slave. These include Richard Hildreth's novel *The Slave; or the Memoirs of Archy Moore* (1836); the narrative of James Williams, which was transcribed and edited by John Greenleaf Whittier; and the narrative of Charles Ball, very freely edited by Isaac Fisher. Hildreth, son of a Unitarian minister and an iconoclastic Whig historian, anticipated by a decade Douglass's searching meditation on the dilemma of the enslaved son of a white master. The Williams narrative, widely distributed by the American Anti-Slavery Society and in many ways the prototype for later slave narratives, lapsed into obscurity after Southern critics successfully disproved its factual details. Ball's narrative, by contrast, contains many accurate details of life in South Carolina and has been widely cited as a source of historical evidence about slavery, but its peculiar literary status—one scholar compares it to "historical fiction based on very extensive research"—has not been analyzed.[17] Editor Fisher claimed, rather implausibly, to have taken his 517-page text "from the mouth" of an illiterate slave, though he also admitted that he was more concerned with "the sense and import" than the "identical words" of Ball's story.[18] I shall take Fisher largely at his word, treating his text, along with those of Hildreth and Whittier, as a hybrid product reflecting an actual conversation with a slave or at least a genuine encounter with slavery.

Second, my approach shares contemporary scholars' conviction that one cannot come to terms with slavery without encountering the voice of the slave, and thus emphasizes the ways in which white abolitionists' desire for identification led them to seek out slave voices. The antebellum project of solidarity in many ways prefigured the contemporary scholarly search for the slaves' authentic voice, even though abolitionist notions of authenticity differed in some profound ways from those held by twentieth-century scholars. My goal is *not* to depict the fugitive slave narrative as a product of the white abolitionist imagination but to show that it emerged from a series of difficult but creative white-black encounters. My account will thus move from the imaginations of such writers as Hildreth, Whittier, and Fisher to the complex responses of Frederick Douglass and other black abolitionists who demanded that their white audience encounter them as full human beings: body, voice, and soul.

Finally, my approach is complementary because it in no way seeks to displace previous readings of the fugitive slave narratives. It is *another* reading, not a better one. It is possible to place the fugitive slave narrative both within a long black literary tradition that stretches back not only to Equiano but also to the African narrative traditions brought by slaves to the Americas *and* within the more intermittent history of white-black solidarity, which enjoyed one of its most creative periods between 1836 and 1860. By focusing on the theological dimension of this period of solidarity, I also hope to provide a particularly close complement to the work of those theological scholars who have been uncovering the "slave theology" of survival and resistance.[19]

The White Desire for Slave Bodies and Voices

White abolitionists composed or edited fugitive slave narratives because they desired to deepen their identification with their brothers and sisters in chains; fugitive slaves told their painful stories because they had been invited to do so by white abolitionists and because they shared the abolitionists' faith that whites were capable of recognizing their common humanity. From the beginning, attempts to promote identification focused on familial relationships. Most whites, abolitionists believed, could relate to the slaves' love for their children and their often frustrated desire to protect them from harm. These were the traits that liberals characteristically invoked as evidence of the essential identity between God and humanity. Thus, the liberal plea for identification was twofold. By identifying with slave families, abolitionists also identified with the parental God whose image they saw in the slaves. In an abolitionist hymn from 1831, Eliza Lee Cabot Follen encapsulated this dual identification by juxtaposing images of a free mother caring for her child, a slave mother whose child has been sold away from her, and a loving God in heaven:

> Mother! whene'er around your child
>   You clasp your arms in love,
> And when, with grateful joy, you raise
>   Your eyes to God above,
> Think of the negro mother, when
>   Her child is torn away,
> Sold for a little slave,—O, then
>   For that poor mother pray![20]

Subsequent verses address fathers, brothers, and sisters: ultimately, the abolitionist goal was to incorporate all humanity into one divine family.

For Follen, it was not enough merely to claim that whites and blacks were alike; it had to be shown that both groups were familially connected and vulnerable to bodily pain. Similar motifs were ubiquitous in abolitionist literature. When abolitionist John Rankin attempted to convert his slaveholding brother to the cause of humanity, he offered a sentimental fantasy of himself, his wife, and his children in a slave coffle, being dragged to sale in a vicious Southern market.[21] And when Frederick Douglass sought support for the fugitive George Latimer, in his very first public letter, he first noted that Latimer was "a man—a brother—a husband—a father, stamped with the likeness of the eternal God." He then asked the "men, husbands and fathers of Massachusetts" to "put yourselves in the place of George Latimer; feel his pain and anxiety of mind; give vent to the groans that are breaking through his fever-parched lips, from a heart emersed in the deepest agony and suffering; rattle his chains; let his prospects be yours."[22]

The leading purveyor of such sentimental images throughout the 1830s was William Lloyd Garrison's newspaper, the *Liberator*. The first issue opened with a poetic "Salutation," written by "a lady, who sustains a high reputation for poetical merit, and whose soul is overflowing with philanthropic emotion." In the poem, the *Liberator* is personified and introduces itself to the world: "My name is 'LIBERATOR'! I propose / to hurl my shafts at freedom's foes!" The journal then addresses its readers not as isolated individuals but as parents, children, brothers, sisters, and lovers. It asks parents to identify with slave parents whose children have been "rent from thy breast, like branches from the tree." It reminds lovers that love is incompatible with slavery because "naught e'er was found / in lover's breast, save cords of love." And it concludes by asking New England pointedly, "Do you not hear your sister States resound / With Afric's cries to have her sons unbound?"[23]

The *Liberator* did more than wax poetic about identification between whites and slaves. From the beginning, Garrison was committed to listening to former slaves and free blacks—indeed, without their input he might never have begun his magazine at all. In 1831 most antislavery whites supported the American Colonization Society, which sought to end slavery gradually by "colonizing" the free blacks in Africa. Most free blacks, by contrast, wanted to remain in the United States and saw colonization as a racist scheme to deprive them of full citizenship. Free blacks had their own organizations and journals in mid-Atlantic seaports like Baltimore and Philadelphia, and Garrison got to know many of them while working for the *Genius of Universal Emancipation* in Baltimore. His innovation was simply to bring the case against colonization—and against racism—to a white audience.[24] By locating his journal in Boston, he ensured that his readership would include not only free blacks (though these accounted for most of his financial support in the early years) but also reform-minded Unitarians, Congregationalists, and Quakers. These white readers were thoroughly familiar with the liberal theology of the *imago dei* and with sentimental literature, but they had scant previous exposure to actual slaves.[25] Garrison thus employed several strategies to introduce his white readers to the slaves.

First, Garrison exposed white readers to the issues that preoccupied the black community. Through the first year of publication, he devoted a considerable portion of his pages to the debate over David Walker's "Appeal to the Colored Citizens of the World." Walker was a leader in Boston's small community of free blacks who had written a pamphlet advocating slave rebellion—and died under mysterious circumstances shortly thereafter. Garrison welcomed the contributions of letter writers who believed Walker had been murdered; for his own part, he disavowed Walker's violence while suggesting that anyone who had supported the United States Revolution should also support slave insurrections. Garrison also embraced the free blacks' campaign to repeal Massachusetts' antimiscegenation statute. Repeatedly, he reprinted the text of the statute under such headlines as "Liberty in Massachusetts!!" or "Disgraceful Enactment." "Why, then," he editorialized ironically on one occasion, "let us have a law prohibiting tall people from marrying short ones, and fat people lean ones."[26]

Second, Garrison made the *Liberator* a forum for African American writers and activists. The fourth issue, for example, contained at least three letters from free blacks, along with an editorial comment that "we are really proud of our paper this week. Our colored brethren prove themselves not only rational beings, but very clever writers." A few weeks later Garrison reprinted the "Address to the Citizens of New-York" by an African American organization there. This text criticized racism as well as slavery, insisting that "a difference of color is not a difference of species." It also appealed to the Declaration of Independence as the basis of shared citizenship: "The time must come when the Declaration of Independence will be felt in the heart, as well as uttered from the mouth, and when the rights of all shall be properly acknowledged and appreciated. God hasten that time. This is our home, and this our country." The same issue contained a letter from black leader Paul Cuffee, who urged his brothers and sisters to more forthright activism: "Why inactive? why asleep? . . . are you not men—formed like any other of the human species—moulded after the pure image of your Creator—endowed with capacity—invested with all the perfections which Deity has given to man?"[27]

Garrison's white readers did not only want to hear black voices, however. They also wanted to see black bodies—that is, they wanted concrete evidence of the ways in which the divine image was systematically effaced by slaveholding violence. And from the beginning, Garrison was committed to giving his New England readers a graphic picture of slavery. When he was working for Benjamin Lundy's *Genius of Universal Emancipation*, he had revived the "Black List," which listed accounts of atrocities from periodicals and private correspondence.[28] Similarly, the first issue of the *Liberator* contains several accounts of slave trading in Washington, D.C., including an article from the *Washington Spectator* contrasting a presidential parade with "another kind of procession . . . that consisted of colored human beings, handcuffed in pairs, and driven along by what had the appearance of a man on a horse!" In the fifth issue a correspondent named "A.L." suggested that the paper print a "Slavery Record" listing "murders of blacks by whites, and of whites by blacks, cruelties inflicted on blacks, insurrections and plots of slaves, separations of families in sales, cases of the internal slave trade, kidnappings of free blacks," along with an annual index of atrocities. The exposure of such "horrors," this correspondent believed, would stir "public opinion" to overthrow the system. He or she saw no tension between the paper's presentation of free black voices and broken black bodies.[29]

The first "Slavery Record," which appeared a week later, was not quite as systematic as "A.L." had imagined. Rather than compiling objective data about slavery's violence, it simply reprinted advertisements, culled from Southern papers, for slave auctions and for the recovery of fugitives. Garrison's editorial comment drew an analogy between Southern slavery and the horrors of hell: "Is this a comprehensive view of the commercial transactions of Pandemonium?"[30] The power of the "Slavery Record" lay in the way it turned the slaveholder's own voice to abolitionist purposes. In runaway advertisements, in particular, the master was forced to give a detailed account of the physical marks of violence—"the marks of the whip on the backs of women, the iron collars about the neck, the gun-shot wounds, and the traces of the branding iron"—in order to identify the fugitive.[31] The slave owner became a witness against himself, testifying that violence was intrinsic to the property relation of slavery. Soon the *Liberator* and other journals became filled with such self-subverting quotations.

Garrison's strategy of using the words of the slaveholders against them was embraced with great enthusiasm by fellow abolitionist Theodore Dwight Weld, who spent the winter of 1838–39 at the New York Commercial Reading Room culling twenty thousand Southern newspapers for evidence of slaveholding atrocity. Combining these stories with anecdotes from abolitionists who had spent time in the South, Weld produced *American Slavery as It Is*, which sold one hundred thousand copies in its first year and became the handbook of the antislavery movement from then on. Subsequently, few fugitive slave narratives were published without an appendix of corroborating evidence from Southern journals.[32]

The self-subverting quotation ironically manipulated the "opposition of body and voice" described by Elaine Scarry. In its original context, a slave advertisement linked the slave's bodily pain to the master's linguistic power. It pointed to a body, and more specifically to a wound or a scar, in a way that did *not* invite the reader to show compassion or seek relation but rather reinforced the accompanying narrative claim that the body was the property of a particular individual who might offer a reward for its recovery. Clearly such a body, deprived of its voice and personhood, could have no moral claim on the reader! Instead, the reader's attention was drawn *from* the slave's body to the owner's voice. Reprinted in the *Liberator*, the same advertisement allowed the Northern reader to move in the opposite direction, from the owner's voice to the slave's body. It thus exposed the owner's voice as founded and dependent on the practice of violence. Yet this exposure and delegitimation of the owner's voice did nothing to overthrow the owner's linguistic monopoly: he was still the only one speaking! Reprinted advertisements offered a static vision of the horrors of slavery without suggesting any way out; they showed the marks of violence but failed to narrate it as an event that might be survived. Like the atrocity stories that filled popular newspapers, they may have inspired revulsion and a desire to retreat into a safe, private world rather than a desire for solidarity.

It did not occur to white abolitionists that their preoccupation with slave bodies might be an impediment to their hearing slave voices and thus recognizing the slaves' full humanity. On the contrary, they assumed that slave bodies and slave voices were inseparable. To hear the slave's voice was simply to enter more deeply into the embodied experience of suffering. The success of the self-subverting quotation thus inspired some abolitionists to seek a more extended, narrative encounter with the enslaved body. By 1837 the *Liberator* was advertising the sale of a handful of book-length slave narratives, along with Richard Hildreth's fictional narrative, *Archy Moore*. Shortly thereafter, a group of abolitionists met a man named James Williams, who claimed to have escaped slavery with a harrowing story to tell. Disavowing "that abstract and delicate philanthropy which hesitates to bring itself in contact with the sufferer," John Greenleaf Whittier edited the story, which became the *Authentic Narrative of James Williams*. "THE SLAVE," Whittier boldly proclaimed, "HAS SPOKEN FOR HIMSELF."[33]

But this claim raised a problem. Could a slave truly have a voice? If slavery was as utterly dehumanizing as the atrocity stories suggested, how could its victims manage to speak at all? Could a human voice really be found in a body dehumanized by violence? The abolitionist editors' lingering doubts appeared in their choice to authenticate the narratives by appealing not to the slave's voice but to the slave's body, on the one hand, and to the master's voice, on the other. Moses Roper, who published his narrative in England in 1837, validated his account of his first whipping by claiming that "this may appear incredible, but the marks which they left at present remain on my body, a standing testimony to the truth of this statement of his severity." Whittier, like nearly every abolitionist editor, established the veracity of his narrative by including four pages of runaway advertisements. And most early producers of fugitive slave narratives, black as well as white, maintained a strictly objective tone, stressing the physical facts of slavery over their existential implications. They withheld the selfhood of the slaves, even though this was what their white readers most deeply desired.[34]

The point of the early fugitive slave narratives, in short, was to offer the reader an authentic slave body rather than an authentic slave *voice*. Telling evidence for this appears in the two introductions to the 1837 New York edition of the Charles Ball narrative, both of which struggle to explain the connection between the illiterate fugitive Charles Ball and his 517-page story. "The narrative," editor Isaac Fisher asserted in his preface, "is taken from the mouth of the adventurer himself; and if the copy does not retain the identical words of the original, the sense and import, at least, are faithfully preserved." The anonymous author of a separate introduction placed even more distance between Ball's voice and Fisher's text by describing a "private communication" in which Fisher had acknowledged his insertion of numerous anecdotes of slave life derived not from Ball but from "other and creditable sources." This seems to have troubled him less than the possibility that Ball's "vanity" and "forgetfulness" might have impaired his ability to tell his own story! The important point, he concluded, was that there was no reason to consider Ball and Fisher's account of the *violence* of slavery to be exaggerated. *That* was amply proven by a series of newspaper accounts of slaves who suffered horrible murders.[35]

Early fugitive slave narrators expressed their concern for the slave body in several ways. Most simply imposed a narrative superstructure on catalogs of violence not unlike Bourne's *Picture of Slavery*, Weld's *American Slavery*, and the advertisements and newspaper clippings printed at the beginning or end of the narrative. This is especially true of the Ball, Williams, and Roper narratives, each of which recounted incident after incident of horrific violence along a relatively undeveloped connecting plot line. These texts placed particular emphasis on the machinery of violence, describing everything from ordinary whips and paddles to "bells" (metal contraptions attached to a slave's neck to prevent escape) and elaborate torture machines—often with illustrations. In the Ball narrative, a description of a whip grew into an extended meditation on the sheer material horror of slavery, as Ball detailed the dimensions of the whip (ten feet long, with a twenty-inch staff and a nine-inch "cracker"); its composition (catgut, lead, buckskin, and sewing silk); its construction (the buckskin is tanned until hard and then closely plaited, the silk is "twisted and knotted"); the skills required to use it; and its effects: "The cow-hide and hickory, bruise and mangle the flesh of the sufferer; but this whip cuts, when expertly applied, almost as keen as a knife, and never bruises the flesh, nor injures the bones." Both Ball and Williams included lengthy accounts of cat-hauling, or the dragging of an angry cat along a slave's back, and Roper included illustrations of a seven-foot-high system of bells and a carousel-like machine on which slaves were hung and spun. Roper told of a South Carolina farmer who placed disobedient slaves in a barrel studded with nails and rolled them down a hill; he also described having his own hands and feet squeezed and pounded until his nails popped out. Williams described a water torture in which the slave was chained to the bottom of a cistern and forced to pump constantly for twenty-four hours to keep from drowning, while Ball characterized the popular shower torture as a "temporary murder," which nevertheless left the slave able to return to work in a day or two.[36]

In most cases, the early narratives provided intimate physical detail for violent events that the slave narrator did not personally suffer but merely witnessed.[37] This is another way in which these narratives failed to restore the link between body and voice: to the extent that they represented a slave with a voice, they distinguished that slave from the slave whose body was broken by violence. The early chapters of the Ball and Williams narratives are essentially travelogues of relatively privileged slaves who witness and occasionally perpetrate the horrors of slavery but rarely suffer them directly. Williams tells of a happy childhood with a kind family, which is only partly interrupted when his young master places him as slave driver (that is, assistant overseer) on an Alabama plantation, where he is required to whip his friends or "feel the accursed lash upon my own back, if feelings of humanity should perchance overcome the selfishness of misery." Though Williams makes much of the psychological dilemma of having to serve under a fiendish, alcoholic overseer who tries to isolate him from his kin, he does not initially dwell on his own physical vulnerability. Instead, he juxtaposes the vulnerability of others to his own privilege. He tells, for example, of his participation, with the overseer and a pack of vicious dogs, in the search for a runaway slave named little John. They find his body "nearly naked, and dreadfully mangled" only after the dogs have done their work.[38] Williams is here at least as detached and complicit as his white readers.

In the Ball narrative, the tension between the body of the victimized slave and the narrative voice of the unvictimized slave emerges in a series of conversations with the less fortunate slaves Ball meets during his travels through the South. A man who was caught cooking a stolen sheep tells Ball of being knocked down with a cane, beaten, tied up, and left overnight with the ropes so tight around his wrists "that before morning the blood had burst out under my finger nails; but I suppose my master slept soundly for all that." An African slave shares a lengthy account of his happy childhood, kidnapping, and horrifying experiences aboard a slave ship. In relating these stories, Ball places particular emphasis on the bodily circumstances of his conversation partner, offering graphic details of slavery's power to transform the human body. One passage describes a runaway African slave, Paul, whose body has been so transformed by punishments and ill treatment that Ball mistakes him for a specter. Paul wears an iron collar around his neck and an "iron rod, extending from one shoulder over his head to the other, with the bells fastened at the top of the arch." Ball also notes the scarred ridges on Paul's back and the "dusky white" discoloration of his skin. A few days after their conversation, Ball discovers Paul's body hanging from a tree and being devoured by carrion birds; he has hung himself.[39]

In this scene Ball figures as a sympathetic but tangential observer of Paul's plight. Often, however, his relation to the violent incidents he describes is more ambivalent. He tells, for example, of his role in the investigation of a neighboring slaveholder's murder. Despite his usual qualms about intervening in conflicts between slaves and masters, he fingers the culprits—the murder victim's enslaved mistress and her mulatto lover. This leads not only to the execution of the culprits but also to the whipping of Billy, an innocent slave who witnessed the murder but was too frightened to report it. Ball watches attentively as Billy receives an astonishing five hundred lashes, noting with horror that the pain is so intense that Billy cannot even groan: "I saw flakes of flesh as long as my finger fall out of the gashes in his back; and I believe he was insensible during all the time that he was receiving the last two hundred lashes." The perpetrators of this outrage are equally insensible in their own way. Once the whipping is over, they gather under a tree to chat, drink punch, and wait for their dinner.[40] By juxtaposing Billy's voicelessness to the unconcerned sociability of the perpetrators, Ball's narration of this event testifies eloquently to the opposition of body and voice inherent in the violent event. But what should we make of an eloquent testimony to the opposition of body and voice that comes from the mouth of one who helped bring about the violent event? Does Ball's ability to witness this event without becoming bodily involved or losing his voice place him on the wrong side of the rift between victim and perpetrator? And does the readers' stance as uninvolved witnesses also place *them* on the wrong side?

The effect of such passages is simultaneously to offer the reader the victimized body of the slave and to withdraw it, substituting the problematic voice of a thus-far unvictimized and perhaps even complicit slave narrator. The northern white abolitionist's desire for an authentic encounter with the slave's body is not met by this text but simply reconstituted: here are the bodies you want, but you cannot have them. As a successful fugitive from slavery, Ball is perhaps not "really" a slave at all; but as undeniably enslaved, Paul and Billy are always fugitive from the reader. Their fugitive status is enhanced for the reader who has read the introduction carefully and knows that Paul and Billy may not have been acquaintances of Charles Ball at all but simply "anecdotes" taken from unknown sources and introduced by Fisher for literary effect. The reader is thus denied the chance to transcend the opposition of body and voice by identifying with a suffering slave. She is trapped in the text.

The reader's dilemma seems to be resolved later in the texts, when Ball and Williams at last describe their own victimization. The two accounts are remarkably similar. Both Ball and Williams are forced to serve for extended periods as slave drivers (a common theme in slave narratives from Equiano on), and in both cases their own humanity exposes them to the very violence they are expected to mete out to others. Williams is flogged for only pretending to whip female slaves, while Ball—who acknowledges his own hardening in the role of driver—is victimized by his mistress's brothers, who decide he is too proud and that "a good whipping would be good for me." Both whippings are placed immediately after the narrator has been complicit in an especially horrific act of violence (Billy's whipping in Ball's text, the whipping murder of a pregnant woman in the Williams narrative). By the standards previously set in their narratives, Ball and Williams themselves receive only garden-variety whippings: Ball, for example, receives three hundred lashes to Billy's five hundred. Their intimate, detailed accounts of the pain they experience thus reinforce the notion that the greatest horrors of slavery are beyond description. Simply being tied to a tree, according to Williams, produces an "almost intolerable" agony: "I felt a sense of painful suffocation, and could scarcely catch my breath." Ball offers a literally blow-by-blow account of his own experience, moving from "a sensation that I can only liken to streams of scalding water, running along my back," to "a dead and painful aching, which seemed to extend to my very backbone."[41]

Both accounts emphasize the linguistic disempowerment, social isolation, and reduction into the body characteristic (according to Scarry) of violent experience. Williams tells of fainting during the whipping and of spending the next three weeks lying "with my face downwards, in consequence of the extreme soreness of my sides and back." Ball concludes his account with a graphic image of his linen shirt incorporated into the scab that covers his back, suggesting the kinship between his violated body and the inanimate material world.[42] But for both Ball and Williams, the experience of violence and the fear of its repetition also provide the impetus for escape. By narrating heroic escapes, they ultimately offer their readers a remarkably comprehensive picture of the slave: as compassionate and complicit *narrator* of violence, as silenced and merely embodied *victim* of violence, and as heroic *repudiator* of violence. The door seems open for identification and genuine solidarity between whites and blacks.

Yet Williams and Ball, despite the ultimate presentation of their full humanity, are withdrawn from the reader in much the same way as the bodies of Billy and Paul. The Williams narrative concludes with Williams en route to England, convinced that "even the soil which is yet greener for the blood of the revolutionary sacrifice—the plains of Lexington and Saratoga—may not be trodden in safety by the scarred and toil-worn fugitive from Southern Slavery." The Ball narrative ends abruptly when Ball discovers his family sold back into slavery and retreats to a Philadelphia suburb, where he fearfully wonders if "as an article of property, I am of sufficient value to be worth pursuing in my old age."[43] Neither, in short, is available to join the abolitionist campaign in the United States. Indeed, when questions were raised about the veracity of these two narratives, the abolitionist community proved unable to locate either Charles Ball or James Williams—or, for that matter, Isaac Fisher. (John Greenleaf Whittier, for his part, was rather befuddled by the whole affair.)

The Williams and Ball narratives failed to translate narrative identification between ex-slaves and white abolitionists into active solidarity within the antislavery movement. That achievement awaited the emergence, in the 1840s, of a community of ex-slave abolitionists who were able to tell their own stories and to join the antislavery movement as lecturers, editors, preachers, community organizers, and politicians. Yet even in their failures, the Ball and Williams narratives succeeded in underscoring the importance and the difficulty of genuine identification. By persistently withdrawing their fugitives from the abolitionist embrace, these narratives demonstrated that a single narrative could never reveal the full humanity of the slave. They also highlighted the ongoing horror of slavery: Billy and Paul were incapable of participating in the antislavery movement because they had not survived or escaped slavery, and perhaps even Williams and Ball could not be located because they had been reenslaved. If these narratives did not *achieve* sentimental identification, they invited their readers to redouble their efforts in the quest to attain it.

Unfortunately, many abolitionists still focused these redoubled efforts exclusively on slave bodies. During the 1840s, when the North seemed swamped with fugitive slaves, many found their bodies reduced to instruments of the white abolitionist agenda. Fugitive slave lecturers, including Frederick Douglass himself, were expected to display publicly the marks of slavery on their bodies, and they were not expected to make autonomous decisions about their own physical safety. When Douglass purchased his freedom to facilitate his safe travel in the United States, he was bitterly rebuked by white colleagues who perhaps resented the fact that his body had slipped out of their control. But no fugitive was so poignantly reenslaved by the abolitionists as Henry "Box" Brown. Brown's nickname derived from the fact that he had mailed himself to freedom, and it tended to reinforce the notion that he was not merely a body but a *boxed* body. He was frequently called upon to demonstrate his method of escape by climbing into a box; on one occasion, in England, he was actually placed in a box and ceremoniously carried from Bradford to Leeds.[44]

In 1849 Brown's story was transcribed and heavily edited by the Garrisonian activist Charles Stearns. James Olney has aptly commented that in this text "there is precious little of Box Brown (other than the representation of the box itself)."[45] In his preface Stearns betrays the fact that he is not merely obsessed with Box Brown's body. He is obsessed with it precisely as a body that is silent, helpless, and confined. These characteristics, Stearns suggests, make Brown a supreme narrative figure: in all history there is no "parallel instance of heroism." Stearns concedes that the story of William and Ellen Craft (who escaped by disguising the light-skinned Ellen as a young master) would make a good theme "for a future Scott," but "they were not entirely helpless; enclosed in a moving tomb, and as utterly destitute of power to control your movements as if death had fastened its icy arm upon you, and yet possessing all the full tide of gushing sensibilities, and a complete knowledge of your existence, as was the case with our friend."

Why exactly would this predicament make one an ideal romantic hero? Stearns does not say, but Scarry's analysis suggests a reason: a body that contains "gushing sensibilities" but cannot let them escape provides a powerful warrant to the voice, in this case Stearns's, that chooses to speak on its behalf. Freely exploiting the opposition between Brown's body and his own voice, Stearns invited his unenslaved readers to join him in "gushing." By letting "the tear of sympathy roll freely from your eyes," he promised, they could be invigorated, purified, and cleansed from all the "pollutions" associated with the sin of slavery. Brown's actual suffering, hard enough to grasp in the first place, is virtually washed away by this effusion.[46]

I am not the first to suggest that some abolitionists were more interested in cleansing themselves (or their region) from the "sin" of slavery than in joining *with* the slaves in concrete emancipatory projects. What is interesting, however, is that most ex-slave abolitionists responded to the problem not by questioning the logic of sentimental identification but by reiterating the sentimental challenge: you must learn to identify with me! Douglass detested the Brown narrative because it publicized Brown's escape method and thus ensured that slaveholders would be vigilant against similar attempts in the future. But his own, equally publicized, refusal to offer his readers a romantic tale of hairsbreadth escapes was itself a sentimental appeal. Implicitly, he asked his readers to identify with the conscientious scruples that prevented him from making identification too easy.

Other fugitive slave narrators withdrew themselves from their readers by withholding details of their violent experiences or by accenting their own lapses from the pure standards of reformist morality. Henry Bibb, for example, wrote of stealing a horse from his last master; Josiah Henson confessed his failure to liberate a whole boatful of slaves when it lay in his power to do so; and Harriet Jacobs described how she escaped sexual abuse at the hands of her master by voluntarily taking another white lover. The point of these withdrawals was never to alienate the reader altogether but to draw him or her more deeply into the complexity of slave life—to demand, in one critic's words, "an imaginative leap into the total situation of the fugitive and the world of the text."[47]

Among white abolitionist writers, Lydia Maria Child was especially successful in making that imaginative leap into the world of the slaves. In the early 1840s—after Frederick Douglass's emergence as an abolitionist lecturer but before the publication of his *Narrative*—she wrote a series of short stories that brilliantly revealed the complexity of identification. She seems to have deliberately chosen characters who stretched her own capacity to identify: male slaves who consider killing their masters, female slaves who succumb to their masters' sexual advances. In telling these stories, Child maintains her personal commitment to nonresistance and monogamy but nevertheless affirms the moral integrity of persons who make difficult choices. Her slave characters emerge not as broken bodies but as thoughtful moral agents.

"The Black Saxons," set during the War of 1812, is narrated by a kindhearted master who becomes suspicious when his slaves request an unusual number of passes to attend Methodist meetings. He secretly follows them into the woods and discovers they are part of a vast slave conspiracy to join the British army and thus procure their freedom. The conspirators cannot agree, however, on whether to kill the masters first. A young man, whom the narrator recognizes as the illegitimate son of a friend, urges that they "ravish wives and daughters before their eyes, as they have done to us!" An older, Methodist man responds that "thanks to the blessed Jesus, I feel it in my poor old heart to forgive them." The debate continues for several pages, and Child takes care to emphasize the thoughtfulness and clarity of each argument. The issue is resolved when a third man argues that the secret of freedom is not violence but knowledge: he has learned to read and thus knows exactly when the British will land. The slaves then decide that it is unnecessary to kill their masters. But the narrator leaves impressed by the cogency of the argument for violence and by the parallel between the slaves and his own freedom-loving ancestors.[48]

In "Annette Gray," also written in 1841, Child tells the story of a fugitive, living in Boston, who was for many years the mistress of her master. The easiest way to gain sympathy for such a character would have been to exaggerate the physical violence directed against her, but Child takes a more subtle approach. She stresses the fact that the master is not directly violent: "His smiles were frequent and most gracious, his flattery most insidious, his presents abundant." Annette resists these advances at first but submits when he threatens to sell her to a violent, alcoholic Mississippian. Child thus makes clear that Annette is still capable of making moral choices, even though those choices are extremely constrained by circumstances. She also traces the emotional complexity of the situation. Annette is glad her master is "not young and handsome," because she knows it "would have been natural" for her to have felt love for such a man. She is keenly aware that his wife feels both resentment and pity for her, and works hard to forgive the wife's angry outbursts. The readers are left with the sense that they have met a whole person, someone who has felt deep affections and made difficult choices. But Child reminds them, at the end, that the work of identification is still incomplete. They cannot meet Annette in person, for she has had to flee Boston to avoid discovery. "Her present prospects are good," writes Child; "I would mention them, if we, of the nominally free States, were really free."[49]

The demand for sentimental identification, in short, was as unending as human life itself. After telling how he stole a horse in order to escape, Henry Bibb asked, "Who would not do the same thing to rescue a wife, child, father, or mother?" Simply by applying them to himself, he breathed new life into these hackneyed words.[50] Bibb's readers may have thought dozens of times about how their familial affections helped them identify with others in general, but they had not yet thought about whether their affections were broad enough to help them identify with Henry Bibb. This quality of the sentimental appeal helps explain why liberalism, despite the stability of its core ideas, has never achieved stable institutional form. The *idea* that all people are created equal and entitled to life, liberty, and the pursuit of happiness may be enshrined in a sacred text and explicated in any number of laws, but ultimately the idea matters less than the concrete recognition of the equality of each individual person. It was this that each fugitive slave narrator asked for when he or she reiterated the sentimental appeal.[51]

In Through the Blood-Stained Gate: Desacralizing Violence

Fugitive slave narrators thus returned again and again to the classic paradigm of a slave mother, separated from her children and beset by a violent master.[52] Unlike some of the violent images discussed earlier, this one founded its claim for identification not merely on the slaves' suffering but also on their relatedness. Each fugitive slave narrator made this stock image uniquely his or her own by treating it as the blood-stained gate through which he or she had passed twice: once in the violent event of becoming a slave, and again in the triumphal escape that restored his or her freedom. The blood-stained gate thus had a twofold theological significance. For the reader looking *in* at the slaves, it revealed a desacralized world, forsaken by God and utterly distorted by human violence. For the reader looking *out* with the fugitive, by contrast, it opened up a vision of the divine image in human form.

The blood-stained gate scene typically appears near the beginning of a fugitive slave narrative; symbolically, it is the "rebirth" by which the human child is reconstituted as a slave. Thus, in the Ball narrative we learn almost immediately of how Charles is separated from his mother when their master sells her to a trader. Despite her pleas for mercy, the trader tears Charles from her arms and lashes her with a rawhide. Ball describes the poignancy of his departing mother's voice and also suggests that the trader's violence ironically solidified his bond with his master: "Frightened at the sight of the cruelties inflicted upon my poor mother, I forgot my own sorrows at parting from her and clung to my new master, as an angel and a saviour, when compared with the hardened fiend into whose power she had fallen." The violent event alters Ball's social and genealogical identity. As Ball forgets his sorrow and clings to his master, the artificial master bond substitutes for the biological maternal bond. Yet in a sense the sacrifice misfires, for Ball does not repress the subversive knowledge that his new identity is founded in violence: "The horrors of that day sank deeply into my heart, and even at this time, though half a century has elapsed, the terrors of the scene return with painful vividness upon my memory." Ball's painful memory prevents him from imagining that his new status has been ordained by either God or nature. The master-slave relationship cannot become a permanent genealogy, for the memory of violence haunts Ball as long as any member of his family is enslaved, and always inspires resistance.[53]

A similar passage appears in the *Narrative of Sojourner Truth*, again suggesting that slave owners used violence to get young slaves to identify with them rather than with their parents. Just prior to Truth's emancipation under New York state law, her young son Peter was illegally sold to a vicious Alabama planter. When Truth sued for Peter's recovery, her ex-master went south to retrieve the boy. By using a good cop/bad cop routine to take personal credit for rescuing Peter from the violent Mr. Fowler, he caused Peter to see him as something of a savior. Thus, when Peter arrives in the courtroom, he denies that Truth is his mother, begs to remain with "his dear master," and explains away his many scars as accidents. Only after the judge restores him to his mother's custody does he reveal the extent of his injuries and confess that even Fowler's wife (herself a victim of abuse) had wished Peter home with his mother.[54]

The blood-stained gate might be described as a half sacrifice: it effaces the natural bond of mother and child but fails to install a new sacred reality in its place. The genealogical failure of slavery's violence also appears in a story Ball hears from another slave, who underwent the Middle Passage from Africa. On board ship, this man recalls, the sailors enacted the blood-stained gate by callously tossing the children overboard. But the mothers refused to accept the new reality imposed by this act of violence. Two jumped overboard determined to rescue their children or drown, while the third broke her arm trying to jump and died of a fever. Here violence destroys an old familial structure and can create nothing to take its place. William Wells Brown gave a more poignant expression of this genealogical failure by describing how, as a young house servant, he was often woken by the sound of the whip and the slaves' screams from the field. On one occasion the victim is his mother, and he must listen in silence to her unanswered prayer for mercy: "Oh! pray—Oh! pray—Oh! pray." This is a scene of pure loss, for the circumstances of enslavement give the boy no resources for reconstituting meaning in his life: "I returned to my bed, and found no consolation but in my tears. It was not yet daylight."[55]

For all these fugitive slave narrators, the world of slavery was marked not by a new sacred genealogy but by the complete failure of religious meaning.[56] The genius of Frederick Douglass was that he made this point explicit, particularly in the second rendition of his blood-stained gate scene, in *My Bondage and My Freedom*. Here he places the beating of Esther in a chapter entitled "Gradual Initiation into the Mysteries of Slavery" and brackets it with explicitly theological reflections. The chapter title evokes liberal stereotypes of the corrupt "mysteries" and superstitions of illiberal religions and reinforces Douglass's earlier account of his separation from his grandmother as an unholy sacrifice: "Born for another's benefit, as the *firstling* of the cabin flock I was soon to be selected as a meet offering to the fearful and inexorable *demi-god*, whose huge image on so many occasions haunted my childhood's imagination." Douglass introduces Esther's story by claiming that the slave system had succeeded in draining the slaves' lives of any immediate religious or moral significance. "It is one of the damning characteristics of the slave system, that it robs its victims of every earthly incentive to a holy life." At best, slaves might be "sustained" by an otherworldly hope of eventually regaining religious meaning, for "this side of God and heaven, a slave-woman is at the mercy of the power, caprice and passion of her owner."[57]

In narrating Esther's beating, Douglass stresses both his aunt's nakedness and physical vulnerability, and the incapacity of language to derive religious meaning from her suffering. Esther's pleas for mercy go unheeded, Captain Anthony's words are all "tantalizing epithets" or "blasphemous curses," and even young Frederick, despite his kindling rage, is "hushed, terrified, stunned, and could do nothing" because of his fear that he will be next to suffer. Yet on the next page Douglass suggests that the religious meaninglessness of slavery, once recognized, was liberatory. Esther's beating led him to ask some difficult questions of theodicy: "*Why am I a slave?*" And why did Esther have to suffer so? The stock answer that God had made the whites masters and the blacks slaves was clearly unacceptable, for slavery's violence could never be squared with divine benevolence. But simply asking the question led Douglass to a better answer. If God could not have created slavery, humans must have, and "what man can make, man can unmake." This knowledge ensured the failure of Douglass's unholy initiation as a slave: "The appalling darkness faded away, and I was master of the subject."[58]

The significance of this scene, in contrast to the catalogs of violence described earlier, is that it is not so much a scene of slavery as of *enslavement*. To suggest that even children born in slavery must be violently enslaved is to renounce all natural, providential, or ontological explanations of slavery. It is to renounce the facile analogy between slavery and original sin. Fugitive slave narrators continued to believe that slavery was a form of sin that steadily effaced the *imago dei* in both its victims and its perpetrators, but—like earlier liberal theologians—they explained sin itself in terms that were contingent, historical, social, and utterly desacralized.

Fugitive slave narrators described the world of slavery as a hell populated by demons, and yet as a hell that was constituted and repeatedly reconstituted by contingent human actions. Charles Ball recalled that since childhood "the name of South Carolina had been little less terrible to me than that of the bottomless pit"; Henry Bibb claimed that an accurate picture of hell "may be sketched from an American slave prison"; and Box Brown declared, "Slavery reigns and rules the councils of this nation, as Satan presides over Pandemonium." James Williams narrated the exploits of his overseer Huckstep, a "drunken demon" who "made the house literally an earthly hell," and even Douglass described slaveholders as demons or "fiends from perdition," and their violence as a "devilish outrage." Yet, clearly, slaveholders and overseers were not ontological demons analogous to the Indians of the Puritan imagination. They had not been born as demons, and they served no divine purpose transcending their own demonic realm. On the contrary, they had become demonic through processes that could be traced by the slave narrators. Huckstep, according to Williams, became a demon by drinking. Douglass's vicious father was "not by nature worse than other men" and in a free society would have been as "humane and respectable" as most of his neighbors.[59]

Douglass gave an extended account of the demonization of his mistress Sophia Auld, in whose Baltimore household he spent much of his youth. Not raised in a slaveholding family, Sophia welcomed young Frederick into her home with an openness that he found amazing and even disconcerting: "Here I saw what I had never seen before; it was a white face beaming with the most kindly emotions." For a time, Sophia became a surɪogate mother for the young slave, but this relationship of spontaneous affection could not withstand the violent conventions of enslavement. Sophia's husband chastised her for teaching Frederick how to read and then required her to enforce a strict antireading policy. Despite her reluctance, this "exercise of irresponsible power" gradually made "her equal to the task of treating me as though I were a brute." The strain of justifying her behavior to herself gradually eroded her conscience, and soon enough her "angelic face gave place to that of a demon."[60]

Slave narrators did not refer to themselves or to other slaves as demons, but they repeatedly suggested that they, too, had lost the *imago dei*. "Slavery brutalizes all who administer it," wrote the editor of Moses Roper's narrative, "and seeks to efface the likeness of God, stamped on the brow of its victims. It makes the former class demons, and reduces the latter to the level of brutes." Richard Hildreth had his fugitive protagonist complain that his enslavement "was like quitting the erect carriage which I had received at God's hand, and learning to crawl on the earth like a base reptile." Solomon Northup, who was literally enslaved as an adult after being kidnapped in Washington, D.C., used his entire narrative to trace the steady loss of his voice and his name. When, early in the narrative, Northup wakes to find himself in the hands of the slave trader Burch, his first lesson is that his voice—and by extension his familial relatedness—is no longer his own. He protests "that I was a free man—a resident of Saratoga, where I had a wife and children, who were also free, and that my name was Northup." Burch denies all of this and demands that Northup deny it, too; when he refuses, Burch begins lashing him. Northup continues to assert his freedom, but as the pain grows more intense, he pleads for mercy. Burch, "an incarnate demon," responds with curses and continues the whipping until Northup is completely silent: "My sufferings I can compare to nothing else than the burning agonies of hell!"[61]

Though Northup never admits to being a slave, the whipping destroys his sense of social connection. Before he had longed for company; now he shudders at the mere thought of a human face. He also takes the linguistic authority of the masters for granted and resolves never to betray the secret of his freedom. When he carelessly tells a potential buyer that he is from New York, a mere glance from Burch reminds him that he must pretend to be from the South. When a new master arbitrarily assigns him the name "Platt," he accepts this and never tells anyone his true identity. Repeatedly he asserts that his ultimate escape depends on his keeping "the secret of my real name and history," but the course of events suggests that the opposite may have been the case.[62] A sympathetic white sends word to Northup's friends in New York, but they nearly fail to locate him because no one in Louisiana knows him as Solomon Northup. If Northup never accepts his imposed identity as a slave, he very nearly loses his original identity altogether.

For fugitive slave narrators, the making of both slaveholders and slaves was a contingent, violent process. Thus, they implicitly rejected the traditional providential explanation, which held that God had caused Africans to be enslaved so that they, and ultimately their whole continent, would convert to Christianity. Frederick Douglass was not alone in explicitly disavowing this view. When Lunsford Lane heard a white preacher discoursing on God's goodness in bringing the slaves to Christianity, he immediately reflected that "God also granted temporal freedom, which *man* without God's consent, had stolen away." Similarly, Peter Randolph acknowledged that God had given Africans dark skins "with an all-wise purpose," but that purpose had no connection to the "crimes" of the slaveholders.[63]

In place of the providential account, slave narrators proffered a *systemic* explanation of slavery's violence. Enslavement was a violent process not because God willed it thus, nor because it was perpetrated by totally depraved individuals, but because its own inner logic made it so. "The slave must be brutalized to keep him as a slave," wrote Frederick Douglass in his second autobiography. "The whip, the chain, the gag, the thumb-screw, the blood-hound, the stocks, and all the other bloody paraphernalia of the slave system, are indispensably necessary to the relation of master and slave." This point impressed at least one contemporary reviewer, who commented that Douglass's "denunciations of slavery and slaveholders are not indiscriminate, while he wars upon the system rather than upon the persons whom that system has made." Douglass's argument was not new, however; it echoed the explanation given two decades earlier in the Ball narrative. The master-slave relationship, Ball suggested, so disrupted the "sentiments that bind together" individuals in free communities that violence became necessary for the maintenance of any order.[64]

The same point was echoed by Lewis Clarke, who insisted that "all the abuses which I have here related are *necessary*, if slavery must continue to exist"; by James W. C. Pennington, who held that "the being of slavery, its soul and body, lives and moves in the chattel principle" and that "the cart-whip, starvation, and nakedness, are its inevitable consequences"; and by Henry Bibb, who said he was not brought up but "*flogged up*, for where I should have received moral, mental, and religious instruction, I received stripes without number, the object of which was to degrade and keep me in subordination." Slave narrators drew their systemic analyses in part from temperance literature, which made the parallel argument that the abuses associated with alcohol were rooted neither in individual pathology nor in the divine plan but in the institutional interactions of rumsellers, community leaders, and drunkards. Thus, Douglass insisted that the cruelty of an individual slave mistress "is as justly chargeable to the upholders of the slave system, as drunkenness is chargeable on those who, by precept and example, or by indifference, uphold the drinking system." But systemic analysis of slavery did nothing to mitigate its horrors. However constituted, the world of slavery was still a hellish place where violence fed on violence. On the plantation, Douglass glumly concluded, "the whip is all in all."[65]

The systemic account of slavery did offer a glimmer of hope in that it implied that the inhabitants of slavery's world—both slaves and masters—might regain the *imago dei* if placed in a new environment. But this was more than outweighed by the gloomy implication that slavery itself existed entirely outside divine Providence. As successful fugitives, slave narrators testified again and again to the utter incommensurability between the worlds of slavery and freedom. (These "worlds" corresponded only occasionally to South and North. Given Northern complicity with slavery, fugitive slave narrators often placed the entire nation within the slave world. Conversely, they could locate natural phenomena in the South outside slavery's realm.) James Williams recalled that his fellow slaves generally held no faith, for on the plantation "they could not keep their minds upon God and the devil (meaning Huckstep) at the same time." Lewis Clarke reported that his escape was nothing short of cosmic in its significance: "I hardly seem to be in the same world that I was then. When I first got into the free states, and saw every body look like they loved one another, sure enough, I thought, this must be the 'Heaven' of LOVE I had heard something about." Jermain Loguen's biographer drew the cosmic divide between the natural world and the social system of slavery: when young Jarm's nature walk is interrupted by the sound of a slave being beaten on a neighboring plantation, the narrator comments that "the infernal act on the opposite bank rudely and suddenly changed a celestial picture into an image of hell."[66]

Henry Bibb, who was reenslaved after a period of freedom, gave his rendition of the cosmic divide a slightly hopeful twist: "I thought I was almost out of humanity's reach, and should never again have the pleasure of hearing the gospel sound, as I could see no way by which I could extricate myself; yet I never omitted to pray for deliverance. I had faith to believe that the Lord could see our wrongs and hear our cries."[67] Bibb's faith, however, only confirmed the limited scope of God's Providence. He did not have faith that God's hand controlled all events in the world of slavery, but only that God might eventually remove him from that world. It is noteworthy, moreover, that Bibb represents himself as speaking and God as merely seeing and hearing. This is a reversal of orthodox providential theology, according to which God speaks and manifests the divine glory in all earthly events, and the proper human role is to watch in awe. Bibb takes for granted the liberal subjectivization of religion, in which human faith has more ultimate significance than divine action.

Fugitive slave narrators underscored the cosmic divide between slavery and freedom by suggesting that the slave world had its own religion, "slaveholding Christianity," which was a demonic mirror image of true Christianity. "Between the Christianity of this land, and the Christianity of Christ," insisted Douglass, "I recognize the widest possible difference." The external trappings of religion confirmed the demonic character of what Henry Watson called "the land of Bibles and whips," for slavery's realm was filled with "devils dressed in angels' robes, and hell presenting the semblance of paradise." Slave narrators repeatedly suggested that the most pious masters were also the cruelest. Henry Bibb told of Deacon Whitfield, who "looked like a saint—talked like the best of slave holding Christians, and acted at home like the devil," while William Wells Brown told of being captured by rough men, one of whom tied him up "with a strong cord" and then turned to Bible reading and praying, "just as though God sanctioned the act he had just committed upon a poor, panting, fugitive slave."[68]

The slaves themselves sought to practice a true Christianity uninfected by this diabolical religion, but most fugitive slave narrators emphasized the obstacles thrown up in their way. On Box Brown's plantation, the young slaves believed that their master was God and their master's son was Jesus Christ, while some neighboring slaves were taught that "*negroes have nothing to do with God.*" James Williams's demonic Huckstep teaches the slaves that heaven is God's reward to the whites for taking care of their slaves, while hell is reserved for blacks. He also torments those who try to worship, coming up behind one old man who is praying, "How long, oh Lord, how long?" and answering, "As long as my whip!" "It was," Williams concludes, "the sport of a demon." Moses Grandy likewise told of how his brother-in-law, caught holding prayer meetings in the woods, saw two of his companions murdered and his wife and infant children sold away. When he himself was sold, he died of a broken heart before he could be carried away.[69]

Some fugitive slave narrators, most notably Frederick Douglass, were viewed by their contemporaries as infidels because of their harsh attacks on slaveholding Christianity, and more recent scholars have sometimes seen them as precursors of "secularism" who replaced traditional Christianity with a religion of abolition.[70] In my view it is more illuminating to regard them as Christian liberals who continued a long tradition of setting the pure gospel message against institutional corruptions. This tradition can be traced back to Reformation notions of the Roman Antichrist, and even to medieval polemics against pope or emperor. For champions of the individual conscience as bearer of the *imago dei*, the papal beast, gloomy orthodoxy, and the slavocracy have played analogous roles as embodiments of institutional evil.

Yet it was comparatively easy for sixteenth-century Reformers and early Unitarians to urge their followers to abandon ecclesiastical institutions, at least after they had created rival institutions of their own, and white abolitionists in the North faced no physical obstacles to "coming out" of "corrupt churches." The dilemma of the fugitive slave narrator was to explain what liberal religion could possibly mean for individuals who were physically bound to the realm of Antichrist. Most often the answer they gave was this: enslaved individuals could certainly pray to God, but so long as they remained in slavery, their prayers would go unanswered. Moses Roper and Solomon Northup both described how slaves could spend entire nights in prayer, only to see the sun rise on an unchanged world. "I poured forth the supplications of a broken spirit," recalled Northup, "imploring strength from on high to bear up against the burden of my troubles, until the morning light aroused the slumberers, ushering in another day of bondage." Sojourner Truth's biographer suggested that Truth could maintain her conviction that God answers prayer because she thought, naively, that only spoken prayers counted. "When I got beaten," Truth recalled, "I never knew it long enough beforehand to pray."[71]

In recounting acts of violence, slave narrators often suggested that the victims were gradually reduced from prayer to silence. "The last sentence which he articulated," Loguen's biographer reported of a slave beaten to death, "was 'O Lord! O Lord!' and he continued to utter it until utterance failed, and no noise broke the stillness around but the sound of the infernal weapon upon the insentient and motionless body." This echoes William Wells Brown's poignant account of the inarticulateness of his mother's suffering, which reduces her prayer to the word "pray": "She cried, 'Oh! pray—Oh! pray—Oh! pray'—these are generally the words of slaves, when imploring mercy at the hands of their oppressors."[72] Her suffering body betrayed both her voice and her faith; violence was the place where speech and prayer became impossible. It is no accident, then, that James Williams concluded his panorama of the slave world with a longing prayer:

> We hear the sound of the horn at daybreak, calling the sick and weary to toil unrequited. Woman, in her appealing delicacy and suffering, about to become a mother, is fainting under the lash, or sinking exhausted beside her cotton row. We hear the prayer for mercy answered with sneers and curses. We look on the instruments of torture, and the corpses of murdered men. We see the dogs, reeking hot from the chase, with their jaws foul with human blood. We see the meek and aged Christian, scarred with the lash, and bowed down with toil, offering the supplication of a broken heart to his Father in Heaven for the forgiveness of his brutal enemy. We hear, and from our inmost hearts repeat, the affecting interrogatory of the aged slave, *"How long, Oh Lord! how long!"*[73]

Out Through the Blood-Stained Gate: Discovering the *Imago Dei*

Probably the best-known account of the godforsaken prayers of the slaves is Frederick Douglass's curious meditation on the "rude and apparently incoherent songs" of his fellow slaves. Though he professed not fully to understand the songs, Douglass did not hesitate to call them prayers: "They breathed the prayer and complaint of souls boiling over with the bitterest anguish. Every tone was a testimony against slavery, and a prayer to God for deliverance from chains." To hear such prayers, Douglass reported, "always depressed my spirit, and filled me with ineffable sadness." In their incomprehensibility they revealed the power of slavery's violence to efface the *imago dei* and exposed the "dehumanizing character and soul-killing effects of slavery."[74]

Yet merely by describing these songs, Douglass shows that his soul has not been killed by slavery, and this is also his point. The songs are for him a liberatory goad; they "follow me, to deepen my hatred of slavery and quicken my sympathies for my brethren in bonds." What Douglass is suggesting is that God's answer to the slaves' unanswered prayer was the prayer itself. The world of slavery might be devoid of providential power and its inhabitants bereft of the divine image, yet a spark of divinity remained in the slaves' very misery and despair over their bereftness. The slave who, like young Douglass, was perceptive enough to recognize both the godforsakenness and the despairing spark could perhaps fan that spark into a flaming desire for freedom.

Both Douglass and other fugitive slave narrators used their blood-stained gate scenes to elaborate this point. The witnessing of a slave mother's violation and bereavement was, as I have shown, the gate through which young slaves entered the hell of slavery, a godforsaken place where speech and prayer were either impossible or impotent. But the young, witnessing slaves also caught a glimpse through the blood-stained gate in the other direction, at a world of freedom where speech and prayer might become possible. To *know* that they were in the hell of slavery was to know that they might escape. Thus, immediately after describing the painful process of his own enslavement, Henry Bibb confidently proclaimed that his situation had "kindled a fire of liberty within my breast which has never yet been quenched. This seemed to me to be a part of my nature; it was first revealed to me by the inevitable laws of nature's God." And James Pennington described his devastation when his father was beaten by a master determined to be "the master of your tongue as well as of your time," then concluded that "although it was some time after this event before I took the decisive step, yet in my mind and spirit, I never was a *Slave* after it."[75]

For Douglass, Bibb, and Pennington, a profound sense of God-given freedom arose directly from the process of enslavement. How could such a powerful conviction flow from such a devastating experience? The answer is that the process of enslavement became reversible as soon as it was recognized as a process rather than a part of the unchangeable constitution of the universe.[76] Fugitive slave narrators affirmed that the act of violence had set up an utterly godforsaken world of slavery, but they also affirmed that *nothing more* than the act of violence had created that world. It was *not* God's creation! This realization was profoundly liberating, for it enabled the slave to imagine, and indeed discover, a larger world beyond that of slavery. The slave narrators insisted on narrating the scene of violence because they hoped that by sharing their experience of liberatory witnessing, they would shatter the hold of the slave world on their white readers' imaginations as well.

By describing the blood-stained gate as a contingent act of enslavement, the fugitive slave narrators discovered the *imago dei* in their own capacity to expose slavery's violence. Their status as speakers and writers was intimately linked to the *imago dei*. But this status involved more than the sheer narration of slavery's horrors. Fugitive slave narrators were also *declarers* who asserted their own freedom as emphatically as the evils of bondage. Frederick Douglass reported that in his early career as a lecturer some of his white handlers pressured him to stick to the facts and let them articulate the abolitionist theory. But "it did not entirely satisfy me to *narrate* wrongs; I felt like *denouncing* them. . . . I must speak just the word that seemed to *me* to be the word to be spoken *by* me."[77]

Douglass, and in his wake dozens of other fugitive slaves, soon realized that the writing of an autobiography was, in one critic's words, a "uniquely self-liberating" act. It gave them the mastery over their own lives that they had been denied as slaves; in a sense it made them masters of the world of slavery itself. It assimilated them to the American Founding Fathers, who had also "declared" their own freedom, and to a divinity often figured as *Logos* or Word. Autobiographical self-liberation was also a way of claiming positive religious value for the assertive self. Douglass skillfully exploited the power of self-assertion as a lecturer, leading one auditor to describe his speech as "the volcanic outbreak of human nature" and Garrison to announce Douglass's "godlike nature." As autobiographers, in short, fugitive slaves exemplified the liberal Christian commitment to the gospel, the revolutionary heritage, and the divinity of the unfettered self.[78]

Fugitive slave narrators discovered the *imago dei* not only in their autobiographical voices but also in concrete events in their lives, particularly their early childhoods and their escapes. Typically, slave narrators preceded their accounts of the blood-stained gate with descriptions of the happiness they had enjoyed earlier. In the days before he was separated from his mother, Bibb claimed, "I knew nothing of my condition then as a slave." "It was a long time before I knew myself to be *a slave*," Douglass reported in *My Bondage and My Freedom*. "I knew many other things before I knew that." Jermain Loguen's biographer claimed that his subject first "blossomed in the shape of an angel" and only subsequently was exposed to the "monster passions" of slavery.[79] Such claims should not be read as literal descriptions of the material conditions of slave infancy. Their narrative purpose, rather, was to assert the priority of the *imago dei* to the process of enslavement.

The *imago dei* became fully manifest, however, only in the act of escape. Many fugitive slave narrators discerned the hand of Providence in their escapes, but they rarely adhered to the rules of orthodox providential theology. Lewis Clarke concluded his narrative by recognizing "the hand of a kind Providence in leading me from the terrible house of bondage," but this invocation seems rather pro forma, as God is scarcely mentioned earlier in the text.[80] Other fugitive slave narrators portrayed Providence not as an all-embracing power with a purpose for every earthly event but simply as a reliable source of strength for the escaping slave. Many found it easiest to see God's hand in natural events, such as the discovery of food or protection from wild animals, and thus left unresolved the question of whether God exercised direct power over the institutions of slavery.[81]

Congregationalist minister James W. C. Pennington was unusual in that he could invoke the categories of orthodox theology, but these only entangled him in deep conundrums. In his narrative, he found significance in the fact that his escape had begun on the Sabbath, repeatedly credited Providence with guiding him to a benevolent Quaker, and affirmed that "my object in writing this tract . . . has been to shew the reader the hand of God with a slave." But Pennington believed that God was providentially involved in his life only because he first obeyed God by seeking his freedom. Thus, he wrote to his former master that "since I have been out of your hands, I have been signally favoured of God, whence I infer that in leaving you, I acted strictly in accordance with his holy will."[82]

Writing to his family, Pennington insisted that "not a solitary decree of the immaculate God . . . has been concerned in the ordination of slavery." God might have "permitted us to be enslaved according to the invention of wicked men," but he "cannot approve of it." Indeed, "He has no need to approve of it, even on account of the good which He will bring out of it, for He could have brought about that good in some other way." Here Pennington seems to be muddling toward the orthodox distinction between providential and moral government, according to which God may providentially cause an event without morally approving it. But his Providence acts only in response to the good or evil actions of human beings, rather than imposing an overarching pattern on human existence. The God he offers to his family members is thus a moral, not a coercive, power: "We have the glorious and total weight of God's moral character in our side of the scale."[83]

Frederick Douglass avoided Pennington's muddle by entirely subordinating the doctrine of Providence to that of the *imago dei*. He regarded himself as a special favorite of Providence, but most of his evidence for this special status was internal, having more to do with his own passion for freedom than with external circumstances. Thus, in the *Narrative* Douglass portrays his youthful sojourn to Baltimore as a providential intervention but concedes that such a view of Providence might be "superstitious" or "egotistical." What is more important than whether God had brought him to Baltimore is the fact that he believed it to be so: "I should be false to the earliest sentiments of my soul, if I suppressed the opinion." The most important gift of Providence was his lifelong "conviction that slavery would not always be able to hold me within its foul embrace," which accompanied him "like ministering angels" even in his "darkest hours." "This good spirit," Douglass could assert without qualification, "was from God, and to him I offer thanksgiving and praise."[84]

Where orthodox writers looked at outward circumstances to glimpse God's hand *upon* their lives, Douglass chose as his theme the process by which his God-given inner freedom found external expression. Thus, after describing the horrors of slavery, he announces his real agenda: "You have seen how a man was made a slave; you shall see how a slave was made a man."[85] Several incidents play key roles in this process: his frequent relocations; his learning to read after discovering that his master believes reading will make him unfit to be a slave; his refusal to be whipped by the notorious slave breaker, Mr. Covey. Each is driven by his own passion for freedom, and each provides new evidence of the special interest of Providence.

Because Douglass's Providence is inside himself, he can portray his struggle with the forces of slavery not as part of the providential plan but as a struggle between Providence and human evil. The outcome of this struggle is not foreordained, for Douglass is surrounded by powers inimical to his own providential faith. Indeed, at the nadir of Douglass's life—six months into his stay with Covey—his providential spark is actually snuffed out by Covey's violence. Even when alone in the woods, he cannot pray, for "the sham religion which everywhere prevailed" has convinced him "that prayers were unavailing and delusive." This dark night of the soul, Douglass makes clear, is not providentially ordained as a chastisement or preparation for grace. Instead, it is a genuine death of the soul: "Mr. Covey succeeded in breaking me. . . . the cheerful spark that lingered about my eye died; the dark night of slavery closed in upon me, and behold a man transformed into a brute!" Douglass's defiance of Covey is thus nothing less than a resurrection: "It was a glorious resurrection, from the tomb of slavery, to the heaven of freedom. . . . However long I might remain a slave in form, the day had passed forever when I could be a slave in fact."[86]

A number of scholars have noted that Douglass's account of his escape both runs parallel to and diverges from the classic conversion paradigm. It has the emotional intensity and life-changing effects of a conversion, and yet Douglass makes very clear that it is not sinful to be a slave, that the fall into slavery was not ordained by God, and that he does not need to acquire a new self.[87] What Douglass does, I would suggest, is offer a conversion that is a resurrection rather than a rebirth. It does not involve replacing an originally corrupt self with a new and purer self but rather restoring the life of an originally pure self that has been killed by violent institutions.

The power that effects this resurrection inheres in the self's divinity rather than in the prevenient grace of an external God. Unlike orthodox conversion, it is not guaranteed in advance by the atoning sacrifice of Jesus Christ. On the contrary, the self and God could, for Douglass, be vindicated only in the concrete event of liberation. He often reminded audiences that, when he was a slave, he "had offered many prayers for freedom," but he got it only when he "prayed with his legs." Up to the eve of his escape, Douglass admitted, he continued to ask fundamental questions of theodicy: "May not this, after all, be God's work? May He not, for wise ends, have doomed me to this lot?" Such questions simply could not be answered *theoretically*, but they were *practically* dissolved by the escape itself: "The contest was now ended; the chain was severed; God and right stood vindicated. I WAS A FREEMAN, and the voice of peace and joy thrilled my heart."[88]

This is what made Douglass's narrative such a powerful response to the white abolitionists' desire for the slave. He wanted them to identify with him as much as they wanted to identity with him, but his standard of identification was awesomely high. To identify with the slave was to be fully committed to the slave's liberation, and the entire validity of liberal theology hinged on the success of that liberation. Identification with the slave was not a luxury to be enjoyed by liberals whose faith was already secured by the more parochial affections of their own families, for the divine image that liberals worshiped lived or died in the breast of the slave. By revealing his own godlike humanity, Douglass challenged liberals to believe that *their* faith depended on *his* freedom.

At the Blood-Stained Gate: The Maternal Sacrifice

Yet could Douglass meet his own religious standard? Could he stake his own faith on the ultimate freedom of those slaves he left behind by escaping? Or did his powerful sense of freedom depend in some perverse way on his alienation from slaves like his mother and aunt, who continued to be sacrificed on the idolatrous altars of slavery? Put somewhat differently, was Douglass's "resurrection" capacious enough to include the entire web of kinship—his relations with his mother, his grandmother, his aunt, perhaps even his sympathetic white half sister, Lucretia Auld—that had nurtured his sense of self in the first place? Or was his resurrected self an abstract individual, free from family ties, as well as from the bonds of slavery? Could his solitary escape vindicate the liberal God of familial affection?

I have argued that at the blood-stained gate Douglass discovered not only the horrors of slavery but also his own divine humanity. Suddenly aware that violence and not God had ordained slavery, he gained a voice, a passion for freedom, and a fierce sense of identification with his suffering aunt. Other scholars, however, have suggested that as he watched Esther writhing in pain, Douglass discovered not his humanity but his manhood—his masculinity. Rather than identifying with her, he realized that women were the primary victims of violence, and thus gained a voice through his voyeuristic identification with the male perpetrator of violence—in this case his own father, Captain Anthony.[89]

This argument is too plausible to be dismissed and too one-sided to be accepted. Douglass's masculinity was an integral component of his identity, and yet his lifelong commitment to women's rights makes it hard to claim that his masculinity itself was founded on violence against women. Moreover, there is a sense—as I shall argue shortly—in which he was willing to stake his own faith not on his mother's literal survival but on her resurrection in memory. The complexity of Douglass's case notwithstanding, however, it is fair to say that male slave narrators as a class did anchor their freedom and humanity in the victimization of female slaves and the failure of slave families. Though as late as 1861 Lydia Maria Child could write that the sexual exploitation of women was a "peculiar phase of slavery" that had "generally been kept veiled," in fact fugitive slave narratives written by men did not downplay women's experience.[90] Just the opposite was the case: male narrators were obsessed with the many special trials of their mothers and sisters. They stressed slave women's victimization at the expense of their resistance and love of freedom, and thus allowed some white abolitionists to avoid confronting the full humanity of the female slave. Male slave narrators could present the bodies but not the voices of their mothers and sisters, and there were few female slave narrators to right the balance. Sojourner Truth was a powerful presence in the abolitionist movement, but she had experienced only the dwindling days of slavery in New York and was thus only a partial representative of Southern slave women. The witness of Harriet Jacobs, moreover, appeared only in 1861 and was not widely read until the twentieth century. If Douglass brought the challenge of fully identifying with a black man to a mass white audience, a similar feat may not have been achieved for black women until the 1980s.[91]

It is interesting, however, that the troubling gender politics of the fugitive slave narrative appear most clearly in the early texts whose composition was dominated by whites. Richard Hildreth's fictional narrative, like some twentieth-century white analyses of alleged black pathology, even went so far as to imply that family affections were impossible in slavery. Hildreth's hero, Archy Moore, is a mulatto whose "family" of origin is a powder keg of exploitation, affection, and desire. His slaveholding father, Colonel

Moore, spouts Jeffersonian doctrine but refuses to acknowledge his enslaved son. Archy secretly marries his half sister, Cassy, but cannot defend her from their father's repeated rape attempts. Their escape attempt leads to vicious punishment and separation, but their eventual reunion leads to something even more tragic: the birth of a son. Looking at the baby boy, Archy sees not the *imago dei* but its inevitable effacement by the hand of slavery: "Whenever I looked upon him, my mind was filled with horrid images. The whole future seemed to come visibly before me. I saw him naked, chained, and bleeding under the lash; I saw him a wretched, trembling creature, cringing to escape it; I saw him utterly debased, and the spirit of manhood extinguished within him." The knowledge that he cannot protect his son haunts Archy through his many adventures, including his successful escape and lengthy career in the British navy. It is "the barbed arrow that still is sticking in my heart; the fatal, fatal wound, that nought can heal."[92]

Hildreth's depiction of Archy's ambivalence about fatherhood echoed the common fear of orthodox parents that their newborn infants would prove to be depraved.[93] He was, in turn, echoed by fugitive slave narrators like Frederick Douglass, who claimed that "there is not beneath the sky an enemy to filial affection so destructive as slavery." Henry Bibb reported that to bear children in slavery was to "propagat[e] victims for . . . torture and cruelty," while Sojourner Truth's biographer expected readers to be shocked at Truth's willingness to bear children as a slave and thus lay "her own children, the 'flesh of her flesh,' on the altar of slavery—a sacrifice to the bloody Moloch!"[94] The lingering implications of the doctrine of original sin proved a potent obstacle to the recognition of the *imago dei* in slave families.

If later expressions of familial despair merely echoed Hildreth, Douglass's generation of fugitive slave narrators could not compete with John Greenleaf Whittier in the depiction of slave women as helpless victims whose divine humanity was utterly destroyed by slavery. The Williams narrative contains not one but three episodes of extreme violence against pregnant women. The latter two (one in the body of the text and one in an appendix of corroborating testimonies) involve women who are whipped until they deliver stillborn babies. The first is quite lengthy and involves Williams's participation in the punishment of a pregnant woman named Sarah, daughter of a slaveholder, who is newly arrived from Virginia. As slave driver, Williams is compelled to administer fifty lashes on Thursday. The overseer adds another fifty on Saturday. On the climactic day, Williams underscores the godforsakenness of slavery by contrasting the scene of violence to the peace that should characterize the Sabbath: "Instead of the tones of the church bell summoning to the house of prayer, she heard the dreadful sound of the lash falling upon the backs of her brethren and sisters in bondage. For the voice of prayer she heard curses; for the songs of Zion obscene and hateful blasphemies." He then describes the murder in almost pornographic detail, noting how the overseer separates his victim's legs with a fence rail, strips off her dress with a penknife, and slices her abdomen entirely open with just two lashes of the whip.[95]

The text may be too gruesome to be read pornographically, but it certainly provides little basis for sentimental identification. We know nothing about the victim with which we might identify. She is described as "wretched," as "sick and despairing," and as "faint and fevered," but her aspirations and relationships are never described. At no point in the narrative does she speak for herself. We are told that she has a sister, Hannah, but the narrator does not say whether Hannah strives to preserve her sister's divine image in memory. If Sarah's victimization has no divinely ordained purpose, neither does her life. Totally consumed by the slave system, she is reduced to a symbol of its profanity, a sign of pure loss.[96]

Seen against the backdrop of *Archy Moore* and the Williams narrative, Douglass's rendition of Esther's beating no longer appears as a facile exploitation of female suffering for the sake of his own identity. It is, rather, a pained and partial step along the path to full identification. Like white abolitionists longing to encounter the slave's humanity and divinity, Douglass truly desired to know his aunt and his mother. He thus gave Esther as much genealogical context as he could—her relation to his mother, her romance with Ned Roberts. Even more significantly, he seems to have been goaded by his failure, in the *Narrative*, to do more than allude to his alienation from his mother. In *My Bondage and My Freedom*, consequently, she somehow becomes a major character.

In the introduction, Douglass's friend James M'Cune Smith sets the stage by highlighting Douglass's characterization of his mother and grandmother and concludes "that for his energy, perseverance, eloquence, invective, sagacity, and wide sympathy, he is indebted to his negro blood." In the text itself, Douglass takes pains to draw out *all* the implications of his fleeting maternal memories. An incident in which his mother intervenes on his behalf against a cruel slave cook demonstrates that he is not entirely an orphan: "That night I learned the fact, that I was not only a child, but *somebody's* child." Douglass testifies simultaneously to the ephemerality of his ties to his mother and to the permanence of his memory of those ties: "It has been a life-long, standing grief to me, that I knew so little of my mother; and that I was so early separated from her. The counsels of her love must have been beneficial to me. The side view of her face is imaged on my memory, and I take few steps in life, without feeling her presence; but the image is mute, and I have no striking words of hers treasured up."[97]

Douglass, in short, had a real dilemma. He was perhaps willing to stake his faith on the divinity of his mother's voice, but he simply had no access to that voice. Perhaps his God could not be vindicated after all. But by including this passage in *My Bondage*, and thus withdrawing his mother from his readers, he succeeded in reconstructing and even sharing the abolitionist desire for a fuller identification. A similar achievement can be found in the 1853 narrative of Solomon Northup, who offered a particularly poignant account of the sufferings of his friend Patsey.

Northup's text seems to have been somewhat dependent on the Williams narrative. Like Williams, Northup is a slave driver who is an accomplice, as well as a witness of his friend's beating. And like Williams, he sets his climactic scene on the Sabbath, juxtaposing the "peace and happiness" of sunny fields and chirping birds to the "demoniac exhibition" of violence. But if his account of the violence itself mirrors Williams's, his description of the victim is utterly different. Patsey has a keen sense of her own genealogy, tracing her roots to Africa via Cuba. She has both an inner dignity and stupendous skill as a field hand: "In cotton picking time, Patsey was the queen of the field." She is resolute in her resistance to her rapacious master and even finds time to console the black concubine of a neighboring planter. This act of defiance leads to her beating. There is thus no doubt that this victim of violence has the image of God's love stamped on her soul.[98]

Patsey also differs from Williams's victim in that she does not die from her whipping. She longs to die and experience heavenly rest, but instead she lives to feel the bittersweet pleasure of seeing her dear friend "Platt" (Northup) redeemed by his New York friends. Northup can thus juxtapose his own liberation to the unanswered prayer of the still godforsaken slave: "You've saved me a good many whippins, Platt; I'm glad you're goin' to be free—but oh! de Lord, de Lord! what'll become of me?"[99] There is a profound realism here, for every successful fugitive left behind dozens or even hundreds of longing, questioning kin.

At their best, fugitive slave narrators juxtaposed the voices of Northup and Patsey—the successful fugitive who boldly proclaims his full humanity and the still-victimized slave who calls her humanity into question by asking, "What'll become of me?" Readers of such narratives were challenged both to recognize the divinity of the survivor and to vindicate that divinity by responding to the victim's question. Such readers were forced to realize that liberal faith left no room for complacency. To acknowledge the inborn divinity of all humanity is also to acknowledge the extent to which institutional violence has effaced the *imago dei*. In every age, thousands of victims of violence await resurrection, and from the liberal perspective that resurrection is the task of other human beings.

6

Epics of Ambivalence

Nonviolent Power in Harriet Beecher Stowe's Antislavery Novels

All the currents of antebellum social reform came together in Harriet Beecher Stowe's wildly popular antislavery epic, *Uncle Tom's Cabin*. A master of many voices, Stowe brought together sentimental celebrations of familial love, heroic tales of escape, lurid pictures of the horrors of violence, theological debates, a mini–temperance tale about an abused and alcoholic slave, and not one but two recapitulations of Christ's passion. She used every literary device she could find to get her nation to recognize the enormous evil of slavery, and the nation did take notice. Yet if Stowe instantly became the nation's leading exponent of radical Christian liberalism, she was also among its most ambivalent supporters. On virtually every page of *Uncle Tom's Cabin* and its sequel, *Dred*, Stowe betrayed a nagging doubt that nonviolent power could not, in fact, defeat the evil of slavery. These doubts did much to shape the political culture of the 1850s, and in this sense Abraham Lincoln was right to call Stowe "the little woman who wrote the book that started this great war!"[1]

Stowe studies have experienced a renaissance in the past generation, and much of the current debate has focused on the role of power in Stowe's work—both the power actually exerted by her novels and the models of social power that they promote. According to some critics, Stowe promoted a self-defeating model of power. Her books trapped those whom they proposed to liberate by suggesting that women could do better without full political equality and that "feeling right" about slavery was an acceptable substitute for antislavery action.[2] Others argue that *Uncle Tom's Cabin* was a "political enterprise" that did "cultural work" by promoting sentimental identification between blacks and whites, thus incorporating blacks into the national community.[3] For critics in both camps, Stowe stands as the classic example of the literary sentimentality and reformist zeal so widespread in the antebellum era.

All these critics err to the extent that they portray Stowe as an innovator of sentimental strategies or as a single-minded exponent of just one model of power. On the contrary, she drew freely on the work of a generation of predecessors, including Catharine Sedgwick, Lydia Maria Child, Frederick Douglass, and William Lloyd Garrison. And her religious ambivalence prevented her from endorsing any single model of the connection between God's power and human activity. An adequate account of Stowe's contribution must therefore place her in the context of her predecessors and carefully analyze her diverse representations of power: the sentimental power exemplified most prominently by the Quaker community in *Uncle Tom's Cabin*; the power of Christic suffering embodied in Little Eva and Uncle Tom; and, finally, the violent apocalypticism hinted at throughout *Uncle Tom's Cabin* and explored more directly in Stowe's second antislavery novel, *Dred*.

Stowe and the Tradition of Radical Christian Liberalism

It is difficult to pin down Stowe's religious and political loyalties. The daughter of the foremost preacher of the day, Stowe was raised a Congregationalist and remained one until her father's death (long after the publication of *Uncle Tom's Cabin*), when she followed her daughters into the Episcopalian Church. Throughout her life she thought of orthodox Congregationalists as her people. Yet Stowe's mother was an Episcopalian, and as a girl she spent several years with Episcopalian relatives. Like her mother, she had a conversion experience that did not conform to orthodox expectations—she felt Jesus' unconditional love but not the grueling conviction of sin supposed to precede it— but that Lyman Beecher chose to accept as authentic. (In fact, none of the Beecher children managed to summon a fully orthodox conversion, a factor that helped move the entire family along the path to liberalism.) Perhaps Stowe was reciprocating her father's favor by remaining a Congregationalist so long, and then honoring her mother by turning Episcopalian. Family loyalty had a high value in the Beecher household, but in her published writings Stowe could be harshly critical of both of her own traditions and was in fact more positive in her accounts of Quakerism and Methodism.

Stowe's novels contain multiple voices—one critic has called *Uncle Tom's Cabin* a "polyphonic oratory of reality"—and in them she represents a wide range of positions with a mixture of sympathy and skepticism.[4] In one of her later novels, *Oldtown Folks*, narrator Horace Holyoke describes his own religious position in terms that fit well with Stowe's authorial practice: "Though Calvinist, Arminian, High-Church Episcopalian, sceptic and simple believer all speak in their turn, I merely listen and endeavor to understand and faithfully represent the inner life of each. I myself am but the observer and reporter, seeing much, doubting much, questioning much, and believing with all my heart in only a few things." If, like Horace, Stowe believed with all her heart in only a few things, one of those things was that God is love. She sounded this theme repeatedly in all her novels, summing it up in an 1883 letter to her sister Isabella Beecher Hooker: "You said you wished there was some name for God that expressed all human affection—Father, lover, Friend. You have it in St. John in the words God is *Love—Love—* Essential Love covers and expresses all." This stress on divine love as equivalent to human affection was, of course, a characteristically liberal starting point.[5]

Like other liberals, Stowe felt that this model of God was incompatible with the orthodox teaching that God is an absolute monarch who arbitrarily saves the elect and condemns the reprobate. In her New England novels, written after the antislavery books, she laid particular emphasis on Samuel Hopkins's theory that Christians ought to be willing to be damned for the greater glory of God, a notion she described as a "refined poetry of torture." (Here she borrowed the central theme of Sedgwick's *New-England*

Tale.) She also linked the orthodox position to monarchical ideology, with its claim that the king "can do no wrong." The orthodox God was a tyrant whose example could be used to justify human tyrannies. Thus, in *Oldtown Folks*, Stowe described a young girl who has the doctrine of divine sovereignty so impressed upon her by her tyrannical guardian that she comes to see God and Miss Asphyxia as one and the same.[6]

The antislavery novels are not so theologically preoccupied, but they also exhibit reservations about divine sovereignty. In *Uncle Tom's Cabin*, for example, Tom's sympathy for a bereaved mother is ironically contrasted with the "enlarged views" of orthodox Christians who see human suffering from the perspective of a complacently sovereign God. And in *Dred*, Stowe has a proslavery lawyer and Presbyterian elder parrot the Edwardsean doctrine of benevolence to justify slavery: since virtue is a "love of the greatest good," powerful masters deserve more happiness than powerless slaves, just as the all-powerful God deserves absolute happiness and glory.[7]

Stowe also borrowed a page or two from Catharine Sedgwick when she described the corrosive effects of the orthodox doctrine of original sin. In *Uncle Tom's Cabin*, the abused slave Topsy cannot learn right from wrong so long as her guardian reinforces her well-established belief in her own innate wickedness, while in *Dred* the Calvinist Aunt Nesbit teaches both the pampered mistress Nina and the playful slave Tomtit that they are beyond redemption. "She only takes it for granted," Nina complains, "in her hateful, quiet way, that I'm going to destruction and that she can't help it, and don't care!" Aunt Nesbit is hardly alone; as Joan Hedrick has observed, virtually all the villains in *Dred* "are, in one way or another, Calvinist theologians."[8]

Interestingly, Stowe's portrayals of poorly educated Methodist revivalists are much more positive, though it is hard to imagine that she personally would have embraced an anti-intellectual faith. Uncle Tom, significantly, is a Methodist. Stowe seems to have believed that the uneducated could access their innate human virtues more easily than the sophisticated. In *Uncle Tom's Cabin*, for example, she says that the "heathenish" Kentucky slaveholder who gallantly helps an escaping fugitive "was betrayed into acting in a sort of Christianized manner, which, if he had been better situated and more enlightened, he would not have been left to do." And in *Dred* a well-educated, very sympathetic character offers a rather Transcendentalist defense of revivalism: "I never repent my share in a popular excitement, provided it be of the higher sentiments; and I do not ask too strictly whether it has produced any tangible result. I reverence the people, as I do the woods, for the wild, grand freedom with which their humanity develops itself."[9]

This ambivalence about intellectual faith shaped Stowe's position on biblical authority, which sidestepped the scholarly debates between liberals and orthodox. The antislavery novels mirror the exegetical preoccupations of the national debate over slavery: again and again, characters wrangle over the curse of Canaan, the book of Philemon, the slaveholding example of the patriarchs, the Golden Rule, and the Exodus. In one case the debate degenerates into a quibble over which exegetes know the most Hebrew and Greek. But Stowe clearly did not think this was the way forward. Typically, antislavery characters "win" their debates only by meeting exegetical logic-chopping with silent appeals to feeling: one "smoke[s] on like a volcano" after having his say; another sits silently; still another "whistle[s] a tune." This strategy has its intended effect on at least one halfhearted defender of slavery, who has "the sense in which some logicians on this particular subject do not excel,—that of saying nothing, where nothing could be said."[10]

Stowe clearly reverenced the Bible; she harshly criticized Garrison for promoting ultraliberal views that threatened, in her view, to deprive Uncle Tom of his Bible.[11] But this reverence had little to do with any doctrinal proposition that might be derived from the biblical text. It was grounded, instead, in a series of associations between the Bible and virtuous human beings. In *Uncle Tom's Cabin*, virtually every model Christian is either symbolized by, or made to symbolize, the Bible: Little Eva is the "evangel" who points her father to Christ; Tom is "all the moral and Christian virtues bound in black morocco, complete"; and Eva's saintly grandmother is "a direct embodiment and personification of the New Testament." The narrator of *Dred* complicates this personalization of biblical authority by suggesting that the intimate link between the Bible and the individual soul accounts for both the Bible's power and its ultimate unreliability: "As the mind, looking on the great volume of nature, sees there a reflection of its own internal passions, and seizes on that in it which sympathizes with itself,—as the fierce and savage soul delights in the roar of torrents, the thunder of avalanches, and the whirl of ocean storms,—so it is in the great answering volume of revelation. There is something there for every phase of man's nature; and hence its endless vitality and stimulating force."[12]

Stowe's most positive presentation of biblical power is her account of Uncle Tom's use of the sacred book. Though only marginally literate, Tom reads regularly, recruits his friends to read with him, and marks the passages he finds most inspiring. When he falls into the hands of Simon Legree, the Bible becomes his lifeline, keeping his spirit alive in a place where the other slaves have been brutalized by toil. Yet this life-giving power seems to depend on Tom's uneducated simplicity: he is not troubled by "a thousand questions of authenticity, and correctness of translation." Unhindered by questions, Tom can reflect that the Bible "must be true; for, if not true, how could he live?"[13] Paradoxically, this passage sets Tom apart from the reader: by asserting that "the possibility of a question never entered [Tom's] simple head," Stowe ensures that such a possibility *will* enter our heads. We are left to admire the Bible's power in Tom's life but also forced to work out a different, unspecified way of accessing biblical power for ourselves.

This complex view of the Bible expresses what I shall call "perspectival liberalism," a position that differs greatly from the rational liberalism of official Unitarianism and somewhat from the sentimental liberalism of Sedgwick, Child, and Lee. Stowe did not want to replace the dogmatic truths of orthodoxy with equally dogmatic liberal truths but rather to expose the limits of *any* grand generalizations. The measure of a doctrine was its effect in particular situations: implicit faith in a poorly understood Bible was a great virtue in Tom and a troubling vice in slaveholders who ranted on about the curse of Canaan. To opt universally for or against such faith is to miss the point, which is to have enough compassion to see things from the perspective of those who suffer. "I can assure you," explains a rebellious slave in *Dred*, "the Bible looks as different to a slave from what it does to a master, as everything else in the world does."[14] This is clearly a form of liberalism, for the criterion used to judge particular religious ideas is that of the equal inclusion of those who suffer or are oppressed.

Stowe turned to a liberal perspectivalism in part because the liberal generalizations of predecessors like Sedgwick and Channing had lost their plausibility for her generation. Early Unitarians believed their doctrine of God as love was confirmed by the benevolence of nature and the progress of human history, while for Stowe the Fugitive

Slave Act of 1850 suggested that historical progress had stalled. Proto-Darwinist developments in science made nature seem indifferent or downright hostile. Stowe repeatedly ascribed a Calvinist lack of fatherly love to nature—"How inflexibly and terribly regular are all his laws! Fire and hail, snow and vapor, storming wind, fulfilling his word—all these have a crushing regularity in their movements, which show he is to be feared as well as loved"—and acknowledged that Providence seemed woefully indifferent to human suffering. In *Uncle Tom's Cabin*, she even ironized scriptural images of benign nature when describing a bereaved slave mother: "The woman looked calm, as the boat went on; and a beautiful soft summer breeze passed like a compassionate spirit over her head,—the gentle breeze, that never inquires whether the brow is dusk or fair that it fans. And she saw sunshine sparkling on the water, in golden ripples, and heard gay voices, full of ease and pleasure, talking around her everywhere, but her heart lay as if a great stone had fallen on it."[15]

Such reflections on the failing power of natural theology drove many of Stowe's contemporaries into outright agnosticism, and Stowe understood the process by which sensitive souls were driven to doubt by encounters with evil.[16] "Great afflictions—those which tear up the roots of the soul," she reflected in *Dred*, "are often succeeded, in the course of the man's history, by a period of skepticism." But personally she followed a different path, back to the orthodox Christology that had been denied or evaded by most previous liberals. Christ was, for Stowe and for many of her heroines and heroes, a reliable resort whenever intellectualized doctrines failed. "Generally speaking, preaching only weakens my faith," a thoughtful character observes in *Dred*, but "I *know* that our moral nature needs a thorough regeneration; and I believe this must come through Christ. This is all I am certain of." His fiancée expresses a similar sensibility when she reports on an interview with an orthodox pastor: "He wanted to know whether I had any just views of sin, as an infinite evil; and I told him I had n't the least idea of what infinite was; and that I had n't any views of anything, but the beauty of Christ."[17]

Such Christomonism obviously made affiliation with the Unitarians unthinkable for Stowe. Yet Stowe's Christology was directed less against liberalism than against what she perceived as the Old Testament legalism of orthodoxy. This was a theme she might have borrowed from Sedgwick, who also feared that the orthodox had betrayed the ethical spirit of the gospels. The difference between the two women writers was that Sedgwick was confident that the gospel vision could be realized by purely natural means, and thus she embraced Jesus but not Christ. Stowe, less confident, needed a divine savior to guarantee that love would triumph after all.

Still, the vision of the ideal society was the same for Sedgwick and Stowe. This was a vision of nonviolence, freedom, and equality—a vision rooted in the Sermon on the Mount as interpreted in the light of the Declaration of Independence. For my purposes, Stowe's commitment to this vision is what marks her as a religious liberal. Her repeated construal of slavery as "sin" is thus not, as some critics have suggested, evidence that she was committed to "Christian morality" rather than "racial equality"; equality was for her an integral part of Christian morality.[18] When Stowe betrayed her own egalitarian vision, it was not because she was a Christian moralist but because she had little faith that Christian morality could triumph without extraordinary divine intervention.

Stowe's relationship with Garrison's brand of radical abolitionism ran parallel to her relationship with Christian liberalism. Though family loyalty compelled her to maintain a certain distance from organized abolitionism—the abolitionist students at Lane Seminary had walked out in protest of Lyman Beecher's colonizationism in 1834, and Catharine Beecher had attacked Angelina Grimké's public speaking in 1837—Stowe held many beliefs that resonated with Garrisonianism. Like Garrison, Stowe advocated a nonviolent solution to slavery even as she insisted that slave rebellion was at least as justifiable as the United States Revolution. She located the evil of slavery in the system rather than its abuse: "The *thing itself* is the essence of all abuse," says one character in *Uncle Tom's Cabin.* She sought to direct the brunt of her attack against the institution rather than the persons who participated in it, though—like Garrison—she also resorted to rhetoric that was perceived to be harshly ad hominem. She believed that the constitutional protections of slavery, and especially the Fugitive Slave Act, implicated the entire nation in slavery's sin. And, perhaps most important, her most basic argument against slavery appealed to the equal humanity of all people. Thus, when in *Uncle Tom's Cabin* the slave mistress Marie St. Clare casually remarks that to place the slaves "on any sort of equality with us, you know, as if we could be compared, why, it's impossible," she shocks her New England cousin Ophelia, who exclaims, "Don't you believe that the Lord made them of one blood with us?" Like Ophelia, Stowe was not free of racial prejudice, but she recognized liberal identification as the divinely ordained goal.[19]

Many readers, nevertheless, have been troubled by Stowe's refusal to end her antislavery novels with the triumph of liberal principles. At the conclusion of *Uncle Tom's Cabin,* Tom is dead, and the most energetic slave characters have lost faith in the United States and embraced the colonizationist scheme of establishing a separate black republic in Liberia. Meanwhile, at Tom's old Kentucky home, the virtuous young master has freed his slaves, but they have chosen to continue as his employees; the plantation has become the sort of benevolently paternalistic institution that proslavery apologists claimed most plantations already were. Nowhere are we allowed to see a community of whites and blacks living and working together in equality. Read in light of this conclusion, Stowe's classic statement of suasionist faith—"There is one thing that every individual can do,—they can see to it that *they feel right*"—has been taken as a disavowal of the reader's responsibility to work politically for an equal society. Such a reading is surely unfair. As the rebellious speeches of Stowe's colonizationist hero make clear, Stowe believed that African Americans had a right to full inclusion in U.S. society, as well as a right to abandon the United States when its racism became intolerable. Yet Stowe must take responsibility for confusing her readers. She proclaimed the power of right feeling, but she could not explain what precisely that power might accomplish. She simply did not know, and so she offered a series of incompatible theories of antislavery power.

Sentimental Power

According to the classic sentimental theory, to "feel right" is to identify with the suffering other, and thus to begin working together for the common good. The theory assumes that identification is an innate capacity of all humans, albeit one that can be either nurtured or neglected. It is a profoundly humanistic theory, and its literary task is to represent the full humanity of persons involved, in various ways, in the inhuman system of slavery. This is what Stowe sets out to do, with a fair measure of success, in the first thirteen chapters of her novel.

The title of the first chapter, "In Which the Reader Is Introduced to a Man of Humanity," states the problem aptly: Who is human? Who is humane? Who gets to decide? We are actually introduced to two men, the Kentucky slaveholder Mr. Shelby and the slave trader Haley, who are discussing the pending sale of Shelby's slave Tom. Both claim to be "humane"; Haley, in fact, says that "humanity . . . is the great pillar of *my* management." But neither has been properly "introduced" to the humanity of Tom himself. Haley's management is actually founded on his belief that "these critters ain't like white folks" and can easily get over the forced separation of families. Shelby has sentiment enough to find Haley repulsive but not enough to reject the sale. Instead, he relies on his devout wife to exercise humanity on his behalf: "If not exactly a believer in the doctrine of the efficiency of the extra good works of saints, he really seemed somehow or other to fancy that his wife had piety and benevolence enough for two." So long as he has all the real power on the plantation, it is clear that her piety is scarcely enough for one.[20]

This opening chapter lays out a challenge for the readers: Can we confirm our own humanity by recognizing that of the slaves? The next two chapters, entitled "The Mother" and "The Husband and Father," employ the classic sentimental tactic of introducing suffering individuals in terms of their relational roles. We first see Eliza Harris fretting over the possibility that her son Harry will be sold, and subsequently we are told of the intense grief she felt when her first two children died. Her husband, George, is the first victim of violence depicted in the novel, and his victimization is linked to his own humane identification with animals. When George tries to stop "young Mas'r Tom" from mistreating a horse, Tom has him tied to a tree and whips him until he is tired. And when George refuses to drown his pet dog, Carlo, he receives another flogging and must watch as Carlo is both drowned and pelted with stones. Clearly, Stowe expected that any reader who had cared for a dog or a horse would have an easier time identifying with George.[21]

Similar tactics recur throughout Stowe's account of the slave community's reaction to the pending sale of Uncle Tom and little Harry, the son of George and Eliza. But Stowe's understanding of sentimental identification appears most clearly in the chapters dealing with Eliza's reception in two northern households after her daring escape across the Ohio River. The first of these is the home of the Birds, an Ohio senator and his benevolent wife, Mary. In this household, "humanity" is at once an innate capacity and a project that must be worked at. The narrator attributes an "unusually gentle and sympathetic" character to Mrs. Bird and "a particularly humane and accessible nature" to her husband but also suggests that the Bird children must be trained to avoid cruelty. One of the first things we see Mrs. Bird doing is telling her daughter not to pull the cat's tail; we are then told that she was recently thrown "into a passion" upon finding her sons "leagued with several graceless boys of the neighborhood, stoning a defenceless kitten." On that occasion she whipped the boys and sent them to bed without supper, and "after that," one of the sons reports, "I heard mother crying outside the door, which made me feel worse than all the rest. I'll tell you what . . . we boys never stoned another kitten!" Like Henry Clarke Wright, this young white man attains nonviolent power only through a complex, relational process.[22]

His father must do much the same. Senator Bird comes onstage from a legislative session in which he had sacrificed his humanity to patriotism by supporting the Fugitive Slave Act. Mrs. Bird remonstrates against this, but the senator explains that "we mustn't suffer our feelings to run away with our judgment" or put "private feeling" ahead of "public interests." This rule quickly dissolves upon the arrival of Eliza Harris: the Birds, recently bereaved of an infant, learn that Eliza has lost two children and fears losing Harry as well, and this knowledge seals their identification. Indeed, the senator is particularly eager to mark the commonality by asking his wife to give Eliza her own clothes, and the lost baby's things for Harry. He also drives Eliza to the home of an abolitionist friend who mentions that he had joined the church only after finding a minister whose "Greek and Hebrew" confirmed his own natural aversion to slavery.[23]

A few chapters later Eliza finds herself in a community that is organized entirely around the sort of sentimental identification newly achieved by Senator Bird. This is the Quaker settlement presided over by "our good friend Rachel Halliday," a woman often cited by critics as the epitome of Stowe's theory of maternal salvation. Rachel spends her time in a squeaky rocking chair that has itself imbibed the motherly spirit: her husband "and children all avowed that they wouldn't miss of hearing mother's chair for anything in the world" because "for twenty years or more, nothing but loving words, and gentle moralities, and motherly loving kindness, had come from that chair." On Eliza's arrival, Rachel immediately calls her "daughter," "for hers was just the face and form that made 'mother' seem the most natural word in the world."[24]

Rachel's talent for identification is mirrored by the other members of the Quaker community. A young woman, Ruth Stedman, insists that Eliza immediately be told of her husband George's presence in the community because that is what she would want in Eliza's situation. "Thee uses thyself only to learn how to love thy neighbor," observes Rachel's husband, to which Ruth replies, "Isn't it what we are made for? If I didn't love John and the baby, I should not know how to feel for her." In subsequent chapters— Eliza and George's later adventures are widely spaced throughout the novel—we learn that the sentimental way has its effect even on such latecomers to Quakerism as Phineas, "a hearty, two-fisted backwoodsman" who has become a Quaker through marriage. Only tepidly committed to nonviolence, Phineas encourages George to arm himself against their slave-catching pursuers, and at a critical moment he pushes the brutal Tom Loker over a precipice. But Phineas, like George himself, is averse to killing and has enough surgical expertise to save the injured slave catcher. There is even a sort of sentimental identification between the two rough-mannered men. After being nursed by the Quakers, Tom Loker advances to Phineas's starting point by embracing a relatively pacific life as a frontiersman.[25]

The sentimental history concentrated in the early chapters of *Uncle Tom's Cabin* is, however, marked by doubts. Stowe's goal is to change the hearts of her readers, and her characterizations of Senator Bird, Phineas, and Tom Loker suggest the means by which a change of heart might take place. But these instructive characters are surrounded by those who either need not or cannot change—by mothers and others who are nonviolent by nature rather than practice, and by white and light men who cannot utterly relinquish coercive power. Many critics have regarded Stowe's romanticization of motherly love and her racialist theory of blacks as "not naturally daring and enterprising, but home-loving and affectionate" as intrinsic to the sentimental strategy.[26] From my perspective, the opposite is the case. Sentimentalism relies on identification, and it is far easier to identify with traits that must be cultivated through struggle than with those that are said to inhere in a gender or racial category. Real-world mothers, I suspect, identified with Mrs. Bird's bereavement and with the "twenty years" of Rachel Halliday's patient efforts far more than with the insinuation that these women had not had to learn to be good mothers. Stowe's romanticizations represent a different, more insidious sort of power: they appeal to those who fear they cannot change, offering the alternative hope that a maternal savior with supernatural powers might do the work for them. Underneath the appeal to such power was the lingering suspicion that mother love could not, after all, save the world.

The doubts implicit in Stowe's appeal to superhuman mothers are quite explicit in her characterization of Eliza's husband, George Harris, in many ways the most complexly human character in the novel. A tragic mulatto like Archy Moore and Frederick Douglass, George flees his cruel master early in the novel, determined to reach Canada if possible, to defend himself when necessary, and to die before returning to slavery. When his plan is questioned, he appeals both to universal human nature—"My master! . . . I'm a man as much as he is. I'm a better man than he is"—and to the example of the Founding Fathers. Again and again Stowe suggests that George is a latter-day Washington or Jefferson; confronted by the slave catchers, he makes a defiant speech, which the narrator calls "his declaration of independence." Yet he is also haunted by Eliza's Christianity and the "gentle system of ethics" she derives from it. "I an't a Christian like you, Eliza," he tells her before his escape, "my heart's full of bitterness; I can't trust in God. Why does he let things be so?" The question Stowe asks through George Harris (and through George Shelby, the impulsive and idealistic heir to Tom's home plantation, who mirrors George in name and sensibility) is whether such a man can *become* a Christian—whether strict Christian nonviolence can ultimately be reconciled with the egalitarian vision of the Declaration. And the answer she gives is profoundly equivocal.[27]

Much has been made of the fact that George, like so many antislavery heroes, is a mulatto. Undoubtedly, Stowe assumed that her white readers would find it easier to identify with a light-skinned hero; probably she personally found it easier. She also assumed that a rebellious spirit was most likely to appear in a body with a considerable measure of Anglo-Saxon blood.[28] Paradoxically, however, Stowe's rigid and conventional thinking about what it means to be a mulatto allowed her to make George emblematically human. If other characters are trapped in single categories, George's multiple categorization places him between the violent freedom of the whites and the nonviolent love of the blacks, free to choose either path—or perhaps to integrate them.

It is fitting, therefore, that George is at once the first victim of violence and the most self-reflective perpetrator of violence depicted in Stowe's novel. Both roles confirm his humanity—his victimization, in that he is punished because of his sympathy for animals, and his violence, in that it appears as a natural reaction against objectification. When his jealous master removes him from a satisfying position in a factory, George is "able to repress every disrespectful word; but the flashing eye, the gloomy and troubled brow, were part of a natural language that could not be repressed,—indubitable signs, which showed too plainly that the man could not become a thing."[29]

At the same time, George's victimization and violence militate against his becoming a Christian. His violence is inconsistent with the Christian ethic, while his victimization makes belief in a providentially sovereign God impossible. From the slave's perspective, he explains to the sympathetic factory owner, faith is not an option: "I've seen things all my life that have made me feel that there can't be a God. You Christians don't know how these things look to us. There's a god for you, but is there any for us?" The best George can propose is that perhaps faith will come when he has escaped the perspective of a slave: "My wife is a Christian," he says, "and I mean to be, if ever I get to where I can."[30]

George does "get to where he can," and he does become a Christian; his religious dilemma, like Frederick Douglass's, is resolved by his escape. Fittingly, the scene of this change is the Quaker settlement, where the Quakers' long-practiced tactics of identification have their full effect.

> This, indeed, was a home,—*home*,—a word that George had never yet known a meaning for; and a belief in God, and trust in his providence, began to encircle his heart, as with a golden cloud of protection and confidence, dark, misanthropic, pining atheistic doubts, and fierce despair, melted away before the light of a living Gospel, breathed in living faces, preached by a thousand unconscious acts of love and good will, which, like the cup of cold water given in the name of a disciple, shall never lose their reward.[31]

When George continues to question the power of Providence, the Quakers patiently read Psalm 73 with him, demonstrating that his doubts and despair had been fully shared by a biblical writer who ultimately found the strength to believe.[32]

Had Stowe fully believed in the power of sentimental identification to conquer slavery, she might have made George's conversion the first step in a program of direct confrontation with Southern slavery—she might, in short, have made George a somewhat more sentimental, nonviolent version of Frederick Douglass. Instead, she imposed on George a series of further removals—first to Canada, then to France, and ultimately to Liberia, where he proposes to confront slavery very indirectly by building a more truly Christian, and less Anglo-Saxon, republic. The implication of these removals is that George has perhaps not quite gotten to where he can be a Christian—and that he certainly cannot return to the South, to confront slavery, while remaining a Christian. Indeed, Stowe's ultimate, very illiberal, message seems to be that a man like George can be fully Christian only in heaven. This message is suggested as early as George's conversation with the factory owner. Mr. Wilson's parting comment is that "everything will be set right,—if not in this life, in another," and these words alone manage to get George's attention. And despite the this-worldly virtues of the Quaker community, the Quakers' clinching argument is strictly otherworldly: "If this world were all, George, . . . thee might, indeed, ask where is the Lord? But it is often those who have least of all in this life whom he chooseth for the kingdom. Put thy trust in him and, no matter what befalls thee here, he will make all right hereafter."[33] Heaven, it seems, is George's only home.

The Power of Death

Even as Stowe gently pushes George out of this world and into heaven, so she also pushes him out of her novel in order to take the narrative where he cannot go—the South. Here we must come to terms with Tom and Eva, the slave sold south and the slaveholder's daughter, two emblems of sentimentality who exert powers that ultimately have nothing whatsoever to do with sentimental identification.[34] To be sure, both are utterly compassionate, and Stowe suggests that this compassion is the source of great power. But neither really thinks that he or she is like other people, and as readers we are repeatedly told *not* to identify ourselves with Tom or Eva.

When Tom learns that he and little Harry are to be sold, he responds by endorsing Eliza's flight—"tan't in *natur* for her to stay"—and yet insisting that he must accept his own sale to redeem the plantation from debt, even though this also involves a family separation. Eva, for her part, knows that she is dying of consumption and thus has a connection to heaven denied most humans. Other characters also see Tom and Eva as unlike other people: Eva's father describes Tom as a "moral miracle" because the trials of slavery have not made him dishonest, and he justifies his own negligent parenting with the observation that no one can corrupt or spoil his daughter because she is "more angel than ordinary" and "evil rolls off Eva's mind like dew off a cabbage leaf,—not a drop sinks in." Both Tom and Eva recognize that the other is superhuman, and Tom loves and "almost" worships Eva "as the Italian sailor gazes on his image of the child Jesus,—with a mixture of reverence and tenderness."[35] The implicit message to the reader is not "go and do likewise" but "don't try this at home."

At first it appears that Tom's and Eva's virtues, however supernatural their origins, operate like those of merer mortals. Eva's spontaneous love for the abused slave Topsy, for example, is both healing for Topsy and morally instructive for Topsy's guardian, Ophelia. Tom's compassionate solicitude for his new master, Augustine St. Clare, immediately inspires the latter to quit drinking and almost brings him to become a Christian and free his slaves. Yet as Eva succumbs to disease and Tom moves on to the heartless plantation of Simon Legree, it becomes increasingly clear that their true power, retroactively involved even in their earthly kindnesses, derives from their deaths. Eva's death—which the narrator refers to as "the victory without the battle,—the crown without the conflict"—enables her to distribute curls of her hair to the community, one of which will eventually have a talismanic power over Simon Legree, and helps her extract from her father a promise to emancipate his slaves. Tom's death guarantees the escape of his friends Cassy and Emmeline and instantly converts Sambo and Quimbo, Legree's brutal accomplices in the murder.[36]

Given the significance Stowe ascribes to these two deaths (and to the deaths of heroines in most of her subsequent novels), there is justice in one critic's comment that "not love but death is Mrs. Stowe's true Muse."[37] Indeed, critics on both sides of the debate over Stowe agree that death is the ultimate power in her universe and assume that this view stems directly from her Christian commitment.[38] Such readings ignore the possibility of a liberal Christianity that places primary emphasis on life in this world, and neglect Stowe's own account of this-worldly Christian power in the Quaker village. Still, it is Stowe's own fault if many readers conclude that for her the deathbed is both more important and more religious than the kitchen. Stowe limits the kitchen's efficacy to the North, treating it as little more than a way station for fugitives en route to Liberia, while leaving to the deathbed the task of actually confronting slavery. And she reserves her most explicitly religious language for scenes of death.

Stowe's two dying saints, Tom and Eva, are for her at once models of (inimitable) human action and divine action. Again and again, Stowe attributes to God both the

absolute sympathy and the apparent powerlessness of Tom and Eva. Effectively elimi-
nating divine omnipotence in order to affirm divine omnipresence in a violent world,
she describes a God who is present at every calamity, who listens to every prayer, but
who rarely responds. This first becomes clear when Tom is en route from Kentucky
to Louisiana on an Ohio River ferryboat filled with other bereaved slaves. Tom over-
hears a slave woman bidding her husband a final farewell, and the narrator comments that the story "of heartstrings rent and broken . . . needs not to be told;—every
day is telling it,—telling it, too, in the ear of One who is not deaf, though he be long
silent."[39] Tom then befriends a woman who has just lost her child; he tells of Jesus'
love and the promise of heaven, but she is too grief-stricken to hear. Stowe's poignant, oddly pacific narration of the woman's suicide exemplifies the theme of the
godforsakenness of violence:

> Night came on,—night calm, unmoved, and glorious, shining down with her innumer-
> able and solemn angel eyes, twinkling, beautiful, but silent. There was no speech nor
> language, no pitying voice or helping hand, from that distant sky. One after another, the
> voices of business or pleasure died away; all on the boat were sleeping, and the ripples at
> the prow were plainly heard. Tom stretched himself out on a box, and there, as he lay, he
> heard, ever and anon, a smothered sob or cry from the prostate creature,—"O! what shall
> I do? O Lord! O good Lord, do help me!" and so, ever and anon, until the murmur died
> away in silence.[40]

Godforsakenness resurfaces in a powerful way three hundred pages later, when Tom
arrives at the Legree plantation in the Red River valley. Here Tom is introduced to Legree's
spurned mistress Cassy, a proud and brilliant woman who has suffered the worst of all
slavery's evils. "The Lord never visits these parts," she assures Tom at their first meeting. Later, when she has told him of her many tribulations and he continues to suggest
that she look to Jesus for living water, she elaborates, "I used to see the picture of him,
over the altar, when I was a girl . . . but *he isn't here!* There's nothing here, but sin and
long, long despair! O!" Gradually, Tom comes to see her point. As the workload in-
creases at the height of the cotton-picking season, as weeks pass without any word from
his Kentucky friends (whom Tom hopes will come to redeem him), and as Tom becomes increasingly aware of slavery's degrading effects on all those around him, he slips
into a dark night of the soul. Physically and spiritually exhausted, he stops reading the
Bible and must even "crush back to his soul bitter thoughts,—that it was vain to serve
God, that God had forgotten him." Noticing Tom's despair, Legree is exultant and invites
Tom to discard his Bible and "join my church!" The best response Tom can muster is
that whether or not the Lord helps him, he will continue to believe.[41]

For Stowe, paradoxically, such scenes of earthly godforsakenness are the places where
God, in Christ, is most fully present. Thus Tom's dark night ends with a mystic vision
of the crucified Christ:

> The atheistic taunts of his cruel master sunk his before dejected soul to the lowest ebb; and,
> though the hand of faith still held to the eternal rock, it was a numb, despairing grasp. Tom
> sat, like one stunned, at the fire. Suddenly everything around him seemed to fade, and a
> vision rose before him of one crowned with thorns, buffeted and bleeding. Tom gazed, in
> awe and wonder, at the majestic patience of the face; the deep, pathetic eyes thrilled him to
> his inmost heart; his soul woke, as, with floods of emotion, he stretched out his hands and

fell upon his knees,—when, gradually, the vision changed: the sharp thorns became rays of glory; and, in splendor inconceivable, he saw that same face bending compassionately towards him, and a voice said, "He that overcometh shall sit down with me on my throne, even as I also overcome, and am set down with my Father on his throne."[42]

This vision both anticipates Tom's death and infuses him with the power to defy Legree to the end. He experiences "an inviolable sphere of peace" that places him beyond "the bleeding of earthly regrets"; indeed, his will is "now entirely merged in the divine."[43]

Tom's vision changes the theological calculus of the novel. The power that was at first dispersed in all the natural affections of this earth—in Eliza's maternal love, in Rachel Halliday's sympathy, in George Harris's fervent sense of his own manhood—is now concentrated in a Christic power that is *always* suffering on earth yet always triumphant in heaven. This theology had already been suggested when, a few chapters earlier, Tom tells Cassy, "Ye said the Lord took sides against us, because he lets us be 'bused and knocked round; but ye see what comes on his own Son,—the blessed Lord of Glory,—wasn't he allays poor? and have we, any on us, yet come so low as he come?" It is reiterated in Stowe's later novels: in *Dred*, the pious slave Milly has a vision of Jesus "suffering, bearing with us, year in and year out—bearing—bearing—bearing so patient! 'Peared like, it wa'n't just on de cross; but, bearing always, everywhar!"[44] And *The Minister's Wooing*, Stowe's most theological novel, contains an elaborate apotheosis that simply identifies Christ with sorrow:

> Sorrow is divine. Sorrow is reigning on the throne of the universe, and the crown of all crowns has been one of thorns. There have been many books that treat of the mystery of sorrow, but only one that bids us glory in tribulation, and count it all joy when we fall into divers afflictions, that so we may be associated with that great fellowship of suffering of which the Incarnate God is the head, and through which He is carrying a redemptive conflict to a glorious victory over evil. If we suffer with Him, we shall also reign with Him.[45]

Here the distance between Stowe and earlier liberals becomes crystal clear. For Sedgwick, Child, and Lee, and even for Garrison, Wright, and Judd, a notion of God as pure love, mirrored in the sentimental identifications of ordinary people, served as a bulwark against the despair liberals associated with both orthodoxy and infidelity. Stowe, by contrast, embraces the despair, labels it Christ, and asserts that it is the mark of heavenly triumph.[46] She does not revive the substitutionary atonement, for she never attributes Tom's or anyone else's death to God's providential plan. Stowe's plot resonates more closely with the ransom theory of the atonement, in that the devilish Simon Legree is responsible for Tom's death, and Tom's defiance ensures the escape of Cassy and Emmeline. (The proximate cause of his murder is his refusal to divulge their escape plan.) But, unlike Mary's death at the hands of Simon Slade in *Ten Nights in a Bar-Room*, Tom's death does not lead to the entire defeat of the devil. Though Cassy and Emmeline escape, and though George Shelby arrives to collect Tom's body and knock Simon Legree down, Legree remains in full control of his hellish plantation: when other slaves ask young George to purchase them, he replies dejectedly that "it's impossible!" What Stowe offers is really a new theory of the atonement in which the perpetrator of the passion and its earthly effects are simply irrelevant: the suffering itself is all in all.[47]

The point can perhaps be clarified through a comparison of Tom's dark night with the experiences of Frederick Douglass just before his decisive fight with Covey. For both slaves, a period of atheistic despair gives way suddenly to a new faith that enables them to confront a diabolically violent white power. But the *goal* of Douglass's confrontation is to live and escape, while Tom's goal (and *not* merely the undesirable consequence of his defiance) is to die. Thus Tom confronts Legree not by saying that he *will* be free, dead or alive, but that he wants to die: "I'd as soon die as not. Ye may whip me, starve me, burn me,—it'll only send me sooner where I want to go." Heaven, it seems, is the only goal that counts.[48]

Apocalyptic Power

Yet Stowe was a relentlessly complex writer, and this is not the last word either in *Uncle Tom's Cabin* or in her career as an antislavery writer. Stowe did not believe what this theology seems to suggest—that slavery is a perfectly useful conduit of virtuous blacks to heaven, which is where they really want to be anyhow. Indeed, she believed that despite her own doubts something—anything—desperately needed to be done. But the logic of *Uncle Tom's Cabin* suggests that the nonviolent power of sentimental identification could be practiced only in the North, or among those who are already nonviolent, and that the nonviolent power of Christic suffering is truly effective only in heaven. This left the door wide open for Stowe to invoke a third sort of power—for her to suggest that slavery will end only with God's violent, apocalyptic intervention. Indeed, this theme is prominent enough in *Uncle Tom's Cabin* that one recent critic has made the seemingly self-evident observation that the novel's "message was an apocalyptic judgment upon America's worst continuing sin."[49]

Stowe touched the apocalyptic theme from the beginning of her career as an antislavery writer. One of the first stories she wrote for the *National Era*—the antislavery journal that serialized *Uncle Tom's Cabin*—was "The Freeman's Dream," a tale of a Northern man who refuses to give food to a runaway slave and then has a terrifying dream of being put with the goats at the Last Judgment.[50] *Uncle Tom's Cabin* is tinged with apocalypticism throughout: the early reference to "one who is not deaf though he be long silent" hints that God will eventually speak loudly, and the narrator comments, after describing a New York firm profiting from the slave trade, that "on the reverse of that draft, so obtained, let them write these words of the great Paymaster, to whom they shall make up their account in a future day: 'When he maketh inquisition for blood, he forgetteth not the cry of the humble!'"[51]

The apocalyptic theme is developed more extensively in Stowe's characterization of Little Eva's father, Augustine St. Clare. St. Clare is a philosophical dilettante, sensitive but cynical, whose scruples about slavery and lack of resolution make him a kind, extremely indulgent master. He has relinquished all direct involvement in the plantation economy but "wasn't up to" actually freeing his slaves. "To hold them as tools for money-making, I could not," he tells his cousin Ophelia, "have them to help spend money, you know, didn't look quite so ugly to me." But he is convinced that the slave system as a whole is headed for a violent cataclysm comparable to that recently experienced in Haiti. He tells his brother, who maintains a plantation with strict discipline, that his position is that of one who would "put on the steam, fasten down the escape-valve, and sit on it, and see where you'll land." In his conversation with Ophelia, he explains his vision of history in more depth, echoing Garrison by linking the slaves' rebellion to waves of working-class revolution: "One thing is certain,—that there is a mustering among the masses, the world over; and there is a *dies irae* coming on, sooner or later. The same thing is working in Europe, in England, and in this country."[52]

This is a naturalistic vision of the apocalypse. It is not clear whether it will come in God's good time or simply when accumulated human resentments bring it about. But this distinction does not seem to matter to Stowe. She has Ophelia validate the religiosity of St. Clare's vision by commenting that her cousin is "not far from the kingdom." And she reiterates St. Clare's theory in her own narrative voice on the concluding page of the novel. An "earthquake" is coming, she suggests, and "every nation that carries in its bosom great and unredressed injustice has in it the elements of this last convulsion." The coming earthquake will be caused by "the spirit of HIM whose kingdom is yet to come," but its goal will be classically liberal: "man's freedom and equality." And it will be violent, a "*day of vengeance*" in which "he shall break in pieces the oppressor." Unless, that is, the nation repents: like Garrison, Stowe is careful to cast her apocalypse in hypothetical language, noting that there is still a "day of grace" in which the Union might be saved "by repentance, justice, and mercy."[53]

When Stowe published her second antislavery novel, *Dred*, in 1856, the chances of this day of grace being obtained seemed dim indeed. The Supreme Court's decision in the Dred Scott case, which established that a master could bring a slave into a free state without forfeiting ownership, confirmed the federal government's commitment to maintaining slavery and further blurred the distinction between North and South. At the same time, proslavery Southerners seemed to be pushing every advantage. A Southern congressman publicly assaulted Massachusetts's antislavery senator Charles Sumner in 1857, and in Kansas, supposedly free to accept or reject slavery, "border ruffians" from Missouri were crossing over to vote in territorial elections and harass free-state settlers. Repeated clashes in "bleeding Kansas" persuaded many Northerners that slavery required a violent solution. Among them was Stowe's brother Henry Ward Beecher, who enthusiastically gathered Sharp's rifles, or "Beecher's Bibles," to send to the Kansas settlers.

In this heated context, Stowe wrote a novel reflecting on the apocalyptic basis of slave rebellion. Like *Uncle Tom's Cabin*, this novel contains two leading male slave characters. Henry Gordon is a mulatto Everyman in the tradition of Frederick Douglass and George Harris. The son of his deceased master, Harry is devoted to his white half sister, fiercely resentful of his debauched half brother, jealous of his manhood, and ambivalent about the role of violence in his own quest for freedom. But where Tom, the embodiment of the New Testament, is George's alter ego, Harry's is the swamp rebel Dred, son of Denmark Vesey and an apocalyptic figure who speaks almost exclusively in quotes from the Hebrew prophets and the Book of Revelation. Dred arrives with a violent challenge whenever Harry has suffered a humiliation at the hands of his brother, prompting Harry to complain, "You are raising the very devil in me!" But Harry is also moved by Dred's challenges, feeling "an uprising within him, vague, tumultuous, overpowering; dim instincts, heroic aspirations; the will to do, the soul to dare."[54] By contrasting Harry with Dred, Stowe implicitly asked if ordinary mortals could appropriate apocalyptic violence any more readily than they could the Christic self-sacrifice of Tom and Eva.

Apparently the answer was no. Dred is as carefully differentiated from the rest of humanity as is Tom; indeed, where Tom is simply superhuman, Dred is at once sub-

and superhuman. He is "of magnificent stature" and "herculean strength" and is pre-
ternaturally well developed in the phrenological areas of perception, morality, and intel-
ligence. But he also has "the agility and stealthy adroitness of a wild animal." In his
eyes "there burned . . . like tongues of flame in a black pool of naphtha, a subtle and
restless fire that betokened habitual excitement to the verge of insanity." But, perhaps
most of all, Dred, who lives secretly in the Carolina swamps, embodies the wildness of
nature: he is as intimately linked to "the nursing influences of nature" as a tree and has
"the rain, the wind, and the thunder" as his "familiar companions."[55]

Stowe was too good a novelist to maintain a character for hundreds of pages as no
more than a symbol of the Old Testament or of wild nature. Gradually, she reveals that
Dred, like Harry, is a human being who must struggle to discern God's will for his life.
But to the extent that Dred is revealed as human, it becomes clear that he, like Harry,
is not really free to choose the path of apocalyptic violence. This emerges in Stowe's
account of his exegetical wrestlings with the prophetic tradition. Dred's "greatest instrument of influence," says the narrator, "was a book that has always been prolific of insurrectionary movements, under all systems of despotism." But the tone suggests that it is
at least in part a misreading to construe the Bible as "not the messenger of peace and
good will, but the herald of woe and wrath!" This becomes clearer and more complicated in a later reflection on the theme, in which the narrator argues that the prophetic
tradition is "not definitely understood" in the revolutionary communities that value it,
but that it nevertheless possesses an "indefinite stimulating power" over them.[56]

Why did Stowe simultaneously endorse and disavow the connection between the
Bible and revolution? The reason is that she was unwilling to endorse the human *decision* to engage in revolution but nevertheless believed it possible that such revolutionary
action might be part of God's plan. Paradoxically, Stowe believed that God was acting
even through the misreading of the Bible.

Ultimately, Stowe wanted to have both a long-suffering Christ and at least the possibility of a final apocalypse in which the tables are turned on those who have inflicted
the suffering. This tension is dramatized in Dred's confrontation with Milly, a devout
Christian slave who is committed to nonviolence. Just as Dred's band of rebels, which
now includes Harry Gordon, is preparing to launch their attack, Milly walks into the
camp singing, "Alas! and did my Saviour bleed." Her testimony to "the eternal principle of intercession and atonement" has its effect on Dred, who has already been wondering if he really has God's green light for the attack. Before he can decide what to do,
he is killed trying to protect another fugitive. Milly, Harry, and the rest of Dred's band
all decide to escape rather than fight.[57]

Milly was modeled on Sojourner Truth, by 1850 a prominent Garrisonian speaker,
and it is significant that Truth, like Stowe, was struggling to make more room for
Christology within a broadly liberal religious framework. Truth's vocation as a reformer
had been shaped during her stay with the Northampton Association, an abolitionist
commune founded in part by Garrison's brother-in-law, George Benson. Her closest friend
there was a Unitarian ministry student, Giles B. Stebbins, who would ultimately preach
at Truth's funeral. But Truth's personal religious synthesis had to take account of the
vision of Jesus she had experienced just after obtaining her freedom, at a time when she
was thinking of returning to the Egypt of slavery. Though at the time she had no idea
that Jesus was more than "an eminent man, like a Washington or a Lafayette," she saw

him as "a form distinct, beaming with the beauty of holiness, and radiant with love." He promised to mediate between her and a God whom she tended to see in the image of her old master, as one who saw and judged all her "delinquencies." If Truth's biographer Olive Gilbert—herself a Garrisonian—is to be trusted, this vision did not convert Truth to orthodox Trinitarianism. Instead, she saw Jesus as the return of the divine image that Adam and Eve had possessed prior to the Fall. To possess Jesus' spirit in one's own heart was thus to be personally committed to a nonviolent ministry of love and mercy.[58]

It was not, however, to be convinced that God's work would always be nonviolent. When the Civil War began, Truth embraced it as God's work more fervently than some Garrisonians, even penning a hymn to the black soldiers who could "shoot a rebel farther than a white man ever saw." Similarly, Stowe's Milly does not deny the possibility of an apocalypse but simply urges against the human promotion of it: "If dere must come a day of vengeance, pray not to be in it! It's de Lord's strange work." The narrator elaborates in terms that are at once psychological and theological: Dred's desire for retribution is a sign of the sense of justice characteristic of the "highest natures." But "the human heart" also contains "a pleading, interceding element . . . which the Scriptures represent by the sublime image of an eternally interceding highpriest," that is, Jesus Christ. Yet this "mysterious *person*" is not merely the "impersonation of divine tenderness" but also "has yet in reserve this awful energy of wrath"—hence the scriptural references to the Lamb as the agent of apocalyptic violence. If Milly's Christ is the antithesis to Dred's apocalyptic thesis, then the synthesis is the coming apocalypse of Christ himself. And the measure of this coming violence is exactly proportionate to the Christic suffering of all humanity: "If we would estimate the forces of almighty justice, let us ask ourselves what a mother might feel for the abuse of her helpless child, and multiply that by infinity."[59]

Stowe concludes this passage with her standard image of God's silence on a starlit night: "But the night wore on, and the stars looked down serene and solemn, as if no prayer had gone through the calm, eternal gloom, and the morning broke in the east resplendent."[60] This mirrors the fact that Stowe's apocalyptic theology offers even fewer guideposts for human action than her Christology. Stowe holds out the possibility that slavery will end through apocalyptic intervention but insists that we not seek or even hope for such an outcome, apparently forgetting that she has given us no reason to hope for any other sort of solution. After all her searching explorations of various forms of power that might be brought to bear against slavery, Stowe is unable to offer her readers even one sort of power that they might deliberately embrace.[61]

One might expect that the effect of such a self-defeating exploration of antislavery power would be a dampening of abolitionist fervor. The actual result of Stowe's novels was, of course, quite the opposite: she helped engineer the broad antislavery consensus in the North that would bring the Republicans into power and thus spark the Civil War. What Stowe's work did dampen, however, was the explicit discussion of the various forms of power that might be used to defeat slavery. By suggesting that apocalyptic intervention was the force most likely to succeed, she encouraged her readers to interpret any event that seemed likely to overturn the system in terms of divine rather than human action. Stowe's influence helps explain why nearly all abolitionists, once the war had begun, interpreted it as *the* way God had chosen to fight slavery, rather than as *a* way that they had chosen.

7

Violent Messiahs

Radical Christian Liberals and the Civil War

The radical liberal theology of nonviolence was radically open-ended. Reformers of many stripes could agree that God required their absolute resistance to the many institutions of social violence, and nonresistants could agree further that active nonviolence was the proper expression of this resistance, but they could only guess as to how God might support their efforts. This open-ended stance can be traced to the liberal willingness to let earthly experience function as a criterion of theological claims. Present earthly experiences, such as that of family affection, allowed them to make strong claims about God's fatherly love, but *future* experiences, such as the longed-for end to violence, could generate only theological hypotheses. Thus, while the orthodox—for whom doctrinal theology provided a sure criterion for judging both past and present experiences—could confidently proclaim that the world is the theater of God's glory, radical liberals could merely ask: *How* (and when) will God's sovereign love shine forth in this violent and loveless world?

Radical liberals were, in short, open to having their theology changed by any person or event that seemed to manifest God's love and power. They were ready, in principle as well as practice, to accept such persons and events as revelatory or even messianic. Most hoped that the coming messiah would be a child, probably female, whose pure human nature, untainted by institutional violence, would spark the millennial transformation of the community. From Hope Leslie and Naomi Worthington to Catharine Anderson and Margaret Hart, from Mary Morgan to Little Eva, such fantasy messiahs were imagined not only by radical liberals and nonresistants but also by less ideologically consistent reformers who temporarily hitched their wagons to the radical liberal star. Taken together, these young messiahs constituted a new model of divine power working through powerless individuals to defeat the violence of history.

Unfortunately, we rarely get the messiah we dream of. Few slave plantations or "Groggy Harbors" were turned upside down by children. Henry Clarke Wright's beloved "Wee Darling" could not even end Scotland's denominational divisions. Perhaps recognizing this possibility, many reformers paired messianic hope with apocalyptic dread, suggesting that, without the intervention of a nonviolent messiah, God might soon sanction the violent conflagration of American society, most likely sparked by a wave of slave insurrections. This pair of alternatives, already clearly posed in the opening issue of the

Liberator, was enshrined in the popular imagination by *Uncle Tom's Cabin*. Yet slave insurrections, even in the 1860s, were scarcely more effective than messianic children.

From 1830 to the Civil War, the diversity of approaches to social reform steadily increased. Garrisonian nonresistance still attracted adherents, but many more reformers were drawn to the revelatory power of individuals and events that lay somewhere between the nonviolent child messiah and the bloody apocalypse. Temperance activists vested their hopes in prohibitionist politicians like Neil Dow—hardly messianic figures but men with programs of pragmatic action. Antislavery activists, meanwhile, were drawn to a series of men whose bold, public stands against slavery *did* seem to give them a messianic status despite their willingness to use violence. Frederick Douglass, John Brown (1800-1859), and Abraham Lincoln (1809-65) took on revelatory significance for the growing community of reformers who awaited God's decisive action against slavery. Each seemed to embody the *imago dei* in a profound way, yet for each the divine image was peculiarly bound up with a willingness to inflict and suffer violence. Each promised, moreover, to bring about what Lincoln would call a "new birth of freedom"—a regeneration of the liberal dream by such illiberal means as violence and death rather than through the natural human functions of generation and nurture.

Douglass, Brown, and Lincoln—these seeming messiahs allowed activists to move, in three easy steps, from a nonviolent theology of identification to a neo-Reformed theology in which violence was an instrument of God's mysterious plan to chasten and regenerate a guilty nation. The steps were easy because they were gradual. Despite his cautious endorsement of violence, Douglass was without doubt a radical Christian liberal. Brown was, paradoxically, an adherent of *both* Douglass's version of radical liberalism and Reformed orthodoxy, though his admirers painted him as a Cromwellian Puritan. Lincoln, for his part, was a curious mix: an admirer of Jefferson's Declaration who was still more fervently committed to the preservation of the Union, and a Reformed providentialist who had no personal faith in Jesus. His paradoxical relation to orthodoxy only enhanced his ability to lead the whole nation to orthodox conclusions.

The three easy steps were *not* inevitable. Adin Ballou vehemently resisted each one, while Garrison retained his nonresistant *ethic* even as he allowed his theology to shift with the course of events: nonviolence remained a duty for true Christians even if God had chosen to end slavery through the instrumentality of individuals not yet fully converted. Despite Ballou's and Garrison's efforts to maintain the faith, however, sentimental theology suffered a decisive defeat during the Civil War years. Though nonviolence still had adherents, what was defeated was Garrison's case that nonviolent theology best expressed the *consensual* values of American Christianity, as embodied in the Declaration of Independence and the New Testament. By the time of Lincoln's Second Inaugural and subsequent "martyrdom," a new American consensus had coalesced around the war experience. The ideas of radical Christian liberalism were pushed back to the margins.

Accommodation to Violence?

In its broad outlines, this chapter's story is a familiar one to historians, who have wrestled for decades with the abolitionists' "accommodation to violence" just before the Civil War.[1] This phrase must be used with caution, for most abolitionists had always accepted the legitimacy of limited violence under certain circumstances. Even among loyal Garrisonians, nonresistance was a minority position from the beginning, and it continued to be held by an articulate minority to the end of the Civil War. Still, the consistently nonresistant Adin Ballou was not being unfair when he complained, in 1859, that "the war-principle and spirit are becoming too dominant" among abolitionists.[2] Important changes had occurred during the 1850s, and they would continue to occur during the Civil War.

What exactly was changing? First, second-generation abolitionists like James Redpath (1833–91) and Thomas Wentworth Higginson (1823–1911) were positively enthusiastic about violence. Some even suggested that the slaves could achieve full freedom and "manhood" only through violence. These leaders rallied many previously uncommitted abolitionists to the cause of violent means. Second, the passage of the Fugitive Slave Act and the publication of *Uncle Tom's Cabin* sparked a massive increase in the Northern constituency that was opposed to slavery but not specifically abolitionist. A variety of Northerners—including racists who opposed the expansion of slavery because they hoped to keep African Americans out of the western territories—flocked to the Free Soil Party and the Republican Party, both of which advocated the nonextension of slavery. The once-despised Garrison discovered that he could express his most outrageous views in public without "a single hiss or note of disapprobation."[3] Third, a series of dramatic events—violent rescues of fugitives captured under the new law, clashes between Free Soil and pro-slavery settlers in Kansas, John Brown's raid on Harpers Ferry, and finally the Civil War itself—suggested that violence might be an effective strategy of liberation. Twenty years earlier, most abolitionists had assumed that any violent resistance would be instantly crushed by the slaveholders and the federal government; now they had to contemplate the possibility that state violence might actually bring an end to slavery.

Nonresistant abolitionists did not cause these changes, but they were quick to respond. In 1854 Angelina Grimké, who had previously waffled on the question of violence, publicly announced that she supported violence if it was necessary to protect a fugitive slave from recapture. A year later Henry Clarke Wright noted the large numbers of young men in an antislavery audience and proposed that they "strike for revolution." A few years later the African American Garrisonian Charles L. Remond proposed a plan to promote insurrection in the South. Around the same time, the devoutly nonresistant Charles Stearns went out to "bloody Kansas," determined to try the effectiveness of peace principles there. Within a year he wrote to Garrison that his nonresistance no longer applied because "God never made these fiends—they are devils' spawn, and are to be killed as you would shoot lions and tigers."[4]

Lydia Maria Child responded to the situation in Kansas with considerably more ambivalence. In a deeply tragic story entitled "The Kansas Emigrants," she told of a Massachusetts family among the Free Soil settlers. Though they are determined to "cheerfully return good for evil," they are repeatedly victimized by "human bloodhounds" and "enemies far worse than wolves." Still, their commitment to moral suasion has an effect when they befriend a chivalrous, proslavery settler who is offended by his associates' attacks on women. But he is quickly "silenced" by more vicious Border Ruffians and thus learns "the uselessness of trying to moderate slavery, or ameliorate murder." Eventually, the Massachusetts settlers decided to arm themselves but to "act *only* on the defensive." This approach has no more effect than moral suasion: at the story's end, Child's hero is dead, and "Free Kansas" exists only in the delirious visions of his dying wife.[5]

Garrison was more optimistic but equally ambivalent about violence. His reply to Charles Stearns reflected a characteristically liberal understanding of sin as social rather than individual. "To a great extent," he explained, the proslavery settlers "are the victims of a horribly false state of society in Missouri, and no doubt fearfully depraved; yet they are not beasts, nor to be treated as beasts." If anyone deserved to be killed, it was "the President and his Cabinet." Garrison also asked why it was so easy to generate Northern sympathy for the Kansas settlers, even though many were not consistently abolitionist. "If such men are deserving of generous sympathy, and ought to be supplied with arms, are not the crushed and bleeding slaves at the South a million times more deserving of pity and succor? Why not, first of all, take measures to furnish them with Sharp's rifles?" A few years later Garrison reiterated his pacifist commitment at the New England Anti-Slavery Convention: "I will not trust the war-spirit anywhere in the universe of God, because the experience of six thousand years proves it not to be at all reliable in such a struggle as ours. . . . Much as I detest the oppression exercised by the Southern slaveholder, he is a man, sacred before me. . . . I have no other weapon to wield against him but the simple truth of God, which is the great instrument for the overthrow of all iniquity, and the salvation of the world."[6]

At the same time, Garrison could not help but be encouraged by the fact that many people who were once willing to use violence against abolitionists were now contemplating using it on behalf of the slaves. This was an important step toward his own position, and his liberal faith in humanity obliged him to recognize it as a manifestation of God's power. Thus, he greeted the rise of the Republican Party with considerable enthusiasm. During the Fremont campaign of 1856, he articulated a position of critical support. His duty, he said, was "to call to repentance our guilty land; to impeach, criticize, admonish, entreat, rebuke every sect, every party, every person, in alliance or sympathy with the oppressors . . . to reject all half-way measures, while hailing with gladness the smallest indications of progress." He reiterated the case for disunion and nonresistance but also said that if it were not for such scruples against voting at all, he would gladly give a million votes to Fremont. Three years later he told the Massachusetts Anti-Slavery Society that "my hope is in the great Republican party—not where it stands, but it has materials for growth."[7]

Language of this sort led Adin Ballou to rebuke Garrison and all those who "while professing to be Non-Resistants themselves, spend their main strength in exhorting fighting people to be sure and fight on the right side." By 1859 he was even prepared "to stand aloof" from Garrisonian abolition. But his reasons only underscored the contrast between Garrison's liberal nonresistance and his own more biblically based faith. He faulted the Garrisonians for their support of "Red Revolutionism" and their "manifest contempt for really valuable established religious institutions." The root of slavery, he explained, was not in the Bible, the church, or any other institution but in "man's animal lusts,—in his lust of dominion, lust of property, and lust of sensual pleasure. . . . It is the same radical selfishness which causes all kinds of sin." Ballou's basic distrust of human nature, in other words, allowed him to root his nonresistance entirely in the supernatural revelation of the Bible and to stick strictly to it no matter what happened in the external world. Garrison's sense of the *imago dei* present in all humanity, by contrast, forced him to contemplate the possibility that God was working even through people who had not yet come up to the high ground of nonresistance. This position grew out of the fundamental principles of radical Christian liberalism.[8]

Garrison's dilemma, and that of radical Christian liberals more generally, was not ethical but theological. Their insistence on the supreme value of human life, free from violence and coercion, placed a clear ethical demand on all true Christians: no end can justify a violent or coercive means! But was this rule also binding on God? To answer yes led to a paradox. If God acts noncoercively, then God acts through the consciences of individual humans, and if those individuals are only partially converted to the divine will—if they accept abolition but not nonresistance—then God's moral influence is some-how caught up in well-intended revolutionary violence. Because liberals believed that God's influence was mediated by God's image in every human heart, moreover, they had no basis for clearly differentiating the converted from the unconverted. Men like George Washington, Nat Turner, and David Walker proved that it was possible to have one foot in and one foot out of the kingdom of God. So long as such individuals were few and far between, this paradox could be relegated to the footnotes of nonviolent theology. But by the 1850s the nonresistants were engulfed by a massive wave of vio-lent abolitionism. It was all they could do to hold themselves slightly aloof from this wave; they could not also deny God's presence in a conscientious movement that prom-ised to fulfill one of their deepest hopes. And so they accepted violent abolition's appar-ent place at the center of God's work in history, relegating nonviolent theology to the historical and social margin.

The Liberal Violence of Frederick Douglass

Nonresistants—at least the Garrisonian rather than Ballouian sort—had always been willing to let events and individuals shape their view of God. In August 1841, when a young fugitive named Frederick Douglass took the podium at an antislavery convention on Nantucket, his presence had a *theological* impact that was immediate and electric. "I think I never hated slavery so intensely as at that moment," recalled Garrison,

> certainly, my perception of the enormous outrage which is inflicted by it, on the godlike nature of its victims, was rendered far more clear than ever. There stood one, in physical proportion and stature commanding and exact—in intellect richly endowed—in natural eloquence a prodigy—in soul manifestly "created but little lower than the angels"—yet a slave, ay, a fugitive slave,—trembling for his safety, hardly daring to believe that on the American soil, a single white person could be found who would befriend him at all haz-ards, for the love of God and humanity![9]

As a radical liberal Garrison assumed that anyone who revealed true humanity also revealed God, and this is what he glimpsed in the "godlike nature" of the handsome young man who already spoke with such power and eloquence. He immediately recruited Douglass as a lecturer for the American Anti-Slavery Society, served as mentor for the early years of Douglass's abolitionist career, and wrote the preface for Douglass's first autobiography, which he praised as an exposé of "how accursed is that system, which entombs the godlike mind of men, defaces the divine image, reduces those who by creation were crowned with glory and honor to a level with four-footed beasts, and exalts the dealer in human flesh above all that is called God!"[10]

Douglass had a messianic appeal for Garrison and other radical liberals because he met their ideological humanism with a fervent defense of his own humanity. In his speeches he repeatedly challenged his audiences to recognize his humanity; later he would recall that his first audiences were surprised that a fugitive slave was even capable of speaking on his own behalf: "I was generally introduced, as a '*chattel*'—a '*thing*'—a piece of southern '*property*'—the chairman assuring the audience that *it* could speak." In his autobiographies he traced both the violence by which "a man was made a slave" and the acts of resistance by which "a slave was made a man."[11] Thus, *My Bondage and My Freedom* reaches a climax when Douglass arrives as a free man in New York City. At this moment both Douglass's humanity and God's divinity are simultaneously vindicated: "A contest had been going on in my mind for years, between the clear consciousness of right and the plausible errors of superstition; between the wisdom of manly courage, and the foolish weakness of timidity. The contest was now ended; the chain was severed; God and right stood vindicated. I WAS A FREEMAN, and the voice of peace and joy thrilled my heart."[12]

Abolitionists were delighted to have such a powerful witness to the power of slave humanity in their midst, and Garrison was doubly delighted that this advocate was also willing to testify to the "divine" cause of nonresistance "with the melting accents of charity on his lips, with the gentleness of love beaming in his eyes!" As a slave, Douglass was one of those "who, of all others, have the most cause to repudiate the doctrine." Indeed, Garrison insisted that "above all men living, the slaves of this country would be justified in resisting their relentless tyrants unto blood." But if revolutionary blacks like David Walker and Nat Turner were admirable, Douglass was exemplary. As an ex-slave who actually accepted nonresistance, he epitomized nonresistant virtue in a way that nonslaves never could: "I could not help thinking how incomparably superior was this 'chattel,' in all the great qualities of the soul, to any warrior whose deeds are recorded on the page of history, and that here was a remarkable instance of Christian magnanimity, and martyr-like devotion to the cause of humanity." Just to look at such a man was to dream that slavery might, after all, be destroyed without a violent conflagration.[13]

For several years thereafter, Douglass did much to confirm Garrison's understanding of him as an apostle of nonviolence. At the end of his first lecture tour of Great Britain, Douglass affirmed that he was a "Peace man," and that if he were not, he would have urged the British to support a slave insurrection. At the National Negro Convention in 1843 he blocked a motion in favor of violent resistance by slaves, and he began an 1848 speech on West Indian emancipation with three paragraphs of pacifist rhetoric celebrating the fact that emancipation had been achieved nonviolently: "We attract your attention to no horrid strife; to no scenes of blood and carnage, where foul and unnatural murder carried its true designation, because regimentally attired." He went on to praise England's "peaceful reformation" over France's "bloody revolution," noting that "friends of freedom rely not upon brute force but moral power. Their courage is not that of the tiger, but that of the Christian." Such sentiments mirrored Garrison's nonresistant philosophy perfectly. And even though Garrison discouraged Douglass's project of editing his own paper in Rochester, New York, Douglass remained "a faithful disciple of William Lloyd Garrison" for the first four years of his editing career.[14]

On the other hand, many of Garrison's "faithful disciples" did not embrace non-resistance, and Douglass himself never joined the Non-Resistance Society. And he seems never to have ruled out the use of violence in self-defense. During the 1840s, Douglass was deeply involved in the Garrisonians' direct action campaign against Northern segregation. On many occasions—especially when Garrison was present—he submitted quietly to the verbal and physical abuse of railroad and hotel employees trying to maintain segregated facilities. But on a few occasions he resisted in a manner that demonstrated his physical prowess, albeit without posing any threat to his attackers. In September 1841, for example, he ripped his seat from the floor while being dragged out of a segregated rail car. Two years later, in Pendleton, Indiana, Douglass swung a piece of lumber at rioters who attacked his speaking partner, and he in turn was beaten unconscious. Recalling this event in 1843, he claimed that he had been a "believer in non-resistance" until he saw "a dear friend assaulted and beaten in a cruel and inhuman manner."[15]

Douglass's *Narrative* (1845) effectively encapsulates his ambivalence about nonresistance. Its theme is "how a slave was made a man," and perhaps the central episode in the process is a scene in which Douglass fights back rather than allow the notorious slave breaker Covey to whip him. This event, Douglass claims, formed "an epoch in my humble history"; immediately thereafter he "resolved that, however long I might remain a slave in form, the day had passed forever when I could be a slave in fact."[16]

What does this episode imply? A few things can be noted. First, it hardly places Douglass in the company of David Walker and Nat Turner. He engaged in a single act of spontaneous, unarmed self-defense; he stopped fighting as soon as Covey let go of him; he drew blood but inflicted no permanent injury on his attacker. As one scholar has rightly noted, in this passage Douglass "goes to extraordinary lengths to portray himself as having exhausted every reasonable alternative before resorting to violence." Surely it was not the violence per se but the simple refusal to be whipped that gave the event its "epochal" quality.[17]

Furthermore, there is nothing inconsistent in a nonresistant acknowledging, and even taking a certain pride in, his or her past resorts to violence. Everyone assumed that nonresistance was an advanced ethical value that could be attained only after a long process, and Garrison was clear that resistance to tyrants was virtuous even in those who had not yet attained the virtue of nonresistance. Indeed, by constantly invoking the Declaration of Independence, Garrison suggested that the United States Revolution had been a noble stage in the American people's path to pure nonresistance. It would thus be quite plausible to see the fight with Covey as a similar stage in a nonresistant Douglass's own life journey.

And indeed, Douglass describes several nonviolent episodes in similar terms as marking decisive shifts from slavery to freedom. His childhood move from a rural plantation to cosmopolitan Baltimore is a providential "interposition" that "laid the foundation, and opened the gateway, to all my subsequent prosperity" by suggesting the possibility and some of the means of escape. His master's attempt to prevent him from learning to read "is a new and special revelation" of "the white man's power to enslave the black man," which enables him to see "the pathway from slavery to freedom." Even his first speech on Nantucket, three years after his escape, is a sort of passage from slavery to freedom. When he is called upon to speak, he hesitates because "I felt myself a slave," but after beginning he "felt a degree of freedom, and said what I desired with considerable ease." All these passages reveal the paradoxical character of Douglass's assertion of his own humanity. In one sense he is *never* truly a slave—"from my earliest recollection, I date the entertainment of a deep conviction that slavery would not always be able to hold me within its foul embrace"—and yet he experiences his full humanity only in the act of achieving freedom. Such a theme would appeal to any nonresistant.[18]

Yet the fight with Covey is narrated with a rhetorical intensity that sets it apart from the other moments in which Douglass achieves a relative freedom. In the other scenes, the freedom Douglass experiences is a *future* freedom, seen through a "gateway" or at the end of a "pathway." Indeed, they are sometimes succeeded by a rebound into present despair. Actually learning to read, for example, only makes Douglass more aware of his wretchedness and unfulfilled humanity: "It opened my eyes to the horrible pit, but to no ladder upon which to get out. In moments of agony, I envied my fellow-slaves for their stupidity. I have often wished myself a beast."[19] The "battle with Mr. Covey," by contrast, is an immediate resurrection into full humanity:

> It rekindled the few expiring embers of freedom, and revived within me a sense of my own manhood. It recalled the departed self-confidence, and inspired me again with a determination to be free. The gratification afforded by the triumph was a full compensa-tion for whatever else might follow, even death itself. He can only understand the deep satisfaction which I experienced, who has himself repelled by force the bloody arm of slavery. I felt as I never felt before. It was a glorious resurrection, from the tomb of slav-ery, to the heaven of freedom. My long-crushed spirit rose, cowardice departed, bold defiance took its place.[20]

Though Douglass does not explicitly step outside the camp of nonresistance in this passage, his claim that only those who have resisted slavery with force can understand suggests that there is no adequate nonresistant substitute for the experience of violence. Douglass made it clear that his experience as a perpetrator of violence was as central to his own story of survival and resistance as his experiences as victim and witness of slaveholding violence. Even the liberatory experience of *telling* the story, upon which Douglass placed so much emphasis, could not substitute for that of breaking one's own bonds.[21] It would take Douglass a lifetime to sort out the implications of these contra-dictory experiences, and he only really began after his break with Garrison.

Whether or not Douglass was a nonresistant in 1845, he clearly was not a decade later. But neither was he a fire-breathing apostle of insurrection. In 1855, when Douglass published *My Bondage and My Freedom*, he was a leading figure in the circle of upstate New York abolitionists organized—and generously funded—by Gerrit Smith.[22] Unlike the Garrisonians, these "revolutionaries" were willing to imagine that a coercive govern-ment might sometimes be an appropriate instrument for Christians seeking to do God's will. As Douglass suggested in 1860, they approved "all methods of proceeding against slavery, politics, religion, peace, war, Bible, Constitution, disunion, Union—every pos-sible way known in opposition to slavery."[23]

But, as radical Christian liberals, they continued to place primary emphasis on ap-peals to conscience. Just after the 1852 election, for example, Douglass wrote that "the way to swell our vote for freedom . . . is to spread anti-slavery light, and to educate the people on the whole subject of slavery—circulate the documents—let the anti-slavery speaker, more than ever, go abroad—let every town be visited, and let truth find its way into every house in the land." Three years later, Douglass said that "the main and most potent weapon with which slavery is to be assailed and overthrown . . . is speech." The "grand secret" of abolition's power was that "in every human breast, it has an advocate which can be silent only when the heart is dead."[24]

The revolutionaries' location in upstate New York placed them in the path of many fugitive slaves fleeing to Canada, and "the constant meeting with these whip-scarred brothers" deepened Douglass's resolution to defeat slavery by any means necessary. Douglass condoned the use of self-defense by fugitives, and in 1851 he assisted a group of fugitives who had recently killed a slave catcher. In his paper, he referred to the incident as "freedom's battle" and defended the right of "hunted men" to "fight with the biped bloodhounds that had tracked them."[25] In October of that year, Gerrit Smith and several of Douglass's closest associates participated in the "Jerry Rescue," in which a fugitive slave was forcibly liberated from the Syracuse police station.

A few years later, after the killing of a slave catcher in Boston, Douglass wrote a careful philosophical justification of the right to kill "kidnappers"—meaning, of course, slave catchers. He begins by admitting that the moral aversion to bloodshed is an important part of God's creation: "These tender feelings so susceptible to pain, are most wisely designed by the Creator, for the preservation of life." But, he goes on, such moral feelings are not absolutely authoritative: "God has not left us solely to the guidance of our feelings, having endowed us with reason." From the perspective of reason, life is not an end in itself but a means to the person's "own good, and the honor of his Creator." The right to life, therefore, is lost by those who abuse the purpose of life by taking the lives of others. Society has a duty to restrain such "aggressors," and when society fails to fulfill this duty, individuals have a right to step in. Interestingly, Douglass buttresses this argument with an appeal to natural law. "When a man flings himself from the top of some lofty monument, against a granite pavement, in that act he forfeits his *right* to live." But this "is no argument against the beneficence of the law of gravitation." It is simply a reminder that human well-being depends on our careful respect for the physical laws established by God. The same applies, Douglass suggests, to the moral laws that are also a part of God's creation.[26]

Douglass then exposes the fallacy of a common nonresistant argument. Some might say, he notes, that while fugitives have the right to resist their captors, they would do better to submit for the sake of the resulting "moral effect." He concedes this point, so long as submission "has some chance of being recognized as a virtue." But this is simply not the case for slaves. "While fugitives quietly cross their hands to be tied, adjust their ankles to be chained, and march off unresistingly to the hell of slavery, there will ever be fiends enough to hunt them and carry them off." Indeed, the meekness of slaves only "creates contempt for them in the public mind." To wipe away this "reproach," slaves must resist enslavement. "Every slaveholder who meets a bloody death in his infernal business, is an argument in favor of the manhood of our race." Here Douglass's rhetoric seems to overstep his meaning, for his real point is that the slaves can achieve manhood by risking the death of themselves or their attackers, not by the shedding of blood in itself.[27]

The article ends with a Garrisonian flourish. Douglass addresses an editor who condemned the killing and challenges him to reconsider his patriotism: "Until he ceases to glory in the deeds of Hancock, Adams, and Warren—and ceases to look with pride and patriotic admiration upon the sombre pile at Bunker Hill . . . it does not look graceful in him to brand as *murderers* . . . [the defenders of] . . . the poor, defenceless Burns."

During the 1850s Douglass also used fictional and autobiographical narrative to sort out his changing views on violence. In 1853 he composed "The Heroic Slave," a brief piece of historical fiction about a slave who led a successful uprising on a slave ship in 1841.[28] The story opens with a long soliloquy in which the hero, Madison Washington, complains that his life "is aimless and worthless" because he was "born a slave, an abject slave,—even before I made part of this breathing world, the scourge was plaited for my back; the fetters were forged for my limbs." A page later, he reconsiders the significance of his birth and concludes that "liberty" is "the inalienable birthright of every man." Significantly, he arrives at this changed view by resolving no longer to submit to enslavement: "Liberty I will have, or die in the attempt to gain it." Douglass implies that it is this resolution, and not the actual use of violence, that frees the slave: "At that moment he was free, at least in spirit. The future gleamed brightly before him, and his fetters lay broken at his feet."[29]

The story goes on to tell of Madison's physical escape—full of adventure but not of violence inflicted by him—and his recapture during an attempt to rescue his wife. After his wife is shot dead during their flight, Madison defends himself physically, though to no real effect, as he is unarmed. He is then placed on a ship bound for the New Orleans slave market. It is here, finally, that the insurrection occurs. Madison smuggles three files on board, frees his fellows, and—armed only with fetters—takes control of the ship. In the process he kills the captain and the slave owner but spares the rest of the crew. He explains his policy to the first mate: "Sir . . . your life is in my hands. I could have killed you a dozen times over during this last half hour, and could kill you now. You call me a black murderer. I am not a murderer. God is my witness that LIBERTY, not malice, is the motive for this night's work. . . . We have done that which you applaud your fathers for doing, and if we are murderers, so were they."[30]

Taken as a whole, the story presents a clear hierarchy of values. The highest value is freedom itself and the willingness to pursue freedom at whatever cost. This implies a willingness to risk one's own death *if* such a risk is necessary to achieve freedom. It also, but secondarily, implies a willingness to inflict violence, especially if the freedom of more than one person is at stake. (Madison is completely nonviolent when fleeing alone, uses very limited violence when with his wife, and is willing to kill only when the freedom of over a hundred people is at stake.) Many of the traditional just war criteria are implicit in the story. Madison's violence serves a just cause, occurs only as a last resort, is limited and proportionate, and is discriminately targeted against only the guiltiest persons.

This just war logic is mixed with considerable ambivalence in Douglass's retelling of his fight with Covey in his second autobiography. Here he adds details about his motives for fighting, the fight itself, and the philosophical implications of the fight. In the *Narrative*, for example, he suggested that his decision to fight back was spontaneous— "from whence came the spirit I don't know"—while in *My Bondage* he claims that he had resolved the day before "to defend and protect myself to the best of my ability." This decision, taken on a Sunday, is portrayed as specifically religious and reflects the perplexity Douglass felt concerning Covey's apparent piety: "My religious views on the subject of resisting my master had suffered a serious shock, by the savage persecution to which I had been subjected, and my hands were no longer tied by my religion." Yet when Douglass comes to the fight itself, he does not present it entirely as the product of a deliberate, conscientious decision but partly disowns agency by suggesting that he was possessed by a bestial spirit: "The fighting madness had come upon me, and I found my strong fingers firmly attached to the throat of my cowardly tormenter. . . . I felt as supple as a cat."[31]

Douglass goes on to narrate the fight in graphic detail, stressing the consequences of each action: "I held him so firmly by the throat, that his blood followed my nails." Yet even as Douglass glories in his own bloodthirstiness, he keeps a careful account of when he was on the defensive and when on the offensive, measuring his every move by a precise moral standard. At first, "I was strictly on the *defensive*, preventing him from injuring me, rather than trying to injure him." When Covey's cousin Hughes intervenes, Douglass shifts to a more aggressive posture: "I was still *defensive* toward Covey, but *aggressive* toward Hughes; and, at the first approach of the latter, I dealt a blow, in my desperation, which fairly sickened my youthful assailant." By the end of the fight Douglass is not sure if he has won a physical or a moral victory: "The fact was, *he had not whipped me at all.* He had not, in all the scuffle, drawn a single drop of blood from me. I had drawn blood from him; and, even without this satisfaction, I should have been victorious, because my aim had not been to injure him, but to prevent his injuring me."[32]

This uncertainty carries over into Douglass's expansion of the "resurrection" passage cited previously. In the original passage, Douglass simply asserts that the fight marked his passage from enslavement to freedom and manhood. Now he explains *why* this was the case: "A man, without force, is without the essential dignity of humanity. Human nature is so constituted, that it cannot *honor* a helpless man, although it can *pity* him; and even this it cannot do long, if the signs of power do not arise." A few sentences later, Douglass offers a significantly different explanation: "I was no longer a servile coward, trembling under the frown of a brother worm of the dust, but, my long-cowed spirit was roused to an attitude of manly independence. I had reached the point, at which I was *not afraid to die.* This spirit made me a freeman in *fact*, while I remained a slave in *form*."[33] Though Douglass does not acknowledge the tension between these two explanations, it is critical: had he achieved "manhood" because he possessed physical "force" and "power," or because he had lost his fear of death? From a nonresistant perspective the former position was anathema, while the latter was quite attractive. Douglass refused to resolve the tension, I suspect, because he remained ambivalent about nonresistance: repelled by its unmanly distaste for power but attracted to its moral high-mindedness. His double stance on violence would appeal to many who felt similarly ambivalent.[34]

However Douglass may have judged his use of violence against Covey, he felt diminishing inclination to repeat it in later years.[35] Indeed, he declined a direct invitation from John Brown to participate in the Harpers Ferry raid. In part this was because Brown's "desperate but sublimely disinterested effort" did not meet Douglass's rigorous standard of feasibility. In part, though, it was because Douglass did not see fighting as central to his own vocation. "I have not one word," he wrote in a public letter on Harpers Ferry, "to say in defence or vindication of my character for courage. I have always been more distinguished for running than fighting."[36] (Indeed, Douglass wrote this letter from Canada, where he had fled to avoid prosecution for his role in the incident.)

Throughout the 1850s, however, Douglass became increasingly convinced that violence would play a leading role in the end of slavery. "I have little hope," he wrote in
1860, "of the freedom of the slave by peaceful means. . . . [The slaveholders] have neither ears nor hearts for the appeals of justice and humanity." The increasingly violent
tone of his speeches provoked the concern of Sojourner Truth, who interrupted him on
one occasion to ask, "Frederick, is God dead?" "No," Douglass answered, "and because
God is not dead slavery can only end in blood."[37]

Douglass explained his dispute with Truth by noting that "my quaint old sister was of
the Garrison school of non-resistants," but this really does not go far to explain their disagreement. When Douglass threatened his audiences with apocalyptic judgment, he was
simply echoing the rhetorical strategy that Garrison himself derived from his open-ended
theology. Douglass's words in an 1857 pamphlet on the Dred Scott decision might almost have been penned by Garrison. If the United States did not voluntarily end slavery,
he argued, "The lightning, whirlwind, and earthquake may come. Jefferson said that he
trembled for his country when he reflected that God is just, and his justice cannot sleep
forever." Douglass did not, to be sure, expect a supernatural apocalypse. Rather, he believed a violent end to slavery would naturally result from continued neglect of the moral
laws God had built into the universe. "Goaded by cruelty, stung by a burning sense of
wrong, in an awful moment of depression and desperation, the bondman and bondwoman
at the South may rush to one wild and deadly struggle for freedom."[38]

Like Garrison, Douglass suggested that God *might* end slavery in a violent apocalypse, and like Garrison he held out an alternate hope that that fate might yet be averted.
Where they differed was not in the apocalyptic vision but in the precise character of the
alternative: while Garrison proposed a spontaneous popular withdrawal of support for
slavery, Douglass envisioned organized (and potentially violent) government action: "The
Constitution, as well as the Declaration of Independence, and the sentiments of the
founders of the Republic, give us a platform broad enough, and strong enough, to support the most comprehensive plans for the freedom and elevation of all the people of
this country, without regard to color, class, or clime." These words opened a path for
those who admired Garrison's rhetoric but did not fully accept his nonresistant principles to endorse the Union war effort.[39]

The Apocalypse of John Brown

Frederick Douglass, in short, offered a qualified justification of political (and human) as
well as apocalyptic (and divine) violence within the rhetorical and theological framework of radical liberalism. He believed that both liberal suasion and governmental violence, both words and deeds, could and should contribute to the liberation of his enslaved brothers and sisters. In the 1850s a second messianic figure, one committed to
deeds *instead* of words, would push the abolitionist community much farther from its
radical liberal center. This was John Brown, an orthodox ex-seminarian and failed wool
merchant who traced his descent to Plymouth Rock. In 1849 Brown settled with his
family in North Elba, New York, a colony of ex-slaves funded by Gerrit Smith, where
Brown hoped to serve as a sort of informal farming instructor. A few years later Brown
followed his sons to Kansas, where Free Soil and proslavery settlers were competing for

control of the territorial government. Brown played a leading role in several military clashes—including an alleged massacre of unarmed Missourians—and inspired a wave of financial and military support for the cause of "Bleeding Kansas." Finally, in 1859, Brown led a small band of ex-slaves and white abolitionists in an attack on the federal armory at Harpers Ferry, Virginia. Their goal was to inspire slave rebellions and create a free republic of escaped slaves in the mountains and swamps of the South, but they were quickly defeated by federal troops. When Brown was executed by the State of Virginia on 2 December 1859, a wide range of Northerners—nonresistants, political abolitionists, Transcendentalists, orthodox ministers—hailed him as a martyr.

What sort of man was this new messiah? Brown frequently summed up his philosophy by saying, "*I believe in the Golden Rule, sir, and the Declaration of Independence. I think they both mean the same thing; and it is better that a whole generation should pass off the face of the earth—men, women, and children—by a violent death, than that one jot of either should fail in this country. I mean exactly so, sir.*" This is yet another variation on the radical liberal theme. All radical liberals affirmed the equality and sanctity of the human individual as their supreme end, but they differed on means. Garrison repudiated any means that compromised the end even slightly; Douglass held that the end was so important that any means could at least be considered; and Brown held that the end was so urgent that the careful consideration of means had to give way to action—even the deliberate provocation of apocalypse. Yet Brown was no lover of violence for its own sake; indeed, the exegesis of the Golden Rule he offered from his jail cell savored more of benevolent sympathy than defiant rebellion. His "principle," he said, was "the golden rule. I pity the poor in bondage that have none to help them. That is why I am here; it is not to gratify any personal animosity, or feeling of revenge, or vindictive spirit. It is my sympathy with the oppressed and the wronged, that are as good as you, and as precious in the sight of God."[40]

If Brown's stress on the Golden Rule linked him to the Smith-Douglass circle of abolitionists, his formal theology was quite different from Douglass's rational skepticism and Smith's ardent come-outerism. Brown maintained the Reformed orthodoxy of his Puritan ancestors and favored for his devotional reading such texts as *Pilgrim's Progress*, Baxter's *Saints' Rest*, a biography of Oliver Cromwell, and of course the Bible. Though theological orthodoxy was not unheard of in the broader abolitionist community, it was very unusual in the radical circles in which Brown moved. Brown's ardent supporter, the radical Unitarian Thomas Wentworth Higginson, thus reflected that "John Brown is almost the only radical abolitionist I have ever known who was not more or less radical in religious matters also. His theology was Puritan, like his practice; and accustomed as we now are to see Puritan doctrines and Puritan virtues separately exhibited, it seems quite strange to behold them combined in one person again."[41]

Brown believed himself to be "an instrument in the hands of providence" and often expressed a conviction that God would work through him whether his specific ventures succeeded or failed. The depth of this faith amazed most of his acquaintances, though Brown was not free of inner doubts. "That 'God reigns,' and most wisely, and controls all events," he wrote from his jail cell, "might, it would seem, reconcile all those who believe it to much that appears to be very disastrous. I am one who have tried to believe that, and still keep trying. Those who die for the truth may prove to be courageous at last; so I continue 'hoping on,' till I shall find that the truth must finally prevail."[42]

Ultimately, the precise balance of faith and doubt, of liberalism and orthodoxy, of violence and sympathy in Brown's consciousness had little bearing on his messianic status, for he was not the creator of his own public image. He believed in actions rather than words and left it to others to say precisely what his actions meant. That task fell primarily to Brown's young admirer James Redpath, a radical British émigré who toured both the slave states and "Bleeding Kansas" as a reporter for Horace Greeley's *New York Tribune*. He became an admirer of Brown while in Kansas and dedicated the account of his travels—*The Roving Editor, or Talks with Slaves in the Southern States*—to the "Old Hero." After Brown's execution, Redpath published two celebratory volumes, a hagiography entitled *The Public Life of Capt. John Brown* and an edited collection of public reactions called *Echoes of Harper's Ferry*. For Redpath, Brown's genius lay in the fact that he linked the Declaration of Independence and the Golden Rule to Bunker Hill and the Book of Judges:

> He was an abolitionist of the Bunker Hill school. He followed neither Garrison, nor Seward, Gerrit Smith nor Wendell Phillips: but the Golden Rule, and the Declaration of Independence, in the spirit of the Hebrew warriors, and in the God-applauded mode that they adopted. "The Bible story of Gideon," records a man who betrayed him, "had manifestly a great influence on his actions." He believed in human brotherhood and in the God of Battles; he admired Nat Turner, the negro patriot, equally with George Washington, the white American deliverer.[43]

Here we see a sharp difference from Douglass's careful endorsement of violence as one legitimate means to liberal equality. For Redpath, Brown's violence was *the* means to achieve the liberal vision, the only legitimate path. Undoubtedly this picture of the "Old Hero" reflects Redpath's own peculiar fascination with violence. In the opening section of *The Roving Editor*, he differentiated his own "creed" from most others by stressing his love of violence. He was "something more" than an "Emancipationist" because he advocated emancipation "with bloodshed and violence, with the torch and the rifle"; he was more than a "Peace-Man" because he "would fight and kill for the sake of peace"; and he was more than a nonresistant because he "would slay every man who attempted to resist the liberation of the slave." Finally, he was "a Democrat—and nothing more. I believe in humanity and human rights. I recognize nothing so sacred on earth. Rather than consent to the infringement of the most insignificant or seemingly unimportant of human rights, let races be swept from the face of the earth—let nations be dismembered—let dynasties be dethroned—let laws and governments, religions and reputations be cast out and trodden under feet of men!"[44]

One might wonder if there is any meaning in a "seemingly unimportant" human right that could justify genocide, but Redpath brushed aside such concerns. By the middle of the book, Redpath's rhetoric reached a chilling extreme: "In an insurrection, if all the slaves in the United States—men, women and helpless babes—were to fall on the field or become the victims of Saxon vengeance, after the event, if one man only survived to relate how his race heroically fell, and to enjoy the freedom they had won, the liberty of that solitary negro, in my opinion, would be cheaply purchased by the universal slaughter of his people and their oppressors."[45]

Even though Redpath dismissed nonresistance—and political abolition—as "cant," there is no denying the Garrisonian influence on his rhetoric. Garrison's favorite trick was to offer such chilling comparisons hypothetically, to underscore the utter evil of slavery, but then to insist that nonresistant activism was the only legitimate means for humans, and the only way to prevent an apocalyptic intervention. Redpath simply claimed for himself the violent rights that Garrison reserved for God and taught that "a few scores of rattling insurrections" would be the best and "speediest" method of abolition.[46]

The purpose of *The Roving Editor*, then, was to demonstrate that the slaves were "morose and savagely brooding over their wrongs" and that a mere spark was needed to commence the insurrectionary end of slavery. To demonstrate this, he conducted dozens of interviews with slaves, carefully cultivating their trust until they would tell him how they truly felt about slavery. But the results went only halfway to proving his thesis: though most of his subjects reported that they and their fellows were truly unhappy as slaves, and though many agreed that they would escape immediately if provided with a pistol and a compass, Redpath reported not a single individual who told him of a desire to launch an insurrection. Undaunted, he read insurrectionary sentiment into the smallest gestures: "There was an ominous light in his eye—the precursor, probably (I thought), of a terrible conflagration which is destined yet to burn up the oppressor and his works." Redpath also included a secondhand account of a failed insurrectionary named Isaac, who told his beloved minister that he would have killed his white friends first to show that he "could sacrifice my love." The story concludes with a sentence that echoes Douglass's connection between violence and manhood: "The record below tells of his crime, and he will be remembered on earth as a felon; but the record above will contain his virtues, and in heaven the good will know and love him—for ISAAC was a MAN." The volume's frontispiece shows a very manly Isaac nobly confronting his minister in a jail cell.[47]

The fact that Redpath had to dedicate his book to a white man and use a secondhand story as a source for his frontispiece suggests that most slaves did not share his assumption that true resistance must take the most violent possible form. Nevertheless, these solitary examples inspired Redpath to stay true to his insurrectionary faith. What is more, they inspired him because they, unlike himself, could ground their insurrectionism in a fervent religious devotion. While Redpath professed a belief in "destiny" that grounded a disregard for his personal safety, both Isaac and John Brown claimed that God had commanded them to enter the battlefield against slavery. Isaac claimed that God spoke within his heart, while Brown—according to Redpath—drew his divine command from the Old Testament: "He was the last of the old Puritan type of Christians. Gideon to him, and Joshua, and Moses, were not interesting historic characters merely,—as, judging from their acts, modern Christians regard them but holy examples set before us, by Deity himself, for our imitation and our guidance." After all the ink that had been spilled demonstrating the New Testament sanction for nonresistance, Redpath was delighted to realize through Brown that those Christians who accepted the infallibility of the entire Bible might be induced to support his violent schemes: "John Brown most earnestly believed the Bible to be the Word of Almighty God—as infallible as it is sacred. Now, in no book, not professedly military, are there more clear and unequivocal approvals of war, 'as a moral agency,' than in the Sacred Volume of Christendom."[48]

Redpath's interpretation of Brown as an Old Testament Puritan willing to fight at God's command touched a popular nerve. By the late 1850s many Northerners—both inside and outside the abolitionist community—were uncomfortable with the apparent implications of radical liberalism. It led to a theology that was too open-ended to galvanize passionate commitment, a style of nonresistant activism that was perhaps utterly ineffective, and a stress on the power of the powerless that was distinctly unmasculine. Perhaps a healthy dose of violent orthodoxy was needed—and yet three decades of liberal critique had rendered orthodoxy simply implausible to much of the educated elite. For those who were unhappy about being liberal and incapable of being orthodox, John Brown was a true messiah—a surrogate Puritan whose vicarious sacrifice might purge them of the effeminate stain of liberalism.

I refer especially to the Transcendentalists. Ralph Waldo Emerson and Henry David Thoreau had long maintained an individualistic distance from organized abolition, but both spoke at commemorative gatherings before or after Brown's execution.[49] For Emerson, Brown's linking of the Bible and Bunker Hill provided a long-needed clue to the inner spirit of American identity. "He was happily a representative of the American Republic," a man who joined "that perfect Puritan faith which brought his fifth ancestor to Plymouth Rock, with his grandfather's ardor in the Revolution." Like many others, Emerson cited with approval Brown's willingness to see "a whole generation of men, women, and children" killed to prevent the abuse of the Golden Rule or the Declaration of Independence.[50] Thoreau, for his part, used Brown's Puritanism as a weapon with which to castigate his own generation's political sins:

> He was one of that class of whom we hear a great deal, but, for the most part, see nothing at all—the Puritans. . . . They were a class that did something else than celebrate their forefathers' day, and eat parched corn in remembrance of that time. They were neither Democrats nor Republicans, but men of simple habits, straightforward, prayerful; not thinking much of rulers who did not fear God, not making many compromises, nor seeking after available candidates.[51]

For Thoreau, there was just a short step from Brown's Puritanism to his manhood: "For once we are lifted out of the trivialness and dust of politics into the region of truth and manhood." Brown possessed a humanity and a masculinity that were all but unattainable for Thoreau and his neighbors. Having abandoned a theological education because of poor eyesight, he had been spared the "pap" dispensed at places like Harvard and instead had "commenced the public practice of Humanity in Kansas, as you all know. Such were his *humanities*, and not any study of grammar. He would have left a Greek accent slanting the wrong way, and righted up a falling man." His preference for actions over words set him apart, as "a living man," from the "*cackling* of political conventions." Above all, his death revealed the true meaning of life: "This event advertises me that there is such a fact as death—the possibility of a man's dying. It seems as if no man had ever died in America before, for in order to die you must first have lived. . . . How many a man who was lately contemplating suicide has now something to live for!"[52]

Thoreau's words, like Douglass's account of his fight with Covey, contain a curious doubleness. It is never clear whether Thoreau's praise of Brown's "manhood" refers to his masculinity or his humanity, to his willingness to kill or his willingness to die. Thoreau's assumption that Brown's devotion was unmatched by Garrisonian activists and his use of words with feminine connotations, like "pap" and "cackling," suggest that what drew him to Brown was the specifically military character of Brown's action, but his ultimate appeal is to a self-sacrificial virtue as characteristic of Little Eva as of John Brown. It is no accident that the ambivalence is left unresolved, for Thoreau's entire point was to avoid the nonresistant's distinction between physical and moral power and thus appeal to both simultaneously.

Other admirers of Brown had similar difficulty deciding whether to admire him for his violent masculinity or his humanitarian ideals. Frederick Douglass called Brown "THE man of the nineteenth century." The Garrisonian activist Stephen S. Foster commented, "I claim to be a Non-Resistant, but not to be a fool. I think John Brown has shown himself a *man*, in comparison with the Non-Resistants." And Edwin M. Wheelock, a Dover, New Hampshire, minister, saw Brown's manliness as an antidote to northern "effeminacy" but refused to distinguish manliness from idealism: "He startled our effeminacy with the sight of a man whose seminal principle was justice, whose polar star was right."[53]

Against the nonresistants, Wheelock insisted that "never yet in the history of man was a tyrant race known to loosen its grasp of the victim's throat, save by the pressure of force," yet he illustrated this principle with a story that might have appealed to the nonresistants. The slave system, he said, was like "the Druid stone, which the united force of a hundred men could not move, while a child's finger rightly applied, rocked to its base." One has to read this twice, for in Wheelock's rendition the "hundred men" represent organized moral suasion, while the "child's finger" is John Brown's violent attack: "Invulnerable to all moral appeals, [slavery] yields, it dissolves, it *dies*, before the onset of force." The apparent duplicity of figuring Brown simultaneously as a man of "force" and a powerless child was, paradoxically, made possible by the very failure of Brown's attempt to overthrow slavery: he was, as Wheelock spoke, "only one old man in a southern prison," and yet perhaps the only person in the nation fully committed to the Declaration of Independence. Wheelock's stress on Brown's solitude suggests yet another dimension of the common emphasis on Brown as a "man." This set him apart not only from women and from subhuman creatures but also from the institutions— states, churches, parties—that could never match Brown's absolute devotion. Thus Wheelock could proclaim that "the cause of human liberty in this land needs speeches and prayers, eloquence and money; but it has now on the banks of the Potomac, for the *second* time, found what it needed more than these; what the Hebrew Exodus found in Moses; what Puritan England hailed in Oliver Cromwell; what revolutionary France has sought in vain—A MAN!"[54]

Wheelock also pointed out, seemingly against the nonresistants (though most would have shared this sentiment) that strictly speaking a peaceful end to slavery was impossible because "in Slavery *blood is always flowing*." He blasted the hypocrisy of those who focused only on the violence of resistance while disregarding the violence of oppression. Compared with slavery's "perpetual war against men, women, and children, unarmed, helpless, and bound," he said, "insurrection is but a transient war, on more equal terms, and with the weaker side capable at least of flight." Wheelock's real difference from the nonresistants was not this insight but rather his assumption that insurrection and "the peace of insensibility" were the *only* possible responses to slavery's warfare. He thus moved quickly to a reassertion of the intrinsic, manly virtue of violence: "The slave, who vainly tries to shake off his fetters, is schooled by every such effort into fuller manhood. No race ever hewed off its chains except by insurrection."[55]

Wheelock's sentiments were shared by the growing cluster of young abolitionists, mostly second-generation liberals such as Theodore Parker and Thomas Wentworth Higginson, who were convinced that the moral suasionist phase of abolition was long over. Several of these men had collaborated in funding the Harpers Ferry raid, and they were quick to articulate a principled defense of the insurrectionary faith. Theodore Parker, in a letter written after Brown's conviction, began with a measured ethical defense of violent resistance: slaves have a natural right and perhaps even a duty to kill those who enslave them, and by extension freemen have a right and perhaps a duty to assist slave rebellions. Parker moved from this ethical analysis to a more metaphysical claim about the necessary link between violence and freedom. Though he had once imagined a peaceful end to slavery, he now saw that "all the great charters of HUMANITY have been writ in blood," and that "our pilgrimage must lead through a Red Sea, wherein many a Pharaoh will go under and perish." Parker praised his correspondent for having supported the Bunker Hill monument, which he had initially opposed but now described as "a great sermon in stone," worth "all the blood it took to lay its corner-stones," because it would guide the North along the true path to freedom.[56]

A more nuanced, and surprising, defense of insurrection came from Wendell Phillips, long a critical fellow traveler of Garrisonian nonresistance. (He advocated disunion but not absolute pacifism, and he dutifully cast "no" votes on most of the resolutions at the New England Non-Resistance Society's founding convention.) Like Parker, Phillips believed that Harpers Ferry marked "a new phase of this great American struggle," and like Parker he characterized this new phase in the strongest possible language. He entitled his first speech on John Brown "The Lesson of the Hour" and boldly proclaimed, "I think the lesson of the hour is insurrection."[57]

Yet Phillips's defense of insurrection appealed less to the inherent virtue of violence than to the long-standing commitments of radical liberalism. What John Brown's revolt, and the wave of public sympathy that followed it, signified to Phillips was that inherent human virtues could never be crushed out by the institutions of tyranny. "As Americans," he explained, "we have never accepted our own civilization," which was founded on the notion that "men do not need any guardian." When ordinary people rise up against tyrannical statutes, by whatever means, they vindicate the liberal faith that "the best power this side of the ocean, is the unfettered average common sense of the masses" and reveal that not they, but tyrannical governments, are the true insurrectionaries. Because it refuses to render "equal justice between man and man," Phillips insisted, Virginia "is only a pirate ship. Virginia, the Commonwealth of Virginia! She is only a chronic insurrection."[58]

Phillips's second speech on Brown was entitled "The Puritan Principle," and here he endeavored to turn even Brown's orthodoxy to his own radically liberal ends. In so doing, he simply continued the long-standing liberal argument that the Puritan tradition was a mixture of tares and wheat and that New England's liberals were the true heirs of Puritan wheat. "I thank God," he began, "for John Calvin. To be sure, he burned Servetus; but the Puritans, or at least, their immediate descendants, hung the witches; George Washington held slaves, and wherever you go up and down history, you find men, not angels. Of course, you find imperfect men; but you find great men; men who have marked their own age, and moulded the succeeding." It was Calvin, not Luther, according to Phillips, who had warded off the forces of reaction and ensured the triumph of the Reformation, and it was Calvin who had bequeathed to Phillips's own day the twin virtues of religious republicanism and religious action.[59]

Phillips identified Calvin as the father of republicanism by conflating Calvin's biography with the subsequent history of England and Scotland, particularly "the triumphs of the people against priestcraft and power." Paradoxically, he traced the liberal faith in human nature to Calvin's doctrine of original sin by suggesting that that doctrine applied even more to corrupt institutions than to human individuals: "The Puritan said, 'Human nature is sinful'; so the earth is accursed since the Fall; but I cannot find any thing better than this old earth to build on; I must put up my corner-stone upon it, cursed as it is; I cannot lay hold of the battlements of heaven.'" For Phillips this justified an anarchist reliance on "the millions" and "the ocean of public thought" as the safest basis of society.[60]

The second legacy of Puritanism that Phillips affirmed was its stress on *action*, that is, on the active incarnation of religious ideas. Once again, he assumed—in quite unpuritan fashion!—that these ideas would be incarnated in individuals rather than in institutions: "Puritanism, therefore, is *action*; it is impersonating ideas; it is distrusting and being willing to shake off, at fitting times, what are called *institutions*." This was the necessary counterpart to Phillips's faith in popular opinion and the "millions": the masses could be trusted precisely insofar as they were, on occasion, educated by an individual willing to "throw himself against society." Phillips's Puritan—like Socrates and like John Brown—was the one man in a thousand who, once persuaded of a principle, would put it into immediate action: "If you tell a man the absolute truth, that if he will plunge into the ocean, and only keep his eyes fixed on heaven, he will never sink. . . . Nine hundred and ninety-nine will throw up their arms to clasp some straw or neighbor, and sink; the thousandth will keep his hands by his body, believing God, and float—and he is the Puritan." Phillips called upon New England liberals of the nineteenth century to emulate the Puritans not by adopting Puritan orthodoxy but rather by being truer to themselves. If the Puritans "lived to any purpose," he insisted, "they produced a generation better than themselves," and thus "the vindication of Puritanism is a New England bound to be better than Puritanism."[61]

Clearly, Phillips conceded nothing to orthodoxy in his exegesis of Brown's Puritanism. Yet the sheer delight that he and so many others took in the fact of Brown's Puritanism, their willingness to invoke Puritanism in such unqualifiedly positive terms, created a major opening for the reassertion of orthodoxy. Thus George Barrell Cheever, the stridently orthodox and abolitionist minister of New York City's Church of the Puritans, found in John Brown an occasion to lambaste the nation's "perversions of the Word of God and of the Constitution" and to call the abolitionist community back to churchgoing, Bible reading, and the discipline of prayer.[62] Interestingly, even Cheever did not fully *identify* with Brown's orthodoxy but romanticized his Puritanism in terms that echoed those of the liberals: "This type of character is of the old Puritan Mayflower stamp. It would seem as if the plates of that character must have been stolen away from that first generation and buried; but now, after two hundred years, a new, fresh, vivid impression is before us." But Cheever drew properly orthodox lessons from this romantic image: Brown's biblical militarism confirmed the shared authority of Old and New Testaments, while his sublime confidence in God's direction proved not the inherent virtues of humanity (à la Phillips) but rather the transcendent power of God.

Brown's character, he asserted oddly, "is God's work, not man's." His words "surpass[ed] all possibility of mere human contrivance" and were "at once the work of a Divine Providence, and the impulse of Divine truth and grace." Like so many others, Cheever described Brown as "A MAN, one of the noblest of his race," but he rejoiced even more that he was "a faithful servant of Christ" who could direct the nation to divine rather than human powers.[63]

The only radical liberals who bothered to protest against the illiberal tendencies of Brown's Puritanism were the ones Redpath classified as nonresistants, and even their protests were tempered with much praise. Garrison initially described Brown's venture as "misguided, wild, and apparently insane," but he went on to insist that "no one who glories in the Revolutionary struggle of 1776, deny the right of the slaves to imitate the example of our fathers." James Freeman Clarke referred disparagingly to "a church, which, binding up in one volume the Old and New Testaments, calls them both the Christian Bible, and gives equal authority to the one as to the other." He said that Brown "shares all the great and noble qualities [Calvinism] has so often produced, together with its frequent alloy"—but went on to illustrate Brown's "strict and impartial sense of justice" with a touching story of Brown's solicitude for the family of a horse thief whom he had helped send to prison. Charles K. Whipple blasted the church's "mischievous doctrine that the true God is the 'God of battles'" who authorizes "some of his children to hang, behead, stab, and shoot others" but suggested that since Brown had never really contemplated the truth of nonresistance, he could be judged by a lower standard: "So far as his light extended, John Brown nobly, gloriously, did his duty to the slave."[64] And John Greenleaf Whittier suggested in verse that when the dying Brown kissed a slave child who had prayed for him, his loving humanity had been purged of its masculine violence:

> The shadows of his stormy life
> That moment fell apart:
> Without, the rash and bloody hand,
> Within, the loving heart.
> That kiss, from all its guilty means,
> Redeemed the good intent,
> And round the grisly fighter's hair
> The Martyr's aureole bent![65]

William Lloyd Garrison objected to even this laudatory poem, pointing out that Whittier had previously written poems on the patriot fathers that did not so insistently invoke images like "the rash and bloody hand." Though Garrison himself characterized the attack on Harpers Ferry as a "well-intended but sadly misguided effort," his assessment of John Brown mirrored his response to Nat Turner nearly three decades earlier. Since the slaves suffered an oppression far greater than anything experienced by the British colonists in the eighteenth century, all admirers of "Concord, Lexington and Bunker Hill" were bound to honor Brown. "If we are justified in striking a blow for freedom, when the question is one of a threepenny tax on tea, then, I say, they are a thousand times more justified, when it is to save fathers, mothers, wives and children from the slave-coffle and the auction-block, and to restore to them their God-given rights."[66]

Garrison had good reason to believe that the spirit of Bunker Hill prevailed not just in the nation but even in the abolitionist community. When he spoke at a gathering on the day of Brown's execution, he asked how many nonresistants were present in the audience and received just one affirmative response. This provided an occasion for Garrison to remind "you who are otherwise" of their duty to admire John Brown, but also for him to clarify the implications of his own radically liberal nonresistance.

The nonresistant's duty, he explained, is to resist tyranny by laboring "unremittingly to effect the peaceful abolition of slavery, by an appeal to the reason and conscience of the slaveholder," and this he had done and continued to do. But by the same token the nonresistant's sympathy must lie entirely with the victims of oppression, and so it is consistent with peace principles to desire the victory of the oppressed in any physical contest with their oppressors. Though nonresistants should urge the enslaved to resist nonviolently, they can nevertheless express a preference for violent resistance over sheer passivity: "Rather than see men wearing their chains in a cowardly and servile spirit, I would, as an advocate of peace, much rather see them breaking the head of the tyrant with their chains." Similarly, a nonresistant can rejoice when men like John Brown "who believe in the right and duty of wielding carnal weapons are so far advanced that they will take those weapons out of the scale of despotism, and throw them into the scale of freedom."[67] The nonresistant, in short, is forbidden from allowing the radically liberal end to justify the violent means, but he or she is entirely free to celebrate the accomplishment of that end by others using whatever means.

For many scholars, as well as for Garrison's former friend Adin Ballou, this characteristically Garrisonian argument clinches the case that the nonresistants had fatally accommodated their position to the cause of violent resistance.[68] But, as I have shown, Garrison had always represented, with utter consistency, a nuanced and paradoxical respect for those who shared his radical liberalism while repudiating his nonresistance. There is no denying that between 1831 and 1859 the tone of abolitionist sentiment had shifted, but what was at stake was not nonresistant principle but a question of tactics: How should one respond when popular opinion suddenly embraces some, but not all, of the principles one has long championed? Is it best to rejoice in the change or to continue enunciating the distance left to be traveled?

It is important to realize how dramatic the shift was in the minds of Garrison and his associates. In the 1830s, Wendell Phillips recalled, abolitionists were regularly mobbed and silenced, but after thirty years of abolitionist testimony, "men that still believe in violence, the five points of whose faith are the fist, the bowie-knife, fire, poison, and the pistol, are ranged on the side of Liberty." The popular reaction to John Brown first revealed the extent of the change to surprised abolitionists such as Theodore Parker, who confessed, "I am surprised to find love for the man, admiration for his conduct, and sympathy with his object, so widespread in the North, especially in New England, and more particularly in dear, good, old Boston!"[69]

For Adin Ballou, whose nonresistant faith had always been grounded in an exclusive if heterodox understanding of biblical authority, the popular groundswell of abolitionist sentiment meant little one way or the other, and his tactic was to lean all the harder on the still-neglected truth of nonresistance. Garrison, on the other hand, had always vested authority in the agreement between Jesus' teaching and the deepest values of the American nation, and his preferred tactic was to point out the ways in which

Americans were gradually becoming conscious of that agreement. He never stopped singing nonresistant solos, but his delight was to join at last in the national chorus that proclaimed John Brown a martyr and Harpers Ferry an apocalyptic event betokening God's imminent victory over slavery.

John Brown as Martyr

"Some eighteen hundred years ago Christ was crucified; this morning, perchance, Captain Brown was hung. These are the two ends of a chain that is not without its links. He is not Old Brown any longer; he is an angel of light." Thoreau's words were the most eloquent expression of a widely shared sentiment that John Brown had become a martyr by dying for freedom. The orthodox George Cheever noted that Brown's death had all the traits of martyrdom: "the false accusations, the prejudice and hatred, the reigning religion and law against him, the abuse, the torture, the present ignominy and shame, the apparent failure of his life, and defeat of all his plans, and perfect triumph of his enemies." The radical Theodore Parker agreed, noting a bit more humanistically that Brown's "noble demeanor, his unflinching bravery, his gentleness, his calm, religious trust in God, and his words of truth and soberness, cannot fail to make a profound impression on the hearts of Northern men; yea, and on Southern men." Louisa May Alcott wrote in her diary that "the execution of Saint John the Just took place today." And William Lloyd Garrison proclaimed on the day of Brown's execution, "Now he no longer needs our sympathy, for he is beyond suffering, and wears the victor's crown."[70]

Others went so far as to suggest that Brown might supersede Jesus Christ. A correspondent to the *Liberator*, for example, commented that "almost every [biblical] passage applied to Christ, as suffering death for the sins of others, may be truthfully applied to John Brown" and predicted that "after fifty years we should find Brown churches all over the South." Henry Clarke Wright, always fond of blasphemy, concluded that "the sin of this nation . . . is to be taken away, not by Christ, but by John Brown. Christ, as represented by those who are called by his name, has proved a dead failure, as a power to free the slaves. . . . The nation is to be saved, not by the blood of Christ, (as that is now administered,) but by the blood of John Brown, which, as administered by Abolitionists, will prove the 'power of God and the wisdom of God' to resist slaveholders, and bring them to repentance."[71]

Adin Ballou, standing almost alone, was disgusted with those who sought to link Jesus and John Brown, noting pointedly that "if these laudations had held up John Brown as a devout Calvinist of the old Puritanic, Cromwellian stamp . . . they would have been truthful, just, and unexceptionable. But when they characterize his enterprise and conduct as pre-eminently *Christ-like*, and canonize him as a *Christian* saint, and some of them as a self-sacrificing *redeemer* more to be honored than the Christ of Calvary, they are untruthful, unjust, and utterly absurd." The dangers of treating Brown as a messiah appear more poignantly in Frederick Douglass's self-effacing praise, written twenty years later: "His zeal in the cause of my race was far greater than mine—it was as the burning sun to my taper light—mine was bounded by time, his stretched away to the boundless shores of eternity. I could live for the slave, but he could die for him. The crown of martyrdom is high, far beyond the reach of ordinary mortals." By treating

Brown's accidental (or suicidal) death as more significant than his own devoted life's work, Douglass betrayed the radical liberal faith that the *living* sentiments of the human heart had the power to overthrow injustice. And by separating the "martyrs" from "ordinary mortals," he implicitly preached passivity—at least to those hearers who regarded themselves as ordinary and mortal.[72]

A range of abolitionists used a similar sacrificial logic to interpret Brown's death as a blow against slavery. "All first class victories, from that of Calvary downwards," said Wheelock, "are defeats." This theme could bring together nonresistants and advocates of violent rebellion. Once Brown was dead, it no longer mattered that he had once sought to kill others. The important thing now was his commitment to principle, his faith in God, and the inspiration he might provide to those who remained behind. Thus, Phillips, Wheelock, and Thoreau all suggested that the nation would receive new life from the realization that "in this Sodom of ours, twenty-two men have been found ready to die for an idea." Thoreau, Parker, and a Rev. Mr. Belcher all invoked the biblical image of martyrs as seeds of the future: "In the moral world, when good seed is planted, good fruit is inevitable, and does not depend on our watering and cultivating; that when you plant, or bury, a hero in his field, a crop of heroes is sure to spring up."[73] Significantly, Garrison gave this image a stridently apocalyptic tone:

> It will be a terribly losing day for all Slavedom when John Brown and his associates are brought to the gallows. It will be sowing seed broadcast for a harvest of retribution. Their blood will cry trumpet-tongued from the ground, and that cry will be responded to by tens of thousands in a manner that shall cause the knees of the Southern slavemongers to smite together as did those of Belshazzar of old! O that they might avoid all this by a timely repentance![74]

This passage suggests the second part of the consensus on John Brown: just as he was a martyr, so the attack on Harpers Ferry was an apocalyptic token, a sign that God's decisive intervention against slavery was surely on its way. Why did a failed, indeed, a rather pathetic, attack on the Slave Power take on such significance? Part of the answer lies in the contrast between Harpers Ferry and the other signal events of the 1850s. The Fugitive Slave Act, the Kansas-Nebraska Act, and the Dred Scott decision all suggested that historical initiative lay with the Slave Power itself, while the white pragmatism of the Free Soil Party and the Republican Party suggested to abolitionists that most of the North still did not truly understand. If Harpers Ferry was a defeat, it was also a sign that the abolitionists themselves might make things happen. Moreover, Harpers Ferry provoked a dramatic national response, galvanizing the attention of Northerners, slaveholders, and even, abolitionists assumed, the slaves themselves. "Never has any single event in our annals," exclaimed Methodist minister Gilbert Haven, "so inthralled the whole nation."[75]

Startled by the sheer power of the event, abolitionists of all theological persuasions turned to providential explanations. Cheever affirmed that "John Brown is God's own protest against this tyranny, against the unrighteous laws that sanction it, against the men and States that support it. God writes out his warning on clear white paper, takes the heart and mind of a Christian, a man of prayer, for its publication." Theodore Parker compared Harpers Ferry to Lexington Green and noted that "great events turn on small hinges, and let mankind march through. How different things happen from what we fancy! . . . But it sometimes happens that the Divine Providence uses quite humble cattle to bear his most precious burdens, both fast and far." James Freeman Clarke described the event as "like the clock, striking the fatal hour—the hour of the beginning of a new era in this conflict."[76]

For Clarke, Harpers Ferry was an apocalyptic warning but not a sure sign of what was to come. For him, belief in Providence meant that the "wide, destroying flame" might still be averted. Apocalypse was not really God's preferred method but the natural consequence of human evil, a consequence that could be defeated only by divinely inspired love: "I have faith in the Divine Providence—faith in the coming Kingdom of Jesus Christ—faith that He, the Master, shall yet come to reign in hearts grateful for his love, and in minds submissive to his will. . . . Condemning all violence, bloodshed, and war, let us overcome evil with good, and whenever we speak the Truth, speak it also in love."[77]

Clarke, like Wendell Phillips and other radical liberals, assumed that even apocalyptic divine intervention would ultimately confirm the liberal faith in the human heart. But their appeals to Harpers Ferry only served to strengthen an alternative theory of Providence that linked God's will not to human hearts but to human blood. On the morning of his execution, John Brown handed the guards a slip of paper that gave *his* final testimony on God's battle against slavery. "I John Brown," he had written, "am now quite *certain* that the crimes of this *guilty, land: will* never be purged *away;* but with Blood. I had *as I now think: vainly* flattered myself that without *verry much* bloodshed; it might be done."[78]

Liberal, Constitutional, and Orthodox: Abraham Lincoln's Political Religion

As Brown had prophesied, an event was coming that would galvanize the nation's attention far more completely than Harpers Ferry. Five years after Brown's execution, millions of Americans shared his belief that the nation's sins demanded a bloody expiation, and they knew too well that the amount of bloodshed required was far greater than he had ever imagined. Yet the Civil War was not quite the sort of national apocalypse anticipated by Brown. It was fought, at least initially, not by African Americans seeking freedom but by European Americans defending the constitutional union. Its result was not a millennium of racial harmony but the triumph of a militarized, industrialized nation-state in which corporations prospered while poor farmers and workers, both white and black, struggled to survive. And its messianic leader, Abraham Lincoln, was a man who led the nation one step further away from the radical liberal dream.

This is not to suggest that Lincoln stood entirely outside the liberal political tradition. In fact, he could celebrate the Jeffersonian heritage as effusively as Brown, Douglass, or Garrison. But Lincoln's political philosophy was complex and multifaceted, if not outright contradictory, and liberalism was just one component. Frederick Douglass's religious and political principles could ultimately be reduced to the central liberal values of freedom and equality. John Brown's faith and politics were bipolar, moving between liberal equality and his orthodox understanding of divine sovereignty. But to understand Lincoln's words and deeds one must recognize three centers of ultimate value: the liberal ideals enshrined in the Declaration of Independence, the tradition of national union symbolized by the Constitution, and an unecclesiastical but deeply orthodox understanding of divine sovereignty.

The Liberal Lincoln

Invocations of Jefferson's Declaration were at the heart of Lincoln's political rhetoric in the 1850s and beyond. "Nearly eighty years ago, we began by declaring that all men are created equal," Lincoln told an Illinois audience in 1854, and he repeated himself at Gettysburg in 1863: "Four score and seven years ago our fathers brought forth on this continent, a new nation, conceived in Liberty, and dedicated to the proposition that all men are created equal." "I have never," he told a crowd at Independence Hall while en route to his first presidential inauguration, "had a feeling politically that did not spring from the sentiments embodied in the Declaration of Independence." Indeed, he added, "I would rather be assassinated on this spot than to surrender" those principles. In campaign speeches, moreover, Lincoln repeatedly suggested that the rival Democrats— once the party of Jefferson—had "assailed, and sneered at, and construed, and hawked at, and torn [the Declaration], till, if its framers could rise from their graves, they could not at all recognize it."[79]

What did Lincoln find so appealing in Jefferson's Declaration? Most important, he valued the Declaration as an eloquent statement of the liberal principles of equality and liberty. The Declaration, he insisted, gave "liberty, not alone to the people of this country, but hope to the world for all future time. It . . . gave promise that in due time the weights should be lifted from the shoulders of all men, and that *all* should have an equal chance." Because chattel slavery, like all forms of tyranny, was inimical to the liberal vision of equality, Lincoln's lifelong aversion to slavery was integrally related to his admiration for the Declaration. Indeed, he once derived a capsule definition of democracy from his antislavery sentiment: "As I would not be a slave, so I would not be a master. This expresses my idea of democracy. Whatever differs from this, to the extent of the difference, is no democracy." "If slavery is not wrong," he later wrote to Albert G. Hodges, "nothing is wrong."[80]

The American founders, Lincoln believed, had conceded their inability to end slavery immediately, but they nevertheless understood that their enterprise hinged on its essential wrongness and ultimate extinction. The debate in the 1850s over the extension of slavery into Kansas, Nebraska, and other western territories was thus a recapitulation of the revolutionary struggle against monarchical tyranny. In his seventh senatorial debate with Stephen Douglas, Lincoln announced grandly that their disagreement over slavery extension was "the eternal struggle between . . . right and wrong." Lincoln believed slavery to be wrong; Douglas believed it to be right and thus placed himself on the side of tyrants of all ages. Freedom and tyranny, Lincoln said, "are the two principles that have stood face to face from the beginning of time; and will ever continue to struggle. The one is the common right of humanity and the other the divine right of kings."[81]

Lincoln, in short, cherished the Declaration for its central idea. He also admired Jefferson for having the audacity to use an idea—rather than, say, an ethnic identity—as the basis for founding a nation. Lincoln often compared Jefferson to Euclid, suggesting that his principles were "the definitions and axioms of free society." The geometric precision of Jefferson's ideas appealed to the canny rationalism of the prairie lawyer. In an 1859 letter Lincoln praised Jefferson for having "had the coolness, forecast, and capacity to introduce into a merely revolutionary document, an abstract truth, applicable to all men and all times." Thus, the nation Jefferson created transcended the normal constraints of nationhood. In a speech in Chicago in 1858, Lincoln noted that perhaps half the people of the United States were recent immigrants who could not "trace their connection with those days [of the Revolution] by blood." But these people could still identify with the national idea, could feel that the equality of all people was "the father of all moral principle in them." By sharing the idea of the fathers, immigrants became heirs of the Revolution. "That is the electric cord in that Declaration that links the hearts of patriotic and liberty-loving men together, that will link those patriotic hearts as long as the love of freedom exists in the minds of men throughout the world."[82]

Paradoxically, Lincoln revered Jefferson both as the expounder of the transcendent idea of human equality and as the founder of a particular nation, albeit a nation dedicated to the idea's ultimate realization. Lincoln may have stressed the ideas of the Declaration, but he took for granted its status as the nation's founding document. By using the phrase "four score and seven years ago," Lincoln dated the nation not to the Constitutional Convention of 1787 nor to the commencement of revolutionary hostilities in 1775 but to Jefferson's Declaration of 1776. The Declaration could thus serve, for Lincoln, as the hermeneutical key to the Constitution. Though the Constitution did not itself mention such abstract ideals as human equality, it could be interpreted only as the chosen vehicle for the realization of those ideals.[83]

Several commentators have pointed out that there was something subtly anti-Jeffersonian about Lincoln's invocation of Jefferson as the national father. Jefferson invoked eternal principles to justify his revolution and anticipated that coming generations would have to fight new revolutions for those same principles. Lincoln praised Jefferson, however, for forging a permanent bond between eternal principle and just one revolution, just one nation. Jefferson opened his Declaration by talking about God and humanity; Lincoln began the Gettysburg Address by talking about the United States of America. And, perhaps most tellingly, while Jefferson considered human equality to be a "self-evident truth," Lincoln referred to it merely as a "proposition."[84]

These differences reflect both personal differences and changes in the intellectual climate between 1776 and 1863. Jefferson breathed the crisp air of Enlightenment rationality and had little doubt that his own moral sense gave him authoritative insight into the laws established by nature's God. Lincoln, chastened by his own upbringing, frequent personal losses, and the national crisis of the 1850s, was equally sure of the existence of divine laws but far less confident of his own ability to discern them. He also shared the romantic emphasis on historical development, assuming that abstract ideas could be realized only through an organic process of development and struggle. The Jeffersonian idea, however compelling, was for Lincoln no more than an untested proposition until a nation emerged that was willing to dedicate itself to human equality.[85]

So long as such a nation had not fully emerged, Lincoln was willing to tolerate violations of human equality in the historical present. The Founding Fathers, he believed, had compromised with slavery in the forging of the Constitution because they had no choice, and well into the Civil War he himself honored the constitutional sanctity of Southern slavery. His political passion was not to destroy slavery immediately but to prevent its extension into the territories—to prevent, that is, a retrograde movement away from human equality. The historical mission of the Founding Fathers, he insisted, was not to produce perfect equality instantaneously but to "set up a standard maxim for free society, which should be familiar to all, and revered by all; constantly looked to, constantly labored for, and even though never perfectly attained, constantly approximated." Tellingly, Lincoln was willing to apply this exegetical principle to the Gospels as well as the Declaration. In a speech in Chicago in 1858, he illustrated his point of view by citing Jesus' teaching, "As your Father in Heaven is perfect, be ye also perfect." Jesus, Lincoln explained, "set that up as a standard, and he who did most toward reaching that standard, attained the highest degree of moral perfection. So I say in relation to the principle that all men are created equal, let it be as nearly reached as we can. If we cannot give freedom to every creature, let us do nothing that will impose slavery upon any other creature."[86]

The National Union

Lincoln's willingness to treat human equality as an ultimate ideal rather than a self-evident truth reflects his prior commitment to the Whig Party's ideal of national union. Lincoln may have revered the Declaration in the 1850s, but even earlier, according to his congressional colleague Alexander Stephens (future vice president of the Confederacy), he spoke of the Union with a mystical fervor. Jefferson thus shared space in Lincoln's pantheon with Henry Clay, the pragmatic Whig politician from Kentucky who was always willing to compromise sectional interests for the sake of the nation.

Clay's "predominant sentiment," Lincoln explained in his 1852 eulogy, "was a deep devotion to the cause of human liberty." But this could be expressed only in his devotion to the preservation and strengthening of the national union: "He loved his country partly because it was his own country, but mostly because it was a free country; and he burned with a zeal for its advancement, prosperity and glory, because he saw in such, the advancement, prosperity and glory, of human liberty, human right and human nature." Clay stood as a bulwark against the disunionism of abolitionists and apologists for slavery, rejecting both "those who would shiver into fragments the Union of these States; tear to tatters its now venerated constitution; and even burn the last copy of the Bible, rather than slavery should continue a single hour," and those "who, for the sake of perpetuating slavery, are beginning to assail and to ridicule the white-man's charter of freedom—the declaration that 'all men are created free and equal.'"[87]

Lincoln was deeply committed to reconciling the abstract ideals of the Declaration with the practical compromises of the Constitution. Where Garrison and other radical liberals stressed the incompatibility of slavery and coercion with liberal ideals, Lincoln insisted that no ideal could ever be achieved without an institutional framework.[88] He also suggested that only a fervent commitment to the national union would allow the nation to preserve its founding ideals for future generations. For, like other antebellum Americans, Lincoln was preoccupied with the problem of generational continuity. How could members of his generation preserve the achievements of their heroic fathers and grandfathers? The Democratic politicians of the "Young America" movement insisted that the new generation needed to assert its own autonomy. Lincoln, however, counted himself with the Whig "old fogies," who thought the task was simply to deepen reverence for the sacrifices of the fathers.[89]

Thus, the central question of the Gettysburg Address—can the nation which "our fathers brought forth . . . long endure"?—guided Lincoln's entire career. As early as 1838 he explained the dilemma to the Young Men's Lyceum of Springfield in classic Whig terms. The United States, he said, possessed both "the fairest portion of the earth" and the world's best "system of political institutions." But the present generation could take no credit for this happy "legacy," which had been earned entirely by a "lamented and departed race of ancestors." The paramount duty of the present generation was to preserve the land "unprofaned by the foot of an invader" and the political institutions "undecayed by the lapse of time, and untorn by usurpation—to the latest generation that fate shall permit the world to know."[90]

In both the Lyceum speech and the lecture "Discoveries and Inventions" (1859), Lincoln offered a Whig analysis of the forces that might prevent this loyal perpetuation of institutions. He dismissed the possibility of threats from outside but suggested that a serious internal threat lay over the horizon in the form of "mob law." Too many Americans were willing to step outside the law in order to redress real or perceived injustices. Too many, moreover, were so enamored of their national "youth" that they failed to see their dependence on earlier generations. As a consequence of the popular disregard for law and tradition, the affections of the people were becoming alienated from the nation as a whole. If no one could count on the government to protect his or her life and property from the mob, who would truly value government? This was troubling because passions and affections could not be relied upon as a bulwark of national union in a postheroic age. During the Revolution itself, Lincoln argued, the passions of ambitious men naturally flowed into the revolutionary cause because they hoped to immortalize themselves through the triumph of democracy. The ambitious men of the future, by contrast, could achieve glory only by destroying what the fathers had created. It was up to the rest of the citizens to guard the nation's institutions against any such attempt. "Let reverence for the laws," Lincoln implored, "become the *political religion* of the nation; and let the old and the young, the rich and the poor, the grave and the gay, of all sexes and tongues, and colors and conditions, sacrifice unceasingly upon its altars."[91]

In the Lyceum speech, then, Lincoln disavowed the liberal faith that genuine freedom would unleash sentimental affections that would, in turn, hold society together far more effectively than any coercive institution. Natural affections were simply too ephemeral to allow freedom to thrive apart from an institutional framework. But such a framework, Lincoln increasingly came to admit, would place significant constraints even on liberal sentiments. Lincoln himself, for example, possessed a strong sentimental aversion to slavery. Despite the congruence of this sentiment with the egalitarian thesis of Jefferson's Declaration, Lincoln felt obliged to subordinate it to his loyalty to constitutional law. Especially after his inauguration as president, he drew a careful and constant distinction between his "abstract judgment and feeling on slavery" and his official duty to "preserve, protect, and defend the Constitution of the United States." This duty forbade any interference with slavery in the Southern states.[92]

Lincoln's insistence on placing national duty above natural feeling was precisely the position that Harriet Beecher Stowe had lampooned in the person of Senator Bird, who like Lincoln believed that political duty mandated support even for the Fugitive Slave

Act. But Lincoln put the best possible face on the matter by arguing that constitutionalism provided the only framework in which slavery could ever be defeated. Had the Founding Fathers not agreed to tolerate slavery, they would have failed to achieve liberty for anyone. They did the best thing possible by simply hiding slavery "in the Constitution, just as an afflicted man hides away a wen or a cancer, which he dares not cut out at once lest he bleed to death; with the promise, nevertheless, that the cutting may begin at the end of a given time." Given this arrangement, Lincoln implored his Southern friends "to appreciate how much the great body of the Northern people do crucify their feelings, in order to maintain their loyalty to the constitution and the Union."[93]

The cash value of all this, in the tumultuous 1850s, was that Lincoln supported the protection of slavery in the South, the Missouri Compromise, and the Fugitive Slave Act, but rejected the Dred Scott decision and the Kansas-Nebraska Act, which threatened to allow slavery to expand unchecked into all western territories and even the Northern states. So long as slavery could not expand, Lincoln believed, it would die out eventually. His complacency about this eventuality (a matter of decades or even centuries rather than years) reflected his underlying race prejudice. He did not believe that whites and blacks were fully equal: they were equally entitled to life, liberty, and the pursuit of happiness but not capable of living together on a basis of full social equality. As a rising politician, he happily pandered to the popular white fear of miscegenation: "I protest against that counterfeit logic which concludes that, because I do not want a black woman for a *slave* I must necessarily want her for a *wife*." Throughout his career he supported colonization (to Central America if not to Africa) as the solution to slavery most compatible with the feelings of "the great mass of white people," himself included. Indeed, on the eve of the issuance of the Emancipation Proclamation he was still scolding free blacks not to allow "selfish" motives to prevent them from supporting colonization.[94]

Lincoln's underlying racism also appeared in the colorful parable he used to criticize the extension of slavery:

> If I saw a venomous snake crawling in the road, any man would say I might seize the nearest stick and kill it; but if I found that snake in bed with my children, that would be another question. I might hurt the children more than the snake, and it might bite them. Much more, if I found it in bed with my neighbor's children, and I had bound myself by a solemn compact not to meddle with his children under any circumstances, it would become me to let that particular mode of getting rid of the gentleman alone. But if there was a bed newly made up, to which the children were to be taken, and it was proposed to take a batch of young snakes and put them there with them, I take it no man would say there was any question how I ought to decide![95]

It is not clear who the "children" threatened by the "snake" of slavery are, but they obviously are *not* the African American children and adults who faced slavery's whips and chains every day. By framing his argument in pseudosentimental terms, Lincoln defused the classic sentimental appeal to the plight of those less metaphorical children.

It would, however, be a mistake to make too much of Lincoln's personal race prejudice.[96] Even had he been free of prejudice, his ideological commitment to the Union would have led him to honor the prejudices of his white compatriots. Such a policy was, for him, not political pandering but a sober acknowledgment of what he saw as the real limits of human nature. For Lincoln was deeply aware of the dilemmas involved in defending institutions that simultaneously support and limit the pursuit of liberal ideals. Could, as the Garrisonians hoped, perfect equality and liberty ever be achieved entirely by means of natural affection? Could the liberal utopia rely, as Gerrit Smith and Frederick Douglass perhaps imagined, exclusively on institutions purged of any taint of illiberalism? Or, as Lincoln insisted, did liberal ideals ultimately depend for their realization on the muddy processes of such highly flawed institutions as a constitutional union with built-in protections for slavery? Was it ever necessary, in other words, for liberal ideals to be sacrificed for the sake of institutions that might at some future date become means to the realization of those ideals? By answering these questions affirmatively, Lincoln made himself vulnerable to another line of questioning. If the sacrifice of liberal ideals is sometimes legitimate, who is to say that it is not *always* legitimate? What is to prevent the entire liberal vision from being sold out to the god of institutional prerogatives?

Lincoln and the Sovereignty of God

For Lincoln, the ultimate safeguard against the collapse of liberal ideals into institutional prerogatives was the sovereignty of God. Lincoln believed that God rules over all human individuals and institutions, directing them toward ends that conform to liberal ideals but yet transcend precise human imaginings. His desire to conform his own life to God's will was a third pole of his political philosophy, as vital a center of concern as either his Jeffersonian liberalism or his Whig constitutionalism. Though he could speak of each of the first two poles as matters of ultimate concern, he could also—especially near the end of his life—insist that God's will transcended them both.

Though the precise content of Lincoln's faith has been hotly disputed, several facts are well established. He was raised in the Baptist milieu of the Indiana-Kentucky frontier. As a teenager he served as the sexton of his parents' church, though he never became a member of it or any other. As a young man he read the works of such notorious infidels as Tom Paine and joined in discussions with local freethinkers. These early associations proved a political liability when Lincoln faced Methodist preacher Peter Cartwright as a congressional opponent. Lincoln deeply resented Cartwright's insinuations about his own infidelity and in response issued a handbill that rebuffed the charges while giving few clues about his actual position: "That I am not a member of any Christian Church, is true; but I have never denied the truth of the Scriptures; and I have never spoken with intentional disrespect of religion in general, or of any denomination of Christians in particular."[97] (It is not clear if this is a politic evasion or a principled refusal to make personal faith a political issue.)

As Lincoln aged, he became increasingly dependent on the Bible both as a source of rhetorical cadences and as a staff of comfort during tribulations. He grew close to several clergymen, especially the Scottish Presbyterian James Smith, who became Lincoln's informal pastor in Springfield. (Mary Todd Lincoln joined Smith's congregation, though her husband did not.) As president, Lincoln did much to incorporate religious categories into political discourse: such now-conventional phrases as "under God" and "In God we trust" originated with Lincoln, and his willingness to declare national days of fasting and thanksgiving helped establish Thanksgiving as an annual holiday. Despite his earlier aversion to wearing his faith on his sleeve, President Lincoln made no secret of his desire to be a "humble instrument in the hands of the Almighty." For this he has been lauded as "one of the greatest theologians of America—not in the technical meaning of producing a system of doctrine, certainly not as the defender of some one denomination, but in the sense of seeing the hand of God intimately in the affairs of nations."[98]

But what was the substance of Lincoln's theology? It is difficult to place Lincoln in the terms of the New England debate between liberals and orthodox. His religious milieu was more fragmented and sectarian; the lines were never drawn in clear ways. Lincoln himself both absorbed and repudiated the faith of his forebears. He was repulsed by the petty squabbling of frontier sects, but his solution to the problem—placing the authority of the Bible above that of any church—would have been endorsed by most of the churches in question. His was the implicit, anticreedal liberalism of frontier primitivism, and as such it followed paths uncharted by Harvard's liberal dogmaticians.

Lincoln rejected the notion that a good God would predestine anyone to damnation, but this led him not to an Arminian doctrine of the will but to a predestinarian universalism—or what one scholar aptly calls a "Calvinized deism." At times his religious rhetoric could sound rather Unitarian. In 1842 he praised the Washingtonian temperance movement for rejecting the doctrine of reprobation implicit in earlier temperance activism. The belief "that all habitual drunkards were utterly incorrigible," Lincoln complained, was "so repugnant to humanity, so uncharitable, so cold-blooded and feelingless, that it never did, nor ever can, enlist the enthusiasm of a popular cause." In 1858 he paraphrased the Founding Fathers in terms worthy of Channing: "In their enlightened belief, nothing stamped with the Divine image and likeness was sent into the world to be trodden on, and degraded, and imbruted by its fellows." He also repeatedly claimed that he would join any church that established no membership requirements beyond Jesus' command to love God and neighbor. Yet when Channing's disciple Jesse Fell arrived in Illinois claiming to bring just such a church, Lincoln responded with benign indifference.[99]

Ultimately, the liberal Lincoln could not shake his sense of God's inscrutable and awesome sovereignty, aptly expressed in one of his favorite Shakespearean quotes: "There's a divinity that shapes our ends, / Rough-hew them how we will." In his freethinking youth, Lincoln espoused the "Doctrine of Necessity"—a belief "that the human mind is impelled to action, or held in rest by some power, over which the mind itself has no control." Lincoln noted, in his political handbill, "I have always understood this same opinion to be held by several of the Christian denominations," and his own perspective gradually fused with more conventional Christian providentialism. At times this took rather complacent forms. Lincoln refused to allow immediate abolition to disrupt the Union because he was confident that slavery, though evil in itself, could be part of God's plan for the "ultimate redemption of the African race and African continent." At other times, however, Lincoln suggested that although God's plan will necessarily prevail, humans must nevertheless strive to conform their own lives to it. In a preinaugural speech, for example, Lincoln told his hearers, "I shall be most happy indeed if I shall be an humble instrument in the hands of the Almighty, and of this, his almost chosen people, for perpetrating the object of that great struggle."[100]

Lincoln's felicitous insertion of the word "almost" suggests the most characteristic theme of his theology, a theme that was not fully articulated until the final months of his life. Lincoln believed that individuals and nations should seek to conform themselves to God's will, but he also believed that discerning God's will was ultimately a matter of guesswork. No one could know it perfectly or adhere to it exactly; no nation or community could claim definitively to be "chosen." The tragic prolongation of the Civil War seems to have driven this point home for Lincoln. He began the war fairly confident that the Northern cause of union and the ultimate extinction of slavery conformed more closely to God's will than the Southern cause, but it soon became clear that divine Providence had not provided for a speedy Northern victory. By September 1862 Lincoln wrote, in a private reflection, that "in the present civil war it is quite possible that God's purpose is something different from the purpose of either party—and yet the human instrumentalities, working just as they do, are of the best adaptation to effect His purpose. I am almost ready to say this is probably true—that God wills this contest, and wills that it shall not end yet." Two years later he reiterated this unsettling thought in a letter to his Quaker friend Eliza P. Gurney and then incorporated it into his powerful Second Inaugural Address.[101] Both sides in the war, he noted then, "read the same Bible, and pray to the same God; and each invokes His aid against the other. It may seem strange that any men should dare to ask a just God's assistance in wringing their bread from the sweat of other men's faces; but let us judge not that we be not judged. The prayers of both could not be answered; that of neither has been answered fully. The Almighty has His own purposes."[102]

Lincoln has been almost universally lauded for the sentiment expressed in this passage. It has been rightly seen as a warning against the ideology of Manifest Destiny, against the constant temptation to domesticate Providence by identifying God's purposes with those of one's own community. It has been praised for its sense of "mystery" and its "subtlety and humility." "Lincoln makes no claim to know God's purposes," one scholar notes, "but claims only to see that they are different from the purposes of men."[103] What may be lost in this chorus of praise is the fact that Lincoln's theology, precisely because it is so open-ended, seems to provide no guidance in resolving the tensions between justice and order, the Declaration and the Constitution, that vexed Lincoln's career. If God's will is unknowable, who can say whether God prefers to see the Union dissolved for the sake of abolition or slavery perpetuated for the sake of the Union?

Yet this reading is not quite right either. Lincoln's theology implicitly points to a resolution of the dilemma of order and justice by introducing a conservative bias in favor of actuality rather than ideality, of what *has* happened in the past rather than what *might* happen in the future. Lincoln comes off as uncertain and humble, and in a sense he is, but he is serenely confident of two things: that human purposes for the future, however noble, do not conform perfectly to God's will, and that historical events of the past, however violent and troubling, *do*. As a postinaugural note to Thurlow Weed makes clear, Lincoln simply could not imagine a theology without these two propositions. "Men are not flattered by being shown that there has been a difference of purpose between the Almighty and them. To deny it, however, in this case, is to deny that there is a God governing the world."[104] Because he was unsure of God's purposes but certain of God's governance, Lincoln's spirituality was more Puritan than liberal. He discerned God's hand not in his own aspirations and agency but in the things that happened to himself and his community.

The Coming of the War

"I claim," Lincoln wrote to a friend in the midst of the war, "not to have controlled events, but confess plainly that events have controlled me."[105] It may seem strange to find such a passive spirituality in a man who presided over a great war that in turn sparked revolutionary change. Yet war has an extraordinary capacity to deprive people of their usual sense of agency. It is so big, so unpredictable, and so capable of transforming everyday life that people accord it the sort of reverence they might ordinarily reserve for God.[106] Lincoln was careful not to divinize the nation, but he unhesitatingly divinized the war. It was too divorced from his own choices and desires to be his work, so it must be God's. Indeed, Lincoln and most of his contemporaries came to see the Civil War not merely as *an* act of God but as *the* definitive act of God.

When Lincoln ran for president in 1860, he did not wish to provoke a war. Few, if any, of those who voted for or against him hoped for such an outcome. Lincoln's intent was to preserve both the constitutional union and the liberal mission of moving steadily toward greater human freedom. As late as the First Inaugural Address, Lincoln was sure that the Revolution was the only war needed to guarantee the success of his mission: "The mystic chords of memory, stretching from every battle-field, and patriot grave, to every living heart and hearthstone, all over this broad land, will yet swell the chorus of the Union, when again touched, as surely they will be, by the better angels of our nature."[107] To Lincoln's right, Northern conservatives pursued the same end, though they believed that some speedy concessions to a wary South would be more effective than Lincoln's lofty rhetoric. Abolitionists, by contrast, were relatively complacent about the threat of disunion. They were willing to bid good riddance to their slaveholding neighbors and saw no point in fighting to preserve an unholy compact.[108]

The firing on Fort Sumter on 12 April 1861 changed everything. Those who had been working hardest for conciliation turned, in James Moorhead's words, "upon the South with the anger of friends betrayed." Preachers of various theological and political persuasions, including those most open to nonviolent models of God's power, joined in declaring that the war had profound eschatological significance. As otherworldly a philosopher as Ralph Waldo Emerson took manly satisfaction in the war, declaring that "gunpowder smells good." Congregationalist theologian Horace Bushnell (1802–76), who had never sympathized much with abolition, spoke for many when he recalled the instantaneous enthusiasm of the war's early days: "This immense enthusiasm, bursting forth spontaneous, in a day, and fusing us into a complete unity—how great and thrilling a surprise has it been to us. . . . It verily seems to be, in some sense, an inspiration of God."[109]

The abolitionists, for their part, sometimes grumbled that a war to save the Union was hardly worth it, but they could scarcely conceal their enthusiasm at the rising tide of antislavery sentiment in the North. William Goodell declared it the "Second American Revolution," Theodore Dwight Weld called it "a vast moral Revolution," and Frederick Douglass lauded the "sudden revolution in Northern Sentiment." William

Lloyd Garrison exulted in the "uprising of the entire North . . . like a general and in-stantaneous resurrection from the dead, in defense of whatever of freedom remains in the land." It was, he said, "a hopeful sign of the times even for the sacred cause of peace, in comparison with that moral paralysis and compromising spirit which have so long held mastery over the minds of the people of the North. God's hand is in it."[110]

Indeed, the onset of the war simply confirmed Garrison's long-standing suspicion that slavery would end through an apocalyptic intervention. "Well, at last the day of visitation has come," he declared after the beginning of hostilities. "And so the whole land is to be scourged with fire and blood." He went on to remind his readers,

> For thirty years the Abolitionists have been faithfully warning the nation that, unless the enslaved were set free, a just God would visit it with tribulation and woe proportional to its great iniquity. Now that their predictions have come to pass, are they to indulge in morbid exclamations against the natural operation of the law of immutable justice, and to see in it no evidence of the growth of conscience, the power of truth, or the approach of the long-wished for jubilee? Surely, this would be to arraign Infinite Wisdom, to be blind to the progress of events. Surely, emancipation is nearer than when we believed, and the present struggle cannot fail to hasten it mightily, in a providential sense.[111]

It is hard to know just what "providential sense" Garrison was referring to. His invo-cation of "the natural operation of the law of immutable justice" suggests that by this time he had conflated Providence with natural law. To say that God was punishing the nation for its sins was simply to say that God had designed the universe so that vio-lence would inevitably bring about its own punishment. This allowed Garrison simul-taneously to take pleasure in the progress of the war and to affirm the continuing valid-ity of his peace principles, since "if they had been long since embraced and carried out by the people, neither slavery nor war would now be filling the land with violence and blood." It also allowed him to hope that the effect of the war would be the triumph of nonviolent liberalism: "The war must go on to its consummation; and among the salu-tary lessons it will teach will be the impossibility of oppressing the poor and the needy, or consenting thereto by entering into 'a covenant with death,' without desolating judg-ments following in its train."[112]

Frederick Douglass, for his part, saw the war in Manichean terms as part of "the eternal conflict between right and wrong, good and evil, liberty and slavery, truth and falsehood, the glorious light of life, and the appalling darkness of human selfishness and sin." It called upon each individual to take sides: "They can be angels, or they may be demons." He anticipated, though, that the war would ultimately vindicate the liberal faith in human nature, for it pitted the violence of slavery against "all the promptings, aspirations, convictions and sympathies of unperverted human nature."[113]

Similarly, Lydia Maria Child continued to believe that human affections, as well as military might, had a role to play in ending slavery. She conceded that the abolitionists had erred in thinking that "moral influence" alone would "regenerate" the South. "A little leaven will, indeed, leaven the whole lump, provided you can get it in; but despotism guarded itself so strictly at the South that the leaven of freedom could be worked in only by the sword." Still, Child insisted that by leavening public sentiment in the North, the abolitionists had made a military solution to slavery possible. She also relied heavily on traditional suasion to push Lincoln toward emancipation. In an 1862 public letter, she promised Lincoln that the army could gain the "*heart*-service" of the slaves by freeing them. She also reported a touching incident in which a union general gave a slave girl a ride on a cannon. Such acts, she said, had a "magnetic power" that "wakened a responsive thrill in other kindly, generous hearts." Child concluded by warning Lincoln of the divine displeasure he faced for "stifl[ing] the moral enthusiasm of noble souls."[114]

Despite abolitionist hopes, the war was initially fought on grounds that were conservative and constitutional rather than liberal and revolutionary. The war, Lincoln explained to Congress on 4 July 1861, was a test of whether a nation that had established a constitutional republic could also *maintain* it "against a formidable internal attempt to overthrow it." It was a test of a constitutional theory that Lincoln had articulated in the First Inaugural by suggesting that the Union existed prior to the individual states and even the Constitution, having been forged in the struggle stretching from the beginning of the Revolution to the Constitutional Convention. To be sure, Lincoln also anticipated that the war would have a salutary effect on the ongoing liberal struggle for human freedom. But this effect was to be indirect. The "People's Contest" would not *advance* the liberal agenda but would simply preserve "that *form, and substance of government,* whose leading object is, to elevate the condition of men." Lincoln assumed that this cause was his religious as well as political duty, but he alluded to this conviction only briefly, in closing. "And having thus chosen our course, without guile, and with pure purpose, let us renew our trust in God, and go forward without fear, and with manly hearts."[115]

The surprising, and bloody, prolongation of the war, coupled with a series of personal tragedies, forced Lincoln to deepen his reflections on God's purposes. Gradually, he began to think of Providence not as a mechanistic "necessity" but as a personal cause, guiding and shaping human actions to a particular end. If God willed the war and did not will a speedy end to it, Lincoln reasoned, then perhaps God had larger purposes for the war than Lincoln himself did. Perhaps the war was, after all, God's means of ending slavery.[116]

Such reflections, in the summer of 1862, led Lincoln to consider issuing a proclamation of emancipation. Significantly, though, Lincoln was not willing to base his decision to emancipate solely on the witness of his own conscience—or even on the witnesses of Lydia Child, Frederick Douglass, and the countless others who were insisting that he obey God by freeing the slaves. He needed a different sort of sign. Secretary of State William Seward had suggested that emancipation would appear desperate unless it occurred after a military victory, and Lincoln took this suggestion very much to heart. As he would later explain to his cabinet, he made a vow "to my Maker" that, as soon as the Confederates were driven from Maryland, he would free the slaves. (This startled the cabinet members, few of whom had ever heard him claim a personal relationship with God.) With the victory at Antietam in September, therefore, "God had decided this question in favor of the slaves."[117]

The War as Sacrifice

Lincoln developed his new theology of war further over the next year. By the time he addressed a war-weary crowd at Gettysburg in November 1863, Lincoln saw the war as a sacrificial process by which God was bringing about a "new birth of freedom." Lincoln had an instrumental role in this process, but it was overshadowed by the work of the soldiers—"brave men, living and dead, who struggled here"—who had "consecrated" the ground through their participation in the violence of warfare. Where liberals had long claimed that freedom from violence was the birthright of all people, Lincoln now countered that a sacrificial war was a prerequisite for rebirth.[118]

Lincoln was not the first to propose a sacrificial interpretation of the Civil War. Such interpretations appealed to many who had little taste for sacrificial theology during peacetime. Even Lydia Maria Child had recently declared that the "self-sacrifice" of the Massachusetts Fifty-fourth Regiment (composed of black soldiers) was "holy and immortal."[119] Lincoln himself took for granted that sins could not be remitted without sacrifice—a position emphasized by his unofficial pastor in Illinois, James Smith.[120] When the United States fell into the sin of slavery extension through the Kansas-Nebraska Act, Lincoln anticipated a sacrificial cleansing—though he still hoped, at that date, that the prior sacrifice of the Revolutionary fathers might cover the sins of their children. "Our republican robe is soiled," he declared, "and trailed in the dust. Let us repurify it. Let us turn and wash it white, in the spirit, if not the blood of the Revolution." Throughout the war itself, he used sacrificial language to console those who had lost loved ones. "I pray that our Heavenly Father may assuage the anguish of your bereavement," Lincoln wrote to Lydia Bixby in 1864, "and leave you only the cherished memory of the loved and lost, and the solemn pride that must be yours, to have laid so costly a sacrifice upon the altar of Freedom."[121]

From the beginning of the war, dozens of Northern preachers offered sacrificial interpretations of the conflict, generally drawing on the classic model of the Puritan jeremiad. The nation had sinned, these preachers argued, and the war was both a divine punishment and the means by which God would reconcile the nation to himself. But these preachers could not agree on the precise nature of the national sin. Some pointed to conventional moral lapses, others to disrespect for ancestors, neglect of the Old Testament, or, of course, the toleration of slavery.[122] Perhaps the most sophisticated sacrificial interpreter of the war was Horace Bushnell. Bushnell was a Congregationalist minister who had done much to make a place for liberal themes—notably the importance of familial nurture and the priority of Christ's life over his death—within orthodox theology. Yet Bushnell celebrated the Civil War as the sacrificial means by which the nation would be purged not of slavery or tyranny but of Jeffersonian liberalism.

Bushnell developed his theory in a sermon preached just after the Union's defeat at the first battle of Bull Run. No doubt to the congregation's surprise, Bushnell greeted the defeat with enthusiasm. Reverses were needed, he suggested in the sermon's title, to transform the nation's initial enthusiasm for war into something more lasting. The loyalty most Americans had felt when Fort Sumter was attacked was ephemeral. "It must be struck in by sacrifice, drilled into the very bone of our substance by persistent struggles with adversity, and then it will stand, then it is loyalty complete."[123]

But why had a lasting sense of national loyalty not been established long before? The problem, Bushnell suggested, was that the nation had not been conceived in liberty but misconceived in abstraction. The New England Puritans had laid a suitable national foundation in faith and history, but during the Revolution they had been preempted by Thomas Jefferson, "who taught abstractively, not religiously, and led the unreligious mind of the time by his abstractions." Jefferson imagined that free individuals could create a lasting social compact without appealing to any authority beyond humanity. Rightly rejecting the divine right of kings, he wrongly assumed that there was no divine right vested in any government. As a result, he failed to create any government at all, only a "copartnership" with no authority over its citizens. "How can a copartnership amount to a governing power over the parties in it? . . . They get no authority till we see them authorized to legislate by God. Nothing touches the conscience and becomes morally binding that is not from above the mere human level." The "grand crowning mischief" of Jeffersonianism was thus the doctrine of states' rights, by which the South justified its withdrawal from constitutional obligations. "We began with a godless theorizing, and we end, just as should, in discovering that we have not so much as made any nation at all."[124]

How does a nation attain a sense of the divine authority of the laws? Near the end of his sermon, Bushnell hinted that one device might have been the inclusion in the Constitution of "a recognition of the fact that the authority of government, in every form, is derivable only from God." But God's decisive act in the war made such verbal devices unnecessary. The nation's spontaneous loyalty, stiffened by sacrifice, was enough to effect a bond between national law and divine authority. For a moment Bushnell equivocated on this point, perhaps sensing that too close an association of God and nation might be considered idolatrous. National loyalty, he conceded, is "not religion certainly . . . yet, in another view, it is no other than the old historic religious element in which our nationality has been grounded from the first." Drawing on the organic theories of *volk* identity promoted by romantic conservatives, Bushnell argued that the forging of national identity through historic violence is an essentially religious process— so much so that the fighting of a battle on the Sabbath was cause for praise: "I know not any cause more worthy of the day."[125] Bushnell summed up his argument thus:

> The true loyalty is never reached, till the laws and the nation are made to appear sacred, or somewhat more than human. And that will not be done till we have made long, weary, terrible sacrifices for it. Without shedding of blood there is no such grace prepared. There must be reverses and losses, and times of deep concern. . . . Then the nation emerges, at last, a true nation, consecrated and made great in our eyes by the sacrifices it has cost! There is no way ever but just this to make a nation great and holy in the feeling of its people. And it is never raised, in this manner, till it has fought up some great man, or hero, in whom its struggles and victories are fitly personated.[126]

Though many Northerners came to see Lincoln as the "great man" anticipated by Bushnell, this was clearly not Lincoln's understanding of sacrifice. Lincoln could never celebrate bloodshed with Bushnell's complacency, and he made more of an effort to separate divine and human agency in the sacrificial process.[127] More important, Lincoln had little affinity with Bushnell's fervent illiberalism. Even at Gettysburg he still treasured the Jeffersonian "proposition" and wished to see it vindicated. But he could not conceal his growing skepticism about its capacity to vindicate itself. Lincoln doubted that a mere verbal declaration could be a determinative force in a history shaped by the violent clash of armies. Hence his rueful comment that "the world will little note, nor long remember, what we say here, but it can never forget what they did here."

Scholars have noted that this is a stock trope of the Athenian oratory that Lincoln admired, and a poignantly ironic one: in fact, the world has remembered Lincoln's words far better than the specific deaths of soldiers at Gettysburg.[128] Yet Lincoln's phrase suggests a dilemma too deep to be resolved by mere verbal alchemy. Could the abstract Jeffersonian proposition be translated into concrete reality without the mediation of violence, suffering, and death? Was the old liberal faith in the power of language—and of sentiment—unfounded? Just four years earlier Lincoln had defended language as the most important discovery of human history because of its capacity to bind individuals together: "The impulse to exchange thoughts with one another is probably an original impulse of our nature. If I be in pain I wish to let you know it, and to ask your sympathy and assistance, and my pleasurable emotions also, I wish to communicate to, and share with you."[129] But at Gettysburg Lincoln conceded that the power of language was parasitic on the very pain that it expressed. And *our* memory of his words does little to refute this. Would either Lincoln's or Jefferson's words be "long remembered" had they not been proposed as explanations of military violence?

What is at stake here, politically, is the question of whether the trajectory of history must *always* run from violent deeds to the words that rationalize them, or instead may sometimes run from verbal propositions to their peaceful realization. What is at stake theologically is the related question of whether divine power follows the trajectory from deeds to words or from words to deeds. Must God's will always come out of the barrel of a gun? If all history, sacred and profane, flows from deeds to words, neither the triumph of democracy after that of the Revolution nor that of emancipation after the Civil War can be meaningfully related to prior liberal aspirations. They must be attributed either to cosmic accident (the wars might have turned out the opposite way) or to a divine necessity utterly independent of human sentiment.

The War as Judgment

In the Second Inaugural, Lincoln chose the last path. Drawing on a theme he had developed in several earlier speeches, he suggested that human agency could explain neither the beginning nor the perpetuation of the war: "Both parties deprecated war; but one of them would *make* war rather than let the nation survive; and the other would *accept* war rather than let it perish. And the war came." The true explanation of the war thus lay in God's righteous indignation against the sin of slavery. Only that could be commensurate with the extent of the war's devastation. In ringing words, Lincoln elaborated his providential theory:

> If we shall suppose that American Slavery is one of those offences which, in the providence of God, must needs come, but which, having continued through His appointed time, He now wills to remove, and that He gives to both North and South, this terrible war, as the woe due to those by whom the offence came, shall we discern therein any departure from those divine attributes which the believers in a Living God always ascribe to Him? Fondly do we hope—fervently do we pray—that this mighty scourge of war may speedily pass away. Yet, if God wills that it continue, until all the wealth piled by the bond-man's two hundred and fifty years of unrequited toil shall be sunk, and until every drop of blood drawn with the lash, shall be paid by another drawn with the sword, as was said three thousand years ago, so still it must be said "the judgments of the Lord, are true and righteous altogether."[130]

This seems to endorse John Brown's apocalyptic theory of the end of slavery, and in a sense it does. But two qualifications must be noted. First, Lincoln uses conditional language: "If we shall suppose. . . . If God wills. . . ." He does not insist or proclaim that God has acted in the manner described.[131] Second, Lincoln spoke these words when the end of the war was in sight. By that time it was clearly unlikely that *all* the wealth piled up by slavery would be sunk by the war. In this context, the accent of Lincoln's words fell as much on divine mercy as on divine justice. However horrible the war, it was less horrible than the sin of slavery actually merited. By pronouncing "a sentence suspended," one scholar has suggested, Lincoln called the nation to "neither self-congratulation nor fear of the future but rather continuing repentance."[132]

This reading only heightens the peculiarity of Lincoln's theology. Why would a God who was free to spare people from the full measure of justice nevertheless inflict four years of horrible war? A more plausible account of God's role in the war is that of the Confederacy's chief of artillery, Edward Porter Alexander, who commented that "it is customary to say that 'Providence did not intend that we should win.' But Providence did not care a row of pins about it. If it did, it was a very unintelligent Providence not to bring the business to a close—the close it wanted—in less than four years of most terrible and bloody war." Of course, it is easier for a loser than a victor to see the absurdity of providential explanations of war. Losers confront death and destruction directly, while for the victors they point beyond themselves to larger purposes—in this case, to the end of slavery. Lincoln's explanation of why God caused the war does not come off as absurd because it does not dwell on the horror of the war but uses it as a measure of the horror that was slavery—which Lincoln does not attribute to God. As one scholar rightly notes, "Lincoln actually finds meaning in the war only by diverting his glance from the war and fixing it on slavery."[133]

This introduces some absurdities of its own. The logic of the Second Inaugural depends on Lincoln's characterization of the war as a divine judgment and of slavery as a human sin. But since war and slavery are at least partly comparable in the depth of their horror, one might ask why the characterizations could not simply be reversed. Might slavery itself be a divine judgment, meted out for some supposed prior sin of the African or American peoples? Proslavery apologists had made precisely that argument for decades. Conversely, what if the war itself, with all its bloodshed, were a human sin that merited its own judgment? Was humanity to be subject to an endless series of catastrophes, each simultaneously a judgment and a new offense?

Lincoln's rhetorical slide from the horror of war to the sin of slavery is further peculiar in that it inverts the logic of his initial justification of the war. As the parable of the snake and the children illustrates, the political Lincoln of the 1850s was eager to translate Northern sentimental concern for the victims of slavery into solicitude for the abstract "children" of constitutional union. For years he had told immediatists that their concern was misplaced, that only if emancipation were delayed for the sake of union could the promise of liberty be fulfilled at all. But when his efforts on behalf of the union had widened the sectional divide into a gaping wound—and thousands of non-metaphorical wounds—he suddenly concluded that the real issue was not the wounds of war but the sin of slavery after all. It appears that Lincoln's rhetoric testifies not, as Garry Wills thinks, to "the power of words" but to the infinite substitutability of deeds and words. Tortured slave children become an imperiled union, the dead bodies at

Gettysburg somehow give birth to freedom, and the nation's most terrible war becomes a tidy morality play.

Perhaps the difficulty can be traced to the first conditional of the Second Inaugural and, lurking behind it, that old "doctrine of necessity." "If we shall suppose that American Slavery is one of those offences which, in the providence of God, must needs come." But why should we suppose any such thing? If every violent offense is both necessary and able to be translated into a good word, how can there ever be either moral accountability or genuine change? Lincoln ruled out both original offenses and original words—acts for which the agents are truly responsible, propositions that open new possibilities to the world. All hope was reduced to substitution.

Lincoln as Messiah

A final substitution lurked beyond Lincoln's rhetoric. When an assassin's bullet felled the sixteenth president on Good Friday 1865, the anguish of four years of war and two centuries of slavery found a center in Lincoln himself. "All the feelings," Matthew Simpson said at Lincoln's funeral, "which had been gathering for four years, in forms of excitement, grief, horror, and joy, turned into one wail of woe—a sadness inexpressible—an anguish unutterable."[134] Suddenly Americans recognized in the fallen president a host of Christic qualities: his humble representativeness, his compassion and sadness, his role as instrument of God's purposes in the war, and now his status as a final sacrifice that brought an end to and somehow stood in for all the others. A Baptist preacher called Lincoln's death "the aftertype of the tragedy which was accomplished on the first Good Friday," while a Methodist proposed that Lincoln's death be remembered not on its specific date but always on Good Friday. Yet another eulogist declared it "a bloody sacrifice, upon the altar of human freedom," for "the painful salvation of the Republic."[135]

If Northerners agreed in perceiving Lincoln's death as an atoning sacrifice, they did not generally adhere to the strictures of the Anselmian substitutionary theory. Their sense of institutional evil led them, like T. S. Arthur and Harriet Beecher Stowe, to an implicit ransom theory in which Satan rather than God demanded the death of their chosen Christ figure. "I charge this murder," said Phillips Brooks, "where it belongs, on Slavery." Henry Clarke Wright said that Lincoln had been "immolated on the altar of that piratical power that has cost [the country] so much blood and treasure." Most others agreed. Yet they enclosed this charge within a larger providential theory that made God, not Satan or slavery, the ultimate agent of Lincoln's death. Some thought that Lincoln had been killed to expose the depths of slaveholding violence, others that it was to prevent his being idolized, to punish the sins of the North, to make way for a sterner leader for Reconstruction, to ensure a broader diffusion of Lincoln's ideas, or simply to unify the sympathies of the North. Despite this diversity, most anticipated that Lincoln's death would lead to the new national birth that he had prophesied at Gettysburg. "Even here, in the cause of Liberty," said George Dana Boardman, "as in the cause of the Church, it shall be found that the blood of the martyrs is the seed of the Republic."[136]

By placing the ransom theory within the providential framework of divine necessity, these preachers combined the worst aspects of liberal and orthodox theologies. The vaguely liberal ransom theory helped them demonize the South and justify harsh reprisals, while the orthodox doctrine of Providence made them sanguine about the military, governmental, financial, and industrial institutions that seemed to have been the instruments of God's victory. At the same time, Lincoln's status as substitutionary victim helped turn the nation's attention away from the deaths of both soldiers and slaves. Even Garrison, who claimed that Lincoln's death had "quickened the march of liberty throughout the world," was almost willing to identify the nation's destiny with God's providential plan:

> How strong, now, are our national foundations! Through suffering and triumph, through the sundering of all chains and the liberation of all the oppressed, our country enters upon a career of prosperity and glory,—if faithful to all the requirements of justice towards all its inhabitants,—that shall culminate in overturning, by the majesty of its greatness and the splendor of its example, all the despotisms of the globe, and leading all nations up to the temple of liberty and peace.[137]

To his credit, Garrison qualified this pronouncement by noting that "there must be no compromise of the self-evident truths of our Declaration of Independence; otherwise there shall again fall upon us the vials of divine retribution." But few were listening. The legacy of the Civil War was neither an end to racism nor a renewed dream of peace but a permanent standing army, the expansion of the central government, an industrial boom in the North, and the lasting impoverishment of the South. This outcome troubled few Northerners. Lincoln's violent death had saved the nation, just as Jesus' death had saved the world, and there was no longer a need to heed his quiet words, echoing the Sermon on the Mount: "Let us strive on to finish the work we are in; to bind up the nation's wounds; to care for him who shall have borne the battle, and for his widow, and his orphan—to do all which may achieve and cherish a just, and a lasting peace, among ourselves, and with all nations."[138]

Conclusion

Liberal Irony

The tradition of radical Christian liberalism poses an exciting challenge for people of today. Can we revive the practice of sentimental identification in a manner appropriate to today's struggles against oppression? Can we tell stories that reveal the image of God in the welfare mother, the migrant worker, and the gang member? Can we speak out of our own deepest experiences of suffering and relatedness, inviting even bitter enemies to recognize their common humanity?

In many ways we can, and we do. The civil rights movement of the 1960s, which continues to shape social activism in the present, revived much of the sentimental politics of the 1830s. The movement challenged white college students to identify with black schoolchildren, President Lyndon Johnson with Baptist preachers, and Mississippi share-croppers with Appalachian coal miners. The Christian liberalism of leaders like Martin Luther King Jr. also blossomed into interfaith dialogue, as they recognized God's image in Hindus like Mohandas Gandhi, Jews like Abraham Joshua Heschel, and Buddhists like Thich Nhat Hanh.

The late twentieth-century peace movement, similarly, produced a substantial body of sentimental literature, despite the fact that few participants would have identified it as such. Countless antiwar songs tell of deep, difficult identification between people on opposite sides of the world wars, the Vietnam War, and the cold war. John McCutcheon's "Christmas in the Trenches," for example, tells of British and German soldiers singing carols together during World War I. In "Walls and Windows," by Judy Small and Pat Humphries, an American mother addresses her Russian counterpart, asking if her sons also send photos home from far-off battlefields.[1] The distant echoes of Lydia Maria Child, Frederick Douglass, and William Lloyd Garrison are unmistakable here.

Other recent literature demonstrates the complexity of sentimental identification. In *Beloved*, Toni Morrison draws on nineteenth-century history to tell the story of a mother who kills her children to save them from slavery. In *The Third Life of Grange Copeland*, Alice Walker challenges us to identify with an abusive husband and father who, like the heroes of *Ten Nights in a Bar-Room* and other temperance tales, must walk a long path to personal transformation. Texts like these respond in a powerful way to James Baldwin's famous critique of sentimentality. *Uncle Tom's Cabin* failed, according to

Baldwin, because of its "rejection of life, the human being, the denial of his beauty, dread, power, in its insistence that it is his categorization alone which is real and which cannot be transcended."[2] Morrison and Walker demonstrate that the antidote to this problem is a still deeper politics of identification, one that moves beyond categories to reveal the full integrity of each individual life.

Despite this revival of sentimental literature, the tradition of radical Christian liberalism has not fully recovered from the setbacks it experienced at the time of the Civil War. Most Americans still have trouble imagining that radical social change might take place without coercion, or that the bonds of affection are strong enough to sustain a complex, technological society. Even many activists, influenced by Marxist class theory, doubt that persons of different races, classes, and genders can identify fully with one another.[3] The fact that the term "sentimentality" now carries an entirely negative connotation is just one index of our lack of faith in humanity.

But this is nothing new. As my analysis has shown, even the pioneers of radical Christian liberalism occasionally betrayed their liberal faith. Harriet Beecher Stowe wanted her readers to "feel right," but she was not sure they would do so unless she misrepresented the slaves as either heroically forgiving or virtually white. Henry Clarke Wright believed that the truest theology was anthropology, but ultimately he saw God less clearly in himself than in his fantasy of Catharine Anderson. William Lloyd Garrison demanded a human ethic of absolute nonviolence, but he could not imagine that God's own power might also be nonviolent. Antebellum activists readily saw God's image in other people, but few managed to see God even in the messiness, vulnerability, and failings of their own lives.

To learn from the mistakes of our predecessors, we must see those mistakes accurately. Conventional wisdom suggests that nineteenth-century liberalism suffered from an excessive faith in human nature. The liberals "failed" because they ignored the unconquerable human propensity for violence and thus diverted their energies away from attainable goals to the fantasy of a world without coercion. In fact, however, radical Christian liberals did *not* ignore the widespread violence and oppression in their society. They were deeply attuned to the violence of slavery, the tyranny of addiction, and the horrors of war, though they insisted that all these were alien to the deepest impulses of human nature. When they faltered in their responses to evil, it was because they were so dazzled by its ubiquity that they forgot its contingency. Their sin was a lack, not an excess, of faith in human nature.

Reinhold Niebuhr, perhaps the twentieth century's most influential critic of theological liberalism, gave strong voice to the conventional critique. His perspective is especially pertinent here, for in his own career he recapitulated much of the historical process described in this book. Originally a pacifist and national officer of the Fellowship of Reconciliation, Niebuhr gradually embraced aspects of just war theory as the basis of a responsible resistance to Fascism. As the nation's leading Christian ethicist during the cold war, Niebuhr promoted both a "neo-orthodox" theology emphasizing God's sovereignty and a political theory emphasizing the pursuit of liberal goals within a distinctly nonutopian institutional framework. A fervent admirer of Abraham Lincoln, Niebuhr helped engineer a narrowing of the political and religious conversation that paralleled that of the post–Civil War period.

For Niebuhr, the rise and fall of radical Christian liberalism was a leading instance of "the irony of American history." The United States began, he argued, with the hope that democratic revolution might rejuvenate all human societies, but as it became more powerful it became less capable of realizing that hope. "Our dreams of bringing the whole of history under the control of the human will," Niebuhr insisted, "are ironically refuted by the fact that no group of idealists can easily move the pattern of history toward the desired goal of peace and justice." This irony is profoundly orthodox, deeply rooted in traditional doctrines of original sin and divine sovereignty. According to Niebuhr, all history is a divinely ordained drama "enacted in a frame of meaning too large for human comprehension or management," and all human individuals are inclined to overreach their limited capacities and significance. This sort of overreaching explains the failures of American liberals: liberals pretentiously imagined that all social evils were contingent and soluble, and they vainly set out to subject all history to their own vision. Fortunately, Niebuhr concluded, such acts occur "under the scrutiny of a divine judge who laughs at human pretensions without being hostile to human aspirations." The ironic recognition of this divine laughter thus tends "to dissolve into the experience of contrition and to an abatement of the pretensions which caused the irony."[4]

In this study I have sought to replace Niebuhr's orthodox irony with a *liberal* irony—an irony that is alert to the diverse manifestations of sin in human affairs but does not conclude that original sin is the all-encompassing context of human existence. Human life is characterized both by profound sins and by profound acts of love and justice. While orthodox ironists see every human misdeed as a species of overreaching, the liberal ironist also recognizes our propensity for *underreaching*. We are capable of identifying with one another and struggling toward solidarity, yet we have trouble trusting ourselves. We cannot always imagine that our capacity for love might be as real or as powerful as the violence surrounding us. Indeed, we are often tempted to worship the violence—to see God's image more clearly in a great war than in a simple act of kindness.

The goal of liberal irony is to expose the sin of underreaching and thus stimulate a renewal of liberal activism. Had Garrison and Stowe recognized the underreaching involved in their perception of the Civil War as God's apocalyptic solution to slavery, they might have been inspired to continue the human struggle against racism in both North and South. Had Niebuhr recognized the underreaching in his endorsement of the atom bomb as a lesser evil, he might have looked harder for an alternative to the cold war arms race. In general, to acknowledge underreaching is to consider the possibility that the failures of American idealists may be rooted not in their hopeful visions but in a lack of faithfulness to those visions. And so while orthodox irony ends in contrition, liberal irony leads to reparation—to the active renewal of utopian hopes. The solution to failed idealism is to revivify and chasten the ideals, not to substitute the chastening for the ideals.

From the perspective of liberal irony, orthodox irony is an instance of what Sharon Welch has called "cultured despair"—an "inability to persist in resistance when problems are seen in their full magnitude."[5] I have shown that both orthodox and liberal Christians have been guilty, again and again, of this "cultured despair." This is not surprising, for the "full magnitude" of our problems grows greater every day. We cannot know, as both Niebuhr and Welch remind us, what will be the result of our nonviolent efforts; we cannot know when or if God's love will triumph over violence. But that uncertainty need not prevent us from embracing our duty and our hope.

Notes

Introduction

1. Stowe, *Uncle Tom*, pp. 144–56.
2. Garrison, "The Great Crisis!" *Liberator*, 29 December 1832, and "The Meeting at Framingham," *Liberator*, 7 July 1854.
3. Similar descriptions of sentimentality appear in Fisher, *Hard Facts*, pp. 87–127; Samuels, *Culture of Sentiment*, p. 6; Camfield, "Moral Aesthetics," pp. 319–45; Fluck, "Power and Failure," p. 327; and Turner, *Without God*, p. 70. By "sentimentality" I do *not* refer to "the ostentatious parading of excessive and spurious emotion" that James Baldwin has identified as the distinguishing mark of sentimentality ("Everybody's Protest Novel," p. 579). Yet a certain conventionality is part of the sentimental strategy. Since the goal, as Philip Fisher notes, is to present "novel objects of feeling" (that is, women, children, slaves) "rather than novel feelings," the feelings and experiences attributed to the newly included individuals must be conventional enough to be readily identified with by the reader (*Hard Facts*, p. 98). I may be fascinated by a man's pursuit of a mysterious white whale, but I am more likely to identify with his pursuit of a childhood sweetheart. This conventionality often leads to an exaggerated representation of emotion, but such rhetorical excess is not integral to the strategy. In fact it betrays a lack of sentimental faith. When authors do not really trust readers to identify with realistically portrayed victims, they may resort to exaggeration as a way of manipulating a sentimental response.
4. My understanding of violent power follows Elaine Scarry's argument that in the violent act the perpetrator steals power from the victim by inflicting physical pain and then refusing to acknowledge the subjective reality of that pain. Because the victim is incapable of expressing her pain, the perpetrator is able to impose her own interpretation on the victim's suffering. Power flows from the victim's body to the perpetrator's voice, as the broken body becomes the "insignia of power" that legitimates whatever the perpetrator says. See Scarry, *Body in Pain*, p. 71.
5. Sánchez-Eppler, "Bodily Bonds," p. 100.
6. My interpretation here dissents from that of Philip Fisher, who overstates the function of the powerlessness of the sentimental reader. Drawing on a parable of Rousseau, Fisher compares the sentimental reader to an imprisoned man who must watch helplessly as a beast rips a child from its mother's arms: the purity of the man's sentimental identification is heightened by his inability to intervene. Fisher goes on to suggest that sentimental narrative concentrates on two temporal moments related to the violent act: the moment of anticipation when the victim sees the attack coming but cannot prevent it, and the moment when the act, with all its conse-

quences, is recalled at a great temporal distance. At these moments, Fisher suggests, the victim's subjectivity is paramount, but his or her helplessness is also most evident—or is it? While Fisher rightly emphasizes that sentimentality is not a violence-stopping power, he fails to acknowledge that there is another sort of power in the victim's maintenance of subjectivity in the face of violence, and in the sheer fact that *there is* a history which comes after the violent event. See Fisher, *Hard Facts*, pp. 105, 116.

7. Child, "Woman and Suffrage," *Independent*, 17 January 1867, in *Child Reader*, p. 400.

8. Fisher, *Hard Facts*, p. 102.

9. Winfried Fluck makes both points in describing how Harriet Beecher Stowe character-ized the hero of *Uncle Tom's Cabin*: "What the metaphor of the family does is to redefine a character such as Tom in a new social role: instead of emphasizing his ethnic identity, he is now presented in the roles of father, husband, and especially that of uncle, which establishes, in the very title of the book, a family relation between white and black" ("Power and Failure," p. 327).

10. Douglass, "A Day, a Deed, an Event, Glorious in the Annals of Philanthropy," 1 August 1848, in *Papers*, ser. 1, 2:136; and Douglass, "The Anti-Slavery Movement," 19 March 1855, in *Papers*, ser. 1, 3:49.

11. Niebuhr, *Kingdom of God*, p. 193.

12. Elkins, *Slavery*, p. 141.

13. Douglas, *Feminization*, p. 12. The "sentimentalism" to which Ann Douglas refers in-cludes not only social reform texts like *Uncle Tom's Cabin* but also many books with no radical social agenda.

14. Yoder, *Politics of Jesus*; Hauerwas, *Peaceable Kingdom*; and Hauerwas, *Dispatches*.

15. Foucault, *Discipline and Punish*.

16. Brodhead, "Sparing the Rod," pp. 68–69.

17. I refer *only*, however, to the most extreme varieties of the politics of identity. In general, the politics of identity has *not* claimed that identification among diverse cultural groups is im-possible, only that it is extremely difficult. It is opposed to a sort of easy sentimentalism that tries to avoid the challenging work of coming to understand those whose experiences are very different from our own, despite our common human identity. From a radical liberal perspective, *this* politics of identity is indispensable.

18. King, "I Have a Dream," in *Testament of Hope*, pp. 217–20.

Chapter 1

Portions of this chapter have appeared as "Tares in the Wheat: Puritan Violence and Puritan Families in the Nineteenth-Century Liberal Imagination," *Religion and American Culture: A Journal of Interpretation* 8 (summer 1998): 205–36.

1. Whittier, *Leaves*, pp. 23–31.

2. This doctrinal tradition is often referred to as "Calvinism" because of the decisive influ-ence of John Calvin (1509-64). But Calvin was just one of several theologians who influenced statements like the Westminster Confession, which was the actual standard of orthodoxy for American Presbyterians, Congregationalists, and some Baptists. I prefer, therefore, to use "Re-formed orthodoxy" rather than "Calvinism."

3. My analysis draws extensively on the following texts: Sedgwick, *New-England Tale*; Sedgwick, *Hope Leslie*; Child, *Hobomok*; Child, *First Settlers*; Sigourney, *Sketch*; Lee, *Delusion*; Lee, *Naomi*; and Lee, *Florence*. Additional texts by these and closely related authors, including Sarah Savage, Henry Ware Jr., and Eliza Cabot Follen, will be used to illustrate certain aspects of the liberal literary vision. Valuable overviews of this literature include Gould, *Covenant*; Bell, *Hawthorne*; Buell, *New England*; and Baym, *American Women Writers*. A study that emphasizes the theologi-

cal dimension of liberal literature, albeit from a perspective vastly different from that developed here, is Douglas, *Feminization*.

4. The term "Arminian" refers to the Dutch theologian Jacobus Arminius (1560–1609), who opposed the hard-line positions on predestination and total depravity adopted by the Dutch church at the Synod of Dort. Though Arminius's personal influence was not far-reaching, his name became a convenient label for anyone who claimed that humans have the moral ability to cooperate in the process of their own salvation.

5. Channing, "A Letter to the Rev. Samuel C. Thacher," 1815, in *Selected Writings*, p. 49; Channing, "Unitarian Christianity," 1819, in *Works*, p. 376; Wright, *Beginnings*, pp. 3, 184; Ahlstrom and Carey, *American Reformation*, p. 37; and Hutchison, *Transcendentalist Ministers*, p. 4.

6. Rose, *Transcendentalism*, p. 2. Conrad Wright has suggested that the explosion of reform societies in the 1820s and 1830s reflected the institutionalization of the Unitarian schism, with orthodox and liberal societies striving to outdo one another. But this competition did not preclude cooperation in many endeavors. See "Institutional Reconstruction in the Unitarian Controversy," in Conrad Edick Wright, *American Unitarianism*.

7. Cited in Kelley, *Private Woman*, p. 290. It has remained a Unitarian tradition to take more pride in the general dissemination of liberalism than in institutional expansion. Thus, George Willis Cooke included many non-Unitarians in his 1902 history of Unitarianism on the grounds that the movement "is not represented merely by a body of churches, but . . . is an individual way of looking at the facts of life and its problems." See Cooke, *Unitarianism*, p. v.

8. Channing, "Likeness to God," 1828, in *Works*, pp. 291–92.

9. Channing, "Unitarian Christianity," p. 377; and Channing, "Likeness to God," pp. 295–96. See also Wright, *Beginnings*, p. 165; Wright, *Liberal Christians*, p. 38; and Cooke, *Unitarianism*, p. 38. Though Channing was quite explicit about the political ideals that led him to prefer the image of God as father to that of God as king, he was apparently unconscious of the gender bias that prevented him from thinking of God as mother. Liberal images of the divine were not, however, exclusively masculine: Henry Ware Jr. invoked both maternal and paternal imagery in his essay "The Personality of Deity," p. 433.

10. Child, *First Settlers*, p. 183.

11. Whittier, *Leaves*, pp. 100, 150.

12. Child, "To Abolitionists," *National Anti-Slavery Standard*, 20 May 1841, in *Child Reader*, p. 192.

13. Though liberals rejected this understanding of benevolence in theory, they recognized that in practice such notions often inspired their adherents to support social reforms with which the liberals sympathized. Channing could not forget that, during his boyhood in Newport, Rhode Island, the minister who most courageously challenged his parishioners' involvement in the slave trade was the orthodox Samuel Hopkins. Channing thus consistently lifted up the concept of "disinterested benevolence" as a bright spot in an otherwise dismal theology. See Wright, *Liberal Christians*, p. 28; David Robinson, "Introduction," in Channing, *Selected Writings*, p. 11; and Joseph Conforti, "Edwardsians, Unitarians, and the Great Awakening," in Conrad Edick Wright, *American Unitarianism*, pp. 41–42. Channing anticipated a much more extensive liberal reading of Hopkinsian benevolence, Harriet Beecher Stowe's novel *The Minister's Wooing*.

14. Child, *First Settlers*, p. 38; and Sedgwick, *New-England Tale*, p. 27.

15. For an overview of this new pedagogy, see Fliegelman, *Prodigals and Pilgrims*.

16. Ibid., p. 2.

17. Ibid., pp. 23–24; Martin, *Instructed Vision*, p. 11; Ahlstrom and Carey, *American Reformation*, pp. 33–34; Turner, *Without God*, p. 62; and May, *Enlightenment*, p. 293.

18. Gay, "Natural Religion," pp. 45–59; Channing, *Memoir*, 1:64; and Sedgwick, *Clarence*, 1:209.

19. Child, *First Settlers*, p. 183. This image, which appears in dozens of liberal texts, comes from Jeremiah 31:33: "I will put my law within them, and I will write it on their hearts" (NRSV). The liberals misconstrued the passage, however: while Jeremiah is prophesying what will happen under God's "new covenant," they understood him to refer to the original constitution of human nature.

20. Fliegelman, *Prodigals and Pilgrims*, pp. 30, 104.

21. Curti, *Human Nature*, p. 67; Channing, "A Letter to the Rev. Samuel C. Thacher," p. 49; and Lee, *Naomi*, p. 367.

22. Cited in Curti, *Human Nature*, p. 38.

23. Ware, "Nature of Man," p. 202.

24. Channing, "Spiritual Freedom," 1830, in *Works*, p. 176; and Sedgwick, "Mary Dyre," in *Tales and Sketches*, p. 164.

25. Ware, "Sober Thoughts," p. 363. The tragedy here is that the liberals' progressive theology of history blinded them to the many values they held in common with Roman Catholics and Jews. Though they were harshly critical of orthodox Protestantism, they believed it had been a step forward and assumed that all of its mistakes derived from the authoritarianism of medieval Catholicism—just as the mistakes of Catholicism stemmed from the primitive violence of the Jews.

26. Lee, *Memoirs*.

27. Sedgwick, "A Reminiscence of Federalism," in *Tales and Sketches*, pp. 9–43.

28. Gould, *Covenant*, p. 62; and Bell, "Conditions," 2:43.

29. Degler, *At Odds*, pp. 8–9, has identified these beliefs as defining characteristics of the "modern American family" that emerged between the Revolution and 1830 and remained normative until the very recent past.

30. Baym, *American Women Writers*, p. 2. Baym is paraphrasing a thesis developed in Tompkins, *Sensational Designs*, and her own *Woman's Fiction*. "Public policy" here does not mean exclusively, or even primarily, *state* policy: liberals assumed that social life would be shaped by a range of voluntary as well as state institutions.

31. Zagarell, "Expanding 'America,'" p. 43.

32. Bell, "Conditions," pp. 11, 37, 42; Baym, *Novels*, p. 29; Kelley, *Private Woman*, pp. 7–19; Hart, *Popular Book*, pp. 88–90; and *Harper's*, October 1867, p. 665. Of the writers considered here, Sedgwick was easily the most popular as a novelist. In 1827 the first edition of *Hope Leslie* earned her $1,100, enough to support a middle-class family for a year. Her most popular work, *Home*, went through twenty editions in a decade; other novels typically generated six to eight editions in the United States and England. Lydia Maria Child, a great admirer of Sedgwick, might have rivaled her in popularity had she not suffered boycotts for her abolitionist views in the 1830s. The *Juvenile Miscellany*, which she edited in the 1820s, along with several domestic handbooks, were her most popular productions. *Hobomok* had just one edition in 1824, though a later novel, *Philothea*, generated at least seven editions between 1836 and 1863. Lydia Sigourney was probably the most popular female poet of the antebellum period, but her *Sketch of Connecticut* also went through just a single edition. Eliza Buckminster Lee, whose works I have selected primarily for their theological interest, was the most obscure of the four writers considered here. None of her novels generated more than three editions, although her biography of the German romantic poet Jean Paul Richter was issued three times in the United States and twice in England.

33. Martin, *Instructed Vision*, pp. 58, 70, 87; Dekker, *American Historical Romance*, pp. 16–17; Kelley, *Private Woman*, p. 113; and Baym, *Novels*, p. 32.

34. Martin, *Instructed Vision*, pp. 79–80; Turner, *Without God*, p. 68; Baym, *American Women Writers*, pp. 17, 23, 152; and Kelley, *Private Woman*, p. 119.

35. Recent scholarship has established that early liberalism was not as "corpse-cold" as Emerson pretended, and that Transcendentalism was as much an extension as a repudiation of the Christian liberal movement. This scholarship has rightly focused on William Ellery Channing—a prominent Unitarian preacher who remained a hero to most Transcendentalists—as the key to this transition. My suggestion here is that careful attention to the ways in which fiction writers fleshed out Channing's theology will clarify the ways in which Transcendentalism both continued and departed from liberal tradition. See Wright, *Liberal Christians*, p. 39.

36. Channing, "On Catholicism," in *Works*, p. 475. Despite the stark contrast depicted by Channing, women like Sedgwick, Child, Lee, and, later, Harriet Beecher Stowe managed to learn much of what was being taught in "theological institutions." Their literary reconstructions of theology were far more sophisticated than this quotation suggests.

37. Channing, "Remarks on National Literature," 1823, in *Works*, pp. 133–34. See also "Likeness to God," p. 295.

38. Baym, *Novels*, pp. 39–42. In describing this sort of power, Baym notes that for antebellum critics of various persuasions, "power and vigor were always good."

39. Sedgwick, *New-England Tale*.

40. Gould, *Covenant*, pp. 8–10; and Buell, *New England*, pp. 218, 213. Against Buell, Gould argues that antebellum fiction writers were far more interested in contemporary politics than in historical theology, and that Puritanism was for them "much less a stable analogue than a protean metaphor for the early republic." Gould fails to see, however, that the liberals' commitment to fighting both "tyranny" and "priestcraft" prevented them from making such sharp distinctions. The political vocation of the new nation was, for them, an extension of the religious work of the Reformation.

41. Gould, *Covenant*, p. 13.

42. Dekker, *American Historical Romance*, pp. 52, 75; and Buell, *New England*, pp. 209, 244–45.

43. In the late twentieth-century context, they might be compared to such socially engaged novelists as Alice Walker and Barbara Kingsolver, who do not hesitate to introduce openly didactic elements into their texts.

44. Sedgwick, *Clarence*, 2:147; and Child, "The Church in the Wilderness," in *Child Reader*, p. 32.

45. Buell, *New England*, p. 247.

46. Child, *First Settlers*, p. 58.

47. Child, *Hobomok*, pp. 5–6. A similar passage appears in Lee, *Delusion*, pp. 1–2.

48. Sedgwick, "Mary Dyre," p. 153; Whittier, *Leaves*, p. 186; and Lee, *Naomi*, pp. 102–3.

49. Baym, *American Women Writers*, pp. 59–61.

50. Sedgwick, *New-England Tale*, pp. 114–15; Sedgwick, *Hope Leslie*, p. 54; and Child, "Appeal for the Indians," in *Hobomok*, p. 221.

51. Child, *First Settlers*, p. 213; Child, "The Church in the Wilderness," in *Lydia Maria Child Reader*, p. 33; and Sedgwick, *Hope Leslie*, pp. 56, 194.

52. Channing, "Unitarian Christianity," p. 377. Channing elaborated his argument in an 1820 essay, which in turn influenced Jared Sparks's essay "The Comparative Moral Tendency of the Leading Doctrines of Calvinism and the Sentiments of Unitarians." See Channing, "The Moral Argument Against Calvinism," in *Works*, pp. 459–67; and Sparks, "Comparative," pp. 332–39.

53. Sedgwick, *New-England Tale*, pp. 19, 149.

54. Child, *First Settlers*, pp. 30–31.

55. May, *Enlightenment*, p. 21. Child herself would go on to write a comprehensive survey of world religions (*The Progress of Religious Ideas*) that was remarkably free of Christian chauvinism. Even then, though, she was more drawn to Eastern traditions than to Judaism. Ultimately,

Child understood Judaism, Catholicism, and Calvinism as three versions of the same error: an illiberal claim to a monopoly on infallible truths.

56. Child, *First Settlers*, pp. v, 32, 114-15.

57. Interestingly, Child attributed a similar depressive effect to Catholic ascetic traditions. The Jesuit hero of "The Church in the Wilderness" had, through "voluntary vows, . . . made the best and must luxurious emotions of our nature a sealed fountain within his own soul." His affections are restored when he adopts two children, but even then he performs "penances . . . for an all-absorbing love, which his erring conscience deemed a sin against that God" (*Child Reader*, p. 36).

58. Lee, *Delusion*, pp. 74, 140, 146.

59. Channing, "Moral Argument," p. 462; and Channing, "Likeness to God," pp. 300-301.

60. Lee, *Florence*, pp. 18-19.

61. Ibid., pp. 24, 36, 70, 78.

62. Child, *First Settlers*, p. 117; and Lee, *Naomi*, pp. 415-16.

63. Lee, *Naomi*, p. 357; and Lee, *Delusion*, pp. 124, 131, 148-49.

64. Lee, *Sketches*, pp. 88-89.

65. Channing, "Likeness to God," p. 301.

66. Ibid., p. 299; and Sedgwick, *New-England Tale*, p. 11.

67. Lee, *Delusion*, p. 92; Sedgwick, *Clarence*, 1:44; Sedgwick, *Home*, p. 60; Sedgwick, *Linwoods*, 1:96; and Sedgwick, *Home*, p. 54.

68. Ware Jr., *David Ellington*, p. 17; Savage, *Factory Girl*, pp. 30-32; and Lee, *Delusion*, pp. 32-33.

69. Channing, "Likeness to God," p. 291; Sedgwick, *Clarence*, 2:190; Sedgwick, *New-England Tale*, p. 67; and Lee, *Naomi*, pp. 164, 185.

70. Sedgwick, *Hope Leslie*, pp. 169, 88; and Lee, *Delusion*, p. 34.

71. Follen, *Skeptic*, pp. 123, 2, 131; and Sedgwick, *Hope Leslie*, p. 65.

72. Sedgwick, *New-England Tale*, p. 102.

73. Sedgwick, *Hope Leslie*, p. 9.

74. Ibid., p. 22; Whittier, *Leaves*, pp. 50-52; Lee, *Delusion*, pp. 26, 77; Lee, *Florence*, p. 8; and Sedgwick, "Huguenot Family," in *Tales and Sketches: Second Series*, p. 288. This device is not limited to fiction related to the Puritans. In Sedgwick's "Huguenot Family," Father Clement is an interloper within a Catholic persecuting community, while in *First Settlers*, Child implausibly depicts Queen Isabella as a classic interloper.

75. Lee, *Delusion*, p. 26; Whittier, *Leaves*, p. 41; Lee, *Naomi*, pp. 92-93; Sedgwick, *Hope Leslie*, p. 294; and Lee, *Naomi*, p. 178.

76. Lee, *Naomi*, pp. 391, 138, 7, 172.

77. The stadialism of Scott and Cooper was more akin to Michel Foucault's theory of historical "epochs," which posits a radical discontinuity and incommensurability between historical eras. It is thus no accident that Foucauldian or semi-Foucauldian historians, such as Philip Gould, have generally perceived the liberal novelists as either naively anachronistic or cynically antihistorical.

78. Sedgwick, *Hope Leslie*, pp. 15-16.

79. Ibid., p. 123.

80. Lee, *Naomi*, pp. 52, 104.

81. Ibid., pp. 444-45.

82. By using the term "Ruthian genealogy," I do not mean to suggest that any of the liberal novelists were consciously mimicking the Book of Ruth. Even Lee, who borrowed her characters' names from that book, does not seem to have been making any particular point: in her novel, Naomi's sister Ruth is a petty and vain girl who offers to free Naomi from jail only if she will renounce Herbert.

83. This reading of Abrahamic genealogy is shaped by the work of feminist sociologist of religion Nancy Jay. Drawing on the Abraham story, Jay suggests that sacrifice may have been invented by societies making the transition from matrilineal to patrilineal systems of genealogy. Matrilineal societies did not need to ritualize generational transitions, for they were marked by the event of childbirth itself. Patrilineal societies, by contrast, needed to create rituals that would displace childbirth in the popular imagination, and thus bind the child to the father rather than the mother. As bloody as childbirth, sacrifice was, in Jay's phrase, a "remedy for having been born of woman." See Jay, *Throughout Your Generations*, p. 40.

84. Indeed, a critique of Abrahamic genealogy can be found by reading between the lines of Genesis itself. Though Ishmael is excluded from God's "everlasting" covenant with Isaac, God cares for Ishmael's mother during her time in the desert and promises that his descendents will also be "a great nation" (Genesis 17:19–20). Similarly, the generational transition from Isaac to Jacob is achieved not by a proper sacrificial ritual but by the maternal affection of Rebecca, who helps Jacob trick his father into blessing him. The most sustained biblical critique of sacrifice appears, of course, in the prophetic books. In the Book of Amos, God tells Israel, "I hate, I spurn your feasts, I take no pleasure in your solemnities" (5:21), while Jeremiah's God goes so far as to say that he had never commanded "holocaust or sacrifice" at all (7:22).

85. Bell, *Hawthorne*, pp. 149–50, also notes the prevalence of marriage comedies in New England historical fiction.

86. Sedgwick, *Hope Leslie*, p. 154.

87. Bell, *Hawthorne*, pp. 19–20, has argued that liberal novelists mapped their ambivalences about the Puritan legacy onto a sharp distinction between good Puritans like Winthrop and bad Puritans like Thomas Dudley. The liberals did this, to be sure, but their real ambivalences came out in their complex characterizations of the "good" Puritans.

88. Sedgwick, *Hope Leslie*, p. 156. Sedgwick's "love the sinner, hate the sin" attitude toward Winthrop echoes Channing's insistence that the orthodox were Christians as well as Calvinists, and that consequently "some of the brightest examples of Christian virtue" were included in their camp. See Channing, "Moral Argument Against Calvinism," p. 105.

89. Sedgwick, *Hope Leslie*, pp. 175, 180.

90. Given Sedgwick's more positive representation, it is odd that Lawrence Buell (*New England*, p. 234) has called *Hobomok* "the first and probably the only antebellum fiction to give any kind of support for miscegenation." Child would go on, however, to promote intermarriage as a solution to racial conflict in the United States.

91. Sigourney, *Sketch*, pp. 264–65, 267, 271. Sigourney thus repudiates the harsh racism of the classic captivity narrative, Mary Rowlandson's *Sovereignty and Goodness of God*.

92. Sigourney, *Sketch*, p. 277.

93. Lee, *Delusion*, p. 34; Lee, *Naomi*, pp. 39–40; and Sedgwick, *Hope Leslie*, p. 241. The condescending tone of Sedgwick's account suggests that she may have been unaware of the actual affinity between her views and the Catholic understanding of nature and grace. Later liberals, notably Isaac Hecker and Sophia Ripley, actually converted to Catholicism after becoming aware of these affinities.

94. Sedgwick, *Hope Leslie*, pp. 332, 287, 37; Child, *First Settlers*, pp. 253–54.

95. Sedgwick, *New-England Tale*, p. 40; Sedgwick, *Home*, pp. 57–60; and Lee, *Naomi*, p. 20.

96. Lee, *Naomi*, p. 174; Sedgwick, *New-England Tale*, p. 132; and Lee, *Naomi*, p. 206.

97. Sedgwick, *Hope Leslie*, p. 68; Lee, *Naomi*, p. 99; and Lee, *Delusion*, pp. 18–19; see also Sedgwick, *Redwood*, 2:139.

98. Sigourney, *Sketch*, pp. 23, 75–76; and Sedgwick, *Clarence*, 2:224; see also Lee, *Naomi*, p. 112.

99. Sedgwick, *Hope Leslie*, pp. 11–12, 201; and Child, *First Settlers*, p. 90.

100. Sedgwick, "Mary Dyre," p. 163. See also Sedgwick, *Linwoods*, 2:208.

101. Lee, *Delusion*, p. iii.
102. Ibid., pp. 57, 72, 83–84.
103. Ibid., pp. 96–99.
104. Ibid., pp. 109, 110, 135.
105. Ibid., pp. 137, 143, 152.
106. Sedgwick, *Redwood*, 2:74; and Sedgwick, *Hope Leslie*, p. 339.
107. Sigourney, *Sketch*, pp. 159–62.
108. Child, *First Settlers*, pp. iii–iv, 42–43.
109. Ibid., pp. 281, 42, 234–35, 159.
110. Sedgwick, *Hope Leslie*, pp. 292–93.
111. Ibid., pp. 49, 53.
112. Ibid., p. 229. Nina Baym cites this episode in order to draw an unfavorable comparison between Sedgwick and Cooper: "The hope that Indians might join white society, when it was expressed, always implied an assumption of white cultural superiority. . . . There are friendships, or at least companionable moments, between white women and Native Americans in antebellum women's historical novels, but they are seldom egalitarian and never resonate emotionally like the tie between Cooper's Natty Bumppo and Chingachgook" (Baym, *American Women Writers*, p. 159). This reading is unfair: it ignores both the egalitarian relationship between Everell and Magawisca and the positive depiction of Oneco and Faith's marriage, and it does not seem to recognize Sedgwick's harsh implicit criticism of Hope. The limits on friendship between the two women might better be interpreted as an acknowledgment of the intransigence of racism that is lacking in Cooper.

Chapter 2

1. Chapman, *Right and Wrong*, pp. 6, 4. Radical Christian liberalism should not be confused with the liberalism of Madison, Hamilton, and Lincoln, or with that of twentieth-century American politics. Those more moderate liberalisms sought to build institutions that would safeguard a gradual increase in human freedom, but they did not envision the creation of a society entirely free of coercion. Indeed, they were quite willing to use violence when it was necessary to safeguard their cherished liberal institutions.
2. Sellers, *Market Revolution*, p. 260.
3. The term "nonresistance" may be somewhat misleading. Twentieth-century peace theorists (Wink, *Engaging*, pp. 184–89) often contrast the "nonresistance" of the historic peace churches with the "active nonviolence" of the movements inspired by Mohandas Gandhi and Martin Luther King Jr. The former respond to social injustices with sectarian withdrawal, while the latter actively resist injustice, albeit with nonviolent means. Using these definitions, nineteenth-century nonresistance was actually a form of active nonviolence. As William Lloyd Garrison explained, "The doctrine of nonresistance has reference exclusively to a resort to carnal weapons—to warlike measures. Moral and spiritual resistance of evil and evildoers is at all times lawful, and constitutes the Christian's warfare" (*Liberator*, 6 August 1836). Indeed, Garrison and his associates pioneered many techniques of nonviolent direct action that are still in use today. These are described in detail in Mabee, *Black Freedom*.
4. Child, *Appeal*, p. 206; and Child, *Letters from New York*, 6 October 1842, 1:208.
5. Child, "Talk About Political Party," *National Anti-Slavery Standard*, 7 July 1842, in *Child Reader*, p. 223.
6. Two recent studies that emphasize the multiple causes of antebellum social reform are Abzug, *Cosmos Crumbling*, and Mintz, *Moralists and Modernizers*. The perspective of Abzug and Mintz, which I share, stands in sharp contrast to that of scholars like David Herbert Donald, who dismiss the reformers as a "displaced social elite" motivated primarily by resentment ("To-

ward a Reconsideration"). It also contrasts with the work of the many scholars who treat the "evangelical" revivals as the primary cause of antebellum social reform. Those scholars build on the work of Gilbert Barnes (*Antislavery Impulse*), Timothy Smith (*Revivalism and Social Reform*), and Whitney Cross (*Burned-Over District*), all of whom explored the ways in which evangelical notions of sin compelled reformers to renounce social evils, evangelical experiences of conversion fired them with reforming zeal, and evangelical mission societies provided organizational models for social reform. (For an analysis of Barnes's contribution, see Dillon, "Gilbert H. Barnes.") Even recent scholarship includes such claims as Donald M. Scott's contention that "abolition in a very precise sense was a form of evangelicalism" ("Abolition," p. 73); John R. McKivigan and Mitchell Snay's assertion that "the degree to which evangelical doctrines affected a denomination generally determined its receptivity to abolitionist arguments" (*Religion*, p. 10); and Richard Carwardine's argument that evangelicals "ensured that the questions of education, Indian removal, war, drink and, above all, slavery were placed firmly at the center of the political agenda" (*Evangelicals*, p. xvii). All of these claims are overstated, but the underlying reason is the failure of scholars to explore nonevangelical currents of reform with the same sophistication that has been devoted to evangelical reform. I hope that the present study will partly correct this failure.

7. Douglass, "Country, Conscience, and the Anti-Slavery Cause," 11 May 1847, in *Papers*, ser. 1, 2:68; Stewart, "Religion and the Pure Principles of Morality, the Sure Foundation on Which We Must Build," *Liberator*, 8 October 1831; Theodore Dwight Weld to Angelina Grimké Weld and Sarah Grimké, 17 February 1842, in Barnes and Dumond, *Letters*, 2:924; and Smith, "Religion of Reason," 1858, in *Sermons and Speeches*, pp. 37–38.

8. Douglass, "The Anti-Slavery Movement," 19 March 1855, in *Papers*, ser. 1, 3:19–21.

9. Opponents of social reform sometimes noted the incongruity of ascribing divine status to the words of Jefferson. Around 1851, for example, a Virginia minister wrote, "I am fully aware that there is a text in some Bibles that is not in mine. Professional abolitionists have made more use of it, than of any passage in the Bible. It came, however, as I trace it, from Saint Voltaire, and was baptized by Thomas Jefferson, and since almost universally regarded as canonical authority '*all men are born free and equal.*'" Cited by Abraham Lincoln, "Eulogy on Henry Clay," 6 July 1852, in *Collected Works*, 2:130–31.

10. Whitehead, *Essays*, p. 153.

11. May, *Enlightenment*, pp. 154, 160, 163. See also Bardes and Gossett, *Declarations*, p. 1; Norton, *Alternative Americas*, p. 20; and Foner, *We, the Other People*.

12. Somkin, *Unquiet Eagle*, p. 5.

13. Members of a third liberal denomination, the Universalists, also contributed to social reform. But because of their concentration on the frontier, they were not as prominent in the leadership of social reform and contributed little of the narrative literature that is the focus of this study. Whitney Cross has helpfully suggested that Universalists played a dual role in upstate New York, as theological critics but social allies of evangelical reformers. Much more study is needed of their role in the movement as a whole. See Cross, *Burned-Over District*, p. 323.

14. Channing, "War," 1816, in *Works*, pp. 642–53; Channing, "War," 1835, in *Works*, pp. 654–64; Channing, "Lecture on War," 1838, in *Works*, pp. 664–79; and Channing, "Slavery," 1836, in *Works*, pp. 688–743.

15. Channing, "Spiritual Freedom," 1830, in *Works*, pp. 182, 176.

16. The best studies of the Hicksite reformation are Ingle, *Quakers in Conflict*, and Doherty, *Hicksite Separation*.

17. Cited in Doherty, *Hicksite Separation*, p. 26.

18. Cited in ibid., p. 18.

19. Yacovone, *May*, pp. 8–19.

20. Ibid., pp. 29–40. It is no accident that the exceptions were the two pastors who would

be most remembered and honored by subsequent generations of Unitarians. Throughout the early nineteenth century, those Unitarian leaders who most fully embodied the principles of liberalism chafed under the cautious leadership of the denomination, only to be regarded later as the founding fathers of the tradition.

21. Hallowell, *James and Lucretia Mott*, p. 92.

22. Ibid., p. 109.

23. Ibid., p. 107.

24. Ibid., pp. 296, 346. The latter quotation is a paraphrase from a *New York Times* article.

25. Wyatt-Brown, *Lewis Tappan*, p. 262.

26. In this study I shall ordinarily use the term "revivalism" to refer to that strand of Protestant Christianity that places primary emphasis on an emotional conversion experience and the zealous moral life that follows. This tradition is primarily opposed not to liberalism but to those Protestant traditions that emphasize liturgy or formal doctrine. It is often referred to as "evangelicalism," but this term can be quite confusing. For some scholars "evangelicalism" designates no more than an emotional style of religion; for some it is identical with revivalism; and for still others it refers to a conservative movement that sought to preserve the central doctrines of the Reformation against the onslaught of liberal humanism. This mix of definitions makes a certain degree of sense, for many people in the early nineteenth century were "evangelical" by all three definitions. But it is better to say that "revivalism," not "evangelicalism," led to social reform, because orthodox or antiliberal attitudes as such made little contribution to the reform impulse. Indeed, those scholars who initially emphasized the links between evangelicalism and social reform regarded evangelicalism as a form of liberalism. For example, Timothy Smith (*Revivalism*, p. 60) wrote that "in the nineteenth century revival measures, being new, usually went hand in hand with progressive theology and humanitarian concern." Gilbert Barnes, who did not use the term "evangelicalism," claimed that the "Great Revival" offered a "new perception of human brotherhood" and repudiated orthodoxy's "damnatory suspicion of mankind." It was, he wrote, the "liberals of the Great Revival" who contributed most to social reform (*Antislavery Impulse*, pp. 3, 18).

27. Scott, "Abolition," p. 54.

28. Lydia Maria Child to Anne Whitney, 25 May 1879, in *Selected Letters*, p. 558; and Garrison and Garrison, *William Lloyd Garrison*, 1:214.

29. A similar argument appears in Stange, *Patterns*, p. 45.

30. "It was less the revival than its passing," comments historian Ronald Walters, "that brought men and women to antislavery" (*Antislavery Appeal*, p. 40). See also Abzug, *Passionate Liberator*, p. 39; and Abzug, *Cosmos Crumbling*, p. 75.

31. Abzug, *Passionate Liberator*, pp. 196, 240, 263, 292. It is telling that Weld's biographer, Robert Abzug, is one of the harshest critics of Gilbert Barnes. Abzug faults Barnes for "making a very complicated man into an unbelievable, two-dimensional Christian hero." Another biography that traces the evolution of a once-evangelical reformer is Goodheart, *Abolitionist, Actuary, Atheist*.

32. Studies that emphasize the "on-going spiritual quest" or "ever-widening gyre of spiritual experimentation" within reform include Walters, *Antislavery Appeal*, p. 45; Abzug, *Cosmos Crumbling*, p. 127; Wyatt-Brown, *Lewis Tappan*, p. 311; and Stewart, *William Lloyd Garrison*, p. 154. Whitney Cross's argument is particularly interesting. He suggests that in western New York the reforming impulse of Charles Finney ultimately diverged into two streams, one leading to the apocalyptic speculations of the Millerites and the other to "liberal religion, Bible criticism, and a social gospel." See Cross, *Burned-Over District*, pp. 278, 283.

33. This is one of the most frequently repeated claims in the literature on social reform. Gilbert Barnes, for example, suggests that revivalists wanted "to denounce slavery as a sin, not to reform slavery as a system" (*Antislavery Impulse*, p. 70). Referring to social reform movements

more generally, Whitney Cross (*Burned-Over District*, p. 208) writes that "once any item of social behavior came to be classified as a sin, it thus lay open to the complete operation of the most radical conceptions. It was the function of Burned-Over District ultraism to expand the category of sin far beyond its accustomed limits." And Steven Mintz (*Moralists and Modernizers*, p. 28) sums up half a century of scholarship when he suggests that "by making it each individual's duty to combat sin, by tying personal piety and social action together, evangelical revivalism made a profound contribution to the reform impulse. For antebellum evangelicals, sin was not an abstraction, nor was it something metaphysical. It was concrete: dueling, fornication, profanity, drinking hard liquor." Other studies that make similar claims about abolitionism in particular include Loveland, "Evangelicalism"; Thomas, "Antislavery and Utopia," pp. 246–47; Mathews, "Abolitionists on Slavery"; Wyatt-Brown, *Lewis Tappan*, pp. 81, 95; Scott, "Abolition," pp. 64, 69, 73; Perry, *Radical Abolitionism*, p. 9; Sorin, *Abolitionism*, p. 44, McKivigan, *War Against Proslavery Religion*, pp. 13–21; Carwardine, *Evangelicals*, pp. 134–35; and McKivigan and Snay, *Religion*, p. 7. Studies that apply the sin paradigm to temperance or to social reform generally include Tyrrell, *Sobering Up*, p. 69; Stewart, *William Lloyd Garrison*, p. 33; and Abzug, *Cosmos Crumbling*, p. 79.

34. Even Timothy Smith, one of the most ardent proponents of the link between revivalism and social reform, acknowledges that "an uncompromising stand against slavery *as a sin* fitted alike the pattern of Methodist perfectionism, New School revivalism, and the intensely ethical concerns of radical Quaker and Unitarian religion" (*Revivalism*, p. 181).

35. A big difference between liberal and revivalist notions of sin was that liberals were more forthright in their repudiation of orthodoxy. Finneyites, by contrast, were Arminian without quite admitting to be such. They presented conversion as *both* an act of human will and an interposition of divine grace. This ambiguity may have made their position more appealing to mainstream Americans. The voluntary renunciation of sin took on extra significance if it was also understood to be a token of elect status. That, at least, is the argument of Whitney Cross, *Burned-Over District*, p. 28; and Wyatt-Brown, *Lewis Tappan*, pp. 60–61.

36. Lydia Maria Child, *Letters from New York*, 6 October 1842, 1:201; and Goodell, cited in Perry, *Radical Abolitionism*, p. 46.

37. John L. Thomas, for example, has influentially argued that evangelical reformers reduced complex social problems to the cumulative sins of unregenerate individuals and could thus propose only "moral rather than social" solutions. Ellen DuBois rightly counters that abolitionists actually saw the institutional character of slavery so clearly that they proposed radical, rather than merely institutional, solutions. Other scholars, for instance, Donald M. Scott, acknowledge the systemic understandings of abolitionists but still insist that temperance activists stigmatized individual alcoholics as sinners. In fact, as I shall demonstrate in chapter 4, temperance leaders after 1830 saw rumsellers and respectable moderate drinkers, *not* drunkards, as the primary perpetrators of what they called the "alcohol system." See Thomas, "Antislavery and Utopia," pp. 246–47; Thomas, "Romantic Reform," pp. 657–61; DuBois, "Women's Rights," p. 242; and Scott, "Abolition," pp. 66–68.

38. Paul Goodman makes this point emphatically in his study of abolitionism, *Of One Blood*, pp. 36–53.

39. For the influence of black activists on Garrison, see ibid., pp. 2–3, 36. For Mott's encounter with Forten, see Sterling, *Lucretia Mott*, pp. 79–80. And for Gerrit Smith's encounter with the drunkards, see Sigourney and Smith, *Intemperate*, pp. 23–25, 37; and Tyrrell, *Sobering Up*, p. 138.

40. Scholars who emphasize the revivalist roots of social reform typically focus on the "Burned-Over District" of upstate New York and on northeastern Ohio. I do not mean to downplay those regions but simply to suggest that Boston was a comparable center for the more liberal wing of social reform.

41. On the "body reforms," see Abzug, *Cosmos Crumbling*, pp. 163–82.

42. Chapman, *Right and Wrong*, p. 154; and Chapman, cited in Hersh, "Abolitionist Beginnings," p. 282.

43. Gilbert Barnes (*Antislavery Impulse*, p. 98) and Timothy Smith (*Revivalism*, pp. 179–81) both fault the ultraists for their neglect of society-building, but this criticism simply ignores the diversity of tactics they employed.

44. Stanton cited in DuBois, "Women's Rights," p. 248; and Douglass, "What to the Slave Is the Fourth of July?" 5 July 1852, in *Papers*, ser. 1, 2:371. Good examinations of abolitionist agitation appear in Zinn, "Abolitionists," pp. 417–51; Kraditor, *Means and Ends*; Wyatt-Brown, *Lewis Tappan*, p. 269; Walters, *Antislavery Appeal*, p. 19; and Mayer, *All on Fire*, pp. xiii–xvi.

45. Cited in Abzug, *Passionate Liberator*, p. 218.

46. Barnes, *Antislavery Impulse*, p. 163.

47. Cited in Walters, *Antislavery Appeal*, pp. 5–6.

48. Wyatt-Brown, *Lewis Tappan*, pp. 199–200; Walters, *Antislavery Appeal*, p. 18.

49. References to the *imago dei* appeared even in connection to relatively minor causes. In a letter to Henry C. Wright, for example, Frederick Douglass alluded to their common opposition to laws restricting free travel across international borders: "You hold, (and so do I,) that the image of our common God ought to be a passport all over the habitable world." Frederick Douglass to Henry C. Wright, 22 December 1846, *Liberator*, 29 January 1847, in *Selected Speeches*, p. 52.

50. Frederick Douglass to William Lloyd Garrison, 1 September 1845, in *Selected Speeches*, p. 14.

51. Douglass, "The Anti-Slavery Movement," 19 March 1855, in *Papers*, ser. 1, 3:15–16, 38.

52. Douglass, "Farewell to the British People," 30 March 1847, in *Papers*, ser. 1, 2:32; and Douglass, "Significance of Emancipation," 3 August 1857, in *Papers*, ser. 1, 3:204.

53. Douglass, "The Anti-Slavery Movement," 19 March 1855, in *Papers*, ser. 1, 3:37.

54. Smith, "Religion of Reason," 1859, in *Speeches and Sermons*, pp. 65–66; and Friedman, *Gregarious Saints*, p. 113.

55. Douglass, "Change of Opinion Announced," *North Star*, 15 May 1851, in *Selected Speeches*, p. 173.

56. Smith, "Religion of Reason," 1858, in *Sermons and Speeches*, pp. 3–4; Smith, "Bible Civil Government," 1860, in *Sermons and Speeches*, p. 105; Smith, "Religion of Reason," 1859, in *Sermons and Speeches*, p. 63; and Smith, "Religion of Reason," 1858, in *Sermons and Speeches*, p. 8.

57. Douglass, "A Reform Absolutely Complete," 9 April 1870, in *Papers*, ser. 1, 4:264. For interpretations of this passage, see Gibson," Faith," p. 92; Aptheker, "Unpublished," pp. 279–80; and Van DeBurg, "Frederick Douglass," pp. 27–43.

58. My two categories of "ultraists" and "revolutionaries" correspond closely to Lawrence Friedman's "insurgents of the Boston Clique" and "voluntarists of the Burned-over-District." Many of Friedman's more theologically orthodox "Stewards of the Lord," such as the Tappan brothers in New York City, would not qualify as radical Christian liberals at all (*Gregarious Saints*).

59. Chapman, *Right and Wrong*, p. 6; and Douglass, "What to the Slave Is the Fourth of July?" 5 July 1852, in *Papers*, ser. 1, 2:376–77. I dissent, therefore, from those historians who claim that reformers "turned religious energy toward secular ends" or participated in "a long-term trend toward the secularization of American idealism." Mayer, *All on Fire*, p. xvii; Wyatt-Brown, *Lewis Tappan*, p. 188; Mintz, *Moralists and Modernizers*, p. xviii. From the perspective of Christian liberalism, the contrast between the "secular" and the "religious" makes little sense, for it is precisely in the midst of "the world" that God's presence is most visible. Robert Abzug offers a good antidote to the secularization thesis with his suggestion that most reformers participated in "an endlessly unfolding spiritual odyssey" (*Cosmos Crumbling*, p. 128). I would only add that this odyssey was usually guided by the liberal principle of the *imago dei*.

60. Walters, *Antislavery Appeal*, pp. 51–52.

61. Channing, "Lecture on War," 1838, in *Works*, p. 679; and Douglass, "Country, Conscience, and the Anti-Slavery Cause," 11 May 1847, in *Papers*, ser. 1, 2:62–63.

62. Phillips cited in Stewart, *Holy Warriors*, p. 3. The abolitionist movement was fundamentally revolutionary, radical historian Herbert Aptheker has pointed out, because it sought the overthrow of the system of property on which social power rested (*Abolitionism*, p. xii).

63. By contrast, Alcoholics Anonymous relies on self-help among alcoholics and makes few demands on society at large.

64. Louis Hartz, for example, argued that the United States lacked its own radical tradition because it was a "naturally liberal" society that had never experienced feudal aristocracy. As such, it was "as indifferent to the challenge of socialism in the later era as it was unfamiliar with the heritage of feudalism in the earlier one" (*Liberal Tradition*, p. 6). Stanley Elkins argued that because of the reformers' extreme individualism, "no institutionalized radicalism has ever existed here" (*Slavery*, p. 159). H. Richard Niebuhr, for his part, claimed that the liberal tradition was inevitably "evolutionary" because it "involved no discontinuities, no crises, no tragedies or sacrifices, no loss of all things, no cross and resurrection." If liberals *seemed* to be revolutionary, it was only because they were living off the accumulated capital of the revivals (Niebuhr, *Kingdom of God*, pp. 191, 194).

65. Given the revolutionary potential of liberal ideals, it might seem odd that more Americans have not taken up Thomas Jefferson's suggestion that we fight a new revolution in each generation. Much of the explanation for this, I suspect, lies in the evangelical tradition itself. Because it blends liberal principles so skillfully with theological orthodoxy, it has defused the revolutionary potential of liberal principles taken in themselves.

66. Douglass, "Country, Conscience, and the Anti-Slavery Cause," 11 May 1847, in *Papers*, ser. 1, 2:60–61; and Douglass to Horace Greeley, 15 April 1846, in *Selected Speeches*, p. 29.

67. This question is explored in O'Connell, "Magic," p. 15.

Chapter 3

1. *Liberator*, 1 January 1831.

2. Garrison and Garrison, *William Lloyd Garrison*, 2:313.

3. Ibid., 1:xi.

4. Some of Garrison's biographers, notably John L. Thomas, have assailed him as "illogical," presumably because they find his logical conclusions unpalatable. Even Bertram Wyatt-Brown, who is much more sympathetic to Garrison, writes that "as a philosophical system, Garrison's conceptual fads made no logical sense at all, but, with Yankee ability to turn absurdities to good advantage, he fashioned perfectionism into an effective tool for immediate emancipation." Wyatt-Brown, *Lewis Tappan*, p. 187. My interpretation is closer to that of Aileen S. Kraditor, who reports that when she first read Garrison's own words—after studying Thomas's biography—she "was increasingly struck by the logical consistency of his thought on all subjects" (*Means and Ends*, p. ix).

5. Historians have reached widely different conclusions about Garrison's place in the abolitionist movement, and in social reform more generally. In the late nineteenth century, he was almost universally recognized as the founding and guiding spirit of abolition. In 1933 Gilbert Barnes (*Antislavery Impulse*) assailed this view as a "legend" concocted by Garrison and his fawning supporters. In fact, Barnes argued, Garrison was a self-aggrandizing fanatic who did the movement more harm than good, while the real work of abolition was accomplished by Finneyite revivalists like Theodore Weld. Interestingly, one of Garrison's biographers, John L. Thomas (*Liberator*), largely shares this view. More appreciative views of Garrison appear in Filler, *Crusade*; Kraditor, *Means and Ends*; Wyatt-Brown, *Lewis Tappan*; Perry,

Radical Abolitionism; Friedman, *Gregarious Saints*; Merrill, *Against Wind and Tide*; and Mayer, *All on Fire*. Filler writes that "Garrison outranked them one and all as a subject for controversy and as an antislavery symbol, in his own time and after" (*Crusade*, p. 56). Even in his biography of Lewis Tappan, Bertram Wyatt-Brown goes so far as to say that "Garrison was the real pioneer of antislavery" (p. 85).

6. Few historians would deny Garrison's eventual heterodoxy, but many lay exaggerated emphasis on his evangelical roots. Steven Mintz erroneously refers to Garrison as a "devout Baptist" and claims that he "epitomized the religious piety and millennial spirit of the Second Great Awakening" (*Moralists and Modernizers*, p. 126). James Brewer Stewart lists Garrison with Arthur Tappan and James Birney as "young evangelicals" who made "soul-wrenching commitments to eradicating the sin of slavery" (*Holy Warriors*, p. 43). Robert Abzug suggests that Garrison became an abolitionist shortly after he had "embraced Beecher's vision of evangelical reform," and that he cast "his appeal in the language of militant New England evangelical reform" (*Cosmos Crumbling*, pp. 129, 130). Bertram Wyatt-Brown cites Garrison's understanding of slavery as sin in support of his claim that abolition "began as a direct extension of evangelical Christianity." He even suggests that "in Garrison's mind the [immediatist] formula was merely an extension of the revivalistic experience of instantaneous conversion—a religious, not a secular, act." Since Garrison had not personally had the experience of conversion, it is hard to see how that experience could have had an "extension" in his mind. Still, Wyatt-Brown is right to note the parallel between the two experiences. Later, he acknowledges the increasingly unorthodox character of Garrison's thought (*Lewis Tappan*, pp. 81, 132, 185).

7. Indeed, when Gilbert Barnes (*Antislavery Impulse*, pp. vii–viii, 56) first insisted on the revivalist character of the antislavery movement, he could do so only by refuting Garrison's claim to leadership in that movement.

8. Ziegler, *Advocates*, pp. 3–4. Ziegler's interpretation is somewhat similar to Aileen Kraditor's characterization of Garrison as a "radical" who "believed that American society, North as well as South, was fundamentally immoral, with slavery only the worst of its many sins, and who looked forward to a thoroughgoing change in its institutional structure and ideology" (*Means and Ends*, p. 8). Yet another scholar who treats Garrison as a "sectarian" is Stange, *Patterns*, pp. 26, 46.

9. William Lloyd Garrison to Elizabeth Pease, 20 June 1849, in *Letters*, 3:629–30.

10. Garrison and Garrison, *William Lloyd Garrison*, 2:258; and *Liberator*, 15 December 1837. The fact that Garrison so clearly disavowed sectarianism does not, of course, prove that he was not a sectarian himself. Indeed, his movement succumbed more than once to the sectarian temptation of withdrawal from others with whom it disagreed only slightly. But this withdrawal never meant a lack of communication, for Garrison's commitment to free speech made him somewhat fanatical about including opposing views in the pages of the *Liberator*. He also took pains to celebrate the moral integrity of those—from Nat Turner to Abraham Lincoln—who shared some, but not all, of his commitments. Most certainly Ziegler is not right to say that "the Garrisonian nonresistants . . . *envisioned themselves* as sectarian radicals" (*Advocates*, p. 3, my emphasis).

11. Mayer, *All on Fire*, pp. xvi, xvii.

12. Ibid., pp. 6–7, 21.

13. Garrison and Garrison, *William Lloyd Garrison*, 1:56.

14. Ibid., 1:84, 157.

15. Mayer, *All on Fire*, p. 214.

16. Child, "William Lloyd Garrison," *Atlantic Monthly*, August 1879, in *Child Reader*, p. 289.

17. Mayer, *All on Fire*, pp. 48–49.

18. *Philanthropist*, 21 March 1828, cited in Garrison and Garrison, *William Lloyd Garrison*, 1:95. Garrison referred back to these three causes throughout his career. When he took on the partisan *Journal of the Times* in Bennington, Vermont, he insisted on continuing to agitate these issues; when he joined the *Genius of Universal Emancipation* he took pains to inform his readers

that "I do not mean to lose sight" of temperance and peace. See Garrison and Garrison, *William Lloyd Garrison*, 1:101, 103, 142.

19. Mayer, *All on Fire*, pp. 19, 179, 354; and Garrison and Garrison, *William Lloyd Garrison*, 1:425–26, 2:66–69.

20. Garrison and Garrison, *William Lloyd Garrison*, 2:51, 70. Garrison might well have joined the Quakers if it were not for such lingering sectarian rules as the one that forbade Quakers to attend non-Quaker weddings. In a letter to his wife on Angelina Grimké's wedding to Theodore Dwight Weld, Garrison blasted this rule as "absurd and despotic." William Lloyd Garrison to Helen E. Garrison, 12 May 1838, in *Letters*, 2:360.

21. Garrison and Garrison, *William Lloyd Garrison*, 1:85, 157.

22. Ibid., 1:214–15, 226–27; and Mayer, *All on Fire*, p. 102.

23. Garrison and Garrison, *William Lloyd Garrison*, 1:462–63.

24. Ibid., 2:109–14.

25. William Lloyd Garrison to Henry E. Benson, 10 December 1835, in *Letters*, 1:574. Garrison's public assessment was more balanced: an initial review focused on the merits of the book, predicting that it "will do great good," while a later review listed twenty-five objections before concluding that the book was "utterly destitute of any redeeming, reforming power" (*Liberator*, 12 December 1835; 27 February 1836). For an extended analysis of Channing's views on slavery, see Stange, *Patterns*, pp. 74–99.

26. Garrison and Garrison, *William Lloyd Garrison*, 2:96–97; William Lloyd Garrison to Helen E. Garrison, 7 March 1836, in *Letters*, 2:59; Garrison and Garrison, *William Lloyd Garrison*, 2:106; *Liberator*, 26 May 1848.

27. Garrison and Garrison, *William Lloyd Garrison*, 4:336.

28. William Lloyd Garrison to Francis Jackson, 3 November 1855, in *Letters*, 4:355.

29. Cited in Mayer, *All on Fire*, p. 301.

30. Garrison and Garrison, *William Lloyd Garrison*, 3:7–9.

31. William Lloyd Garrison to Elizabeth Pease, 1 June 1841, in *Letters*, 3:22–23.

32. *Liberator*, 26 November 1841.

33. A good treatment of Garrison's shifting views on the Bible appears in Kraditor, *Means and Ends*, pp. 91–95.

34. Garrison and Garrison, *William Lloyd Garrison*, 1:407.

35. *Liberator*, 29 January 1841; and Garrison and Garrison, *William Lloyd Garrison*, 3:8, 145–46.

36. Garrison, "Interview with Father Mathew," *Liberator*, 10 August 1849; Joseph Barker, "The Bible and Slavery," *Liberator*, 14 May 1852; *Liberator*, 22 April 1853; and Garrison and Garrison, *William Lloyd Garrison*, 3:386.

37. Edmund Quincy to R. D. Webb, 27 November 1843, in Garrison and Garrison, *William Lloyd Garrison*, 3:95; and *Liberator*, 18 May 1860.

38. Garrison and Garrison, *William Lloyd Garrison*, 4:336.

39. Ibid., 1:66, 131; and *Liberator*, 1 January 1831.

40. "Declaration of the National Anti-Slavery Convention," *Liberator*, 14 December 1833.

41. *Liberator*, 29 December 1832; and Garrison and Garrison, *William Lloyd Garrison*, 3:412.

42. *Liberator*, 12 January 1838. Several historians have stressed the positive value of Garrisonian agitation. Bertram Wyatt-Brown emphasizes the nonviolent character of Garrison's harsh language, which was, he says, "a conscious attempt to arouse angry reaction in others (not dissimilar to nonviolent provocations of public anger through mass demonstrations, a technique of agitation of more recent development)" (*Lewis Tappan*, p. 289). Aileen Kraditor explains that "if politics is the art of the possible, agitation is the art of the desirable. Agitation by the reformer or radical helps define one possible policy as more desirable than another, and if skillful and uncompromising, the agitation may help make the desirable possible. . . . the agitator helps

define the value, the principle, for which the politician bargains" (*Means and Ends*, p. 28). See also Mayer, *All on Fire*, p. xiii.

43. *Non-Resistant*, 7 December 1839, cited in Perry, *Radical Abolitionism*, p. 79.

44. William Lloyd Garrison to Theodore Parker, 3 June 1858, in *Letters*, 4:534–35. Similarly, when Garrison spoke at the Hopedale Community in July 1862, he addressed virtually every issue on which he disagreed with the community's founder, Adin Ballou. While Parker appreciated Garrison's commitment to free speech, however, Ballou was deeply offended. See Ballou, *Autobiography*, pp. 438–49.

45. Garrison, "Speech at the Disunion Convention," 15 January 1857, in *Liberator*, 23 January 1857. Garrison's commitment to agitation also explains his insistence on using the slogan of "immediate abolition," even though he recognized that slavery would most likely end through a gradual process. "Urge immediate abolition as earnestly as we may," he wrote in the *Liberator*, "it will, alas! be gradual abolition in the end. We have never said that slavery would be overthrown at a single blow; that it ought to be, we shall always contend" (*Liberator*, 13 August 1831).

46. Maria Weston Chapman to Henry Clarke Wright, 31 March 1843, in Garrison and Garrison, *William Lloyd Garrison*, 3:80; and Garrison and Garrison, *William Lloyd Garrison*, 1:xiv.

47. Judd cited in Brock, *Freedom*, p. 334.

48. Ladd, *Brief Illustration*, p. iii.

49. Curti, *American Peace Crusade*, pp. 12–13.

50. Ziegler, *Advocates*, p. 35. For Ziegler, Dodge exemplifies the "sectarian" temperament, which she also ascribes to Garrison. The connection between the two men is quite misleading. Though they shared an absolute pacifism and antipathy to more moderate approaches, they had little in common theologically. Garrisonian nonresistance is better understood as a radicalization of Worcester's liberalism than as an extension of Dodge's sectarian orthodoxy.

51. Ziegler, *Advocates*, p. 3; Curti, *American Peace Crusade*, pp. 12, 25; and Cooke, *Unitarianism*, pp. 99, 244.

52. Channing, "War," 1816, in *Works*, p. 648; and Curti, *American Peace Crusade*, pp. 21–22.

53. Chapman, *Right and Wrong*, p. 25.

54. Garrison and Garrison, *William Lloyd Garrison*, 1:201, 409.

55. Wright cited in Mayer, *All on Fire*, p. 222; and William Lloyd Garrison to Mary Benson, 27 November 1835, in *Letters*, 1:563.

56. *Liberator*, 8 September 1837.

57. *Liberator*, 14 December 1837; *Liberator*, 21 July 1837.

58. William Lloyd Garrison to Helen E. Garrison, 21 September 1938, in *Letters*, 2:391; and "Declaration of the Sentiments Adopted by the Peace Convention," *Liberator*, 28 September 1838, in Garrison and Garrison, *William Lloyd Garrison*, 2:230.

59. Ballou, *Christian Non-Resistance*, p. 11.

60. Grimké, *Address*, pp. 42, 47, 48. Grimké, a leader in several benevolent societies and the brother of Sarah and Angelina Grimké, died of cholera in 1834. It is thus not possible to place him in one or the other factions that emerged later in the history of the peace movement.

61. *Liberator*, 8 January 1831.

62. Lydia Maria Child, in *Liberator*, 2 April 1836.

63. *Liberator*, 23 July 1836; and Wright, *Kiss for a Blow*, p. 41.

64. Garrison and Garrison, *William Lloyd Garrison*, 2:326–27.

65. Dodge, *War Inconsistent*, p. 44; Worcester, *Solemn Review*, p. 29; "Declaration of Sentiments," in Garrison and Garrison, *William Lloyd Garrison*, 2:232; and Wright, *Anthropology*, pp. 9, 20.

66. Worcester, *Solemn Review*, p. 30.

67. Dodge, *War Inconsistent*, pp. 22, 90–91; and Grimké, *Address*, pp. 26–27.

68. Worcester, *Solemn Review*, p. 10; Ladd, *Brief Illustration*, pp. 72–73; and Ballou, *Christian Non-Resistance*, pp. 66, 72–73.

69. Sarah Grimké rejected what she saw as the dispensationalism of Garrison's Declaration on these grounds, noting that "it seemed impossible to me that God, who is unchangeable, could issue commandments at one period touching the morality of his people, and at another annul them and institute others apparently quite opposite." Her solution, however, was to assert a harmony between the two testaments that was beyond her own comprehension, rather than to reject the authority of the Old Testament passages advocating violence. Sarah M. Grimké to Henry Clarke Wright, 19 November 1838, in Barnes and Dumond, *Letters*, 2:708.

70. "Declaration of Sentiments," in Garrison and Garrison, *William Lloyd Garrison*, 2:233.

71. *Liberator*, 2 January 1846; Wright, cited in Perry, *Childhood*, p. 143; William Lloyd Garrison to Elizabeth Pease, 20 June 1849, in *Letters*, 3:634; and Wright, *Human Life*, pp. 285–86. This insistence on the stability of moral laws runs parallel to the "uniformitarian" theory of contemporary geologists, who insisted that the earth had been shaped not by a sudden creation or cataclysmic flood but by the gradual effects of unchanging physical laws.

72. Worcester, *Solemn Review*, pp. 28, 6; Channing, "War," 1816, p. 648; and Ladd, *Brief Illustration*, p. 110. Dodge's position on this issue was rather curious. As an avowed Calvinist, he theoretically affirmed the doctrine of the Fall. But many of his arguments closely paralleled those of Ladd and Worcester. *War Inconsistent with the Religion of Jesus Christ* opens, for example, with an appeal to the inherent goodness of humanity: "Humanity, wisdom and goodness at once combine all that can be great and lovely in man." The book's very first argument is that war is inhuman "because it hardens the heart and blunts the tender feelings of mankind." By contrasting the callousness of those who have been desensitized by war to the ready sympathy people feel when someone has an accident, Dodge betrays his assumption that some natural benevolence survived the fall. Dodge, *War Inconsistent*, pp. 1, 2, 5.

73. "Declaration of Sentiments," in Garrison and Garrison, *William Lloyd Garrison*, 2:232.

74. Dodge, *War Inconsistent*, p. 32; Worcester, *Solemn Review*, pp. 13, 31; Ladd, *Brief Illustration*, p. 7; and Ballou, *Christian Non-Resistance*, p. 130.

75. Grimké, *Address*, p. 3; Ladd, *Brief Illustration*, p. 5; Grimké, *Address*, pp. 11–12; and Ballou, *Christian Non-Resistance*, p. 114.

76. Wright, *Anthropology*, p. 87. Wright began to develop these views as early as his student days at Andover Seminary, where he filled his notebooks with such comments as "he who best knows, loves, respects man—best knows, loves & honors God." Cited in Perry, *Childhood*, p. 117.

77. Wright, *Anthropology*, pp. 52, 10–11, 55.

78. "Declaration of Sentiments," in Garrison and Garrison, *William Lloyd Garrison*, 2:231–32. The most extensive study of the governmental principle, and of anarchist tendencies in reformist thought, is Lewis Perry's *Radical Abolitionism*. Perry, who sees abolition as an outgrowth of the evangelicalism of the Second Great Awakening, places particular emphasis on the orthodox Protestant doctrine of God's sovereignty. He suggests that for radical reformers all human authority was "sinfully presumptuous" insofar as it ascribed to humans what belonged only to God (pp. 22, 34–48). Such arguments do appear in nonresistant literature, but more commonly in the writings of Adin Ballou and John Humphrey Noyes than in those of Garrison and his allies. Garrisonian nonresistance owes more to the liberal doctrine of the *imago dei* and thus sees human government as a blasphemous assault on the divinity within the individual rather than as a presumptuous assumption of divine authority. In any case, the two claims flow together in the work of Henry Clarke Wright, for whom the only God is the one present in the individual conscience.

79. "Declaration of Sentiments," in Garrison and Garrison, *William Lloyd Garrison*, 1:410; *Liberator*, 4 July 1835; and *Liberator*, 16 December 1859. Even in 1835, though, Garrison does

not appear to have been a literalist, for he goes on to say that "whatsoever requirement of man I believe is opposed to the *spirit* of the gospel, I will at all hazards disobey" (my emphasis).

80. Dodge, *War Inconsistent*, p. 6; and Noyes to Garrison, 22 March 1837, in Garrison and Garrison, *William Lloyd Garrison*, 2:147. For a more extended analysis of Garrison's relationship with Noyes, see Perry, *Radical Abolitionism*, pp. 65–69.

81. Noyes to Garrison, 22 March 1837, in Garrison and Garrison, *William Lloyd Garrison*, 2:147.

82. *Liberator*, 10 January 1845. Another index of the distance between Noyes and Garrison is the fact that Noyes went on to found the Oneida community, a commune in which the members were strictly subordinated to his own charismatic authority, while Garrison continued to renounce any authority beyond that of his words. As Garrison's sons aptly noted, "Noyes's scheme of human regeneration involved a species of church organization, with the Bible as interpreted by himself for authority—in other words, had a purely sectarian basis." Garrison and Garrison, *William Lloyd Garrison*, 2:207. Garrison also repudiated Noyes's controversial system of plural marriage. See *Liberator*, 12 November 1841.

83. Dodge, *War Inconsistent*, pp. 102, 80, 36.

84. *Liberator*, 10 January 1845.

85. "Declaration of Sentiments," in Garrison and Garrison, *William Lloyd Garrison*, 2:231.

86. *Liberator*, 1 January 1831.

87. *Liberator*, 8 March 1839.

88. Worcester, *Solemn Review*, p. 7.

89. Wright, *Anthropology*, pp. 46–47, 12, 43. It is interesting that this resolution, which began with Wright's repudiation of the "idolatrous" God of violence, led him to endorse another practice often labeled idolatrous—the direction of one's utmost devotion toward particular, finite beings. "My soul must idolize something," he insisted; "must have something on which to exhaust its entire love and devotion." Wright, *Anthropology*, p. 54.

90. Ladd, *Brief Illustration*, p. iv; Ballou, *Christian Non-Resistance*, pp. 30–31; and Wright, *Kiss*, p. 50.

91. Ballou, *Christian Non-Resistance*, p. 121; and Ladd, *Brief Illustration*, pp. 10, 46.

92. Wright, *Anthropology*, pp. 56, 57.

93. *Liberator*, 1 January 1831; "Declaration of Sentiments," in Garrison and Garrison, *William Lloyd Garrison*, 2:234; and Wright, *Kiss for a Blow*, p. vii.

94. Wright, *Kiss for a Blow*, p. 171.

95. Garrison and Garrison, *William Lloyd Garrison*, 1:136; and *Liberator*, 5 February 1831 and 1 January 1831.

96. *Liberator*, 1 January 1831.

97. *Liberator*, 3 September 1831. Even after the Civil War, Garrison retained a sense of God's impending punishment. In a Fourth of July speech in 1876, he blasted the continuing oppression of women, ex-slaves, and Native Americans, concluding that "if we rejoice at all let it be with contrite hearts that we have not been utterly consumed" (Mayer, *All on Fire*, p. 614).

98. William Lloyd Garrison to Elizabeth Pease, 6 November 1837, in *Letters*, 2:324–25. A similar letter, to Elizabeth's father, Joseph Pease, appears in *Letters*, 2:673–75.

99. *Liberator*, 8 March 1839 and 23 December 1853.

100. Judd was a sympathizer but not an actual member of the Non-Resistance Society. His sermon "A Moral Review of the Revolutionary War" was reprinted in the *Liberator*, 27 May 1842 and 3 June 1842.

101. Wright, *Anthropology*, p. 10; and Wright, *Human Life*, p. 9.

102. Wright, *Human Life*, pp. 9–10.

103. Ibid., pp. 170, 324.

104. Ibid., pp. 115, 22, 82, 86, 87, 90, 94, 88–89, 104. Commenting on passages of this

sort, Lewis Perry notes that "the warfare between heart and head, ending in reconciliation with tough intellectual doctrines, belonged to the conventions of revivalism" (*Childhood*, p. 103). Wright departed from those conventions, however, by rejecting the traditional revivalist solution, which was the implanting of a new heart by divine grace.

105. Wright, *Human Life*, pp. 99, 104, 88, 89, 28, 50–52. Wright's account of this school-teacher is remarkably similar to Frederick Douglass's description of the education he received at the hands of an elderly slave, "Uncle" Isaac Cooper.

106. Ibid., p. 95.

107. Ibid., pp. 32, 45, 33.

108. Ibid., pp. 78, 35, 78–79.

109. Channing, *Memoir*, 1:39, cited in Delbanco, *William Ellery Channing*, p. 15; and Ware, "Nature of Man," p. 204.

110. Augustine, *Confessions*, II.iv (9); and Wright, *Human Life*, pp. 79–80. Theodore Parker told of a similar experience, in which he nearly killed a turtle but was stopped by what his mother called "the voice of God in the soul of man." "No event in my life," Parker claimed, "has made so deep an impression upon me" (cited in Wyatt-Brown, *Yankee Saints*, p. 51). Psychologist Allison Davis has similarly argued that "children at the age of two or three . . . are likely to be cruel to both animals and siblings, but eventually they *learn* to become kind and even merciful" (*Leadership*, pp. 89–90).

111. Wright, *Human Life*, pp. 60–61.

112. Ibid., pp. 127, 130.

113. Ibid., pp. 139, 198.

114. Even Garrison complained of the lack of "unity" in Wright's text, noting that the inclusion of so many letters to himself "break[s] the charm of consecutive narration." William Lloyd Garrison to Elizabeth Pease, 20 June 1849, in *Letters*, 3:624.

115. Wright, *Human Life*, pp. 245, 277.

116. Wright, *Anthropology*, p. 17; and Wright, *Human Life*, pp. 327, 71, 117.

117. Wright, *Human Life*, pp. 75, 326.

118. Ibid., p. 303.

119. For another interpretation of Wright's relationship with Catharine, see Perry, *Childhood*, pp. 184–86.

120. Judd, *Young Man's Account*, pp. 19, 21, 29.

121. Judd, *Margaret*, pp. 3–4.

122. Ibid., pp. 72, 75.

123. Ibid., p. 208.

124. Ibid., pp. 91, 92, 99, 108.

125. Ibid., pp. 212–16.

126. Ibid., pp. 217–19, 226.

127. Ibid., p. 20.

128. Ibid., pp. 78, 280–82.

129. Ibid., p. 82.

130. Ibid., pp. 288–89, 302, 304.

131. Ibid., pp. 351, 361, 366, 370, 372, 393.

132. Ibid., pp. 376, 378.

Chapter 4

1. Katie G. Cannon has developed an ethical theory that does not treat the situation of the unconstrained moral agent as normative in *Black Womanist Ethics*.

2. A handful of texts described the experiences of female alcoholics, and of the husbands

and children who suffered from their addiction. (See, for example, Shepard, *Confessions*.) But temperance activists clearly assumed that the majority of "drunkards" were men.

3. Nadelhaft, "Alcohol and Wife Abuse," p. 23; Reynolds, *Faith in Fiction*, p. 108; Crowley, *Drunkard's Progress*, pp. xiii, 4; and Koch, "Timothy Shay Arthur," p. 3.

4. Blocker, *American Temperance Movements*, p. 4. Charles Sellers's divergent figures tell much the same story: he reports per capita consumption of 5.1 gallons in 1710, 5.8 gallons in 1790, and 7.1 gallons in 1830–followed by a precipitous decline to 3.1 gallons in 1840 and 1.8 gallons in 1845 (*Market Revolution*, p. 260). W. J. Rorabaugh (*Alcoholic Republic*, pp. 175–83) has helpfully suggested that the Industrial Revolution at first raised aspirations it could not fulfill and thus sparked heavy drinking, and then successfully channeled those aspirations into disciplined production.

5. Sellers *Market Revolution*, p. 260.

6. Twentieth-century research suggests that alcohol consumption does not "cause" violence in any physiological sense. But in cultures that believe there is a causal relationship, alcohol consumption often serves as an occasion of or an excuse for violence. See MacAndrew and Edgerton, *Drunken Comportment*; Gelles and Cornell, *Intimate Violence*, pp. 18–19; Berk et al., "Mutual Combat," pp. 18–19; Blocker, *American Temperance Movements*, p. 109; and Gordon, *Heroes*, pp. 264–66.

7. Rohrer, "Origins."

8. Sellers, *Market Revolution*, p. 214, 265; Tyrrell, *Sobering Up*, pp. 33–34, 54–59; Crowley, *Drunkard's Progress*, p. 5; and Blocker, *American Temperance Movements*, p. 12.

9. Tyrrell, *Sobering Up*, pp. 87, 59.

10. Sigourney and Smith, *Intemperate*, pp. 25, 23, 24, 37.

11. Woodman, *Narrative*, p. 95.

12. In his study of temperance activism in Taunton, Massachusetts, Robert Hampel (*Temperance*, p. 113) found that only 10 percent of Washingtonians (including the society president) had a documented history of drunkenness, but that the society as a whole revealed stark ideological differences from the earlier temperance movement. Washingtonians were less than half as likely to be orthodox Congregationalists or members of the Whig Party (though both groups were still well represented) and considerably more likely to be Methodist, Baptist, Episcopal, or Unitarian.

13. Hampel, *Temperance*, pp. 118, 123.

14. Sellers, *Market Revolution*, pp. 152–53.

15. Sánchez-Eppler, "Temperance," p. 5.

16. Arthur, "Julia Forrester," in *Temperance Tales*, 2:149.

17. I shall cite a later version of this text, entitled *The Drunkard's Looking Glass*, which appears in *Three Discourses*. Given Weems's preoccupation with extreme violence, and the more restrained character of many later temperance texts, it is hard to sustain David Reynolds's thesis that temperance literature evolved from a didactic, nonsensational, "conventional" genre into one that was "subversive" and sensational (Reynolds, *Beneath*, p. 68). Indeed, Reynolds greatly errs in beginning his survey of temperance literature not with Weems but with *Edmund and Margaret* and *The Lottery Ticket*, two obscure liberal tracts published in 1822, neither of which has temperance as its primary focus. Yet Reynolds is correct to see temperance literature as an ambivalent mixture of didactic and sensational styles, and also correct to treat the 1820s as the high point of the more didactic and optimistic liberal approach.

18. Weems, *Three Discourses*, pp. 111, 88–89.

19. Weems, *God's Revenge Against Murder*, pp. 7, 24–29.

20. Weems, *Three Discourses*, p. 119.

21. Ibid., pp. 84, 97.

22. Sargent, "Fritz Hazell," in *Temperance Tales*, 1:113; and Brown, *Minnie Hermon*, p. 204.

23. Sigourney, "Letter to Females," in *Water-Drops*, p. 261; and Rose, *Nora Wilmot*, p. 350.

24. Marsh, *Putnam*, p. 12; Rose, *Nora Wilmot*, p. 350; and Brown, *Minnie Hermon*, p. 428.

25. Sargent, "Kitty Grafton," in *Temperance Tales*, 2:39.

26. Sargent, "My Mother's Gold Ring," in *Temperance Tales*, 1:5–12.

27. Fox, *George Allen*, pp. 112, 22. Similar plot devices appear in Sigourney, "Lost Hopes," in *Water-Drops*, p. 201; Arthur, "The Ruined Family," in *Temperance Tales*, 1:9–56; and Rose, *Nora Wilmot*, p. 55.

28. This is perhaps a conscious or unconscious reference to the very similar character of the same name in Weems's *God's Revenge Against Adultery*, in *Three Discourses*.

29. Fox, *George Allen*, pp. 29, 34.

30. Ibid., pp. 90, 119, 135–136.

31. Woodman, *Narrative*, pp. 84–85.

32. Gough, *Autobiography* (1845), pp. 113, 122, 154.

33. "Mather," *Autobiography*, pp. 109–10.

34. Gough, *Autobiography* (1845), pp. 155, 160.

35. Woodman, *Narrative*, p. 90.

36. Arthur, "Autobiography," in *Illustrated Temperance Tales*, pp. 3–7.

37. Rose, *Nora Wilmot*, p. 286.

38. Fox, *Ruined Deacon*, p. iii; and Arthur, *Six Nights*, pp. 21.

39. Arthur, *Six Nights*, p. 74; Lamas, *Glass*, p. 32; and "J. T.," "Introduction," in Sigourney and Smith, *Intemperate*, p. 3.

40. McGinn, *Foundations*, pp. xviii–xix. The oscillating pattern I have described is perhaps best illustrated in the writings of Pseudo-Dionysius the Areopagite, especially *The Divine Names* and *The Mystical Theology*. See *Complete Works*, pp. 47–142.

41. Woodman, *Narrative*, p. 91.

42. Gough, *Autobiography* (1847), p. 128.

43. Sargent, "My Mother's Gold Ring," in *Temperance Tales*, 1:5.

44. Brown, *Minnie Hermon*, p. 26.

45. I have also seen female characters of this type in postbellum temperance fiction, such as Margaret Hosmer's *Subtle Spell*, but Arthur provides the dominant example in antebellum texts.

46. Arthur, *Six Nights*, pp. 21–22.

47. Ibid., pp. 69–72.

48. Ibid., pp. 73–74, 78. Sargent gives a closely parallel psychological account in "Seed Time and Harvest," in *Temperance Tales*, 1:169.

49. Sargent, "Fritz Hazell," 1:109.

50. Marsh, *Putnam*, p. 15; Arthur, *Ten Nights*, p. 57; Sargent, "Nancy LeBaron," in *Temperance Tales*, 1:300; Rose, *Nora Wilmot*, p. 58; Brown, *Minnie Hermon*, pp. 96, 99, 203; Sargent, "An Irish Heart," in *Temperance Tales*, 1:215; Marsh, *Putnam*, p. 4; Lamas, *Glass*, p. 3; Brown, *Minnie Hermon*, pp. 36–37; Arthur, *Ten Nights*, p. 57; Rose, *Nora Wilmot*, p. 343; and Brown, *Minnie Hermon*, pp. 433, 194.

51. Gough, *Autobiography* (1845), p. 180.

52. Cheever, *Dream*, p. 9.

53. Ibid., pp. 7, 9–10. First published in the *Salem Landmark*, February 1835. The orthodox agenda of Cheever's tale was not lost on William Lloyd Garrison, who complained that Cheever's decision to make Deacon Giles a member of a liberal church was "influenced by a sectarian spirit." But Garrison also faulted the Unitarian attorney general for making too much of an issue of this. In general, the *Liberator*'s coverage of the Cheever case was extremely positive, and the entire fable was reprinted in the journal. *Liberator*, 4 July 1835 and 21 February 1835. A few years later, Cheever would offend Garrison and other radical liberals by issuing a pamphlet in support of capital punishment. See *Liberator*, 1 July 1842.

54. Arthur, *Six Nights*, p. 64; and Brown, *Minnie Hermon*, p. 116.

55. Sigourney and Smith, *Intemperate*, pp. 9–10. See Rowlandson, *Sovereignty*.

56. Sigourney and Smith, *Intemperate*, pp. 15, 12, 15.

57. Ibid., pp. 14–18.

58. At least one orthodox writer recognized the awkwardness of reformist angelology. In his fanciful *Tales of the Devils*, J. P. Brace—a onetime teacher of Harriet Beecher Stowe—asserted that while the souls of the damned are assigned as guardian demons to the living (and constrained to serve God's left-handed purposes), the saved are whisked away to a distant planet where they can relax, knowing that Christ will defeat the devil single-handedly. But Brace knew he was swimming against the tide. His demons appear infrequently in New England because no one believes in them, and his hero resists temptation by recalling his angelic mother's deathbed warning to "beware the first sin!" (pp. 18–19, 68, 207). Evidently by 1846 no U.S. writer could entirely avoid angelology.

59. Gough, *Autobiography* (1847), p. 114; and Rose, *Nora Wilmot*, p. 44.

60. In addition to Sargent's "My Mother's Gold Ring," see especially Arthur, "The Bottle and the Pledge," in *Six Nights*, pp. 265–339, in which demonic and angelic talismans are set against one another. Another temperance writer, Andrus V. Green, referred to the pledge as "the Declaration of Independence" (*Life*, p. 187).

61. Rose, *Nora Wilmot*, p. 12.

62. Sigourney, "The Widow and Her Son," in *Water-Drops*, pp. 45–46, 56, 63; Brown, *Minnie Hermon*, p. 239; and Rose, *Nora Wilmot*, p. 361.

63. Brown, *Minnie Hermon*, p. 320; and Rose, *Nora Wilmot*, pp. 318–19.

64. Sigourney and Smith, *Intemperate*, pp. 37, 6; and Rose, *Nora Wilmot*, p. 354.

65. Arthur, "The Touching Reproof," in *Temperance Tales*, 2:109–14.

66. Sargent, "Well Enough for the Vulgar," in *Temperance Tales*, 1:231–67; and "Nancy LeBaron," in *Temperance Tales*, 1:280. The most elaborate picture of this children's millennium that I have seen is in a postbellum temperance novel, Mary Dwinell Chellis, *Old Times*.

67. Sánchez-Eppler, "Temperance," p. 2.

68. Gough, *Autobiography* (1845), p. 150.

69. Sánchez-Eppler, "Temperance," pp. 8, 13. Another dimension of Sánchez-Eppler's argument is her claim that temperance writers were unwilling to embrace social reforms—such as the liberalizing of divorce law—that would have altered the balance of power within the family. Their appeals to child power thus subtly reinforced "traditional domestic and patriarchal structures" (p. 7). But here she is simply mistaken. T. S. Arthur and other temperance writers generally supported divorce reform and women's suffrage, while women's rights activists were almost invariably strong advocates of temperance.

70. Brown, *Minnie Hermon*, p. 275; and Rose, *Nora Wilmot*, p. 361.

71. Arthur, *Ten Nights*, pp. 23, 57, 73.

72. Ibid., pp. 78, 87. It should be noted, in light of Sánchez-Eppler's suggestion that physical intimacy between fathers and daughters exacerbates previous abuse, that Arthur does *not* depict Joe Morgan as physically or emotionally abusive to his family. Instead, Arthur represents the violence of men like Slade and the alcoholism of men like Morgan as separate effects of the alcohol system.

73. Arthur, *Ten Nights*, pp. 91–94.

74. Ibid., pp. 190–95.

75. Ibid., pp. 9, 233–35. My reading of *Ten Nights*, and in particular of Joe Morgan's centrality in its drama of salvation, may startle readers of Joseph R. Gusfield's influential study, *Symbolic Crusade*. In order to buttress his claim that temperance writers applied an individualistic model of sin to the problem of intemperance, Gusfield describes Joe Morgan thus: "The author of this classic implies that although Joe Morgan's self-indulgence led him to lose owner-

ship of his mill, he wasn't much of a businessman anyway. His character was already spotted and drinking was as much a sign of this as a contributor to further decline" (p. 32). Gusfield thus attributes to Arthur a doctrine of reprobation that is diametrically opposed to the universalist, millennial vision found in the novel.

Chapter 5

1. Douglass, *Narrative*, pp. 18–19. This is one of the most commented upon passages in Douglass's *Narrative* and, indeed, in the entire corpus of fugitive slave narratives. Treatments that have been helpful to me include Franchot, "Punishment"; Van Leer, "Reading Slavery," p. 131; Davis, *Leadership*, p. 28; and Hartman, *Scenes*, p. 3.

2. H. Bruce Franklin has similarly suggested that the persistent question in Douglass's *Narrative* is "What is a human being?" See "Animal Farm," p. 30.

3. Douglass, *My Bondage*, p. 179. This passage echoes Douglass's formulation in a letter to his former master, Thomas Auld: Frederick Douglass to Thomas Auld, 3 September 1848, in *Selected Speeches*, p. 113.

4. These anxieties are forcefully expressed by Baker, *Journey Back*, pp. 38–39; and Ziolkowski, "Antitheses," pp. 148–65.

5. Scarry, *Body in Pain*, p. 6. Unlike critics who see violence as intrinsic to language per se, Scarry is too good a liberal to locate the birth of language in the act of torture. For her, torture is not an original sin but a tyrannical usurpation of linguistic power.

6. Saidiya V. Hartman (*Scenes*, p. 3) makes a pointed case for the dangers of narrating violence. She refuses even to summarize Douglass's account of Esther's beating and instead calls "attention to the ease with which such stories are usually reiterated, the casualness with which they are circulated, and the consequences of this routine display of the slave's ravaged body." Hartman points out that the spectacle of violence can dull sensibilities and reinforce a view of slaves as no more than victims. These dangers must not be forgotten! But the dilemma cannot be solved by a once-for-all decision for or against the narration of violence. After all, the persistent turning away from scenes of violence can also lead to desensitization and outright denial. Ultimately, the task of coming to terms with violence, and with the full humanity of its victims, is an infinite one. The only path, it seems to me, is to look squarely at the violence of slavery while placing it in the context of the inexhaustible complexity of slave humanity.

7. In the wake of the Holocaust, Irving Greenberg proposed as a rule that "no statement, theological or otherwise, should be made that would not be credible in the presence of the burning children." Cited in Roth and Berenbaum, *Holocaust*, p. 262.

8. Garrison, "Preface," in Douglass, *Narrative*, pp. 3–4.

9. William Andrews has noted that in slave autobiographies prior to 1836 "the slavery of sin received much more condemnation than the sin of slavery" (*To Tell*, p. 44).

10. Douglass, *My Bondage*, p. 366.

11. Freeborn blacks, including David Walker, Maria Stewart, Henry Highland Garnet, and Martin Delany, played leading roles within abolitionism from the very beginning.

12. Andrews, *To Tell*, pp. 138, 97–98, 306; Gates, "Binary Oppositions," p. 62; Sundquist, *Frederick Douglass*, p. 3; and Stone, "Identity," p. 8. By comparison, Henry David Thoreau's *Week on the Concord and Merrimack Rivers* sold 219 copies between 1849 and 1853; Nathaniel Hawthorne's *Blithedale Romance* sold out a first edition of 5,000 but stalled in its second edition; Fanny Fern's *Fern Leaves from Fanny's Portfolio* sold 70,000 copies in 1853; and Harriet Beecher Stowe's *Uncle Tom's Cabin* broke the 300,000 mark within a year of publication. See Hart, *Popular Book*, pp. 92–93, 112.

13. Gates, "Wheatley to Douglass," pp. 47–65.

14. Douglass, "The Anti-Slavery Movement," 19 March 1855, in *Papers*, ser. 1, 3:47. In

addition to Douglass's narratives, fugitive slave narratives to be examined here include those of Charles Ball, Moses Roper, James Williams, Moses Grandy, Lewis and Milton Clarke, William Wells Brown, Henry Watson, Henry Bibb, James W. C. Pennington, Henry Box Brown, Sojourner Truth, John Brown, Solomon Northup, Peter Randolph, Austin Steward, J. W. Loguen, and Harriet Jacobs. The Sojourner Truth and Solomon Northup narratives do not exactly fit my definition of the fugitive slave narrative (neither Truth nor Northup was precisely a "fugitive"), but I have included them because they were published under abolitionist auspices and follow many of the conventions established by such fugitive slave narrators as Douglass. The Ball, Roper, Clarke, Wells Brown, Henson, Bibb, Pennington, and John Brown narratives, among others, appear in a new edition, *I Was Born a Slave*, which I have used for my citations. Citations to the Douglass autobiographies are from the Library of America edition.

15. Both of these approaches have proliferated dramatically in recent decades. The most significant examples of the former approach include Blassingame, *Slave Community*; Rawick, *Sundown to Sunup*; Genovese, *Roll, Jordan, Roll*; Levine, *Black Culture*; Raboteau, *Slave Religion*; and Stuckey, *Slave Culture*. Literary treatments of the slave narrative include Starling, *Slave Narrative*; Foster, *Witnessing Slavery*; Stepto, *From Behind the Veil*; Andrews, *To Tell*; and Smith, *Self-Discovery*. Central essays from both scholarly traditions appear in Davis and Gates, *Slave's Narrative*.

16. Winks, "Making," p. 113.

17. Gates, "Wheatley to Douglass," p. 59; Blassingame, "Using the Testimony," p. 81; and Olney, "'I Was Born,'" p. 154.

18. Ball, *Slavery*, 1:264.

19. Harding, *There Is a River*; Hopkins and Cummings, *Cut Loose*; Pinn, *Why Lord?*; and Goatley, *Were You There?*

20. Follen, "Remember the Slave," p. 317.

21. Cited in Hartman, *Scenes*, p. 19.

22. Frederick Douglass to William Lloyd Garrison, 8 November 1842, in *Selected Speeches*, pp. 6, 8. In a letter to his former master, Douglass similarly asked how he would feel "were I some dark night in company with a band of hardened villains, to enter the precincts of your elegant dwelling and seize the person of your own lovely daughter Amanda." Douglass to Thomas Auld, 3 September 1848, *Liberator*, 22 September 1848, in *Selected Speeches*, p. 116.

23. *Liberator*, 1 January 1831. Garrison never tired of this sort of poetry. When his first child was born, for example, he wrote a celebratory poem to this "dearest child of all this populous earth / Yet no more precious than the meanest slave!" He even used a sentimental appeal in the letter he wrote to Massachusetts merchant Francis Todd, while he was in jail for slandering Todd by accusing him of slave trading. "Suppose you and your family," Garrison asked, "were seized on execution, and sold at public auction: a New Orleans planter buys your children—a Georgian, your wife—a South Carolinian, yourself: would one of your townsmen . . . be blameless for transporting you all thither, though familiar with all these afflicting circumstances?" See Garrison and Garrison, *William Lloyd Garrison*, 2:101, 1:180.

24. Two recent studies that emphasize Garrison's dependence on the black movement against colonizationism are Goodman, *Of One Blood*, pp. 36–37, 57; and Aptheker, *Abolitionism*, p. 67. Aptheker (p. xiii) rightly highlights the fact that there was a well-established black abolitionist movement—with journals, organizations, and a variety of activist strategies—well before the period of "black-white united efforts" discussed in this chapter.

25. Huston, "Experiential Basis," pp. 633–34.

26. *Liberator*, 12 February 1831.

27. *Liberator*, 22 January 1831 and 12 February 1831.

28. Mayer, *All on Fire*, p. 75.

29. *Liberator*, 1 January 1831 and 29 January 1831.

30. *Liberator*, 5 February 1831.

31 Williams, *Authentic Narrative*, p. xvii.

32. Weld, *American Slavery*; Barnes, *Antislavery Impulse*, p. 139; Abzug, *Passionate Liberator*, p. 211; and Clark, 'Sacred Rights.' Ironically, Weld had previously expressed reservations about abolitionists' reliance on such "*instances of cruelty.*" They "have a tendency," he wrote to a friend, "to turn the public mind from the crowning horror of slavery, to a mere incidental. . . . At the *present crisis*, the inflictions of slavery on mind—its prostration of conscience—its reduction of accountability to a chattel—its destruction of personality—its death-stab into the soul of the slave—should constitute the main prominence before the public mind." Barnes and Dumond, *Letters*, 1:296; and Abzug, *Passionate Liberator*, p. 134.

33. *Liberator*, 21 August 1837; and Williams, *Authentic Narrative*, pp. xx, xix. The *Liberator*'s announcement of this publication noted that Williams's testimony had been heard not only by Whittier but also by James Mott, Lewis Tappan, Elizur Wright Jr., Charles Follen, James Birney, and other leading abolitionists. *Liberator*, 13 July 1838.

34. Roper, *Narrative*, 1:496; Andrews, *To Tell*, pp. 6, 63, 90.

35. Ball, *Slavery* (1837), pp. xi, ii.

36. Ball, *Slavery*, 1:329-30, 419-20, 477; Williams, *Authentic Narrative*, pp. 52, 78-79; and Roper, *Narrative*, 1:497, 505, 498, 506.

37. This was true even of early oral versions of Frederick Douglass's narrative. In an 1845 speech, "My Slave Experience in Maryland," he actually focused entirely on the experiences of *other* slaves victimized by harsh masters and overseers. Douglass, "My Slave Experience in Maryland," 6 May 1845, in *Papers*, ser. 1, 1:31-32.

38. Williams, *Authentic Narrative*, pp. 43, 51.

39. Ball, *Slavery*, 1:307-8, 332-40, 401-4, 406.

40. Ibid., 1:422-24.

41. Ball, *Slavery*, 1:426; Williams, *Authentic Narrative*, pp. 66-67.

42. Williams, *Authentic Narrative*, p. 67; and Ball, *Slavery*, 1:427.

43. Williams, *Authentic Narrative*, p. 101; and Ball, *Slavery*, 1:485.

44. Starling, *Slave Narrative*, p. 241.

45. Olney, "'I Was Born,'" p. 161.

46. Box Brown, *Narrative*, pp. vi, vii, v. Such passages, Saidiya Hartman rightly points out, "increase the difficulty of beholding black suffering since the endeavor to bring pain close exploits the spectacle of the body in pain and oddly confirms the spectral character of suffering and the inability to witness the captive's pain." Hartman, *Scenes of Subjection*, p. 20.

47. Andrews, *To Tell*, p. 138.

48. "The Black Saxons," in *Child Reader*, pp. 182-91.

49. "Annette Gray," in *Child Reader*, pp. 200-208.

50. Bibb, *Narrative*, 2:80.

51. I am thus skeptical of arguments that use the failings of putatively liberal institutions to indict liberalism as such. Saidiya Hartman, for example, argues that both during and after slavery "violence and domination [were] enabled by the recognition of humanity, licensed by the invocation of rights, and justified on the grounds of liberty and freedom" (*Scenes*, p. 6). But her examples all hinge on either the partial adherence to liberal ideals or their flawed institutionalization. Slaveholders recognized their slaves' humanity only when they perpetrated crimes. The Constitution made possession of property the basis of recognizable humanity. The agents of Reconstruction failed to look deeply enough into the ex-slaves' humanity to see the "burdens" of racism and debt they still carried. The solution to all these problems was more liberalism, not less; without "recognition of humanity" as a guiding norm, they could not even be identified *as* problems. Hartman's critique of liberal institutions actually continues the liberal tradition as embodied in Thomas Jefferson's call for a new revolution in every generation and William Lloyd Garrison's hostility to the Constitution.

52. "The atrocities of slavery," Jenny Franchot has aptly commented, "find their most powerful synecdoche in the silenced figure of the slave mother forced to endure rape, concubinage, and the theft of her children" ("Punishment," p. 141).

53. Ball, *Slavery*, 1:267. My reading follows Nancy Jay's analysis of sacrifice in *Throughout Your Generations*.

54. Gilbert, *Sojourner Truth*, pp. 52–53.

55. Ball, *Slavery*, 1:340; and Wells Brown, *Narrative*, 1:684–85.

56. In interpreting these texts, it is important to remember that fugitive slave narrators did not speak for all slaves. Because escape was the central religious event of their lives, they had trouble imagining the religious meaning of a life that did not include escape. But, as recent studies of "slave culture" have shown, many slaves found profound meaning in family life or participation in the slave church, escaping spiritually without ever leaving the plantation. Yet their experience may be no more representative than that of the fugitive slave narrators. Many other slaves escaped neither physically nor spiritually but succumbed to despair or violent death.

57. Douglass, *My Bondage*, pp. 147, 176.

58. Ibid., pp. 177–79.

59. Ball, *Slavery*, 1:289; Bibb, *Narrative*, 2:48; Box Brown, *Narrative*, p. 35; Williams, *Authentic Narrative*, pp. 57, 59; Douglass, *Narrative*, pp. 17, 78; and Douglass, *My Bondage*, pp. 201, 171.

60. Douglass, *Narrative*, pp. 35, 40, 37; and Douglass, *My Bondage*, p. 223.

61. Roper, *Narrative*, 1:491; Hildreth, *Archy Moore*, 1:31; and Northup, *Narrative*, 2:183–84.

62. Northup, *Narrative*, 2:264.

63. Lane, *Narrative*, p. 20; and Randolph, *Sketches*, p. 73.

64. Douglass, *My Bondage*, pp. 402–3; *Putnam's Monthly Magazine*, November 1855, in Davis and Gates, *Slave's Narrative*, p. 30; and Ball, *Slavery*, 1:424.

65. Clarke and Clarke, *Narratives*, 1:662; Pennington, *Fugitive Blacksmith*, 2:108; Bibb, *Narrative*, 2:13; and Douglass, *My Bondage*, pp. 220, 165.

66. Williams, *Authentic Narrative*, p. 71; Clarke and Clark, *Narratives*, 1:611; and Loguen, *J. W. Loguen*, pp. 44–45.

67. Bibb, *Narrative*, 2:59.

68. Douglass, *My Bondage*, pp. 97–98; Watson, *Narrative*, p. 39; Bibb, *Narrative*, 2:57; and Wells Brown, *Narrative*, 1:703.

69. Box Brown, *Narrative*, pp. 16, 28; Williams, *Authentic Narrative*, pp. 71–73; and Grandy, *Narrative*, pp. 35–36.

70. Gibson, "Faith," pp. 84–98; and O'Meally, "Text," p. 93.

71. Northup, *Narrative*, 2:198; Roper, *Narrative*; 1:505; Gilbert, *Sojourner Truth*, p. 27.

72. Loguen, *J. W. Loguen*, p. 48; and Wells Brown, *Narrative*, 1:684.

73. Williams, *Authentic Narrative*, pp. xix-xx.

74. Douglass, *Narrative*, p. 24.

75. Bibb, *Narrative*, 2:15; Pennington, *Fugitive Blacksmith*, 2:117.

76. One might ask, of course, if Douglass, Bibb, and Pennington were entirely honest in suggesting that their recognition of the process of enslavement was simultaneous with their actual experience of slavery's violence. It may be that in writing their narratives they conflated later reflections on the blood-stained gate experience with the experience itself.

77. Douglass, *My Bondage*, p. 367.

78. Andrews, *To Tell*, p. xi; and Starling, *Slave Narrative*, p. 333. The significance of the fugitive slave narrators' status as autobiographical creators has been emphasized by many scholars, including Andrews, *To Tell*, pp. 7, 99–105; and Smith, *Self-Discovery*, p. 2. The continuity between the liberal tradition of the Declaration of Independence and the fugitive

slave narrative has been noted by Andrews, *To Tell*, p. 14; and Fishkin and Peterson, "'We Hold,'" pp. 190, 193.

79. Bibb, *Narrative*, 2:13; Douglass, *My Bondage*, p. 139; and Loguen, *J. W. Loguen*, p. 28. See also Williams, *Authentic Narrative*, p. 29, Hildreth, *Archy Moore*, 1:14; Lane, *Narrative*, pp. 5–6; and Henson, *Life*, 1:725.

80. Clarke and Clark, *Narratives*, 1:634.

81. Ball, *Slavery*, 1:442, 454; Grandy, *Narrative*, p. 25; Wells Brown, *Narrative*, 1:712; and Bibb, *Narrative*, 2:64.

82. Pennington, *Fugitive Blacksmith*, 2:119, 140, 153.

83. Ibid., 2:151.

84. Douglass, *Narrative*, p. 36; see also Douglass, *My Bondage*, p. 213.

85. Douglass, *Narrative*, p. 60.

86. Douglass, *My Bondage*, p. 278; and Douglass, *Narrative*, pp. 58, 65. This passage closely parallels the account of Uncle Tom's despair in *Uncle Tom's Cabin*.

87. Van Leer, "Reading Slavery," pp. 126–27; Kibbey, "Language," pp. 149–50; and Kibbey and Stepto, "Antilanguage," p. 168. Indeed, Douglass may have seen the analogy between the despair he experienced as a slave and the despair liberals attributed to the doctrine of original sin. At least, in 1848 he referred to the widespread belief in black inferiority as a "gloomy doctrine" under which "many of us have sunk under the pall of despondency." Unitarian liberals often used the phrase "gloomy doctrine" to describe the belief in original sin. See Douglass, "An Address to the Colored People of the United States," 29 September 1848, in *Selected Speeches*, p. 118.

88. Douglass, cited in Gibson, "Faith," p. 91; and Douglass, *My Bondage*, p. 350. By suggesting that God and right had been vindicated only in the moment of escape, Douglass implicitly anticipated the controversial thesis of historian Stanley Elkins, who described Southern slavery as a "total institution"—like a Nazi concentration camp—that partly succeeded in dehumanizing its victims. More recent historians have suggested that slave humanity was vindicated not only in escape but also in the autonomy of slave culture, most particularly in the family and the "invisible institution" of slave religion. It is probably significant that Douglass and other fugitive slave narrators had limited exposure to either slave families or the slave church, and may not have appreciated the analogies between these institutions and their own experience of freedom. Still, Elkins is right to insist that research on slave culture not be used to deny the "damage" of slavery. Neither the North, the family, nor the church could provide a refuge capacious enough for everyone whose soul and body were maimed by slavery's violence. See Elkins, *Slavery*; and Lane, *Debate over Slavery*.

89. This is the argument of Franchot, "Punishment"; Van Leer, "Reading Slavery"; and McDowell, "First Place."

90. Lydia Maria Child, "Introduction," in Jacobs, *Incidents*, p. 4.

91. Scholars have only gradually clarified the fact that what was new about woman-authored slave narratives like that of Harriet Jacobs was their representation not of women's bodies but of women's voices. Many earlier accounts seem to take Child's assertion about the "veiling" of sexual exploitation at face value. Thus, in 1985 Jean Fagan Yellin introduced the Jacobs narrative to the scholarly world by asserting that it was "to my knowledge, the only slave narrative that takes as its subject the sexual exploitation of female slaves—thus centering on sexual oppression as well as oppression of race and condition." By 1987, when her edition of the narrative came out, she had substantially clarified the claim: "Jacobs's achievement was the transformation of herself into a literary subject in and through the creation of her narrator, Linda Brent. . . . What finally dominates is a new voice." Unfortunately, Yellin's earlier formulation continues to echo in the work of scholars who have incorporated Jacobs's witness, as interpreted by Yellin, into theological or other constructive projects. Thus, in 1996 James Poling wrote that Jacobs's

text was "one of the few slave narratives to . . . speak openly about sexual abuse of Black women by slaveholders." See Yellin, "Texts and Contexts," p. 263; Yellin, "Introduction," in Jacobs, *Incidents*, pp. xiii–xiv; and Poling, *Deliver Us*, p. 6.

92. Hildreth, *Archy Moore*, 2:37–38, 115.

93. Greven, *Protestant Temperament*, p. 28.

94. Douglass, *My Bondage*, p. 157; Bibb, *Narrative*, 2:22; and Gilbert, *Sojourner Truth*, p. 37.

95. Williams, *Authentic Narrative*, pp. 62–64.

96. Ibid., pp. 61–62.

97. Douglass, *My Bondage*, pp. 136, 155. In his letter to his former master, Douglass did not mention his mother at all but stressed the ill-treatment of his sisters and demanded that the master "send me my grandmother!" because "she was to me a mother, and a father, so far as hard toil for my comfort could make her such." Douglass to Thomas Auld, 3 September 1848, *Liberator*, 22 September 1848, in *Selected Speeches*, p. 116.

98. Northup, *Narrative*, 2:247, 275–78.

99. Ibid., 2:300.

Chapter 6

1. Hedrick, *Stowe*, p. vii.

2. Douglas, *Feminization*, p. 12; and Yellin, "Doing It Herself," p. 102.

3. Tompkins, *Sensational Designs*, p. 126; and Fisher, *Hard Facts*, pp. 3–4.

4. Douglas, "Introduction," in Stowe, *Uncle Tom*, p. 34. Other critics who have highlighted Stowe's mastery of multiple voices include Wilson, *Patriotic Gore*, pp. 5–6; O'Connell, "Magic," p. 13; and Kirsthardt, "Flirting," pp. 37–56.

5. Stowe, *Oldtown Folks*, p. 48; and Stowe cited in Kelley, *Private Woman*, p. 292. In characterizing Stowe as primarily a Christian liberal—albeit an idiosyncratic and ambivalent one—I am dissenting from the judgments of many critics. Charles H. Foster, for example, refers to "the insistently Puritan nature" of Stowe's work and claims that she abandoned Edwardsean orthodoxy only after reading Oliver Wendell Holmes's *Elsie Venner* in 1860. Josephine Donovan claims that the "dominant religious ethos" of *Uncle Tom's Cabin* is "Edwardsean Calvinism." And Helen Petter Westra suggests that Stowe was "a self-described product of Calvinism" who "generally upheld its views of God's sovereignty, humanity's fall, Christ's redemptive work, and the Bible's infallibility." Though I think Westra is simply wrong about sovereignty and infallibility, I do not regard these arguments as wholly without merit. Stowe shared many of Edwards's key themes: millennialism, divine benevolence, the religious affections. These were precisely the Edwardsean themes most valued by such liberals as Sedgwick, Lee, and Child—not to mention Ralph Waldo Emerson. It is useful, for some purposes, to talk about an Edwardsean tradition that includes *all* these figures. But if one is using "orthodox" and "liberal" to designate competing theological options in the nineteenth-century United States, as I am, it is *not* useful to classify Stowe as orthodox. See Foster, *Rungless Ladder*, pp. 100, 134; Donovan, *Uncle Tom*, 7; and Westra, "Confronting Antichrist," p. 141. My assessment of Stowe is similar to that of Dorothy Berkson, who argues that Stowe regarded the Edwardseanism of her youth as a "masculine, Old Testament Calvinism" and a "patriarchal system of values" diametrically opposed to her own millennial outlook ("Millennial Politics," pp. 244–51).

6. Stowe, *Minister's Wooing*, p. 189; and Stowe, *Oldtown Folks*, pp. 398, 161–62.

7. Stowe, *Uncle Tom*, p. 209; and Stowe, *Dred*, 1:209.

8. Stowe, *Uncle Tom*, pp. 367, 408; Stowe, *Dred*, 1:83, 81; and Hedrick, *Stowe*, p. 261. Hedrick suggests that Stowe was reacting against the stifling masculine culture of Andover Seminary, where Calvin Stowe became professor of Bible shortly after the completion of *Uncle Tom's Cabin*.

This is persuasive, yet I would add that Stowe would not have been able to react in this way had she not been familiar and sympathetic with the liberal novelistic tradition pioneered by Sedgwick.

9. Stowe, *Uncle Tom*, p. 119; and Stowe, *Dred*, 1:319.

10. Stowe, *Dred*, 2:57–58; and Stowe, *Uncle Tom*, pp. 201, 272, 184.

11. Cain, *William Lloyd Garrison*, p. 134.

12. Stowe, *Uncle Tom*, pp. 278, 234–35, 333; and Stowe, *Dred*, 1:263.

13. Stowe, *Uncle Tom*, p. 229.

14. Stowe, *Dred*, 2:67.

15. Stowe, *Dred*, 1:327; and Stowe, *Uncle Tom*, p. 204.

16. This process is explored in detail in Turner, *Without God*, pp. 171–202.

17. Stowe, *Dred*, 2:134, 1:327, 1:435–36.

18. Nuernberg, "Rhetoric of Race," p. 255.

19. Stowe, *Dred*, 2:66, 90; and Stowe, *Uncle Tom*, pp. 332, 268.

20. Stowe, *Uncle Tom*, pp. 47, 46–47, 53. Stowe thus makes it clear at the outset that she does not accept the conservative view of woman's "sphere." Mrs. Shelby's humanity must be exercised beyond her "sphere" in order to be effective.

21. Ibid., pp. 52, 57, 61, 62.

22. Ibid., pp. 141–44.

23. Ibid., pp. 144, 160.

24. Ibid., pp. 215–16.

25. Ibid., pp. 220, 288, 544.

26. Stowe's racialism can perhaps be traced to the 1837–38 Cincinnati lectures of Alexander Kinmont, who argued that African civilization would ultimately preempt European because the Africans' superior capacities for mercy and benevolence enabled them to be more truly Christian. See Frederickson, *Black Image*, pp. 104–106; and Nuernberg, "Rhetoric of Race," p. 259. (Lydia Maria Child, another admirer of Kinmont, similarly claimed that Africans "have the strongest tendency to devotion" of all people. She predicted that they would take the leading role "whenever the age of Moral Sentiment arrives." See "Letters from New York, No. 12," 2 December 1841, in *Child Reader*, pp. 213–14.) A number of critics have pointed out that Stowe's romantic racialism went hand in hand with a tendency to dehumanize blacks. In describing the slave drivers Sambo and Quimbo, for example, Stowe comments that "brutal men are lower even than the animals," and in *Dred* she refers to the "large, rough, black paws" of a sympathetic black character (*Uncle Tom*, p. 493; and *Dred*, 1:120). Sarah Ducksworth has even shown that Stowe depicted Uncle Tom's children as playful, greedy animals indifferent to their parents' plight. "Stowe's Construction," p. 218.

27. Stowe, *Uncle Tom*, pp. 60, 298, 62.

28. The presence of so many mulattos and quadroons in antislavery writing is also, as Karen Sánchez-Eppler points out, a subtle but persistent reminder of the repeated rapes perpetrated against slave women. Sánchez-Eppler, "Bodily Bonds," p. 104.

29. Stowe, *Uncle Tom*, p. 56.

30. Ibid., pp. 191, 183.

31. Ibid., p. 224.

32. Ibid., p. 291.

33. Ibid., pp. 191, 292.

34. Richard Yarborough's acid comment on Tom and George is appropriate here: "One can imagine that, like matter and antimatter, if they were forced into contact, the result would be an explosion of immeasurable force that would leave only Tom, for he, not George, is Stowe's real hero." "Strategies," p. 45.

35. Stowe, *Uncle Tom*, pp. 90, 382, 318, 344, 365, 379.

36. Ibid., p. 429.

37. Fiedler, *Love and Death*, p. 266.

38. James Baldwin, most pointedly, accused Stowe of promoting "theological terror," leading another critic to comment that her real problem was "a profound theological *despair*—and . . . an equally profound *mortal* terror. . . . it is the terror of *living*, of facing a world in which unendurable atrocities must be endured and in which worse atrocities may loom in the future—rather than the terror of dying—that infuses the novel" (Bellin, "Up to Heaven's Gate," p. 288). But even among Stowe's defenders, Jane Tompkins suggests that "in *Uncle Tom's Cabin*, death is the equivalent not of defeat but of victory; it brings an access of power, not a loss of it; it is not only the crowning achievement of life, it *is* life." Isabelle White agrees, insisting on the significance of Stowe's conviction "that death is victory and brings an access to power." Both suggest that this is a characteristically *religious* theory of power and that its underlying principle is a stark inversion of nonreligious models of power. In this theory, Tompkins states, "the ordinary or 'common sense' view of what is efficacious and what is not . . . is simply reversed." "Death," White elaborates, "can be a means of breaking through ordinary human limitations, or in the cases of a child and a slave, extraordinary human limitations. Dying, the only complete release from the self-concern of extreme individualism, provides the occasion for a dramatic condemnation of an unsatisfying world." Embedded here are the profoundly illiberal assumptions that there is an inevitable conflict between communal solidarity and individual self-concern, and that what is "unsatisfying" is the world itself rather than the evils that afflict it. Thomas P. Joswick, who is far less sympathetic to this position than Tompkins and White, has likewise suggested that an illiberal disdain for earthly affairs is characteristic of both Stowe's religion and religion in general. "Does the 'crown without the conflict,'" he asks, "characterize the one belief that shapes a coherent system of religious virtues—the conviction that a divine, which is to say an excessive, power is everywhere invested in this life at little cost to those whose fortunes will be gloriously transformed into an eternal victory?" The assumption that sheer secularism (indeed, a secularism that is characteristically masculine and violent) is the only alternative to religious otherworldliness is common among twentieth-century academics; indeed, it is one of the few assumptions that Tompkins and White share with Ann Douglas and Perry Miller. But it is a dangerous assumption to bring to the antebellum period, when the very character of religion in a democratic society was still being determined. See Tompkins, *Sensational Designs*, pp. 127–28; White, "Sentimentality," p. 103; and Joswick, "'Crown,'" p. 254.

39. Stowe, *Uncle Tom*, p. 202.

40. Ibid., p. 210.

41. Ibid., pp. 504, 523, 553.

42. Ibid., p. 554. Curiously, Stowe introduces Tom's vision by suggesting a purely naturalistic explanation for it: "When a heavy weight presses the soul to the lowest level at which endurance is possible, there is an instant and desperate effort of every physical and moral nerve to throw off the weight; and hence the heaviest anguish often precedes a return tide of joy and courage." It is not quite clear how she means this to shape our reading of the vision itself, but I would suggest that the effect is one of second naïveté: we know there are all sorts of psychological explanations for Tom's experience, but yet the power still inheres in the experience itself.

43. Ibid., p. 556.

44. Ibid., p. 514; and Stowe, *Dred*, 1:227.

45. Stowe, *Minister's Wooing*, p. 263.

46. Laurence Buell has called Uncle Tom the first Christ figure in American literature. My reading of *Margaret* and *Ten Nights in a Bar-Room*, however, suggests, that Tom was not so much the first as the most prominent of a pantheon of midcentury Christs that also included Margaret Hart, Mary Morgan, Little Eva, and Billy Budd. Even the *Liberator* added an image of the risen Christ to its masthead on 31 May 1850, though there he is clearly represented as a liberator rather than a sacrificial victim. See Buell, *New England*, p. 186; and Wolff, "'Masculinity,'" p. 602.

47. Cassy herself might be considered a Christ figure in terms of the ransom theory, for her escape from Legree involves an elaborate subterfuge in which she allows Legree's own violence to defeat itself. (He is superstitious, and she persuades him that a garret is haunted by his past victims and then hides there.) But there are no clues to suggest that Stowe actually regarded Cassy as a Christ figure. This interpretation occurred to me after reading Kathleen Margaret Lant's article on Cassy, "Unsung Hero," pp. 47–71. Lant herself, however, sees Cassy's subterfuge not as a nonviolent manipulation of Legree's violence but as a psychological rape of Legree.

48. Stowe, *Uncle Tom*, p. 540. The consequences of Stowe's messianic vision of Uncle Tom for subsequent African American culture are traced in Moses, *Black Messiahs*.

49. Sundquist, *New Essays*, p. 6.

50. Stowe, "The Freeman's Dream; A Parable," *National Era*, 1 August 1850, in *Oxford*, pp. 57–58. See Hedrick, *Stowe*, p. 206.

51. Stowe, *Uncle Tom*, pp. 202, 479.

52. Ibid., pp. 342–43, 391, 344.

53. Ibid., pp. 344, 629.

54. Stowe, *Dred*, 1:249, 251.

55. Ibid., 1:247–48, 331, 341.

56. Ibid., 1:257, 263, 2:79.

57. Ibid., 2:98, 143.

58. Gilbert, *Sojourner Truth*, pp. 33, 69.

59. Stowe, *Dred*, 2:98, 142–45.

60. Ibid., 2:145.

61. Both Jane Tompkins and Isabelle White make similar points. Tompkins argues that "in terms of its own conception of power . . . the novel was a political failure. Stowe conceived [*Uncle Tom's Cabin*] as an instrument for bringing about the day when the world would be ruled not by force, but by Christian love." White suggests that "the novel calls for action but reveals the ultimate insignificance of that action." Tompkins, *Sensational Designs*, p. 141; and White, "Sentimentality," p. 112.

Chapter 7

1. Perry, *Radical Abolitionism*, pp. 231–67. For other scholarly accounts, see Demos, "Antislavery Movement," and Friedman, "Antebellum American Abolitionism."

2. *Liberator*, 16 September 1859.

3. William Lloyd Garrison to Helen Eliza Garrison, 16 February 1854, in *Letters*, 4:292.

4. *Liberator*, 7 July 1854; Wright cited in Garrison and Garrison, *William Lloyd Garrison*, 3:425; Aptheker, *Abolitionism*, 127; and *Liberator*, 4 January 1856. See also Ziegler, *Advocates*, p. 116.

5. Child, "The Kansas Emigrants," in *Autumnal Leaves*, pp. 328, 344, 356–57, 360, 361, 363.

6. Garrison, "The Gospel and Sharp's Rifles," *Liberator*, 14 March 1856; Garrison, "Peace and War," *Liberator*, 4 April 1856; and *Liberator*, 6 June 1858.

7. Garrison, "The Presidential Election," *Liberator*, 17 October 1856; and Garrison and Garrison, *William Lloyd Garrison*, 3:447, 484.

8. *Liberator*, 28 July 1854 and 16 September 1859. Lewis Perry (*Radical Abolitionism*, pp. 239, 233, 248–49) makes a similar point when he argues that the nonresistant "accommodation" stemmed from "intellectual loopholes in their doctrine" that were "discernible almost from the start of nonresistance." Perry suggests that because the nonresistants acknowledged no authority apart from the divine will as revealed to the individual, they lacked a secure ethical criterion for distinguishing among various tactics for fulfilling God's will. "Private judgment"

was their supreme value, and "In their fight to vindicate the virtues of voluntarism and independent understanding over the vices of coercion and corporate declarations, their own doctrine allowed wide toleration of *means*." It is not clear, though, just what Perry means by "toleration." If it means only that the Garrisonians were willing to honor those who used a variety of means, then he is certainly correct. But if he means that they were personally willing to use a variety of means, then he is not correct—at least not in Garrison's case.

9. Garrison, "Preface," in Douglass, *Narrative*, pp. 3–4.

10. Ibid., p. 8.

11. Douglass, *My Bondage*, p. 366; and Douglass, *Narrative*, p. 60.

12. Douglass, *My Bondage*, p. 350. Interestingly, Douglass's actual escape is not a climactic moment in the 1845 *Narrative*, which suggests that Douglass did not truly feel free until he commenced his lecturing career. Perhaps Douglass placed this passage in *My Bondage* to downplay his dependence on the Garrisonian abolitionists.

13. Garrison, "Anti-Slavery Excursion to Cape Cod," *Liberator*, 1 July 1842.

14. Douglass, "Country, Conscience, and the Anti-Slavery Cause," 11 May 1847, in *Papers*, ser. 1, 2:68; Martin, *Mind*, p. 57; Douglass, "A Day, a Deed, an Event, Glorious in the Annals of Philanthropy," 1 August 1848, in *Papers*, ser. 1, 2:133, 142; and Douglass, *My Bondage*, p. 367.

15. Cook, "Fighting with Breath," pp. 131–32. Douglass biographer Waldo E. Martin Jr. expresses a general consensus when he writes that the young Douglass "apparently could not embrace and thus deemphasized the Garrisonian doctrine of nonresistance" (Martin, *Mind*, p. 24).

16. Douglass, *Narrative*, pp. 60, 65.

17. Yarborough, "Race, Violence," p. 174. Yarborough suggests that Douglass's tortured language reflects the constraints placed on his writing by white expectations, which deprived blacks of full freedom of action and then condemned them for resorting to violence and other socially unacceptable practices. But it seems to me that the damned-if-you-do-and-damned-if-you-don't attitude of white readers may have had a paradoxically liberating effect on Douglass. Since he knew he could be dehumanized either for resorting to violence or for refusing to defend himself, what was to prevent him from saying what he truly thought?

18. Douglass, *Narrative*, pp. 36, 37–38, 96, 36.

19. Ibid., p. 42.

20. Ibid., p. 65.

21. For this reason, H. Bruce Franklin has suggested that this passage is a stumbling block for professors of literature, who would rather rely on powerful words than on violent deeds. Though a professor of theology, not literature, the present author might be included among this group. See Franklin, "Animal Farm," p. 40. Similarly, Thad Ziolkowski argues that the *Narrative*'s "project of representation . . . occurs between the spectacle of violence (both physical and symbolic) and the acquisition of literacy." "Antitheses," pp. 148–65.

22. Douglass had not intended for his friendship with Smith to lead to a radical break with Garrison, but their subsequent conflict was marked by harsh and vindictive rhetoric on both sides. In 1853, for example, Garrison wrote that Douglass was "as thoroughly changed in his spirit as was ever 'arch-angel ruined'" (*Liberator*, 16 December 1853). The harshness probably had less to do with ideological differences than with the psychological dynamics of their relationship. Both Douglass and Garrison had been abandoned in their youth by violent and alcoholic fathers, and their friendship often echoed the difficult dynamics of their childhoods. By contrast, Garrison and Smith were actually on good terms in the 1850s. Smith participated in the American Anti-Slavery Society meeting in Syracuse in 1851 and later that year wrote Garrison a letter praising his collected speeches (Garrison and Garrison, *William Lloyd Garrison*, 3:337–38). For more on Douglass and Smith, see McKivigan, "Frederick Douglass–Gerrit Smith."

23. Douglass, "Speech on John Brown," 3 December 1860, in *Papers*, ser. 1, 3:413.

24. Douglass, "A Call to Work," *Frederick Douglass' Paper*, 19 November 1852, in *Selected Speeches*, p. 212; and Douglass, "The Anti-Slavery Movement," 19 March 1855, in *Papers*, ser. 1, 3:44, 46.

25. Douglass to William Still, 2 July 1860, in *Selected Speeches*, p. 398; and Douglass, "Freedom's Battle at Christiana," *Frederick Douglass' Paper*, 25 September 1851, in *Selected Speeches*, p. 179.

26. Douglass, "Is It Right and Wise to Kill a Kidnapper?" *Frederick Douglass' Paper*, 2 June 1854, in *Selected Speeches*, pp. 277–80.

27. The fact that Douglass found no inherent value in the shedding of blood is evidenced by his consistent opposition to capital punishment. At an 1858 meeting, for example, he proposed resolutions that "the degree to which the sacredness of human life has been exemplified in all ages of the world, has been the truest index of the measure of human progress," and that capital punishment violated "the law of eternal goodness written on the constitution of man by his Maker" ("Resolutions," 7 October 1858, *Liberator*, 22 October 1858, in *Selected Speeches*, p. 370).

28. In so doing he built on a long tradition of abolitionist reflection on this event. For an analysis of this tradition, see Harrold, "Romanticizing."

29. Douglass, "The Heroic Slave," in *Selected Speeches*, pp. 221–22.

30. Ibid., p. 245.

31. Douglass, *Narrative*, p. 64; and Douglass, *My Bondage*, pp. 282–83.

32. Douglass, *My Bondage*, pp. 283–86.

33. Ibid., p. 286.

34. Douglass also failed to clarify whether "man" in this passage means "human" or "male," and thus does not indicate whether he is charting a universal or a gender-specific path to freedom. Certainly, he did not expressly advocate violence by female slaves. For a reflection on this problem, see Yarborough, "Race, Violence," p. 166.

35. In a provocative and persuasive article, James H. Cook suggests that Douglass's rhetorical support for violence intensified at the same time as his actual exposure to violent situations diminished. See Cook, "Fighting with Breath."

36. Frederick Douglass to the *Rochester Democrat and American*, 31 October 1859, in *Selected Speeches*, p. 377.

37. Douglass to James Redpath, 29 June 1860, *Liberator*, 27 July 1860, in *Selected Speeches*, p. 396; and Douglass, *Life and Times*, p. 719. A few years later Gerrit Smith would make a similar argument to defend his growing fear that bullets rather than ballots would bring an end to slavery. To lack faith in the voters, he insisted, is not to lack faith in God but in the devil. To have faith in God is precisely to believe that God will end slavery in a way of God's own choosing. Smith, "Bible Civil Government," 1860, in *Sermons and Speeches*, p. 111.

38. Douglass, "The Dred Scott Decision," May 1857, in *Papers*, ser. 1, 3:169–70. Some years after the war, Douglass offered a fuller explanation of his understanding of moral laws. "There is," he wrote, "in the world's government, a force which has in all ages been recognized, sometimes as Nemesis, sometimes as the judgment of God and sometimes as retributive justice; but under whatever name, all history attests to the wisdom and beneficence of its chastisements. . . . The universe, of which we are a part, is continually proving itself a stupendous whole, a system of law and order, eternal and perfect. Every seed bears fruit after its kind, and nothing is reaped which was not sowed. The distance between seed time and harvest, in the moral world, may not be quite so well defined or as clearly intelligible as in the physical, but there is a seed time, and there is a harvest time, and though ages may intervene, and neither he who ploughed nor he who sowed may reap in person, yet the harvest nevertheless will surely come; and as in the physical world there are century plants, so it may be in the moral world, and their fruitage is as

certain in the one as in the other." See Douglass, "Did John Brown Fail?" 30 May 1881, in *Papers*, ser. 1, 5:10–11.

39. Douglass, "The Dred Scott Decision," in *Papers*, ser. 1, 3:171–72. For another analysis of Douglass's lifelong ambivalence about violence, see Takaki, *Violence*, pp. 17–35.

40. John Brown, cited in Redpath, *Public Life*, pp. 190, 280.

41. Ibid., p. 69.

42. Ibid., pp. 65, 363.

43. Ibid., p. 105.

44. Redpath, *Roving Editor*, pp. 7–8.

45. Ibid., p. 87.

46. Ibid., p. 119.

47. Ibid., pp. 59, 93, 235, 239.

48. Ibid., pp. 134, 235; Redpath, *Public Life*, p. 39; and Redpath, *Echoes*, p. 9.

49. Emerson disliked abolitionism in part because he believed that each individual is responsible for his or her own freedom, and that no one can truly oppress or liberate another person: "Nobody can oppress me but myself. Once more, the degradation of that black race, though now lost in the starless spaces of the past, did not come without sin. The condition is inevitable to the men they are, & nobody can redeem them but themselves." This callous attitude is quite resonant with Brown and Redpath's belief that only slave rebellion could lead to the recognition of slave humanity. Cited in Kazin, *God*, p. 67.

50. Emerson, "Speech Delivered at Tremont Temple," pp. 67–68.

51. Thoreau, "Plea," pp. 19–20.

52. Ibid., pp. 30, 19, 27, 38–39.

53. Douglass to James Redpath, 29 June 1860, *Liberator*, 27 July 1860, in *Selected Speeches*, p. 396; Foster cited in Perry, *Radical Abolitionism*, p. 259; and Wheelock, "Sermon," p. 184.

54. Wheelock, "Sermon," pp. 179, 187, 189.

55. Ibid., pp. 180–81.

56. Parker, "Two Letters," pp. 74–76, 77, 86.

57. Phillips, "Lesson," p. 43.

58. Ibid., pp. 43–44, 51.

59. Phillips, "Puritan Principle," p. 105.

60. Ibid., pp. 106, 112.

61. Ibid., pp. 107–10.

62. Cheever, "Example," p. 163.

63. Cheever, "Martyr's Death," pp. 234, 233, 216, 231.

64. *Liberator*, 21 October 1859; Clarke, "Causes," p. 326; and Whipple, "Brief Testimony," p. 302.

65. Whittier, "Brown of Osawatomie," p. 304.

66. *Liberator*, 28 October 1859; and *Liberator*, 16 December 1859.

67. *Liberator*, 16 December 1859.

68. George Frederickson, for example, suggests that Garrison's speech on Brown "constituted a repudiation of much that Garrison had come to represent" and contained only "a shred of consistency" (Frederickson, *Inner Civil War*, p. 42), while James Brewer Stewart writes that Garrison had "revis[ed] his nonresistance doctrines to the point of near meaninglessness," and that his continued refusal to vote was merely a "habit of ritual" (Stewart, *William Lloyd Garrison*, pp. 169–70).

69. Phillips, "Lesson," pp. 54–55; and Parker, "Two Letters," p. 88.

70. Thoreau, "Plea," p. 41; Cheever, "Martyr's Death," p. 226; Parker, "Two Letters," p. 87; Aptheker, *Abolitionism*, p. 137; and *Liberator*, 16 December 1859, in Cain, *William Lloyd Garrison*, p. 157.

71. *Liberator,* 31 December 1859; and Wright cited in Perry, *Radical Abolitionism,* p. 258.

72. Ballou cited in Perry, *Radical Abolitionism,* pp. 265–66; and Douglass, "Did John Brown Fail?" 30 May 1881, in *Papers,* ser. 1, 5:12. Such sentiments were not entirely new for Douglass. In 1845, for example, he had told the American Anti-Slavery Society that, if he were reenslaved, he would "have the gratification to know . . . that every drop of blood which I shall shed, every groan which I shall utter, every pain which shall rack my frame, every sob in which I shall indulge, shall be the instrument, under God, of tearing down the bloody pillar of Slavery" ("My Slave Experience in Maryland," 6 May 1845, in *Papers,* ser. 1, 1:30).

73. Wheelock, "Sermon," p. 188; Phillips, "Lesson," p. 54; and Thoreau, "Plea," pp. 24–25.

74. Garrison, "The Tragedy at Harper's Ferry," *Liberator,* 28 October 1859.

75. Haven, "Beginning," p. 126.

76. Cheever, "Example," pp. 157–58; Parker, "Two Letters," p. 89; and Clarke, "Causes," p. 327.

77. Clarke, "Causes," p. 331.

78. Brown, cited in Ruchames, *John Brown,* p. 159.

79. "Speech at Peoria, Illinois," 16 October 1854, in *Collected Works,* 2:275; "Gettysburg Address," 19 November 1863, in *Collected Works,* 7:17–23; "Speech at Independence Hall, Philadelphia, Pennsylvania," 22 February 1861, in *Collected Works,* 4:240; and "Speech at Springfield, Illinois," 26 June 1857, in *Collected Works,* 2:404. Lincoln biographer David Herbert Donald calls the proposition of human equality "the bedrock of [Lincoln's] political faith" (*Lincoln,* p. 176), while historian Garry Wills rightly suggests that Thomas Jefferson, not George Washington, was the central father figure in Lincoln's personal drama (Wills, *Lincoln,* p. 84).

80. "Speech at Independence Hall," 4:240; Lincoln, "Definition of Democracy," in *Collected Works,* 2:532; and Lincoln to Albert G. Hodges, 4 April 1864, in *Collected Works,* 7:281.

81. "Seventh Lincoln-Douglas Debate," 15 October 1858, in *Collected Works,* 3:315.

82. Lincoln to Henry L. Pierce and Others, 6 April 1859, in *Collected Works,* 3:375–76; and "Speech at Chicago, Illinois," 10 July 1858, in *Collected Works,* 2:499–500. See also Wills, *Lincoln,* p. 86.

83. Thurow, *Abraham Lincoln,* p. 82; and Wills, *Lincoln,* pp. 130, 145.

84. Wills, *Lincoln,* p. 103; Thurow, *Abraham Lincoln,* p. 72; Wolf, *Almost Chosen,* p. 171; and Guelzo, *Abraham Lincoln,* pp. 193–96.

85. Wills, *Lincoln,* p. 103; and Guelzo, *Abraham Lincoln,* pp. 370–72.

86. "Speech at Springfield," 2:406; and "Speech at Chicago," 2:501.

87. "Eulogy on Henry Clay," 6 July 1852, in *Collected Works,* 2:126.

88. Lincoln's scholarly admirers have found in this idea particular cause for praise. Philip Paludan, for example, suggests that for Lincoln "the writing of the Declaration in 1776 and the writing of the Constitution in 1787 . . . were essentially one meeting, bonded in the act of founding the country." These two documents established a "political-constitutional" system in which egalitarian ideals and constitutional institutions were simply inseparable. To stress one at the expense of the other, as Paludan thinks Garry Wills does, is to betray the national vision. By treating Lincoln only as a Jeffersonian, Paludan insists, "we weaken our faith in the ability of political-constitutional institutions to achieve our egalitarian ideals. When we lose that faith, we have seriously crippled our ability to reach such ideals at all. Ironically, if Lincoln the emancipator overcomes Lincoln the constitutionalist, the possibility for securing equality will be weakened" (Paludan, "Emancipating, pp. 54, 48). David Herbert Donald, similarly, has suggested that by the time of Lincoln's presidency "the concept of the Union . . . had become the premise on which all his other political beliefs rested" (*Lincoln,* p. 269). See also Thurow, *Abraham Lincoln,* p. 52.

89. Forgie, *Patricide,* pp. 6, 11–12; and Somkin, *Unquiet Eagle,* p. 4.

90. "Address Before the Young Men's Lyceum of Springfield, Illinois," 27 January 1838, in *Collected Works*, 1:108.

91. "Lyceum Address," 1:109–15; and "Second Lecture on Discoveries and Inventions," 11 February 1959, in *Collected Works*, 3:356–63.

92. Lincoln to Albert G. Hodges, 7:281.

93. "Speech at Peoria, Illinois," 16 October 1854, in *Collected Works*, 2:274; and Lincoln to Joshua F. Speed, 24 August 1855, in *Collected Works*, 2:320.

94. "Speech at Springfield," 2:405; "Speech at Peoria," 2:256; and "Address on Colonization," 14 August 1862, in *Collected Works*, 5:372.

95. "Speech at New Haven, Connecticut," 6 March 1860, in *Collected Works*, 4:18.

96. Melvin Endy, for example, has questioned Reinhold Niebuhr's assumption that Lincoln's reluctance to free the slaves "exhibited not his own ambiguity but the moral ambiguity of the political order itself." In fact, says Endy, Lincoln's evident racism demonstrated that his "commitment to the Declaration of Independence and his understanding of human rights were more flawed than Niebuhr, among others, recognized" ("Abraham Lincoln," 235, 241). Endy is certainly right to see Lincoln's views of slavery as "morally ambiguous," but he fails to demonstrate that this personal ambiguity is what determined Lincoln's policy.

97. "Handbill Replying to Charges of Infidelity," 31 July 1846, in *Collected Works*, 1:382.

98. Trueblood, *Abraham Lincoln*, pp. 7, 85; "Address to the New Jersey Senate at Trenton, New Jersey," 21 February 1861, in *Collected Works*, 4:236; and Wolf, *Almost Chosen*, p. 24.

99. Guelzo, *Abraham Lincoln*; "Temperance Address," 22 February 1842, in *Collected Works*, 1:275; "Address at Lewistown, Illinois," 17 August 1858, in *Collected Works*, 2:546; and Wolf, *Almost Chosen*, pp. 74–75, 106–7.

100. Donald, *Lincoln*, pp. 15, 337; "Handbill," 1:382; "Eulogy on Henry Clay," 2:132; and "Address to the New Jersey Senate," 4:236. See also Endy, "Abraham Lincoln," p. 233.

101. "Meditation on the Divine Will," c. early September 1862, in *Collected Works*, 5:404; and Abraham Lincoln to Eliza P. Gurney, 4 September 1864, in *Collected Works*, 7:535. See also "Remarks to a Delegation of Progressive Friends," 20 June 1862, in *Collected Works*, 5:278–79.

102. "Second Inaugural Address," 4 March 1865, in *Collected Works*, 8:333.

103. Hein, "Lincoln's Theology," p. 134; Kazin, *God*, p. 133; and Thurow, *Abraham Lincoln*, p. 100.

104. Lincoln to Thurlow Weed, 15 March 1865, in *Collected Works*, 8:356.

105. Lincoln to Albert G. Hodges, in *Collected Works*, 7:282.

106. Of the many attempts to explain this phenomenon, the theories of Elaine Scarry and Barbara Ehrenreich are particularly suggestive. War is, according to Scarry, "reality conferring" in that it juxtaposes unresolved issues with the inescapable reality of injured bodies. Even the victors may be more struck by the awesomeness of this process than by their own role in bringing it about (*Body in Pain*, p. 124). Ehrenreich suggests that the human psyche still bears traces of our early vulnerability to predation and our need to bond with the group for protection. In times of crisis, therefore, we easily feel the "passion" of group solidarity but rarely perceive ourselves as aggressors or initiators of conflict (*Blood Rites*).

107. "First Inaugural Address," 4 March 1861, in *Collected Works*, 4:271.

108. Frederick Douglass, for example, hoped that once the slave states achieved independence it would be possible to mount a guerrilla war to destroy slavery, with the "sympathy" though not the military support of the North. Douglass, "John Brown's Contributions," 3 December 1860, in *Papers*, ser. 1, 3:417–19.

109. Emerson cited in Kazin, *God*, p. 69; and Bushnell, *Reverses Needed*, p. 8.

110. Aptheker, *Abolitionism*, p. 143; Abzug, *Passionate Liberator*, p. 276; Douglass, "Sudden Revolution in Northern Sentiment," *Douglass' Monthly*, May 1861, in *Selected Speeches*, p. 445; and *Liberator*, 10 May 1861.

111 *Liberator*, 10 May 1861.

112. *Liberator*, 14 June 1861.

113. Douglass, "The American Apocalypse," 16 June 1861, in *Papers*, ser. 1, 3:437; and Douglass, "The Union and How to Save It," *Douglass' Monthly*, February 1861, in *Selected Speeches*, p. 430.

114. Child, "Through the Red Sea into the Wilderness," *Independent*, 21 December 1865, in *Child Reader*, p. 281; and "Mrs. L. Maria Child to the President of the United States," *National Anti-Slavery Standard*, 6 September 1862, in *Child Reader*, pp. 269, 267, 270.

115. "Message to Congress in Special Session," 4 July 1861, in *Collected Works*, 4:438–41, my italics. See also "First Inaugural," 4:265.

116. Guelzo, *Abraham Lincoln*, pp. 325–27, 336–37.

117. Ibid., pp. 341–42. "To do liberalism's greatest deed," Guelzo astutely comments, "Lincoln had to step outside liberalism and surrender himself to the direction of an overruling divine providence whose conclusions he had by no means prejudged" (p. 447).

118. "Gettysburg Address," 19 November 1863, in *Collected Works*, 7:17–23. Republican diarist George Templeton Strong offered an even more vivid image of rebirth at the end of the war: "The people has (I think) just been bringing forth a new American republic—an amazingly large baby—after a terribly protracted and severe labor, without chloroform." Cited in Guelzo, *Abraham Lincoln*, p. 458.

119. Child, "A Tribute to Col. Robert G. Shaw," *National Anti-Slavery Standard*, 15 August 1863, in *Child Reader*, p. 267.

120. Wolf, *Almost Chosen*, p. 85.

121. "Speech at Peoria," 2:276; and Lincoln to Lydia Bixby, 21 November 1864, in *Collected Works*, 8:117. Lincoln's authorship of the letter to Lydia Bixby is debated by historians, as his secretary John Hay claimed to have written it on Lincoln's behalf. The relevant point here, however, is simply that a theology of sacrifice was taken for granted within the circle surrounding Lincoln. See Donald, *Lincoln*, p. 680.

122. Moorhead, *American Apocalypse*, pp. 43–46.

123. Bushnell, *Reverses Needed*, p. 9.

124. Ibid., p. 10, 15–21. Bushnell's argument against social compact theory mirrors his insistence, in *Christian Nurture*, on the priority of the Christian community over the individual. This, in turn, suggests that Bushnell's argument in that treatise only seemed to continue the liberal campaign for a recognition of the religious significance of child rearing. True liberals emphasized nurture because they believed that human individuals are born with a natural connection to the divine that obviates the need for supernatural conversion. Bushnell was as supernaturalist as the revivalists; he simply found his supernature in the organic community rather than the ecstatic conversion.

125. Ibid., pp. 26, 22, 6. See Moorhead, *American Apocalypse*, p. 6 Evidently the notion that the Sabbath was an especially good day to fight also figured in Zachary Taylor's campaign literature of 1848, for in the 13 April 1849 *Liberator* Henry Clarke Wright wrote that "Zachary Taylor waged an aggressive war against the Mexicans, and chose the Sabbath as the most suitable day to fight his great battles—to extend and perpetrate slavery and the slave trade."

126. Bushnell, *Reverses Needed*, p. 23.

127. Hein, "Lincoln's Theology," pp. 140–41.

128. Despite Lincoln's own skepticism, Garry Wills argues, "the power of words has rarely been given a more compelling demonstration" than in Lincoln's 272-word performance. Lincoln took "all this muddle, these missed chances, all the senseless deaths" and created from them "something rich and strange," a "symbol of national purpose, pride, and ideals" (Wills, *Lincoln*, pp. 56, 20). See also Trueblood, *Abraham Lincoln*, p. 46; and Thurow, *Abraham Lincoln*, pp. 85–86.

129. "Second Lecture on Discoveries and Inventions," 3:359.

130. "Second Inaugural," 8:333. Frederick Douglass called the speech "a sacred effort," and Garrison would later write that Lincoln's words were "worthy to be written in starry letters upon the sky." See Donald, *Lincoln*, p. 568; and Garrison, "Address on the Assassination of Abraham Lincoln," Providence, Rhode Island, 1 June 1865, in *Liberator*, 7 July 1865.

131. Instead, as Alfred Kazin has suggested, he acknowledges the strangeness of his theology and his inability to imagine an alternative: "To suppose anything like this is actually to suppose a very peculiar God. But since it all happened as described, and believers hold God accountable for all things, one can yield to the enigma of having such a God at all" (*God*, p. 138).

132. This is the argument of David Hein, "Lincoln's Theology," pp. 129–30. But Garrison, at least, missed this point, writing, "Yes, dollar for dollar, blood for blood, torture for torture, life for life have been retributively exacted in full." Garrison, "Address on the Assassination of Abraham Lincoln," Providence, Rhode Island, 1 June 1865, in *Liberator*, 7 July 1865.

133. Kazin, *God*, p. 136; and Thurow, *Abraham Lincoln*, p. 104.

134. Matthew Simpson, "Oration at Lincoln's Burial at Springfield, Illinois," 4 May 1865, in Chesebrough, "*No Sorrow*," p. 130.

135. Guelzo, *Abraham Lincoln*, p. 440; and Moorhead, *American Apocalypse*, p. 176. Sarah Grimké, interestingly, had hoped that the war would produce a black Messiah: "Earnestly do I pray that from among the ranks of our colored brethren a Savior will arise, who will make this war resplendent with his deeds of valor, courage, wisdom and fortitude, and who will be deservedly hailed as the final Deliverer of his people." Cited in Abzug, *Passionate Liberator*, p. 279.

136. Brooks cited in Chesebrough, "*No Sorrow*," p. 17; *Liberator*, 28 April 1865; Boardman cited in Chesebrough, "*No Sorrow*," pp. 66, 74–77.

137. Garrison, "Address on the Assassination of Abraham Lincoln," Providence, Rhode Island, 1 June 1865, in *Liberator*, 7 July 1865.

138. "Second Inaugural," 8:333.

Conclusion

1. Small and Humphries, "Walls and Windows."

2. Baldwin, "Everybody's Protest Novel," p. 585.

3. Though orthodox Marxism is inconsistent with radical Christian liberalism, liberal activists can still learn from the Marxist insight that the material conditions of life often shape beliefs and values. If this is taken as a general pattern rather than an inescapable reality, it suggests that sentimental identification will become easier as we change our daily practices to reflect values of freedom and equality.

4. Niebuhr, *Irony*, pp. 2–3, 88, 17, 155, 169.

5. Welch, *Feminist Ethic*, p. 14.

Bibliography

Primary Sources

Ahlstrom, Sydney E., and Jonathan S. Carey, eds. *An American Reformation: A Documentary History of Unitarian Christianity*. Middletown, Conn.: Wesleyan University Press, 1985.

Andrews, William L. *Slave Narratives*. New York: Library of America, 2000.

Arthur, T. S. *Six Nights with the Washingtonians: A Series of Temperance Tales*. New York: E. Ferrett, 1842.

——. *Temperance Tales*. 2 vols. Philadelphia: Godey and M'Michael, 1843.

——. *Illustrated Temperance Tales, with an Autobiography, and a Portrait of the Author*. Philadelphia: J. W. Bradley, 1850.

——. *Ten Nights in a Bar-Room, and What I Saw There*. Boston: L. Crown, 1854.

——. *Six Nights with the Washingtonians; and Other Temperance Tales*. Philadelphia: T. B. Peterson, 1871.

Augustine of Hippo. *Confessions*. Trans. Henry Chadwick. Oxford: Oxford University Press, 1991.

Ball, Charles. *Slavery in the United States: A Narrative of the Life and Adventures of Charles Ball. . . .* Lewistown, Pa.: John W. Shugert, 1836. In Taylor, *I Was Born*, 1:260–486.

——. *Slavery in the United States: A Narrative of the Life and Adventures of Charles Ball. . . .* New York: John S. Taylor, 1837.

Ballou, Adin. *Christian Non-Resistance, in All Its Important Bearings, Illustrated and Defended*. Philadelphia: J. Miller M'Kim, 1846.

——. *Autobiography of Adin Ballou, 1803–1890*. Lowell, Mass.: Vox Populi Press, 1896.

Barnes, Gilbert H., and Dwight L. Dumond, eds. *Letters of Theodore Dwight Weld, Angelina Grimké Weld, and Sarah Grimké, 1822–1844*. 2 vols. American Historical Association, 1934. Reprint, Gloucester, Mass.: Peter Smith, 1965.

Bibb, Henry. *Narrative of the Life and Adventures of Henry Bibb, an American Slave. Written by Himself*. New York: by the author, 1849. In Taylor, *I Was Born*, 2:2–101.

Birney, Catherine H. *The Grimké Sisters: Sarah and Angelina Grimké, the First American Women Advocates of Abolition and Women's Rights*. 1885. Reprint, Westport, Conn.: Greenwood, 1969.

Blassingame, John W., ed. *Slave Testimony: Two Centuries of Letters, Speeches, Interviews, and Autobiographies*. Baton Rouge: Louisiana State University Press, 1977.

Bontemps, Arna, ed. *Five Black Lives: The Autobiographies of Venture Smith, James Mars, William Grimes, the Rev. G. W. Offley, and James L. Smith*. Middletown, Conn.: Wesleyan University Press, 1971.

Bourne, George. *Picture of Slavery in the United States of America.* Middletown, Conn.: Edwin Hunt, 1834.

——. *Slavery Illustrated in Its Effects upon Women and Domestic Society.* Boston: Isaac Knapp, 1837.

Brace, J. P. *Tales of the Devils.* Hartford, Conn.: S. Andrus and Son, 1846.

Bray, Gerald, ed. *Documents of the English Reformation.* Minneapolis, Minn.: Fortress, 1994.

Brown, Henry Box. *Narrative of Henry Box Brown, Who Escaped from Slavery in a Box 3 Feet Long and 2 Wide, Written from a Statement of Facts Made by Himself, with Remarks upon the Remedy for Slavery.* Ed. Charles Stearns. Boston: Brown and Stearns/Bela Marsh, 1849.

Brown, John. *Slave Life in Georgia: A Narrative of the Life of John Brown.* Ed. L. A. Chamerovzow. London: by the editor, 1855. In Taylor, *I Was Born,* 2:320–411.

Brown, Thurlow Weed. *Minnie Hermon: or, The Night and Its Morning. A Tale for the Times.* Auburn and Buffalo, N.Y.: Miller, Orton and Mulligan, 1854.

Brown, William Wells. *Narrative of William W. Brown, a Fugitive Slave.* Boston: Anti-Slavery Office, 1847. In Taylor, *I Was Born,* 1:674–717.

Bushnell, Horace. *Reverses Needed: A Discourse Delivered on the Sunday After the Disaster of Bull Run, in the North Church, Hartford.* Hartford, Conn.: L. E. Hunt, 1861.

——. *The Vicarious Sacrifice, Grounded in Principles of Universal Obligation.* New York: Scribner, 1869.

Cain, William E., ed. *William Lloyd Garrison and the Fight Against Slavery: Selections from* The Liberator. Boston: Saint Martin's, 1995.

Calvin, John. *Institutes of the Christian Religion.* Ed. John T. McNeill. Trans. Ford Lewis Battles. Philadelphia: Westminster, 1960.

Ceplair, Larry, ed. *The Public Years of Sarah and Angelina Grimke: Selected Writings, 1835–1839.* New York: Columbia University Press, 1989.

Channing, William Ellery. *Slavery.* Boston: James Munroe, 1836. Reprint, New York: Arno Press, 1969.

——. *Memoir of William Ellery Channing.* Boston: Crosby and Nichols, 1848.

——. *Works of William E. Channing.* 1882. Reprint, New York: Burt Franklin, 1970.

——. *Discourses on War.* Ed. Edwin D. Mead. Boston: Ginn and Company, 1903.

——. *Selected Writings.* Ed. David Robinson. New York: Paulist Press, 1985.

Chapman, Maria Weston. *Right and Wrong in Massachusetts.* Boston: Dow and Jackson Anti-Slavery Press, 1839. Reprint, New York: Negro Universities Press, 1969.

Cheever, George B. *The Dream: or The True History of Deacon Giles's Distillery, and Deacon Jones's Brewery.* New York: Thomas Hamilton, 1859.

——. "The Example and the Method of Emancipation by the Constitution of Our Country and the Word of God." In Redpath, *Echoes,* pp. 141–75.

——. "The Martyr's Death and the Martyr's Triumph." In Redpath, *Echoes,* pp. 213–35.

Chellis, Mary Dwinell. *Old Times.* New York: National Temperance Society and Publication House, 1873.

Cheney, Harriet Vaughan. *A Peep at the Puritans in Sixteen Hundred Thirty-Six: A Tale of Olden Times.* Boston: Wells and Lilly, 1824.

Child, Lydia Maria. *Hobomok and Other Writings on Indians.* 1824. Ed. Carolyn L. Karcher. New Brunswick, N.J.: Rutgers University Press, 1986.

——. *The First Settlers of New England: or, Conquest of the Pequods, Narragansetts and Pokanokets. As Related by a Mother to Her Children. By a Lady of Massachusetts.* Boston: Munroe and Francis, 1829.

——. *An Appeal in Favor of That Class of Americans Called Africans.* 1833. Ed. Carolyn L. Karcher. Amherst: University of Massachusetts Press, 1996.

——. *Philothea: A Grecian Romance.* Boston: Otis, Broader, 1836.

———. *Letters from New York.* 2 vols. New York: C. S. Francis, 1845.

———. *The Progress of Religious Ideas, Through Successive Ages.* New York: C. S. Francis, 1855.

———. *Autumnal Leaves: Tales and Sketches in Prose and Rhyme.* New York: C. S. Francis, 1857.

———. *Selected Letters, 1817–1880.* Ed. Milton Meltzer and Patricia G. Holland. Amherst: University of Massachusetts Press, 1982.

———. *A Lydia Maria Child Reader.* Ed. Carolyn Karcher. Durham, N.C.: Duke University Press, 1997.

Clarke, James Freeman. "Causes and Consequences of the Affair at Harper's Ferry." In Redpath, *Echoes,* p. 326.

Clarke, Lewis, and Milton Clarke. *Narratives of the Sufferings of Lewis and Milton Clarke, Sons of a Soldier of the Revolution, During a Captivity of More Than Twenty Years Among the Slaveholders of Kentucky, One of the So Called Christian States of North America. Dictated by Themselves.* Boston: Bela Marsh, 1846. In Taylor, *I Was Born,* 1:602–72.

Craft, William, and Ellen Craft. *Running a Thousand Miles for Freedom: or, The Escape of William and Ellen Craft from Slavery.* London: William Tweedie, 1860. In Taylor, *I Was Born,* 2:482–531.

Crowley, John W., ed. *Drunkard's Progress: Narratives of Addiction, Despair, and Recovery.* Baltimore: Johns Hopkins University Press, 1999.

Dodge, David Low. *War Inconsistent with the Religion of Jesus Christ.* 1812. Ed. Edwin D. Mead. Boston: Ginn and Company, 1905.

Douglass, Frederick. *Narrative of the Life of Frederick Douglass, an American Slave.* 1845. In *Autobiographies,* pp. 1–102.

———. *My Bondage and My Freedom.* 1855. In *Autobiographies,* pp. 103–452.

———. *Life and Times of Frederick Douglass.* 1893. In *Autobiographies,* pp. 453–1045.

———. *The Frederick Douglass Papers.* Series 1, *Speeches, Debates, and Interviews.* Ed. John W. Blassingame. 4 vols. New Haven, Conn.: Yale University Press, 1979–85.

———. *Autobiographies.* Ed. Henry Louis Gates Jr. New York: Library of America, 1994.

———. *Frederick Douglass: Selected Speeches and Writings.* Ed. Philip S. Foner. Abridged and adapted by Yuval Taylor. Chicago: Chicago Review Press, 1999.

Drew, Benjamin. *The Refugee: or the Narratives of Fugitive Slaves in Canada.* Boston: John P. Jewett, 1856.

Edmund and Margaret; or Sobriety and Faithfulness Rewarded. Cambridge, Mass.: Printed for the Trustees of the Publishing Fund, by Hilliard and Metcalf, 1822.

Emerson, Ralph Waldo. "Speech Delivered at Tremont Temple." In Redpath, *Echoes,* pp. 67–71.

———. "Speech Delivered at Salem." In Redpath, *Echoes,* pp. 119–22.

———. *Emerson's Antislavery Writings.* Ed. Len Gougen and Joel Myerson. New Haven, Conn.: Yale University Press, 1995.

Experience and Personal Narrative of Uncle Tom Jones: Who Was for Forty Years a Slave. Also the Surprising Adventures of Wild Tom, of the Island Retreat, a Fugitive Negro from South Carolina. Boston: Skinner's Rooms, n.d.

Follen, Eliza Lee Cabot. "Remember the Slave." 1831. In Ahlstrom and Carey, *American Reformation,* pp. 317–18.

———. *The Skeptic.* Boston: James Munroe, 1835.

Foner, Philip S., ed. *We, the Other People: Alternative Declarations of Independence by Labor Groups, Farmers, Woman's Rights Advocates, Socialists, and Blacks, 1829–1975.* Urbana.: University of Illinois Press, 1976.

Fox, Mary Anna. *George Allen, the Only Son. By a Lady of Boston.* Boston: William Peirce, 1835.

Fox, Mary L. *The Ruined Deacon. A True Story. By a Lady.* Boston: Ford and Damrell, 1834.

Frederickson, George M., ed. *William Lloyd Garrison.* Englewood Cliffs, N.J.: Prentice-Hall, 1968.

Garrison, Wendell Phillips, and Francis Jackson Garrison. *William Lloyd Garrison, 1805–1879: The Story of His Life, Told by His Children.* 4 vols. New York: Century Company, 1885.

Garrison, William Lloyd. *The Letters of William Lloyd Garrison.* Ed. Walter M. Merrill. 6 vols. Cambridge, Mass.: Belknap Press of Harvard University Press.

Gates, Henry Louis, ed. *The Classic Slave Narratives.* New York: Mentor, 1987.

Gay, Ebenezer. "Natural Religion as Distinguished from Revealed." 1759. In Ahlstrom and Carey, *American Reformation,* pp. 45–59.

Gilbert, Olive. *Narrative of Sojourner Truth; A Bondswoman of Olden Time, with a History of Her Labors and Correspondence Drawn from Her "Book of Life."* 1850. Ed. Jeffrey C. Stewart. New York: Oxford University Press, 1991.

Goodell, William. *Come-Outerism: The Duty of Secession from a Corrupt Church.* New York: American Anti-Slavery Society, 1845.

Gough, John Bartholomew. *An Autobiography.* 1845. In Crowley, *Drunkard's Progress,* pp. 111–72.

——. *An Autobiography.* 20th ed. Boston: for the author, 1847.

Grandy, Moses. *Narrative of the Life of Moses Grandy, Late a Slave in the United States of America.* 2d ed. Boston: Oliver Johnson, 1844.

Green, Andrus V. *The Life and Experience of A. V. Green.* 1848. In Crowley, *Drunkard's Progress,* pp. 173–90.

Grimké, Thomas S. *Address on the Truth, Dignity, Power and Beauty of the Principles of Peace. . . .* Hartford, Conn.: George F. Olmsted, 1832.

Hale, Sarah Josepha. *Sketches of American Character.* Boston: Putnam and Hunt, 1829.

——. *Traits of American Life.* Philadelphia: Carey and Hart, 1835.

——. *Northwood; or, Life North and South: Showing the True Character of Both.* 2d ed. New York: H. Long and Brother, 1852.

Hall, James. *Tales of the Border.* Philadelphia: Harrison Hall, 1835.

Haven, Gilbert. "The Beginning of the End of American Slavery." In Redpath, *Echoes,* pp. 125–40.

Henson, Josiah. *The Life of Josiah Henson, Formerly a Slave, Now an Inhabitant of Canada, as Narrated by Himself.* Boston: Arthur D. Phelps, 1849. In Taylor, *I Was Born,* 1:720–56.

Hildreth, Richard. *The Slave: or Memoirs of Archy Moore.* 2 vols. 2d ed. Boston: Whipple and Damrell, 1840. First published in 1836.

Hosmer, Margaret. *The Subtle Spell.* Philadelphia: Alfred Martien, 1873.

Jacobs, Harriet. *Incidents in the Life of a Slave Girl: Written by Herself.* 1861. Ed. Jean Fagan Yellin. Cambridge, Mass.: Harvard University Press, 1987.

Judd, Sylvester. *A Young Man's Account of His Conversion from Calvinism.* Boston: American Unitarian Association, 184-.

——. *A Moral Review of the Revolutionary War.* Hollowell, Maine: Glazier, Masters, and Smith, 1842.

——. *Philo: An Evangeliad.* Boston: Phillips, Sampson, and Company, 1850.

——. *Richard Edney and the Governor's Family: A Rus-Urban Tale.* Boston: Phillips, Sampson, and Company, 1850.

——. *Margaret: A Tale of the Real and the Ideal, Blight and Bloom.* 2d ed. 1851. Reprint, Upper Saddle River, N.J.: Gregg Press, 1968.

King, Martin Luther, Jr. *A Testament of Hope: The Essential Writings and Speeches of Martin Luther King, Jr.* Ed. James M. Washington. San Francisco: HarperSanFrancisco, 1986.

Kuklick, Bruce, ed. *The Unitarian Controversy, 1819–1823.* New York: Garland, 1987.

Ladd, William. *A Brief Illustration of the Principles of War and Peace. . . . By Philanthropus.* Albany, N.Y.: Packard and Van Benthuysen, 1831.

——. *The Essays of Philanthropos on Peace and War.* Ed. Peter Brock. New York: Garland, 1972.

Lamas, Maria, ed. *The Glass; or, The Trials of Helen More: A Thrilling Temperance Tale*. Philadelphia: Martin E. Harmstead, 1849.

Lane, Lunsford. *The Narrative of Lunsford Lane, formerly of Raleigh, N.C.* Boston: published by himself, 1842.

Lee, Eliza Buckminster. *Sketches of a New England Village, in the Last Century*. Boston: James Munroe and Company, 1838.

——. *Delusion; or the Witch of New England*. Boston: Hilliard, Gray, and Company, 1840.

——. *Life of Jean Paul Richter*. Boston: C. C. Little and J. Brown, 1842.

——. *Naomi; or, Boston, Two Hundred Years Ago*. Boston: William Crosby and H. P. Nichols, 1848.

——. *Memoirs of Rev. Joseph Buckminster, D.D., and of His Son, Rev. Joseph Stevens Buckminster*. Boston: W. Crosby and H. P. Nichols, 1849.

——. *Florence, the Parish Orphan; and A Sketch of the Village in the Last Century*. Boston: Ticknor, Reed, and Fields, 1852.

Lincoln, Abraham. *Collected Works*. Ed. Roy P. Basler. 8 vols. New Brunswick, N.J.: Rutgers University Press, 1953.

——. *Selected Speeches and Writings*. Ed. Gore Vidal. New York: Library of America, 1992.

Loguen, J. W. *The Rev. J. W. Loguen, as a Slave and as a Freeman: A Narrative of Real Life*. 1859. Reprint, New York: Negro Universities Press, 1968.

The Lottery Ticket: An American Tale. Cambridge, Mass.: Printed for the Trustees of the Publishing Fund, by Hilliard and Metcalf, 1822.

Lynd, Staughton, and Alice Lynd. *Nonviolence in America: A Documentary History*. Rev. ed. Maryknoll, N.Y.: Orbis Books, 1995.

Lynn, Corra. *Durham Village; A Temperance Tale*. Boston: John P. Jewett, 1854.

Marsh, John P. *Putnam and the Wolf; or, The Monster Destroyed. An Address, Originally Delivered at Pomfret, Connecticut*. New York: American Tract Society, n.d.

Mather, Cotton. *Magnalia Christi Americana: or, The Ecclesiastical History of New England*. Hartford, Conn.: Silas Andrus, 1820.

Mather, John Cotton [pseud.]. *Autobiography of a Reformed Drunkard*. 1845. In Crowley, *Drunkard's Progress*, pp. 97–110.

Mather, Increase. *An Essay for the Recording of Illustrious Providences*. 1684. Reprint, Delmar, N.Y.: Scholars' Facsimiles and Reprints, 1977.

Neal, John. *Rachel Dyer: A North American Story*. 1828. Reprint, Gainesville, Fla.: Scholars' Facsimiles and Reprints, 1964.

Nelson, Truman, ed. *Documents of Upheaval: Selections from William Lloyd Garrison's The Liberator, 1831–1865*. New York: Hill and Wang, 1966.

Newman, Richard, Patrick Rael, and Phillip Lapsansky, eds. *Pamphlets of Protest: An Anthology of Early African-American Protest Literature, 1790–1860*. New York: Routledge, 2000.

Northup, Solomon. *Twelve Years a Slave: Narrative of Solomon Northup*. Auburn, N.Y.: Derby and Miller, 1853. In Taylor, *I Was Born*, 2:160–317.

Osofsky, Gilbert, ed. *Puttin' On Ole Massa: The Slave Narratives of Henry Bibb, William Wells Brown, and Solomon Northup*. New York: Harper and Row, 1969.

Parker, Theodore. "Two Letters." In Redpath, *Echoes*, pp. 73–92.

Peabody, Ephraim. "Narratives of Fugitive Slaves." *Christian Examiner* 47 (July 1849): 64.

Pennington, James W. C. *The Fugitive Blacksmith; or, Events in the History of James W. C. Pennington. . . .* 2d ed. London: Charles Gilpin, 1849. In Taylor, *I Was Born*, 2:104–58.

Phillips, Wendell. "The Lesson of the Hour." In Redpath, *Echoes*, pp. 43–66.

——. "The Puritan Principle." In Redpath, *Echoes*, pp. 105–18.

Pseudo-Dionysius the Areopagite. *The Complete Works*. Trans. Colm Luibheid. New York: Paulist Press, 1987.

Quarles, Benjamin, ed. *Frederick Douglass.* Englewood Cliffs, N.J.: Prentice-Hall, 1968.

——. *Blacks on John Brown.* Urbana: University of Illinois Press, 1972.

Randolph, Peter. *Sketches of Slave Life: or, Illustrations of the "Peculiar Institution."* 2d ed. Boston: for the author, 1855.

Redpath, James. *The Roving Editor; or Talks with Slaves in the Southern States.* 1859. Ed. John R. McKivigan. University Park: Pennsylvania State University Press, 1996.

——. *The Public Life of Capt. John Brown, with an Auto-Biography of His Childhood and Youth.* Boston: Thayer and Eldridge, 1860.

——, ed. *Echoes of Harper's Ferry.* Boston: Thayer and Eldridge, 1860.

Ripley, C. Peter, ed. *Witness for Freedom: African American Voices on Race, Slavery, and Emancipation.* Chapel Hill: University of North Carolina Press, 1993.

Robinson, David, ed. *William Ellery Channing: Selected Writings.* New York: Paulist Press, 1985.

Roper, Moses. *A Narrative of the Adventures and Escape of Moses Roper, from American Slavery; with a Preface by the Rev. T. Price, D.D.* Philadelphia: Merrihew and Gunn, 1838. In Taylor, *I Was Born,* 1:488–521.

Rose, Henrietta. *Nora Wilmot: A Tale of Temperance and Woman's Rights.* Columbus, Ind.: Osgood and Pearce, 1858.

Rowlandson, Mary. *The Sovereignty and Goodness of God.* 1682. Ed. Neal Salisbury. Boston: Bedford, 1997.

Ruchames, Louis, ed. *A John Brown Reader.* London: Abelard-Schuman, 1959.

——. *The Abolitionists: A Collection of Their Writings.* New York: Putnam, 1963.

Sargent, Lucius M. *The Temperance Tales.* 2 vols. New ed. Boston: John P. Jewett and Company, 1852.

Savage, Sarah. *The Factory Girl. By a Lady.* Boston: Munroe, Francis, and Parker, 1814.

——. *Filial Affection; or, The Clergyman's Granddaughter.* Boston: Cummings and Hilliard, 1820.

——. *James Talbot.* Cambridge, Mass.: Hilliard and Metcalf, 1821.

——. *Trial and Self-Discipline.* Boston: J. Munroe, 1835.

Sedgwick, Catharine Maria. *A New-England Tale; or, Sketches of New-England Characters and Manners.* 1822. Ed. Victoria Clements. New York: Oxford University Press, 1995.

——. *Redwood; A Tale.* New York: Bliss and White, 1824.

——. *Hope Leslie: or, Early Times in the Massachusetts.* 1827. Ed. Mary Kelley. New Brunswick, N.J.: Rutgers University Press, 1987.

——. *Clarence; or, A Tale of Our Own Times.* 2 vols. Philadelphia: Carey and Lea, 1830.

——. *Home.* Boston: James Munroe and Company, 1835.

——. *The Linwoods; or "Sixty Years Since" in America.* New York: Harper and Brothers, 1835.

——. *Tales and Sketches.* Philadelphia: Carey, Lea, and Blanchard, 1835.

——. *Tales and Sketches: Second Series.* New York: Harper and Brothers, 1844.

——. *The Power of Her Sympathy: The Autobiography and Journal of Catharine Maria Sedgwick.* Ed. Mary Kelley. Boston: Massachusetts Historical Society, 1993.

[Shepherd, Isaac F.]. *Confessions of a Female Inebriate.* 1842. In Crowley, *Drunkard's Progress,* pp. 69–79.

Sigourney, Lydia Huntley. *Traits of the Aborigines of America.* Cambridge, Mass.: Hilliard and Metcalf, 1822.

——. *Sketch of Connecticut, Forty Years Since.* Hartford, Conn.: Oliver D. Cooke and Sons, 1824.

——. *Olive Buds.* Hartford, Conn.: William Watson, 1836.

——. *Sketches.* Amherst, Mass.: J. S. and C. Adams, 1840.

——. *Myrtis, with Other Etchings and Sketchings.* New York: Harper and Brothers, 1846.

——. *Water-Drops.* New York: Robert Carter, 1848.

——. *Olive Leaves.* New York: Robert Carter and Brothers, 1852.

Sigourney, Lydia Huntley, and Gerrit Smith. *The Intemperate, and the Reformed. Shewing the Awful*

Consequences of Intemperance and the Blessed Effects of the Temperance Reformation. Boston: Seth Bliss, 1833.

Small, Judy, and Pat Humphries. "Walls and Windows." Recorded by Priscilla Herdman. *Darkness into Light.* Flying Fish Records, 1987.

Smith, Gerrit. *Sermons and Speeches.* New York: Ross and Tousey, 1861.

Sparks, Jared. "The Comparative Moral Tendency of the Leading Doctrines of Calvinism and the Sentiments of Unitarians." In Ahlstrom and Carey, *American Reformation*, pp. 332–39.

Steward, Austin. *Twenty-two Years a Slave, and Forty Years a Freeman.* Rochester, N.Y.: William Alling, 1857.

Stewart, Maria W. *Maria W. Stewart, America's First Black Woman Political Writer: Essays and Speeches.* Ed. Marilyn Richardson. Bloomington: Indiana University Press, 1987.

Stowe, Harriet Beecher. *The Mayflower; or, Sketches of Scenes and Characters Among the Descendants of the Pilgrims.* New York: Harper and Brothers, 1844.

———. "The Freeman's Dream; A Parable." *National Era*, 1 August 1850.

———. *Uncle Tom's Cabin or, Life Among the Lowly.* 1851. Ed. Ann Douglas. New York: Penguin, 1981.

———. *Dred: A Tale of the Great Dismal Swamp.* 1856. New York: AMS Press, 1967.

———. *The Minister's Wooing.* 1859. New York: AMS Press, 1967.

———. *Oldtown Folks.* 1869. Ed. Henry F. May. Cambridge, Mass.: Harvard University Press, 1966.

———. *The Oxford Harriet Beecher Stowe Reader.* Ed. Joan D. Hedrick. New York: Oxford University Press, 1999.

Taylor, Yuval, ed. *I Was Born a Slave: An Anthology of Classic Slave Narratives.* 2 vols. Library of Black America. Chicago: Lawrence Hill Books, 1999.

Thoreau, Henry David. "A Plea for Capt. John Brown." In Redpath, *Echoes*, pp. 17–42.

Thornton, John Wingate, ed. *The Pulpit of the American Revolution: or, The Political Sermons of the Period of 1776.* Boston: Gould and Lincoln, 1860.

VanDerBeets, Richard. *Held Captive by Indians: Selected Narratives, 1642–1836.* Knoxville: University of Tennessee Press, 1973.

Ware, Henry. "The Nature of Man." 1820. In Ahlstrom and Carey, *American Reformation*, pp. 199–209.

Ware, Henry, Jr. *The Recollections of Jotham Anderson, Minister of the Gospel.* Boston: Christian Register Office, 1824.

———. "Sober Thoughts on the Signs of the Times." 1835. In Ahlstrom and Carey, *American Reformation*, pp. 362–70.

———. "The Personality of Deity." 1838. In Ahlstrom and Carey, *American Reformation*, pp. 432–40.

———. *David Ellington. With Other Extracts from His Writings.* Boston: William Crosby and H. P. Nichols, 1846.

Watson, Henry. *Narrative of Henry Watson, a Fugitive Slave. Written by Himself.* Boston: Bela Marsh, 1848.

Weems, Mason Locke. *God's Revenge Against Murder; or The Drown'd Wife. . . .* 11th ed. Philadelphia: for the author, 1823.

———. *Three Discourses.* Ed. Emily E. F. Skeel. New York: Random House, 1929.

Weld, Theodore Dwight. *American Slavery as It Is: Testimony of a Thousand Witnesses.* New York: American Anti-Slavery Society, 1839.

Wheelock, Edwin M. "Sermon." In Redpath, *Echoes*, pp. 179–94.

Whipple, Charles K. "Brief Testimony." In Redpath, *Echoes*, p. 302.

Whittier, John Greenleaf. *Leaves from Margaret Smith's Journal in the Province of Massachusetts Bay, 1678–9.* Boston: Ticknor, Reed, and Fields, 1849.

——. "Brown of Osawatomie." In Redpath, *Echoes*, pp. 303–15.

Williams, David R., ed. *Revolutionary War Sermons*. Delmar, N.Y.: Scholars' Facsimiles and Reprints, 1984.

Williams, James. *Authentic Narrative of James Williams, an American Slave*. Ed. John Greenleaf Whittier. Boston: Isaac Knapp, 1838.

Woodman, Charles T. *Narrative of Charles T. Woodman, a Reformed Inebriate*. 1843. In Crowley, *Drunkard's Progress*, pp. 80–96.

Worcester, Noah. *A Solemn Review of the Custom of War; Showing That War Is the Effect of Popular Delusion, and Proposing a Remedy*. 5th ed. Cambridge, Mass.: Hilliard and Metcalf, 1816.

Wright, Henry Clarke. *A Kiss for a Blow: or, A Collection of Stories for Children; Showing Them How to Prevent Quarreling*. Boston: B. B. Mussey, 1842.

——. *Human Life: Illustrated in My Individual Experience as a Child, a Youth, and a Man*. Boston: Bela Marsh, 1849.

——. *Anthropology; or the Science of Man; in Its Bearing on War and Slavery*. Boston: Bela Marsh, 1850.

Secondary Sources

Abzug, Robert H. *Passionate Liberator: Theodore Dwight Weld and the Dilemma of Reform*. New York: Oxford University Press, 1980.

——. *Cosmos Crumbling: American Reform and the Religious Imagination*. New York: Oxford University Press, 1994.

Adams, David K., and Cornelius van Minnen, eds. *Religious and Secular Reform in America: Ideas, Beliefs, and Social Change*. New York: New York University Press, 1999.

Albanese, Catherine. *Corresponding Motion: Transcendental Religion and the New America*. Philadelphia: Temple University Press, 1977.

Alexander, Ruth M. "'We Are Engaged as a Band of Sisters': Class and Domesticity in the Washingtonian Temperance Movement, 1840–1850." *Journal of American History* 75 (December 1988): 763–85.

Altschuler, Glenn C., and Stuart M. Blumin. "'Where Is the Real America?': Politics and Popular Consciousness in the Antebellum Era." *American Quarterly* 49 (June 1997): 225–67.

Ammons, Elizabeth, ed. *Critical Essays on Harriet Beecher Stowe*. Boston: G. K. Hall, 1980.

——. "Stowe's Dream of the Mother-Savior: *Uncle Tom's Cabin* and American Women Writers Before the 1920s." In Sundquist, *New Essays*, pp. 155–95.

Andrews, William L. *To Tell a Free Story: The First Century of Afro-American Autobiography, 1760–1865*. Urbana: University of Illinois Press, 1986.

——, ed. *Critical Essays on Frederick Douglass*. Boston: G. K. Hall, 1991.

——. *African American Autobiography: A Collection of Critical Essays*. Englewood Cliffs, N.J.: Prentice Hall, 1993.

Armstrong, Nancy. *Desire and Domestic Fiction: A Political History of the Novel*. Oxford: Oxford University Press, 1989.

Aptheker, Herbert. "An Unpublished Frederick Douglass Letter." *Journal of Negro History* 44 (July 1959): 277–81.

——. *Abolitionism: A Revolutionary Movement*. Boston: Twayne, 1989.

Bacon, Margaret Hope. *Mothers of Feminism: The Story of Quaker Women in America*. San Francisco: Harper and Row, 1986.

——. *Valiant Friend: The Life of Lucretia Mott*. New York: Walker and Company, 1980.

Bailie, Gil. *Violence Unveiled: Humanity at the Crossroads*. New York: Crossroad, 1995.

Baker, Houston A., Jr. *The Journey Back: Issues in Black Literature and Criticism*. Chicago: University of Chicago Press, 1980.

——. *Blues, Ideology, and Afro-American Literature: A Vernacular Theory.* Chicago: University of Chicago Press, 1984.

Baker, Houston A., Jr., and Patricia Redmond, eds. *Afro-American Literary Study in the 1990s.* Chicago: University of Chicago Press, 1989.

Baldwin, James. "Everybody's Protest Novel." *Partisan Review* 16 (June 1949): 578-85.

Bardes, Barbara, and Suzanne Gossett. *Declarations of Independence: Women and Political Power in Nineteenth-Century American Fiction.* New Brunswick, N.J.: Rutgers University Press, 1990.

Barnes, Gilbert Hobbs. *The Antislavery Impulse, 1830-1844.* With a new introduction by William G. McLoughlin. New York: Harcourt, Brace, and World, 1964.

Baym, Nina. *Novels, Readers, and Reviewers: Responses to Fiction in Antebellum America.* Ithaca, N.Y.: Cornell University Press, 1984.

——. *Feminism and American Literary History: Essays.* New Brunswick, N.J.: Rutgers University Press, 1992.

——. *Woman's Fiction: A Guide to Novels by and About Women in America, 1820-1870.* 2d ed. Urbana: University of Illinois Press, 1993.

——. *American Women Writers and the Work of History, 1790-1860.* New Brunswick, N.J.: Rutgers University Press, 1995.

Bebbington, David W. *Evangelicalism in Modern Britain: A History from the 1730s to the 1980s.* London: Unwin Hyman, 1989.

Bell, Michael Davitt. *Hawthorne and the Historical Romance of New England.* Princeton, N.J.: Princeton University Press, 1971.

——. "Conditions of Literary Vocation." In Bercovitch, *Cambridge History,* 2:9-123.

Bellin, Joshua D. "Up to Heaven's Gate, Down in Earth's Dust: The Politics of Judgment in *Uncle Tom's Cabin.*" *American Literature* 65 (June 1993): 275-95.

Bender, Thomas, ed. *The Antislavery Debate: Capitalism and Abolitionism as a Problem in Historical Interpretation.* Berkeley: University of California Press, 1992.

Bensel, Richard Franklin. *Yankee Leviathan: The Origins of Central State Authority in America, 1859-1877.* Cambridge: Cambridge University Press, 1990.

Bentley, Nancy. "White Slaves: The Mulatto Hero in Antebellum Fiction." *American Literature* 65 (September 1993): 501-22.

Bercovitch, Sacvan, ed. *The Cambridge History of American Literature.* Cambridge: Cambridge University Press, 1995.

Berens, John F. *Providence and Patriotism in Early America, 1640-1815.* Charlottesville: University Press of Virginia, 1978.

Berk, Richard A., Sarah Fenstermaker Berk, Donileen R. Loseke, and David Rauma. "Mutual Combat and Other Family Violence Myths." In Finkelhor et al., *Dark Side,* pp. 197-212.

Berkson, Dorothy. "Millennial Politics and the Feminine Fiction of Harriet Beecher Stowe." In Ammons, *Critical Essays,* pp. 244-58.

Blassingame, John W. *The Slave Community: Plantation Life in the Antebellum South.* Rev. ed. New York: Oxford University Press, 1979.

——. "Using the Testimony of Ex-Slaves: Approaches and Problems." In Davis and Gates, *Slave's Narrative,* pp. 78-97.

Blight, David W. *Frederick Douglass' Civil War: Keeping Faith in Jubilee.* Baton Rouge: Louisiana State University Press, 1989.

Bloch, Ruth. *Visionary Republic: Millennial Themes in American Thought, 1756-1800.* New York: Cambridge University Press, 1985.

Blocker, Jack. *American Temperance Movements: Cycles of Reform.* Boston: Twayne, 1989.

Bloom, Harold, ed. *Frederick Douglass's Narrative of the Life of Frederick Douglass: Modern Critical Interpretations.* New York: Chelsea House, 1988.

Boyd, Richard. "Models of Power in Harriet Beecher Stowe's *Dred*." *Studies in American Fiction* 19 (spring 1991): 15–30.

———. "Violence and Sacrificial Displacement in Harriet Beecher Stowe's *Dred*." *Arizona Quarterly* 50 (summer 1994): 51–72.

Breitweiser, Mitchell Robert. *American Puritanism and the Defense of Mourning: Religion, Grief, and Ethnology in Mary White Rowlandson's Captivity Narrative*. Madison: University of Wisconsin Press, 1990.

Brock, Peter. *Pacifism in the United States from the Colonial Era to the First World War*. Princeton, N.J.: Princeton University Press, 1968.

———. *Freedom from War: Nonsectarian Pacifism, 1814–1914* . Toronto: University of Toronto Press, 1991.

Brodhead, Richard. "Sparing the Rod: Discipline and Fiction in Antebellum America." *Representations* 21 (winter 1988): 67–96.

Brown, Gillian. "Getting in the Kitchen with Dinah: Domestic Politics in *Uncle Tom's Cabin*." *American Quarterly* 36 (fall 1984): 503–23.

———. *Domestic Individualism: Imagining Self in Nineteenth-Century America*. Berkeley: University of California Press, 1990.

Brown, Herbert Ross. *The Sentimental Novel in America, 1789–1860*. Durham, N.C.: Duke University Press, 1940.

Browne, Stephen Howard. *Angelina Grimké: Rhetoric, Identity, and the Radical Imagination*. East Lansing: Michigan State University Press, 1999.

Buchanan, Daniel P. "Tares in the Wheat: Puritan Violence and Puritan Families in the Nineteenth-Century Liberal Imagination." *Religion and American Culture: A Journal of Interpretation* 8 (summer 1998): 205–36.

Buell, Lawrence. "Calvinism Romanticized: Harriet Beecher Stowe, Samuel Hopkins, and *The Minister's Wooing*." In Ammons, *Critical Essays*, pp. 259–75.

———. *New England Literary Culture: From Revolution Through Renaissance*. Cambridge: Cambridge University Press, 1986.

Butler, Jon. *Awash in a Sea of Faith: Christianizing the American People*. Cambridge, Mass.: Harvard University Press, 1990.

Camfield, Gregg. "The Moral Aesthetics of Sentimentality: A Missing Key to *Uncle Tom's Cabin*." *Nineteenth-Century Literature* 43 (December 1988): 319–45.

Cannon, Katie G. *Black Womanist Ethics*. Atlanta, Ga.: Scholars Press, 1988.

Carwardine, Richard. *Evangelicals and Politics in Antebellum America*. New Haven, Conn.: Yale University Press, 1993.

Chapman, Mary, and Glenn Hendler, eds. *Sentimental Men: Masculinity and the Politics of Affect in American Culture*. Berkeley: University of California Press, 1999.

Chatfield, Charles. *The American Peace Movement: Ideals and Activism*. New York: Twayne, 1992.

———, ed. *Peace Movements in America*. New York: Schocken, 1973.

Cherry, Conrad. *God's New Israel: Religious Interpretations of American Destiny*. Englewood Cliffs, N.J.: Prentice-Hall, 1971.

Chesebrough, David B. *"No Sorrow Like Our Sorrow": Northern Protestant Ministers and the Assassination of Lincoln*. Kent, Ohio: Kent State University Press, 1994.

Clark, Elizabeth. "'The Sacred Rights of the Weak': Pain, Sympathy, and the Culture of Individual Rights in Antebellum America." *Journal of American History* 82 (September 1995): 463–93.

Clebsch, William A. *From Sacred to Profane America: The Role of Religion in American History*. New York: Harper and Row, 1968.

Clifford, Deborah Pickman. *Crusader for Freedom: A Life of Lydia Maria Child*. Boston: Beacon Press, 1992.

Conforti, Joseph. "Edwardsians, Unitarians, and the Memory of the Great Awakening, 1800–1840." In Wright, *American Unitarianism*, pp. 31–52.

Conkin, Paul K. *The Uneasy Center: Reformed Christianity in Antebellum America*. Chapel Hill: University of North Carolina Press, 1995.

Cook, James H. "Fighting with Breath, Not Blows: Frederick Douglass and Antislavery Violence." In McKivigan and Harrold, *Antislavery Violence*, pp. 128–63.

Cooke, George Willis. *Unitarianism in America: A History of Its Origin and Development*. Boston: American Unitarian Association, 1902.

Costanzo, Angelo. *Surprizing Narrative: Olaudah Equiano and the Beginnings of Black Autobiography*. Westport, Conn.: Greenwood, 1987.

Cott, Nancy F. *The Bonds of Womanhood: "Woman's Sphere" in New England, 1780–1835*. New Haven, Conn.: Yale University Press, 1977.

Crane, Gregg D. "Dangerous Sentiments: Sympathy, Rights and Revolution in Stowe's Antislavery Novels." *Nineteenth-Century Literature* 51 (September 1996): 176–204.

Cromwell, Otelia. *Lucretia Mott*. New York: Russell and Russell, 1958.

Cross, Whitney R. *The Burned-Over District: The Social and Intellectual History of Enthusiastic Religion in Western New York, 1800–1850*. Ithaca, N.Y.: Cornell University Press, 1950.

Curti, Merle Eugene. *The American Peace Crusade, 1815–1860*. Durham, N.C.: Duke University Press, 1929.

———. *Human Nature in American Thought: A History*. Madison: University of Wisconsin Press, 1980.

Dannenbaum, Jed. *Drink and Disorder: Temperance Reform in Cincinnati from the Washingtonian Revival to the WCTU*. Urbana: University of Illinois Press, 1984.

Davidson, Cathy N. *Revolution and the Word: The Rise of the Novel in America*. New York: Oxford University Press, 1986.

———, ed. *Reading in America: Literature and Social History*. Baltimore: Johns Hopkins University Press, 1989.

Davis, Allison. *Leadership, Love, and Aggression*. New York: Harcourt Brace Jovanovich, 1983.

Davis, Charles T., and Henry Louis Gates Jr., eds. *The Slave's Narrative*. Oxford: Oxford University Press, 1985.

Davis, David Brion. *Homicide in American Fiction, 1798–1860*. Ithaca, N.Y.: Cornell University Press, 1957.

———. "Slavery and Sin: The Cultural Background." In Duberman, *Antislavery Vanguard*, pp. 3–31.

———. *The Problem of Slavery in Western Culture*. Ithaca, N.Y.: Cornell University Press, 1966.

———. *The Slave Power Conspiracy and the Paranoid Style*. Baton Rouge: Louisiana State University Press, 1969.

———. *The Problem of Slavery in the Age of Revolution*. Ithaca, N.Y.: Cornell University Press, 1975.

———. *Slavery and Human Progress*. New York: Oxford University Press, 1984.

Davis, Hugh. *Joshua Leavitt: Evangelical Abolitionist*. Baton Rouge: Louisiana State University Press, 1990.

Davis, Thomas J. "Images of Intolerance: John Calvin in Nineteenth-Century History Textbooks." *Church History* 65 (June 1996): 234–48.

Dawson, Hugh J. "Mason Locke Weems." In *Dictionary of Literary Biography*. Vol. 37, *American Writers of the Early Republic*. Ed. Emory Elliot. Detroit: Gale, 1985.

DeBenedetti, Charles. *The Peace Reform in American History*. Bloomington: Indiana University Press, 1980.

Dedmond, Francis B. *Sylvester Judd*. Boston: Twayne, 1980.

Degler, Carl. *At Odds: Women and the Family in America, from the Revolution to the Present*. New York: Oxford University Press, 1980.

Dekker, George. *The American Historical Romance.* Cambridge: Cambridge University Press, 1987.

Delbanco, Andrew. *William Ellery Channing: An Essay on the Liberal Spirit in America.* Cambridge, Mass.: Harvard University Press, 1981.

——. *The Death of Satan: How Americans Have Lost the Sense of Evil.* New York: Farrar, Straus and Giroux, 1995.

Demos, John. "The Antislavery Movement and the Problem of Violent Means." *New England Quarterly* 37 (December 1964): 501-26.

Dillon, Merton L. "Gilbert H. Barnes and Dwight L. Dumond: An Appraisal." *Reviews in American History* 21 (September 1993): 539-52.

Doherty, Robert W. *The Hicksite Separation: A Sociological Analysis of Religious Schism in Early Nineteenth Century America.* New Brunswick, N.J.: Rutgers University Press, 1967.

Donald, David. *Lincoln.* New York: Simon and Schuster, 1995.

——. "Toward a Reconsideration of Abolitionists." In *Lincoln Reconsidered: Essays on the Civil War Era*, pp. 31-43. 3d ed. New York: Vintage, 2001.

Donovan, Josephine. *Uncle Tom's Cabin: Evil, Affliction, and Redemptive Love.* Boston: Twayne, 1991.

Dorsey, Peter. "De-authorizing Slavery: Realism in Stowe's *Uncle Tom's Cabin* and Brown's *Clotel.*" *ESQ: A Journal of the American Renaissance* 41 (1995): 256-88.

Douglas, Ann. *The Feminization of American Culture.* New York: Knopf, 1977.

Duban, James. "Conscience and Consciousness: The Liberal Christian Context of Thoreau's Political Ethics." *New England Quarterly* 60 (June 1987): 208-22.

Duberman, Martin, ed. *The Antislavery Vanguard: New Essays on the Abolitionists.* Princeton, N.J.: Princeton University Press, 1965.

DuBois, Ellen. "Women's Rights and Abolition: The Nature of the Connection." In Perry and Fellman, *Antislavery*, pp. 238-51.

Ducksworth, Sarah Smith. "Stowe's Construction of an African Persona and the Creation of White Identity for a New World Order." In Lowance, Westbrooks, and DeProspo, *Stowe Debate*, pp. 205-35.

Ebersole, Gary. *Captured by Texts: Puritan to Postmodern Images of Indian Captivity.* Charlottesville: University Press of Virginia, 1995.

Ehrenreich, Barbara. *Blood Rites: Origins and History of the Passions of War.* New York: Henry Holt, 1997.

Elkins, Stanley M. *Slavery: A Problem in American Institutional and Intellectual Life.* 3d ed. Chicago: University of Chicago Press, 1976.

Elliott, Emory, ed. *The Columbia History of the American Novel.* New York: Columbia University Press, 1991.

Endy, Melvin B., Jr. "Abraham Lincoln and American Civil Religion: A Reinterpretation." *Church History* 44 (June 1975): 229-41.

Ericson, David F. *The Debate over Slavery: Antislavery and Proslavery Liberalism in Antebellum America.* New York: New York University Press, 2000.

Farrison, Edward. *William Wells Brown: Author and Reformer.* Chicago: University of Chicago Press, 1969.

Felker, Christopher D. *Reinventing Cotton Mather in the American Renaissance:* Magnalia Christi Americana *in Hawthorne, Stowe, and Stoddard.* Boston: Northeastern University Press, 1993.

Fiedler, Leslie. *Love and Death in the American Novel.* Rev. ed. New York: Stein and Day, 1966.

——. *The Inadvertent Epic: From Uncle Tom's Cabin to Roots.* New York: Simon and Schuster, 1979.

——. "Home as Haven, Home as Hell: *Uncle Tom's Cabin.*" In *Rewriting the Dream: Reflections on the Changing American Literary Canon.* Ed. W.M. Verhoeven. Amsterdam: Rodopi, 1992.

Filler, Louis. *The Crusade Against Slavery, 1830-1860.* New York: Harper and Row, 1960.

Finkelhor, David, Richard J. Gelles, Gerald T. Hotaling, and Murray A. Straus, eds. *The Dark Side of Families*. Beverly Hills, Calif.: Sage, 1983.

Finkelman, Paul, ed. *Articles on American Slavery*. Vol. 14, *Antislavery*. New York: Garland, 1989.

———. *His Soul Goes Marching On: Responses to John Brown and the Harpers Ferry Raid*. Charlottesville: University Press of Virginia, 1995.

Fisher, Dexter, and Robert B. Stepto. *Afro-American Literature: The Reconstruction of Instruction*. New York: Modern Language Association of America, 1979.

Fisher, Philip. *Hard Facts: Setting and Form in the American Novel*. New York: Oxford University Press, 1987.

Fishkin, Shelley Fisher, and Carla L. Peterson. "'We Hold These Truths to Be Self-Evident': The Rhetoric of Frederick Douglass's Journalism." In Sundquist, *Frederick Douglass*, pp. 189–204.

Fladeland, Betty. *James Gillespie Birney*. Ithaca, N.Y.: Cornell University Press, 1955.

Fleischner, Jennifer. *Mastering Slavery: Memory, Family, and Identity in Women's Slave Narratives*. New York: New York University Press, 1996.

Fliegelman, Jay. *Prodigals and Pilgrims: The American Revolution Against Patriarchal Authority, 1750–1800*. Cambridge: Cambridge University Press, 1982.

———. *Declaring Independence: Jefferson, Natural Language, and the Culture of Performance*. Stanford, Calif.: Stanford University Press, 1993.

Fluck, Winfried. "The Power and Failure of Representation in Harriet Beecher Stowe's *Uncle Tom's Cabin*." *New Literary History* 23 (spring 1992): 319–38.

Forbes, Robert P. "Slavery and the Evangelical Enlightenment." In McKivigan and Snay, *Religion*, pp. 68–106.

Forgie, George B. *Patricide in the House Divided: A Psychological Interpretation of Lincoln and His Age*. New York: Norton, 1979.

Foster, Charles H. *The Rungless Ladder: Harriet Beecher Stowe and New England Puritanism*. Durham, N.C.: Duke University Press, 1954.

Foster, Edward Halsey. *Catharine Maria Sedgwick*. New York: Twayne, 1974.

Foster, Frances Smith. *Witnessing Slavery: The Development of Ante-Bellum Slave Narratives*. 2d ed. Madison: University of Wisconsin Press, 1994.

Foucault, Michel. *Discipline and Punish: The Birth of the Prison*. Trans. Alan Sheridan. New York: Pantheon, 1977.

Franchot, Jenny. "The Punishment of Esther: Frederick Douglass and the Construction of the Feminine." In Sundquist, *Frederick Douglass*, pp. 141–65.

Franklin, H. Bruce. "Animal Farm Unbound." In Bloom, *Frederick Douglass*, pp. 29–44.

Frederickson, George M. *The Black Image in the White Mind: The Debate on Afro-American Character and Destiny, 1817–1914*. New York: Harper and Row, 1971.

———. *The Inner Civil War: Northern Intellectuals and the Crisis of the Union*. New York: Harper and Row, 1965.

Friedman, Lawrence J. "Antebellum American Abolitionism and the Problem of Violent Means." *Psychohistory Review* 9 (fall 1980): 23–58.

———. *Gregarious Saints: Self and Community in American Abolitionism, 1830–1870*. Cambridge: Cambridge University Press, 1982.

Fuller, Robert C. *Naming the Antichrist: The History of an American Obsession*. New York: Oxford University Press, 1995.

Gates, Henry Louis, Jr. "From Wheatley to Douglass: The Politics of Displacement." In Sundquist, *Frederick Douglass*, pp. 47–65.

———. "Binary Oppositions in Chapter One of the *Narrative*." In Bloom, *Frederick Douglass*, pp. 59–76.

Gelles, Richard J., and Claire Pedrick Cornell. *Intimate Violence in Families*. 2d ed. Newbury Park, Calif.: Sage, 1990.

Genovese, Eugene D. *Roll, Jordan, Roll: The World the Slaves Made.* New York: Random House, 1974.

Gerteis, Louis S. *Morality and Utility in American Antislavery Reform.* Chapel Hill: University of North Carolina Press, 1987.

Gibson, Donald B. "Faith, Doubt, and Apostasy: Evidence of Things Unseen in Frederick Douglass's *Narrative.*" In Sundquist, *Frederick Douglass*, pp. 84–98.

Girard, René. *Violence and the Sacred.* Trans. Patrick Gregory. Baltimore: Johns Hopkins University Press, 1977.

———. *Things Hidden Since the Foundation of the World.* Trans. Stephen Bann and Michael Metteer. Stanford, Calif.: Stanford University Press, 1987.

Glenn, Myra. *Campaigns Against Corporal Punishment: Prisoners, Sailors, Women and Children in Antebellum America.* Albany: State University of New York Press, 1984.

Goatley, David. *Were You There? Godforsakenness in Slave Religion.* Maryknoll, N.Y.: Orbis, 1996.

Goodheart, Lawrence B. *Abolitionist, Actuary, Atheist: Elizur Wright and the Reform Impulse.* Kent, Ohio: Kent State University Press, 1990.

Goodman, Paul. *Of One Blood: Abolitionism and the Origins of Racial Equality.* Berkeley: University of California Press, 1998.

Gordon, Linda. *Heroes of Their Own Lives: The Politics and History of Family Violence, Boston, 1880–1960.* New York: Viking, 1988.

Gould, Philip. *Covenant and Republic: Historical Romance and the Politics of Puritanism.* Cambridge: Cambridge University Press, 1996.

Greven, Philip. *The Protestant Temperament: Patterns of Child-Rearing, Religious Experience, and the Self in Early America.* New York: Knopf, 1977.

Guelzo, Allen C. *Abraham Lincoln: Redeemer President.* Grand Rapids, Mich.: Eerdmans, 1999.

Gusfield, Joseph R. *Symbolic Crusade: Status Politics and the American Temperance Movement.* Urbana: University of Illinois Press, 1963.

Gutman, Herbert G. *The Black Family in Slavery and Freedom, 1750–1925.* New York: Pantheon, 1976.

Hallowell, Anna Davis. *James and Lucretia Mott: Life and Letters.* Boston: Houghton, Mifflin, 1884.

Hampel, Robert L. *Temperance and Prohibition in Massachusetts, 1813–1852.* Ann Arbor, Mich.: UMI Research Press, 1982.

Handy, Robert T. *A Christian America: Protestant Hopes and Historical Realities.* New York: Oxford University Press, 1971.

Harding, Vincent. *There Is a River: The Black Struggle for Freedom in America.* New York: Harcourt Brace Jovanovich, 1981.

Haroutunian, Joseph. *Piety Versus Moralism: The Passing of the New England Theology.* New York: Henry Holt, 1932.

Harris, Sharon M. "Early American Slave Narratives and the Reconfiguration of Place." *Journal of the American Studies Association of Texas* 21 (October 1993): 15–23.

———, ed. *Redefining the Political Novel: American Women Writers, 1797–1901.* Knoxville: University of Tennessee Press, 1995.

Harris, Susan K. *Nineteenth-Century American Women's Novels: Interpretive Strategies.* New York: Cambridge University Press, 1990.

Harrold, Stanley. "Romanticizing Slave Revolt: Madison Washington, the *Creole* Mutiny, and Abolitionist Celebration of Violent Means." In McKivigan and Harrold, *Antislavery Violence*, pp. 89–107.

Hart, James D. *The Popular Book: A History of America's Literary Taste.* New York: Oxford University Press, 1950.

Hartman, Saidiya V. *Scenes of Subjection: Terror, Slavery, and Self-Making in Nineteenth-Century America.* New York: Oxford University Press, 1997.

Hartz, Louis. *The Liberal Tradition in America: An Interpretation of American Political Thought Since the Revolution.* New York: Harcourt, Brace and World, 1955.

Hatch, Nathan O. *The Democratization of American Christianity.* New Haven, Conn.: Yale University Press, 1989.

Hauerwas, Stanley. *The Peaceable Kingdom: A Primer in Christian Ethics.* Notre Dame, Ind.: Notre Dame University Press, 1983.

———. *Dispatches from the Front: Theological Engagements with the Secular.* Durham, N.C.: Duke University Press, 1994.

Hedrick, Joan D. *Harriet Beecher Stowe: A Life.* New York: Oxford University Press, 1994.

Hein, David. "Lincoln's Theology and Political Ethics." In *Essays on Lincoln's Faith and Politics,* edited by Kenneth W. Thompson. Lanham, Md.: University Press of America, 1983.

Henry, Katherine. "Angelina Grimké's Rhetoric of Exposure." *American Quarterly* 49 (June 1997): 328–55.

Hersh, Blanche Glassman. "'Am I Not a Woman and a Sister?' Abolitionist Beginnings of Nineteenth-Century Feminism." In Perry and Fellman, *Antislavery,* pp. 252–83.

Hopkins, Dwight N., and George C.L. Cummings, eds. *Cut Loose Your Stammering Tongue: Black Theology in the Slave Narratives.* Maryknoll, N.Y.: Orbis, 1991.

Hovet, Theodore R. "Christian Revolution: Harriet Beecher Stowe's Response to Slavery and the Civil War." *New England Quarterly* 47 (December 1974): 535–49.

Howe, Daniel Walker. *The Unitarian Conscience: Harvard Moral Philosophy, 1805–1861.* Cambridge, Mass.: Harvard University Press, 1970.

Huston, James L. "The Experiential Basis of the Northern Antislavery Impulse." *Journal of Southern History* 56 (November 1990): 609–40.

Hutchison, William R. *The Transcendentalist Ministers: Church Reform in the New England Renaissance.* New Haven, Conn.: Yale University Press, 1959.

———. *The Modernist Impulse in American Protestantism.* Durham, N.C.: Duke University Press, 1992.

Ingle, Larry. *Quakers in Conflict: The Hicksite Reformation.* Knoxville: University of Tennessee Press, 1986.

Jay, Nancy. *Throughout Your Generations Forever: Sacrifice, Religion, and Paternity.* Foreword by Karen E. Fields. Chicago: University of Chicago Press, 1992.

Jeffrey, Julie Roy. *The Great Silent Army of Abolitionism: Ordinary Women in the Antislavery Movement.* Chapel Hill: University of North Carolina Press, 1998.

Jehlen, Myra. "The Family Militant: Domesticity Versus Slavery in *Uncle Tom's Cabin.*" *Criticism* 31 (fall 1989): 383–400.

Johnson, Paul E. *A Shopkeeper's Millennium: Society and Revivals in Rochester, New York, 1815–1837.* New York: Hill and Wang, 1978.

Joswick, Thomas P. "'The Crown Without the Conflict': Religious Values and Moral Reasoning in *Uncle Tom's Cabin.*" *Nineteenth Century Literature* 39 (December 1984): 253–74.

Juster, Susan. *Disorderly Women: Sexual Politics and Evangelicalism in Revolutionary New England.* Ithaca, N.Y.: Cornell University Press, 1994.

Karcher, Carolyn. "Rape, Murder, and Revenge in 'Slavery's Pleasant Homes': Lydia Maria Child's Antislavery Fiction and the Limits of Genre." In Samuels, *Culture of Sentiment,* pp. 58–72.

———. *The First Woman in the Republic: A Cultural Biography of Lydia Maria Child.* Durham, N.C.: Duke University Press, 1994.

Kazin, Alfred. *God and the American Writer.* New York: Knopf, 1997.

Kelley, Mary. *Private Woman, Public Stage: Literary Domesticity in Nineteenth-Century America.* New York: Oxford University Press, 1984.

Kerber, Linda K. *Women of the Republic: Intellect and Ideology in Revolutionary America.* Chapel Hill: University of North Carolina Press, 1980.

———. "Separate Spheres, Female Worlds, Woman's Place: The Rhetoric of Women's History." *Journal of American History* 75 (1988): 9–39.

Kibbey, Ann. "Language in Slavery." In Bloom, *Frederick Douglass*, pp. 131–52.

Kibbey, Ann, and Michele Stepto. "The Antilanguage of Slavery: Frederick Douglass's 1845 *Narrative*." In Andrews, *Critical Essays*, pp. 166–91.

Kilcup, Karen L. "Lydia Howard Huntley Sigourney (1791–1865)." In *Nineteenth-Century American Women Writers: A Bio-Bibliographical Critical Sourcebook*, edited by Denise D. Knight. Westport, Conn.: Greenwood, 1997.

Kimball, Gayle. *The Religious Ideas of Harriet Beecher Stowe: Her Gospel of Womanhood*. New York: Edwin Mellen Press, 1982.

Kirsthardt, Melanie J. "Flirting with Patriarchy: Feminist Dialogics." In Lowance, Westbrook, and DeProspo, *Stowe Debate*, pp. 37–56.

Klein, Lawrence E. *Shaftesbury and the Culture of Politeness: Moral Discourse and Cultural Politics in Early Eighteenth-Century England*. Cambridge: Cambridge University Press, 1994.

Koch, Donald A. "Timothy Shay Arthur." In *Dictionary of Literary Biography*. Vol. 3, *Antebellum Writers in New York and the South*. Ed. Joel Myerson. Detroit: Gale, 1979.

Kraditor, Aileen S. *Means and Ends in American Abolitionism: Garrison and His Critics on Strategy and Tactics*. New York: Pantheon, 1969.

Lane, Ann J. *The Debate over Slavery: Stanley Elkins and His Critics*. Urbana: University of Illinois Press, 1971.

Lang, Amy Schrager. "Slavery and Sentimentalism: The Strange Career of Augustine St. Clare." *Women's Studies: An Interdisciplinary Journal* 12 (1986): 31–54.

Lant, Kathleen Margaret. "The Unsung Hero of *Uncle Tom's Cabin*." *American Studies* 28 (spring 1987): 47–71.

Lawson, Bill E. *Frederick Douglass: A Critical Reader*. Malden, Mass.: Blackwell, 1998.

Leary, Lewis. *The Book-Peddling Parson: An Account of the Life and Works of Mason Locke Weems*. Chapel Hill, N.C.: Algonquin, 1984.

Lehman-Haupt, Helmut, ed. *The Book in America: A History of the Making, the Selling, and the Collecting of Books in the United States*. New York: Bowker, 1939.

Lerner, Gerda. *The Grimké Sisters from South Carolina: Rebels Against Slavery*. Boston: Houghton Mifflin, 1967.

Levine, Lawrence W. *Black Culture and Black Consciousness: Afro-American Folk Thought from Slavery to Freedom*. New York: Oxford University Press, 1977.

Levine, Robert S. *Martin Delaney, Frederick Douglass, and the Politics of Representative Identity*. Chapel Hill: University of North Carolina Press, 1997.

Loveland, Anne C. "Evangelicalism and 'Immediate Abolition' in American Antislavery Thought." *Journal of Social History* 32 (May 1966): 172–88.

Lowance, Mason I., Jr., Ellen E. Westbrook, and R. C. DeProspo, eds. *The Stowe Debate: Rhetorical Strategies in Uncle Tom's Cabin*. Amherst: University of Massachusetts Press, 1994.

Mabee, Carleton. *Black Freedom: The Nonviolent Abolitionists from 1830 Through the Civil War*. New York: Macmillan, 1970.

Mabee, Carleton, with Susan Mabee Newhouse. *Sojourner Truth: Slave, Prophet, Legend*. New York: New York University Press, 1993.

MacAndrew, Craig, and Robert B. Edgerton. *Drunken Comportment: A Social Explanation*. Chicago: Aldine, 1969.

MacFarlane, Lisa Watt. "'If I Ever Get to Where I Can': The Competing Rhetorics of Reform in *Uncle Tom's Cabin*." *American Transcendental Quarterly* 4 (June 1990): 135–47.

Machor, James L., ed. *Readers in History: Nineteenth-Century American Literature and the Contexts of Response*. Baltimore: Johns Hopkins University Press, 1993.

Magdol, Edward. *The Antislavery Rank and File: A Social Profile of the Abolitionists' Constituency.* Westport, Conn.: Greenwood, 1986.

Martin, Terence. *The Instructed Vision: Scottish Common Sense Philosophy and the Origins of American Fiction.* Bloomington: Indiana University Press, 1961.

———. *Parables of Possibility: The American Need for Beginnings.* New York: Columbia University Press, 1995.

Martin, Waldo E., Jr. *The Mind of Frederick Douglass.* Chapel Hill: University of North Carolina Press, 1984.

Marty, Martin E. *Righteous Empire: The Protestant Experience in America.* New York: Dial, 1970.

Marvin, Carolyn, and David W. Ingle, "Blood Sacrifice and the Nation: Revisiting Civil Religion." *Journal of the American Academy of Religion* 64 (winter 1996): 767–80.

Mathews, Donald G. "The Abolitionists on Slavery: The Critique Behind the Social Movement." *Journal of Social History* 33 (May 1967): 163–82.

Mattingly, Carol. *Well-Tempered Women: Nineteenth-Century Temperance Rhetoric.* Carbondale: Southern Illinois University Press, 1998.

May, Henry F. *The Enlightenment in America.* New York: Oxford University Press, 1976.

Mayer, Henry. *All on Fire: William Lloyd Garrison and the Abolition of Slavery.* New York: St. Martin's, 1998.

McCall, Laura. "'The Reign of Brute Force Is Now Over': A Content Analysis of *Godey's Lady's Book*, 1830–1860." *Journal of the Early Republic* 9 (1989): 217–36.

McDowell, Deborah E. "In the First Place: Making Frederick Douglass and the Afro-American Narrative Tradition." In Andrews, *Critical Essays*, pp. 192–214.

McDowell, Deborah E., and Arnold Rampersad, eds. *Slavery and the Literary Imagination: Selected Papers from the English Institute, 1987.* Baltimore: Johns Hopkins University Press, 1989.

McFeeley, William S. *Frederick Douglass.* New York: Norton, 1991.

McGinn, Bernard. *The Foundations of Mysticism: Origins to the Fifth Century.* New York: Crossroad, 1991.

McKivigan, John R. *The War Against Proslavery Religion: Abolitionism and the Northern Churches, 1830–1865.* Ithaca, N.Y.: Cornell University Press, 1984.

———. "The Frederick Douglass–Gerrit Smith Friendship and Political Abolitionism in the 1850s." In Sundquist, *Frederick Douglass*, pp. 205–32.

———. "James Redpath, John Brown, and Abolitionist Advocacy of Slave Insurrection." *Civil War History* 37 (1991): 293–313.

McKivigan, John R., and Stanley Harrold, eds. *Antislavery Violence: Sectional, Racial, and Cultural Conflict in Antebellum America.* Knoxville: University of Tennessee Press, 1999.

McKivigan, John R., and Mitchell Snay, eds. *Religion and the Antebellum Debate over Slavery.* Athens: University of Georgia Press, 1998.

McLoughlin, William G. *Revivals, Awakenings, and Reform: An Essay on Religion and Social Change in America, 1607–1977.* Chicago: University of Chicago Press, 1978.

McPherson, James M. *"We Cannot Escape History": Lincoln and the Last Best Hope of Earth.* Urbana: University of Illinois Press, 1995.

Mead, Sidney. "Abraham Lincoln's 'Last, Best Hope of Earth': The American Dream of Destiny and Democracy." *Church History* 23 (March 1954): 3–16.

———. *The Lively Experiment: The Shaping of Christianity in America.* New York: Harper and Row, 1963.

Merish, Lori. "Sentimental Consumption: Harriet Beecher Stowe and the Aesthetics of Middle-Class Ownership." *American Literary History* 8 (spring 1996): 1–33.

Merrill, Walter M. *Against Wind and Tide: A Biography of William Lloyd Garrison.* Cambridge, Mass.: Harvard University Press, 1963.

Meyer, Michael. "Thoreau's Rescue of John Brown from History." *Studies in the American Renaissance* (1980): 301–16.

Meyers, Marvin. *The Jacksonian Persuasion: Politics and Belief.* Stanford, Calif.: Stanford University Press, 1957.

Michaels, Walter Benn, and Donald E. Pease, eds. *The American Renaissance Reconsidered.* Baltimore: Johns Hopkins University Press, 1985.

Miller, Perry. *The Life of the Mind in America: From the Revolution to the Civil War.* New York: Harcourt, Brace and World, 1965.

——. *The New England Mind: The Seventeenth Century.* Cambridge, Mass.: Harvard University Press, 1967.

——. *The New England Mind: From Colony to Province.* Boston: Beacon, 1971.

Mintz, Steven. *Moralists and Modernizers: America's Pre–Civil War Reformers.* Baltimore: Johns Hopkins University Press, 1995.

Moorhead, James H. *American Apocalypse: Yankee Protestants and the Civil War, 1860–1869.* New Haven, Conn.: Yale University Press, 1978.

Morrison, Karl. *The Mimetic Tradition of Reform in the West.* Princeton, N.J.: Princeton University Press, 1982.

——. *I Am You: The Hermeneutics of Empathy in Western Literature, Theology, and Art.* Princeton, N.J.: Princeton University Press, 1988.

Moses, Wilson Jeremiah. *Black Messiahs and Uncle Toms: Social and Literary Manipulations of a Religious Myth.* University Park: Pennsylvania State University Press, 1982.

Nadelhaft, Jerome. "Wife Torture: A Known Phenomenon in Nineteenth-Century America." *Journal of American Culture* 10 (fall 1987): 39–59.

——. "Alcohol and Wife Abuse in Antebellum Male Temperance Literature." *Canadian Review of American Studies* 25 (winter 1995): 15–43.

Nelson, Dana. "Sympathy as Strategy in Sedgwick's *Hope Leslie.*" In Samuels, *Culture of Sentiment,* pp. 191–202.

Nichols, Charles H. "Who Read the Slave Narratives?" *Phylon* 20 (summer 1959): 149–62.

——. *Many Thousand Gone: The Ex-Slaves' Account of Their Bondage and Freedom.* Leiden: Brill, 1963.

Niebuhr, H. Richard. *The Kingdom of God in America.* New York: Harper and Row, 1937.

Niebuhr, Reinhold. *The Irony of American History.* New York: Scribner, 1952.

Noll, Mark A., David W. Bebbington, and George A. Rawlyk, eds. *Evangelicalism: Comparative Studies of Popular Protestantism in North America, the British Isles, and Beyond, 1700–1990.* New York: Oxford University Press, 1994.

Norton, Anne. *Alternative Americas: A Reading of Antebellum Political Culture.* Chicago: University of Chicago Press, 1986.

Norton, Mary Beth. *Liberty's Daughters: The Revolutionary Experiences of American Women, 1750–1800.* New ed. Ithaca, N.Y.: Cornell University Press, 1996.

Nuernberg, Susan Marie. "The Rhetoric of Race." In Lowance, Westbrook, and DeProspo, *Stowe Debate,* pp. 255–70.

Oates, Stephen B. *To Purge This Land with Blood: A Biography of John Brown.* New York: Harper Collins, 1970.

O'Connell, Catharine E. "'The Magic of the Real Presence of Distress': Sentimentality and Competing Rhetorics of Authority." In Lowance, Westbrook, and DeProspo, *Stowe Debate,* pp. 13–36.

Olney, James. "'I Was Born': Slave Narratives, Their Status as Autobiography and as Literature." In Davis and Gates, *Slave's Narrative,* pp. 148–74.

O'Meally, Robert G. "The Text Was Meant to Be Preached." In Bloom, *Frederick Douglass,* pp. 77–94.

Osborne, William S. *Lydia Maria Child.* Boston: Twayne, 1980.

Packer, Barbara L. "The Transcendentalists." In Bercovitch, *Cambridge History,* 2:329–604.

Painter, Nell Irvin. *Sojourner Truth: A Life, a Symbol.* New York: Norton, 1996.

Paludan, Philip Shaw. "Emancipating the Republic: Lincoln and the Means and Ends of Antislavery." In McPherson, "*We Cannot,*" pp. 45–60.

Pateman, Carole. *The Disorder of Women: Democracy, Feminism, and Political Theory.* Stanford, Calif.: Stanford University Press, 1989.

Pegram, Thomas R. *Battling Demon Rum: The Struggle for a Dry America, 1800–1933.* Chicago: Ivan R. Dee, 1998.

Perry, Lewis. *Childhood, Marriage, and Reform: Henry Clarke Wright, 1797–1870.* Chicago: University of Chicago Press, 1980.

———. *Radical Abolitionism: Anarchy and the Government of God in Antislavery Thought.* New ed. Knoxville: University of Tennessee Press, 1995.

Perry, Lewis, and Michael Fellman, eds. *Antislavery Reconsidered: New Perspectives on the Abolitionists.* Baton Rouge: Louisiana State University Press, 1979.

Pinn, Anthony B. *Why Lord? Suffering and Evil in Black Theology.* New York: Continuum, 1995.

Pleck, Elizabeth. *Domestic Tyranny: The Makings of Social Policy Against Family Violence from Colonial Times to the Present.* New York: Oxford University Press, 1987.

Poling, James Newton. *Deliver Us from Evil: Resisting Racial and Gender Oppression.* Minneapolis, Minn.: Fortress, 1996.

Preston, Dickson J. *Young Frederick Douglass: The Maryland Years.* Baltimore: Johns Hopkins University Press, 1980.

Quarles, Benjamin. *Black Abolitionists.* New York: Oxford University Press, 1969.

———. *Allies for Freedom: Blacks and John Brown.* New York: Oxford University Press, 1974.

Raboteau, Albert J. *Slave Religion: The "Invisible Institution" in the Antebellum South.* New York: Oxford University Press, 1978.

Rawick, George P. *From Sundown to Sunup: The Making of the Black Community.* Westport, Conn.: Greenwood, 1972.

Reynolds, David. *Faith in Fiction: The Emergence of Religious Literature in America.* Cambridge, Mass.: Harvard University Press, 1981.

———. *Beneath the American Renaissance: The Subversive Imagination in the Age of Emerson and Melville.* Cambridge, Mass.: Harvard University Press, 1988.

Reynolds, David J., and Debra J. Rosenthal. *The Serpent in the Cup: Temperance in American Literature.* Amherst: University of Massachusetts Press, 1997.

Robertson, Stacey M. *Parker Pillsbury: Radical Abolitionist, Male Feminist.* Ithaca, N.Y.: Cornell University Press, 2000.

Rogers, William B. "*We Are All Together Now*": *Frederick Douglass, William Lloyd Garrison, and the Prophetic Tradition.* New York: Garland, 1995.

Rohrer, James R. "The Origins of the Temperance Movement: A Reinterpretation." *Journal of American Studies* 24 (August 1990): 228–35.

Romero, Lora. "Bio-Political Resistance in Domestic Ideology and *Uncle Tom's Cabin.*" *American Literary History* 1 (winter 1989): 715–34.

———. "Vanishing Americans: Gender, Empire, and New Historicism." In Samuels, *Culture of Sentiment,* pp. 115–27.

Rorabaugh, W. J. *The Alcoholic Republic: An American Tradition.* New York: Oxford University Press, 1979.

Rose, Anne C. *Transcendentalism as a Social Movement, 1830–1850.* New Haven, Conn.: Yale University Press, 1981.

———. *Voices of the Marketplace: American Thought and Culture, 1830–1860.* New York: Twayne, 1995.

Rossbach, Jeffrey. *Ambivalent Conspirators: John Brown, the Secret Six, and a Theory of Slave Violence.* Philadelphia: University of Pennsylvania Press, 1982.

Roth, John K., and Michael Berenbaum, eds. *Holocaust: Religious and Philosophical Implications.* New York: Paragon House, 1989.

Rumbarger, John. *Profits, Power, and Prohibition: Alcohol Reform and the Industrializing of America, 1800–1930.* Albany: State University of New York Press, 1989.

Saiving, Valerie. "The Human Situation: A Feminine View." *Journal of Religion* 40 (April 1960): 100–112.

Samuels, Shirley. "The Identity of Slavery." In Samuels, *Culture of Sentiment,* pp. 157–71.

———. *Romances of the Republic: Women, the Family, and Violence in the Literature of the Early American Nation.* New York: Oxford University Press, 1996.

———, ed. *The Culture of Sentiment: Race, Gender, and Sentimentality in Nineteenth-Century America.* New York: Oxford University Press, 1992.

Sánchez-Eppler, Karen. "Bodily Bonds: The Intersecting Rhetorics of Feminism and Abolition." In Samuels, *Culture of Sentiment,* pp. 92–114.

———. *Touching Liberty: Abolition, Feminism, and the Politics of the Body.* Berkeley: University of California Press, 1993.

———. "Temperance in the Bed of a Child: Incest and Social Order in Nineteenth-Century America." *American Quarterly* 47 (March 1995): 1–33.

Saum, Lewis O. *The Popular Mood of Pre–Civil War America.* Westport, Conn.: Greenwood, 1980.

Scarry, Elaine. *The Body in Pain: The Making and Unmaking of the World.* New York: Oxford University Press, 1985.

———. *Resisting Representation.* New York: Oxford University Press, 1994.

Schwager, Raymund. *Must There Be Scapegoats? Violence and Redemption in the Bible.* Trans. Maria L. Assad. San Francisco: Harper and Row, 1987.

Scott, Donald M. "Abolition as a Sacred Vocation." In Perry and Fellman, *Antislavery,* pp. 51–74.

Sellers, Charles. *The Market Revolution: Jacksonian America, 1815–1846.* New York: Oxford University Press, 1991.

Shea, Daniel B., Jr. *Spiritual Autobiography in Early America.* Princeton, N.J.: Princeton University Press, 1968.

Shea, William M., and Peter A. Huff, eds. *Knowledge and Belief in America: Enlightenment Traditions and Modern Religious Thought.* Cambridge: Cambridge University Press, 1995.

Slotkin, Richard. *Regeneration Through Violence: The Mythology of the American Frontier, 1600–1860.* Hanover, N.H.: Wesleyan University Press, 1973.

Smith, Sidonie. *Where I'm Bound: Patterns of Slavery and Freedom in Black American Autobiography.* Westport, Conn.: Greenwood, 1974.

Smith, Timothy. *Revivalism and Social Reform: American Protestantism on the Eve of the Civil War.* New ed. Baltimore: Johns Hopkins University Press, 1980.

Smith, Valerie. *Self-Discovery and Authority in Afro-American Narrative.* Cambridge, Mass.: Harvard University Press, 1987.

Soderlund, Jean R. *Quakers and Slavery: A Divided Spirit.* Princeton, N.J.: Princeton University Press, 1985.

Somkin, Fred. *Unquiet Eagle: Memory and Desire in the Idea of American Freedom, 1815–1860.* Ithaca, N.Y.: Cornell University Press, 1967.

Sorin, Gerald. *The New York Abolitionists: A Case Study of Political Radicalism.* Westport, Conn.: Greenwood, 1971.

———. *Abolitionism: A New Perspective.* New York: Praeger, 1972.

Speicher, Anna M. *The Religious World of Antislavery Women: Spirituality in the Lives of Five Abolitionist Lecturers.* Syracuse, N.Y.: Syracuse University Press, 2000.

Stange, Douglas C. *Patterns of Antislavery Among American Unitarians, 1831–1860.* Rutherford, N.J.: Fairleigh Dickinson University Press, 1977.

Starling, Marion Wilson. *The Slave Narrative: Its Place in American History.* Boston: G. K. Hall, 1982.

Stepto, Robert B. *From Behind the Veil: A Study of Afro-American Narrative.* Urbana: University of Illinois Press, 1979.

Sterling, Dorothy. *Lucretia Mott.* New York: Feminist Press at the City University of New York, 1999.

Stewart, James Brewer. "Peaceful Hopes and Violent Experiences: The Evolution of Reforming and Radical, 1831–1837." *Civil War History* 17 (December 1971): 293–309.

——. *Holy Warriors: The Abolitionists and American Slavery.* New York: Hill and Wang, 1976.

——. *Wendell Phillips: Liberty's Hero.* Baton Rouge: Louisiana State University Press, 1986.

——. *William Lloyd Garrison and the Challenge of Emancipation.* Arlington Heights, Ill.: Harlan Davidson, 1992.

Stone, Albert E. "Identity and Art in Frederick Douglass's *Narrative.*" In Bloom, *Frederick Douglass*, pp. 7–28.

Strong, Douglas M. *Perfectionist Politics: Abolitionism and the Religious Tensions of American Democracy.* Syracuse, N.Y.: Syracuse University Press, 1999.

Stuckey, Sterling. *Slave Culture: Nationalist Theory and the Foundations of Black America.* New York: Oxford University Press, 1987.

Sundquist, Eric J., ed. *New Essays on* Uncle Tom's Cabin. Cambridge: Cambridge University Press, 1986.

——. *Frederick Douglass: New Literary and Historical Essays.* Cambridge: Cambridge University Press, 1990.

Takaki, Ronald T., ed. *Violence in the Black Imagination: Essays and Documents.* New York: Oxford University Press, 1993.

Thomas, Helen. *Romanticism and the Slave Narratives: Transatlantic Testimonies.* New York: Cambridge University Press, 2000.

Thomas, John L. *The Liberator: William Lloyd Garrison.* Boston: Little, Brown, 1963.

——. "Antislavery and Utopia." In Duberman, *Antislavery Vanguard*, pp. 240–69.

——. "Romantic Reform in America, 1815–1865." *American Quarterly* 17 (winter 1965): 656–81.

——, ed. *Abraham Lincoln and the American Political Tradition.* Amherst: University of Massachusetts Press, 1986.

Thurow, Glen E. *Abraham Lincoln and American Political Religion.* Albany: State University of New York Press, 1976.

Tompkins, Jane. *Sensational Designs: The Cultural Work of American Fiction, 1790–1860.* New York: Oxford University Press, 1985.

Tompkins, Silvan S. "The Psychology of Commitment: The Constructive Role of Violence and Suffering for the Individual and for His Society." In Duberman, *Antislavery Vanguard*, pp. 270–98.

Toulouse, Teresa. *The Art of Prophesying: New England Sermons and the Shaping of Belief.* Athens: University of Georgia Press, 1987.

Trueblood, Elton. *Abraham Lincoln: Theologian of American Anguish.* New York: Harper and Row, 1973.

Turner, Darwin T., and John Sekora. *The Art of the Slave Narrative: Original Essays in Criticism and Theory.* Macomb: Western Illinois University Press, 1982.

Turner, James. *Without God, Without Creed: The Origins of Unbelief in America.* Baltimore: Johns Hopkins University Press, 1985.

Tyrrell, Ian R. *Sobering Up: From Temperance to Prohibition in Antebellum America, 1800–1860.* Westport, Conn.: Greenwood, 1979.

Valeri, Mark. *Law and Providence in Joseph Bellamy's New England: The Origins of the New Divinity in Revolutionary America.* New York: Oxford University Press, 1994.

Van De Burg, William L. "Frederick Douglass: Maryland Slave to Religious Liberal." *Maryland Historical Magazine* 69 (spring 1974): 27–43.

VanDerBeets, Richard. "A Surfeit of Style: The Indian Captivity Narrative as Penny Dreadful." *Research Studies* 39 (December 1971): 297–301.

——. "The Indian Captivity Narrative as Ritual." *American Literature* 43 (January 1972): 548–62.

Van Leer, David. "Reading Slavery: The Anxiety of Ethnicity in Douglass's *Narrative.*" In Sundquist, *Frederick Douglass,* pp. 118–40.

Walker, Peter. *Moral Choices: Memory, Desire, and Imagination in Nineteenth-Century American Abolition.* Baton Rouge: Louisiana State University Press, 1978.

Walters, Ronald G. *The Antislavery Appeal: American Abolitionism After 1830.* Baltimore: Johns Hopkins University Press, 1976.

——. *American Reformers, 1815–1860.* New York: Hill and Wang, 1978.

——. "The Boundaries of Abolitionism." In Perry and Fellman, *Antislavery,* pp. 3–23.

Wartley, Lynn. "Relic, Fetish, Femmage: The Aesthetics of Sentiment in the Work of Stowe." *Yale Journal of Criticism* 5 (fall 1992): 165–91.

Welch, Sharon D. *A Feminist Ethic of Risk.* Minneapolis, Minn.: Fortress, 1990.

Westra, Helen Petter. "Confronting Antichrist: The Influence of Jonathan Edwards's Millennial Vision." In Lowance, Westbrook, and Deprospo, *Stowe Debate,* pp. 141–58.

Wexler, Laura. "Tender Violence: Literary Eavesdropping, Domestic Fiction, and Educational Reform." In Samuels, *Culture of Sentiment,* pp. 9–38.

White, Isabelle. "Sentimentality and the Uses of Death." In Lowance, Westbrook, and Deprospo, *Stowe Debate,* pp. 99–115.

Whitehead, Alfred North. *Essays in Science and Philosophy.* New York: Philosophical Library, 1948.

Wiener, Philip P., and John Fisher, eds. *Violence and Aggression in the History of Ideas.* New Brunswick, N.J.: Rutgers University Press, 1974.

Wills, Garry. *Inventing America: Jefferson's Declaration of Independence.* New York: Random House, 1978.

——. *Lincoln at Gettysburg: The Words That Remade America.* New York: Simon and Schuster, 1992.

Wilson, Edmund. *Patriotic Gore: Studies in the Literature of the American Civil War.* With a new introduction by Malcolm Bradbury. London: Hogarth Press, 1987.

Wink, Walter. *Engaging the Powers: Discernment and Resistance in a World of Domination.* Minneapolis, Minn.: Fortress, 1992.

Winks, Robin W. "The Making of a Fugitive Slave Narrative: Josiah Henson and Uncle Tom—A Case History." In Davis and Gates, *Slave's Narrative,* pp. 112–46.

Wolf, William J. *The Almost Chosen People: A Study of the Religion of Abraham Lincoln.* Garden City, N.Y.: Doubleday, 1959.

Wolff, Cynthia Griffin. "'Masculinity' in *Uncle Tom's Cabin.*" *American Quarterly* 47 (December 1995): 595–618.

Wright, Conrad. *The Beginnings of Unitarianism in America.* Boston: Starr King Press, 1955.

——. *The Liberal Christians: Essays on American Unitarian History.* Boston: Beacon, 1970.

——. "Institutional Reconstruction in the Unitarian Controversy." In Wright, *American Unitarianism,* pp. 3–30.

——. *The Unitarian Controversy: Essays on American Unitarian History.* Boston: Skinner House, 1994.

Wright, Conrad Edick, ed. *American Unitarianism, 1805–1865.* Boston: Massachusetts Historical Society and Northeastern University Press, 1989.

Wyatt-Brown, Bertram. *Lewis Tappan and the Evangelical War Against Slavery.* Cleveland, Ohio: The Press of Case Western Reserve University, 1969.

——. "John Brown, Weathermen, and the Psychology of Antinomian Violence." *Soundings* 55 (winter 1975): 417–440.

——. *Yankee Saints and Southern Sinners.* Baton Rouge: Louisiana State University Press, 1985.

Yacovone, Donald. *Samuel Joseph May and the Dilemma of the Liberal Persuasion, 1797–1871.* Philadelphia: Temple University Press, 1991.

Yarborough, Richard. "Race, Violence, and Manhood: The Masculine Ideal in Frederick Douglass's 'The Heroic Slave.'" In Sundquist, *Frederick Douglass*, pp. 166–88.

——. "Strategies of Black Characterization in *Uncle Tom's Cabin* and the Early Afro-American Novel." In Sundquist, *New Essays*, pp. 45–84.

Yellin, Jean Fagan. *The Intricate Knot: Black Figures in American Literature, 1776–1863.* New York: New York University Press, 1972.

——. "Written by Herself: Harriet Jacobs' Slave Narrative." *American Literature* 53 (November 1981): 479–86.

——. "Texts and Contexts of Harriet Jacobs's *Incidents in the Life of a Slave Girl: Written by Herself.* In Davis and Gates, *Slave's Narrative*, pp. 262–82.

——. "Doing It Herself: *Uncle Tom's Cabin* and Woman's Role in the Slavery Crisis." In Sundquist, *New Essays*, pp. 85–106.

——. *Women and Sisters: The Antislavery Feminists in American Culture.* New Haven, Conn.: Yale University Press, 1989.

Yellin, Jean Fagan, and John C. Van Horne, eds. *The Abolitionist Sisterhood: Women's Political Culture in Antebellum America.* Ithaca, N.Y.: Cornell University Press, 1994.

Yoder, John Howard. *The Politics of Jesus.* Grand Rapids, Mich.: Eerdmans, 1972.

Zagarell, Sandra A. "Expanding 'America': Lydia Sigourney's *Sketch of Connecticut*, Catharine Sedgwick's *Hope Leslie*." In Harris, *Redefining*, pp. 43–65.

Zboray, Ronald J. *A Fictive People: Antebellum Economic Development and the American Reading Public.* New York: Oxford University Press, 1993.

Ziegler, Valarie H. *The Advocates of Peace in Antebellum America.* Bloomington: Indiana University Press, 1992.

Zinn, Howard. "Abolitionists, Freedom-Riders, and the Tactics of Agitation." In Duberman, *Antislavery Vanguard*, pp. 417–51.

Ziolkowski, Thad. "Antitheses: The Dialectic of Violence and Literacy in Frederick Douglass's *Narrative* of 1845." In Andrews, *Critical Essays*, pp. 148–65.

Zur, Ofer. "The Psychohistory of Warfare: The Co-Evolution of Culture, Psyche and Enemy." *Journal of Peace Research* 24 (1987): 125–34.

Index

abolitionists, 47 (*see also* Douglass, Frederick; Garrison, William Lloyd; Stowe, Harriet Beecher)
  attitudes toward violence, 175-78
  criticisms of, 8
  divisions among, 58-59
  and fugitive slave narratives, 129-42
  and the *imago dei*, 49
  responses to Brown, John, 187-97
  responses to Civil War, 206-8
  and revivalism, 55, 226n6, 228n26, 228n30, 228n33, 229n34, 229n37
  and ultra reform, 66, 230n43
Abraham, 29, 35-36, 119, 128, 225n83, 225n84
Abzug, Robert H., 226n6, 228n31, 230n59, 232n6
Adams, John, 14, 77, 101
agitation, 58, 73-76, 233n42
Alcoholics Anonymous, 231n63
Alcott, A. Bronson, 73
Alcott, Louisa May, 195
Alexander, Edward Porter, 212
Alline, Henry, 69
ambivalence of radical Christian liberals
  about God's power, 12-13, 40-45, 64-65, 67-68, 81, 86-90, 174, 216
  about the use of violence, 176-78, 180-81, 183-84, 189-90, 250n17, 252n39
American and Foreign Anti-Slavery Society, 59
American Anti-Slavery Society, 48, 53, 59, 131, 178, 250n22, 253n72
  "Declaration of Sentiments," 50, 72, 74, 78, 85

American Colonization Society, 52, 54, 133
American Peace Society, 50, 78-79
American Revolution. *See* Revolution, United States
American Temperance Society, 54, 103, 104-6, 117, 122
American Unitarian Association, 14, 22, 52, 54
Amos, 225n84
Anarchism, 235n78 (*see also* nonresistance; ultra reform)
Anderson, Catharine, 92, 96-97
Andover Seminary, 91, 93, 246n8
Andrews, William, 130, 241n9
angels, 32-33, 98, 120-21, 123-26, 240n58
Antitrinitarianism, 14
Apocalypticism, 67, 89-90, 100-101, 170-73, 174, 185-97, 217, 236n97
Aptheker, Herbert, 231n62, 242n24
Arminianism, 14, 55, 221n4, 229n35 (*see also* liberal theology; Unitarianism)
Arthur, T. S.
  representation of fathers and daughters, 121-22, 124-26, 240n72
  as sentimental reformer, 60, 107, 113-16
  Six Nights with the Washingtonians, 113-16
  success as an author, 103
  Ten Nights in a Bar-Room, 5, 103, 115, 124-26, 169, 240n75
  and women's rights, 240n69